COLLINS GEM
ANTIQUE MARKS

C000135515

COLLINS GEM
CRICKET

COLLINS GEM
DIETING

COLLINS GEM
DOGS

COLLINS GEM
FIRST AID

COLLINS GEM
INTERNET

COLLINS GEM
PREDICTING

COLLINS GEM
Ready REFERENCE

COLLINS GEM
SHARKS

COLLINS GEM
WHALES & DOLPHINS

COLLINS GEM
WHISKY

COLLINS GEM
WORD PROCESSING

COLLINS GEM
Your PC

CROSSWORD
PUZZLE SOLVER

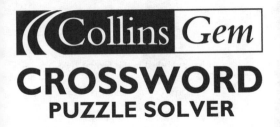

Collins *Gem*

CROSSWORD
PUZZLE SOLVER

CollinsGem

An Imprint of HarperCollins*Publishers*

First published 1986
First published in this format 2000

© HarperCollins Publishers 1986

ISBN 0-00-710136-8

The HarperCollins website address is
www.**fire**and**water**.com

10 9 8 7 6 5 4 3 2 1

A catalogue record for this book
is available from the British Library

Computer typeset by Barbers Ltd.
Wrotham, England
Printed in Italy by Amadeus S.p.A.

CONTENTS

v

CONTENTS, *cont.*

FOREWORD

This new version of the popular GEM CROSSWORD PUZZLE SOLVER has been completely revised and reorganized. The content has been expanded by increasing the word length to include words of up to 15 letters, thus making the coverage more relevant to the standard cryptic crossword grid. The word count now totals over 55,000 items.

This increased content has been arranged in a larger number of separate fields - 81 in all - alphabetically arranged, from Abbreviations to Writers. This greater degree of subdivision should significantly reduce the search time required. Additional help in this respect is provided by a short Index which relates some possible alternative categories to their relevant fields.

The fact that the author is a practising crossword compiler has meant that he has been able to draw on his experience in this area to tailor the content to items that crossword solvers actually meet. Irrelevant items have been excluded and the coverage has been generally updated to include the kind of material today's compilers make use of.

FOREWORD

These improvements make this new *Gem Crossword Puzzle Solver* the ideal aid for all crossword fans.

NOTE: In order to facilitate scrutiny for letter placement within words a special typeface has been used that keeps the letters of each word vertically in line with those of the words above and below it.

To preserve this helpful columnar arrangement the following symbols have been used:

| = word space, as in speed|the|plough
, = hyphen, as in dairy,farm
' = apostrophe, as in lady's|finger

Abbreviations

3D	CB	DJ	GI	JP	mk
AA	CC	DM	Gk	Jr	ml
AB	cc	do	GM	KB	mm
AC	CD	DP	gm	KC	MM
ac	CF	Dr	GP	KG	MN
AD	cf	DS	GR	km	MO
ad	CH	DV	gr	KO	MP
AG	Ch	EC	GS	kr	MR
AI	ch	Ed	gs	KT	Mr
am	CI	ed	GT	Kt	MS
AV	cl	eg	gu	LA	Ms
av	cm	EP	HC	lb	Mt
BA	c/o	ER	HE	lc	mv
BB	CO	Ex	hf	Ld	MW
BC	Co	Ez	HM	lh	NB
BD	CP	FA	ho	LM	nd
bf	cp	FD	HP	LP	NE
bk	CR	ff	HQ	LT	NI
BL	cr	fl	hr	Lt	nl
BM	CS	FM	HT	LV	no
bn	ct	FO	ib	MA	nr
BP	Cu	FP	i/c	mb	NS
Bp	cu	Fr	id	MB	NT
BR	cv	Fr	ie	MC	NW
Br	DA	fr	in	MD	NY
br	DC	FT	IQ	mf	NZ
Bt	DD	ft	Ir	MG	OB
CA	DF	GB	Is	mg	ob
ca	DG	GC	It	MI	OC

OE	qr	SU	yr	Aug	CBI
OK	qt	SW	AAA	AVM	CCF
OM	qv	TA	ABC	bar	Cdr
OP	RA	TB	Abp	BBC	CET
op	RB	TD	acc	BCC	cfi
OR	RC	Th	act	BEd	CGS
OS	RD	tp	ADC	BEF	ChB
OT	Rd	tr	adj	BEM	Chr
OU	rd	TT	adv	bhp	CIA
oz	RE	Tu	AEC	BHS	Cia
pa	RF	TV	aet	BIM	CID
PA	rh	UK	AEU	BMA	Cie
PC	RI	UN	AFC	BMJ	cif
pc	RN	UP	AFM	BMW	CMG
pd	ro	US	agm	BOC	CMS
PE	RS	UU	agr	bor	CND
PG	RT	ux	AID	BOT	COD
pH	RU	vb	aka	Bro	cod
pl	RV	VC	Ald	BRS	COI
pm	ry	VD	alt	BSA	Col
PM	s/c	VE	amp	BSc	col
PO	sc	VJ	amt	BSM	con
po	sd	vo	ans	BST	Cor
pp	SE	VP	aob	BTA	cos
PR	SF	vs	aor	BTU	cot
Pr	SI	vt	APR	Btu	Cpl
pr	SJ	VW	Apr	BVM	CPR
PS	SM	wc	APT	BWV	CRE
Ps	SO	WD	ARP	CAB	CSE
PT	SP	WI	arr	cal	CST
pt	sp	wk	ASA	Cal	CSV
PU	sq	WO	ASH	CAP	CTC
pw	Sr	wp	ATC	cap	CUP
QC	SS	WS	ATS	car	CVO
ql	St	wt	ATV	CAT	cwo
QM	st	yd	AUC	CBE	CWS

cwt	DTs	Feb	GPI	int	lit
Dan	EBU	fec	GTC	IOM	LLB
dau	ECG	fem	GUS	IOU	log
DBE	ECO	fig	Hab	IOW	loq
db l	EDC	fob	HAC	IPC	LPO
DCL	EEC	foc	Hag	IRA	LSA
DCM	EEG	for	HCF	ITN	LSD
DDR	EFL	for	Heb	ITV	LSE
DDT	EIS	her	HGV	Jan	LSO
DEA	EMI	FPA	HLI	Jas	LTA
Dec	ENE	Fri	HMC	JCR	Ltd
dec	Eng	FRS	HMG	jct	LWT
def	eng	fur	HMI	Jer	mag
deg	ENT	fut	HMS	Jno	Maj
del	Eph	fwd	HMV	Jnr	Mal
DEP	ESE	Gal	HNC	Jud	Mar
Dep	ESN	GBA	HND	Jul	max
dep	ESP	gbh	Hon	KBE	MBE
DES	esp	GBS	hor	KCB	MCC
DFC	Esq	GCB	Hos	KGB	Mc/s
DFM	est	GCE	HRH	KKK	MEP
Dip	ESU	GDP	HSE	KLM	met
Dir	ETA	GDR	HTV	km/h	mfd
div	etc	GEC	IBA	kt l	MFH
DIY	ETD	Gen	IBM	Lab	Mgr
DNA	ETU	gen	ICI	lab	Mic
DNB	Exc	Geo	ICS	Lat	mil
dob	fam	ger	ill	lat	Min
DOE	FAO	GHQ	ILO	lbw	min
dom	fas	Gib	ILP	LCC	mis
doz	FBA	GLC	IMF	LCJ	MIT
DPP	FBI	GMC	imp	1cm	MLR
DSC	FCA	GMT	inc	LDS	Mme
DSO	FCO	GNP	ind	LDV	MOD
dsp	fcp	GOC	inc	LEA	mod
DTI	FDR	GOM	inf	Lev	MOH

Mon	NSW	PLA	rep	SDP	TSB
MOT	NUJ	PLC	rev	Sec	TUC
mph	NUM	PLO	RFA	SEN	Tue
MPS	Num	PLP	RFC	Sen	TVA
MRA	NUR	PLR	RFU	seq	UAE
MRC	NUS	PMG	RGS	ser	UAR
Mrs	NUT	PMO	RHA	SET	UDC
MSC	NYO	pop	RHS	SFA	UDI
ms l	OAP	pos	RIC	sfz	UDR
mss	OAS	POW	RIP	sin	UFO
MTB	OBE	ppc	Rly	SMO	UHF
mus	obj	PPE	RMA	SMP	UHT
MVO	Oct	PPS	RMO	SNP	ult
Nat	oct	PRO	RMP	sob	UNO
nat	OED	psc	RMS	Soc	USA
nav	ONC	PTA	ROC	sol	USN
NBC	OND	Pte	Rom	sop	USS
nbg	ono	PTO	RPI	SOS	usu
NCB	opp	PVC	RPM	sqn	usw
NCO	Ops	QED	rpm	SRN	VAD
NEB	opt	QEF	RPO	SSE	val
NEC	ord	QEH	RRE	SSW	var
neg	OSB	QMG	RSA	STD	VAT
Neh	OTC	QPR	RSM	std	VDU
NFS	OUP	qty	RTE	str	veg
NFT	Oxf	RAC	RTZ	STV	vel
NFU	pap	rad	RUC	sub	Ven
NGA	par	RAF	RYS	Sun	VHF
NHI	pat	RAM	sae	tan	vid
NHS	PBI	RBA	SAM	TCD	VIP
NNE	PCC	RCM	Sam	tel	viz
NNW	PEN	RCO	SAS	ten	voc
nom	PEP	RCT	Sat	Thu	vol
NOP	PGA	RDC	SCE	Tim	VSO
Nov	PhD	rec	SCM	Tit	WEA
NPL	phr	ref	SCR	TNT	Wed

wef	biog	cosh	FIFA	kilo	orig
WHO	biol	coth	floz	lang	ORTF
WNW	bldg	CPRE	FRCP	L|of|C	OUDS
wpb	BMus	CRMP	FRCS	Lond	Oxon
wpm	BNOC	CSYS	GATT	long	pass
WSW	BOAC	DAAG	GCMG	LRAM	PAYE
WVS	Brig	D|day	GCVO	LRCP	PDSA
YOP	Brit	decl	Gdns	LRCS	perf
abbr	Bros	dept	gent	mach	perh
ABTA	BThU	derv	geog	marg	pers
ACAS	BUPA	Deut	geol	masc	Phil
ACGB	caps	DHSS	geom	math	phon
AERE	Capt	dial	Glam	Matt	phot
AIDS	CARD	diam	Glos	mech	phys
AMDG	Card	dict	guin	memo	pinx
ammo	Cath	diff	HIDB	MIRV	plup
anat	cath	dist	hist	Mlle	plur
anon	CCPR	DMus	hi|fi	Mods	Preb
arch	CEGB	DUKW	HMSO	MORI	prep
asap	cent	Ebor	Hons	morn	Pres
Asst	cert	Eccl	IATA	MRCP	Prin
at|no	chap	Edin	ICBM	NADA	prob
at|wt	Chas	EFTA	ILEA	NATO	Prof
AUEW	Chem	E l|A l	incl	naut	prop
AWOL	choc	ELDO	INRI	Nazi	Prot
AWRE	CIGS	elec	Inst	NCCL	Prov
BAOR	C|i n|C	ENSA	NEDC	prox
Bart	circ	EOKA	IOUS	neut	PSBR
B|Cal	co|ed	EPNS	Irel	NFER	RADA
B|Com	C|o f|E	Esth	ital	non|U	RADC
Beds	C|o f|I	et|al	Josh	Obad	RAEC
Belg	C|o f|S	exec	Judg	obdt	RAMC
B|è s|L	comp	Exon	junc	OCTU	RAOC
B|è s|S	conj	Ezek	KCMG	OEEC	RAPC
BFPO	co|op	FIAT	KCVO	OHMS	RAVC
Bibl	Corp	FIDO	KGCB	OPEC	RCMP

5

recd	Thur	Assoc	in|loc	SOGAT
regt	TocH	ASTMS	intro	SSAFA
REME	trig	BALPA	Lancs	STOPP
rhet	Trin	B|and|B	LASER	subst
RIBA	Tues	b|and|s	Leics	SWALK
RNAS	UCCA	Bart's	Lieut	SWAPO
RNIB	UEFA	BASIC	Lincs	theol
RNLI	Univ	Berks	Lt,Col	Thess
RNVR	USAF	BLitt	Lt,Gen	trans
ro,ro	USSR	Bucks	maths	treas
RSPB	VSOP	Cambs	meths	UMIST
RSVP	VTOL	CAMRA	Middx	UNRRA
SALT	vulg	CENTO	NAAFI	UWIST
SATB	WAAC	Chron	Notts	V|and|A
Scot	WAAF	circs	NSPCC	vocab
SDLP	WACS	COBOL	op|cit	WAACS
sect	WAVE	COHSE	OXFAM	WAAFS
Sept	W/Cdr	Comdr	P|and|O	Wilts
Serg	WFTU	contd	PLUTO	Worcs
sing	WRAC	cosec	pro|am	WRACS
sinh	WRAF	cresc	pseud	Xtian
SNCF	WRNS	cusec	R|and|A	Yorks
Solr	WRVS	D|and|C	R|and|D	ab|init
SPCK	Xmas	Dip|Ed	ROSLA	approx
SPQR	YMCA	DLitt	RoSPA	attrib
STOL	AAQMG	DPhil	RSPCA	Cantab
subj	ad|lib	ERNIE	Rt|Hon	cet|par
Supt	admin	et|seq	Rt|Rev	cosech
syst	ad|val	ex|lib	Salop	Dunelm
tanh	ALGOL	G|and|S	Sarum	E|and|OE
TASS	Anzac	h|and|c	sci|fi	Fid|Def
TCCB	ANZUS	Hants	SCUBA	Hon|Sec
tech	appro	Herts	SEATO	incorp
temp	arith	Hunts	SHAEF	indecl
TGWU	Asdic	indef	SHAPE	Lit|Hum
Thos	ASLEF	indiv	SLADE	loc|cit

6/9 LETTERS

Londin	SABENA	Nat|West
Lonrho	sculpt	non|obst
Man|Dir	Staffs	per|cent
Messrs	transf	Pol|Econ
mod|con	UNESCO	prox|acc
Mus|Bac	UNICEF	Reg|Prof
Mus|Doc	Winton	var|lect
Nat|Sci	Benelux	verb|sap
nem|con	Cantuar	infra|dig
NIBMAR	COMECON	Interpol
non|com	Consols	Northumb
Noncon	Dip|Tech	Oxbridge
non|seq	Euratom	Cominform
Norvic	FORTRAN	Comintern
pro|tem	intrans	Northants
QARANC	nat|hist	
quango	NATSOPA	

Agriculture

ear	corn	mare	silo	ditch	mower
hay	crop	milk	skep	drill	mulch
lea	dung	neat	soil	fruit	ovine
mow	farm	neep	till	grain	plant
rye	herd	oats	vega	grass	ranch
bale	husk	peat	weed	graze	rumen
barn	jess	pest	baler	guano	sheep
bull	kine	rake	bothy	haulm	shoat
byre	lamb	rape	calve	hedge	stock
calf	lime	root	churn	horse	straw
cart	loam	seed	crops	humus	tilth
clay	lush	shaw	dairy	maize	tuber

AGRICULTURE

veldt	potato	prairie
wagon	reaper	rancher
wheat	roller	reaping
yield	sheave	rearing
animal	silage	rustler
arable	sowing	savanna
barley	stable	stubble
binder	trough	subsoil
butter	turnip	tillage
cattle	warble	tilling
cereal	weevil	tractor
clover	anthrax	wagoner
colter	bullock	agronomy
cowman	cabbage	breeding
cutter	calving	clippers
digger	combine	cropping
fallow	compost	drainage
farmer	cowherd	elevator
fodder	cowshed	ensilage
forage	digging	farmyard
furrow	drought	forestry
gimmer	erosion	gleaning
grains	farming	hayfield
grange	fertile	haymaker
harrow	harvest	haystack
heifer	haycart	landgirl
hopper	hayrick	loosebox
manger	lambing	pedigree
manure	lucerne	pigswill
meadow	milkcan	rootcrop
merino	milking	rotation
millet	newmown	rotavate
piglet	paddock	rotovate
pigsty	pasture	shearing
plough	piggery	sheepdip
porker	poultry	vineyard

8

allotment	agriculture
cornfield	chicken farm
dairy farm	cultivation
dairymaid	farm produce
fertility	germination
grassland	insecticide
harvester	pasture land
haymaking	poultry farm
husbandry	agricultural
implement	horticulture
incubator	insemination
livestock	market garden
pasturage	smallholding
phosphate	agriculturist
pig trough	agrobiologist
ploughing	cattle breeder
root house	cattle farming
rotavator	chicken farmer
rotovator	electric fence
shorthorn	horticultural
sugar beet	kitchen garden
swineherd	sheep shearing
threshing	stock breeding
wasteland	tea plantation
winnowing	viticulturist
agronomist	collective farm
battery hen	market gardener
cattle cake	milking machine
cultivator	milking parlour
fertilizer	speed the plough
harvesting	agriculturalist
husbandman	market gardening
irrigation	rotation of crops
weed killer	

Animals

ai	moo	byre	hoof	paca	toad
ox	nag	cage	horn	pack	tusk
ape	pad	calf	howl	pard	tyke
ass	paw	cavy	hump	peba	unau
bat	pet	chow	ibex	pelt	ursa
bay	pig	claw	jill	pest	urus
cat	pod	colt	kine	pika	urva
cob	pom	cony	kudu	poll	vole
cow	pug	coon	lair	pony	wolf
cry	pup	deer	lamb	prad	yelp
cub	ram	dray	ling	prey	yoke
cur	rat	drey	lion	puma	yowl
dam	run	fang	lynx	puss	zebu
den	set	fawn	mane	rein	addax
doe	sow	Fido	mare	roan	apery
dog	sty	foal	meow	roar	beast
elk	teg	form	mews	rout	billy
ewe	tod	frog	mink	runt	biped
fox	tom	gaur	moke	saki	bison
fur	tup	goat	mole	seal	bitch
gam	yak	hack	mona	sett	bleat
gnu	zoo	hare	mule	stag	bongo
hob	Arab	hart	musk	stot	borer
hog	beak	herd	mutt	stud	boxer
kid	bear	hern	myna	tail	brock
kit	boar	hide	neat	teal	brood
kob	bray	hind	oont	team	Bruin
low	buck	hock	oryx	tike	brush
mew	bull	hole	oxen	titi	brute

5/6 LETTERS

bunny	horse	panda	stray	basset
burro	hound	pidog	swine	bayard
camel	husky	piggy	tabby	beagle
caple	hutch	pinto	takin	beaver
capul	hutia	pongo	talon	bellow
catch	hyena	pooch	tapir	beluga
civet	hyrax	potto	tatou	bharal
coati	izard	pouch	tiger	bident
coney	jenny	pound	tigon	bobcat
coypu	Jumbo	pride	troop	borzoi
crawl	kaama	puppy	trunk	bovine
cuddy	kiang	pussy	udder	bow,wow
daman	kitty	rache	urial	Briard
dhole	koala	rasse	vixen	bridle
dingo	kulan	ratel	waler	bronco
dogie	lapin	reins	whale	burrow
drill	leash	rhino	whelp	cackle
drove	lemur	sable	zebra	canine
earth	liger	saiga	zibet	castor
eland	llama	sasin	zoril	cat,nap
fauna	loris	satyr	zorro	cattle
feral	manis	sheep	agouta	cayman
field	manul	shire	agouti	chacma
filly	miaow	shoat	albino	circus
fitch	moose	shrew	alpaca	coaita
flock	morse	skunk	angora	cocker
fossa	mount	slink	antler	collie
gayal	mouse	sloth	aoudad	colugo
genet	nanny	snarl	argali	corral
genus	Neddy	snort	aye,aye	cougar
girth	neigh	snout	baboon	coyote
grice	okapi	spitz	badger	coypou
growl	orang	stall	baleen	cruive
grunt	otary	steed	bandog	curtal
hinny	otter	steer	barren	cus,cus
hippo	ounce	stoat	barton	dassie

11

ANIMALS

desman	hograt	margay	saddle
dewlap	hooves	marmot	saluki
dikdik	houdah	marten	sambar
dobbin	howdah	merino	school
donkey	humble	merlin	seaape
dragon	hummel	monkey	seacow
dugong	hunter	mouser	seadog
embryo	hyaena	mousse	serval
entire	hybrid	mulish	setter
equine	impala	muskox	shelty
ermine	instar	muster	simian
farrow	jackal	muzzle	sleuth
feline	jaeger	nilgai	sorrel
fennec	jaguar	nilgau	sphinx
ferine	jennet	ocelot	stable
ferret	jerboa	onager	string
fossil	jumart	pallah	summer
foxbat	jungle	pariah	tarpan
garron	kennel	pastor	taurus
geegee	killer	phylum	teetee
genera	kindle	piglet	teledu
gennet	kitfox	pigrat	tenrec
gerbil	kitten	pigsty	tomcat
gibbon	koodoo	poodle	toydog
gnawer	langur	porker	tracer
gobble	lapdog	possum	tusker
gopher	lionet	pugdog	ursine
grison	litter	pyedog	vermin
grivet	lowing	quagga	vervet
guenon	lowrie	rabbit	vicuna
gundog	lupine	racoon	walrus
hackee	maddog	ranger	wapiti
hackle	mammal	redfox	warren
hegoat	manati	reebok	weasel
heifer	manege	rhesus	wether
hogget	manger	rodent	whinny

wild|ox	chimera	griffin	manatee
wombat	colobus	griffon	Manx|cat
wyvern	coon|cat	gryphon	markhor
ant|bear	courser	grysbok	marmose
asinine	cowshed	guanaco	mastiff
aurochs	croaker	guereza	meerkat
barking	dasyure	habitat	metazoa
basenji	deerdog	hackney	milk|cow
bear|cat	deer|hog	half|ape	mole|rat
beavery	deerlet	hamster	mongrel
bestial	denizen	hanuman	monster
big|game	dew|claw	harness	mouflon
bighorn	dolphin	harrier	muridae
bird|dog	echinus	hexapod	musimon
blesbok	epizoon	hindleg	musk|hog
blue|fox	ewe|lamb	hindpaw	musk|rat
brocket	extinct	hircine	mustang
buffalo	fetlock	hog|deer	nandine
bull|bat	finback	hogwash	narwhal
bulldog	fitchet	ice|bear	nosebag
bullock	fitchew	jacchus	opossum
bush|cat	foreleg	jackass	pack|rat
caracal	forepaw	karakul	paddock
carcase	foumart	keitloa	painter
carcass	fur|seal	lambkin	palfrey
caribou	gambrel	land|rat	palmcat
catling	gazelle	lemming	panther
cattalo	gelding	leonine	pastern
centaur	gemsbok	leopard	peccary
cervine	giraffe	leveret	Pegasus
cetacea	gizzard	linsang	piebald
chamois	glutton	lioness	pig|deer
charger	gnu|goat	lurcher	pit|pony
cheetah	gorilla	macaque	pole|cat
Cheviot	grampus	madoqua	polypod
chikara	grey|fox	mammoth	

13

porcine	twinter	brancard	dog|pound
pricket	unicorn	brown|rat	dog's|life
primate	urodele	bull|calf	dormouse
raccoon	vaccine	bull|frog	duckbill
rathole	vampire	bush|baby	earth|hog
rattler	vulpine	bush|buck	edentate
red|deer	wallaby	cachalot	elephant
redpoll	warthog	cachelot	elkhound
Reynard	water|ox	cannibal	entellus
roebuck	web|toed	capuchin	entrails
roe|deer	whippet	capybara	fin|whale
rorqual	whisker	carapace	foxhound
rotifer	wild|ass	carcajou	frogling
saimiri	wild|cat	cariacou	fruit|bat
Samoyed	wistiti	castrate	Galloway
sapajou	withers	cave|bear	grey|mare
sea|lion	wolf|dog	cavicorn	grey|wolf
she|goat	wood|rat	ceratops	hair|seal
shippon	aardvark	Cerberus	hair|tail
siamang	aardwolf	cetacean	hedgehog
sirenia	abattoir	chestnut	hedgepig
sondeli	Airedale	chimaera	hoggerel
sounder	animalia	chipmuck	horse|box
sounder	anteater	chipmunk	hound|dog
spaniel	antelope	chowchow	house|dog
spouter	Antilope	civet|cat	humpback
sumpter	argonaut	coach|dog	hydrozoa
sun|bear	bactrian	cowhouse	Irish|elk
tadpole	black|cat	creature	jenny|ass
tamarin	black|fox	dairy|cow	kangaroo
tanager	black|rat	deer|park	keeshond
tarsier	blauwbok	demi|wolf	kinkajou
terrier	blinkers	Derby|dog	kitty|cat
tigress	blow|hole	dinosaur	kolinsky
tree|fox	blue|buck	Doberman	labrador
trotter	blue|hare	dog|house	lancelet

14

leporine	predator	turnspit
lion'sden	protozoa	turn tail
longhorn	pussycat	ungulate
loosebox	rabbitry	viscacha
mandrill	reindeer	vivarium
maneater	rhizopod	wanderoo
mangabey	riverhog	warhorse
marmoset	ruminant	warragal
mastodon	sandmole	watchdog
maverick	sapiutan	watercow
Minotaur	sauropod	waterdog
mongoose	seahorse	waterrat
monkseal	sealyham	wharfrat
muledeer	seaotter	whistler
musquash	seaswine	whitefox
nautilus	serotine	wildboar
neatherd	sheepdog	wildgoat
nightape	shepherd	wildlife
noseband	Shetland	wolfpack
oliphant	skewbald	woofwoof
omnivore	spitzdog	yeanling
ouistiti	squirrel	yearling
packmule	stallion	amphibian
palomino	stegodon	Angoracat
pangolin	steinbok	Arcticfox
Pekinese	straycat	armadillo
pennydog	straydog	arthropod
pinniped	suborder	babirussa
pinscher	suricate	babyrussa
platanna	tabbycat	badgerdog
platypus	terrapin	bandicoot
polarfox	theropod	bangsring
polliwog	tigercat	beaverrat
polopony	tortoise	billygoat
porkling	treefrog	binturong
porpoise	troutlet	blackbear

15

Black|Bess	dog|collar	lamp,shell
blackbuck	dog|kennel	latration
blue|sheep	dray|horse	lion,heart
blue|whale	dromedary	livestock
boarhound	dziggetai	Lowrie|Tod
brood|mare	earth|wolf	mammalian
brown|bear	Eskimo|dog	manticora
brush|deer	feralized	manticore
brush|wolf	fill|horse	March|hare
buck|hound	flying|fox	mare's|nest
burro|deer	frog|spawn	marsupial
caballine	gazehound	marsupium
Caffre|cat	gift|horse	megathere
camass,rat	ginger|tom	menagerie
caparison	Great|Dane	monoceros
carnivore	greyhound	monotreme
cart|horse	grimalkin	mouldwarp
catamount	ground,hog	mouse,deer
cat|and|dog	guinea,pig	mousehole
caterwaul	herbivore	mule,train
ceratodus	herpestes	musk,shrew
chickaree	high|horse	Nandi|bear
chihuahua	honey|bear	nanny|goat
coleopter	hoofprint	native|cat
cotton|rat	horse,shoe	neat,house
crocodile	horse|whip	neat,stall
curry|comb	Houyhnhnm	on|the|hoof
dachshund	ichneumon	orangutan
dairy|herd	iguanodon	oviparous
Dalmatian	Incitatus	pachyderm
dark|horse	infusoria	pademelon
deerhound	Jersey|cow	palm,civet
deer,mouse	Judas|goat	pariah|dog
deer,tiger	jungle|law	Pekingese
desert|rat	Kerry|blue	percheron
dinothere	koala|bear	phalanger

pinnipede	tiffen|bat	black|sheep
pipistrel	tiger|wolf	blood|horse
pocket|rat	Tod|Lowrie	bloodhound
polar|bear	toy|poodle	bottle|nose
police|dog	tree|shrew	Bucephalus
poodle|dog	trilobite	bull|roarer
porcupine	ululation	Burmese|cat
prayer|dog	waterbuck	camelopard
predatory	water|bull	camel|train
proboscis	water|deer	cannon|bone
pronghorn	water|mole	cattle|grid
protozoan	water|vole	cephalopod
quadruped	Welsh|pony	chevrotain
racehorse	whalebone	chimpanzee
razor|back	white|bear	chinchilla
red|setter	wild|sheep	Clydesdale
rescue|dog	wolfhound	coach|horse
retriever	wolverine	cottontail
ridgeback	woodchuck	crio|sphinx
Rosinante	wood|mouse	dachshound
sarcodina	woodshock	dapple|grey
scavenger	yellow|dog	dermoptera
schnauzer	youngling	dog's|chance
sea|canary	zeuglodon	dumb|animal
sea|squirt	Angora|goat	dumb|friend
shorthorn	angwantibo	equestrian
shrew|mole	animalcule	Evangeline
silver|fox	animal|life	fallow|deer
skunk|bear	arthropoda	fatted|calf
sloth|bear	babiroussa	field|mouse
springbok	Barbary|ape	flagellata
staghound	bear|garden	fox|terrier
St|Bernard	Bedlington	freemartin
stegosaur	bell|the|cat	giant|panda
studhorse	bellwether	golden|mole
tarantula	bezoar|goat	ground|game

hammerhead	pig in a poke	sucking pig
hartebeest	pine marten	Syrian bear
heterocera	Pomeranian	tail wagger
hippogriff	pouched rat	tantony pig
hippogryph	prairie dog	tardigrade
honey mouse	prairie fox	thill horse
horned toad	raccoon dog	Tiergarten
horn footed	radiolaria	timber wolf
horseflesh	rat terrier	toy spaniel
horse sense	rhinoceros	toy terrier
hunting dog	right whale	trace horse
Iceland dog	river horse	tracker dog
Indian pony	rock badger	Turkish cat
jack rabbit	Russian cat	vampire bat
jaguarundi	sabre tooth	vertebrate
Kodiak bear	saddleback	water mouse
kookaburra	sand hopper	Weimaraner
leopardess	sausage dog	white whale
lion's share	schipperke	wild animal
loggerhead	sea blubber	wildebeest
Maltese cat	sea leopard	woolly bear
Maltese dog	sea monster	xiphopagus
martingale	sea unicorn	Afghan hound
megalosaur	sheep's eyes	basset hound
molluscoid	Shire horse	beast of prey
neat cattle	short sheep	Belgian hare
omnivorous	shrew mouse	black cattle
ornithopod	Siamese cat	bloodsucker
otterhound	snaffle bit	buffalo wolf
otter shrew	sperm whale	bull mastiff
pack animal	spring buck	bull terrier
pack of dogs	spring hare	bunny rabbit
pantheress	spring tail	Buridan's ass
paradoxure	stock horse	Cape buffalo
Persian cat	stone horse	cardophagus
phyllopoda	sub species	carriage dog

cat's pyjamas	plantigrade	catamountain
cat squirrel	pocket mouse	cat's whiskers
Cheshire cat	prairie wolf	cattle market
church mouse	rabbit hutch	cinnamon bear
crown antler	red squirrel	dog in a manger
dairy cattle	reservation	draught horse
daisy cutter	rhynchodont	dumb creature
Diana monkey	saddle girth	field spaniel
eager beaver	saddle horse	French poodle
Egyptian cat	sand skipper	gazelle hound
elephantine	sea elephant	goat antelope
entire horse	shepherd dog	grey squirrel
fishing frog	sleuth hound	Guinea baboon
flickertail	snaffle rein	hare and hound
flying lemur	snow leopard	harvest mouse
globigerina	social whale	hippopotamus
green turtle	sorrel horse	hoofed animal
grizzly bear	sporting dog	horse blanket
ground sloth	stone marten	Irish terrier
hibernation	sumpter mule	jumping mouse
Highland cow	swamp rabbit	jumping shrew
hircocervus	titanothere	king of beasts
honey badger	wheel animal	marmalade cat
horned horse	white ermine	mating season
insectivore	wishtonwish	mountain goat
Irish setter	wolf whistle	mountain hare
kangaroo rat	American lion	mountain lion
Kilkenny cat	Archangel cat	national park
killer whale	baby elephant	Newfoundland
land spaniel	bay at the moon	pantophagous
lion hearted	beard the lion	platanna frog
Malayan bear	bonnet monkey	pocket gopher
orang outang	bottom animal	quarter horse
ornithosaur	Cairn terrier	rhesus monkey
paper sailor	Cashmere goat	rock squirrel
Pavlov's dogs		Saint Bernard

19

ANIMALS

Shetland pony	draught animal
Spanish horse	echinodermata
Spanish sheep	gadarene swine
spider monkey	mountain sheep
Suffolk punch	nature reserve
sumpter horse	rogue elephant
thoroughbred	Scotch terrier
tree squirrel	sheep and goats
ursine monkey	tortoise shell
Virginia deer	Clumber spaniel
water buffalo	domestic animal
water spaniel	Highland cattle
Welsh terrier	horse of the year
Aberdeen Angus	Indian elephant
affenpinscher	man's best friend
ailourophilia	pedigree cattle
ailourophobia	Aberdeen terrier
animalisation	animal magnetism
animal kingdom	golden retriever
animal worship	miniature poodle
baggage animal	Newfoundland dog
beast of burden	Scottish terrier
Boston terrier	Sealyham terrier
cocker spaniel	springer spaniel
Dandie Dinmont	

Architecture

3D	bay	inn	rib	arch	barn
RA	cot	kip	tie	area	base
wc	den	nef	adit	aula	bead
bar	hut	pub	apse	balk	beam

4/5 LETTERS

bell	list	site	cabin	helix	plaza
bema	loft	slab	cella	hinge	porch
berm	mews	slum	cheek	hoist	pylon
boss	mill	span	close	hotel	quoin
byre	moat	step	coign	hotel	ranch
cell	mole	stoa	court	house	range
coin	naos	tent	croft	hovel	revet
cote	nave	tige	crown	hutch	ridge
cove	nook	tile	crypt	igloo	riser
cusp	ogee	toft	decor	ingle	rooms
cyma	pale	tope	ditch	inlay	salle
dado	pane	vane	domus	Ionic	salon
dais	park	wall	Doric	jetty	scale
digs	path	weir	dowel	joint	sewer
dome	pier	well	drain	joist	shack
door	pile	wing	drive	jutty	shaft
drip	plan	yard	eaves	kiosk	shore
drum	post	zeta	entry	ledge	slate
eave	quad	abbey	facia	level	slums
exit	rail	abode	fanal	lobby	socie
face	ramp	adobe	fence	lodge	sough
farm	raze	adyta	flats	lotus	speos
flag	reed	agora	floor	mains	spire
flat	rima	aisle	flush	manor	splay
flue	rind	alley	flute	manse	stage
fort	rise	ancon	folly	mitre	stair
foss	road	arena	forum	motel	stall
fret	roof	arris	fosse	newel	stele
gate	roof	attic	foyer	niche	stile
haha	room	berth	gable	ogive	stoep
hall	sash	booth	glass	order	stone
head	seat	bothy	glebe	oriel	stria
home	shed	bower	glyph	ovolo	strut
jamb	shop	brick	grate	panel	study
keep	sill	broch	groin	patio	stupa
lift	silo	brogh	hatch	pitch	suite

talon	castle	fillet	listel	rafter
tepee	cellar	finial	loggia	recess
torus	cement	fleche	lounge	refuge
tower	centre	fluted	louvre	reglet
trave	chalet	founds	lyceum	regula
tread	chapel	fresco	maison	relief
trunk	church	frieze	mantel	rococo
tupek	circus	garage	marble	rubble
tupik	closet	garden	metope	saloon
usine	coffer	garret	milieu	school
vault	column	gazebo	module	sconce
villa	concha	ghetto	mortar	scotia
adytum	convex	girder	mosaic	screen
alcove	coping	godown	mosque	scroll
annexe	corbel	gopura	mud|hut	shanty
arbour	corner	Gothic	muntin	sluice
arcade	corona	gradin	museum	soffit
aspect	course	grange	mutule	spence
atrium	cranny	granny	oculus	spiral
avenue	crenel	gravel	office	spring
awning	cupola	griffe	pagoda	square
bagnio	damper	grille	palace	stable
barrow	dentil	ground	palais	storey
barton	donjon	gutter	paling	street
batten	dormer	hangar	parget	stucco
bedsit	dorsal	hawhaw	parvis	studio
belfry	dosser	header	pharos	suburb
billet	dry|rot	hearth	piazza	summer
bistro	duplex	hostel	picket	tablet
bridge	durbar	hostel	pillar	taenia
brough	estate	impost	plinth	tavern
by,room	exedra	insula	podium	temple
camber	fabric	kennel	portal	thatch
camera	facade	lancet	posada	tholos
canopy	facing	lean,to	prefab	tholus
canopy	fascia	lintel	purlin	timber

22

toilet	capital	estrade	lowrise
torsel	caracol	eustyle	lunette
trench	carving	factory	mansard
tunnel	cavetto	fencing	mansion
turret	ceiling	festoon	marquee
vallum	chamber	fitment	masonry
volute	chambre	fixture	megaron
wicket	chancel	fluting	minaret
wigwam	chapter	Fossway	mirador
window	charnel	freelend	moellon
zoning	chateau	fusarol	mudsill
academy	chezmoi	galilee	mullion
address	chimney	gallery	munting
airduct	choltry	garland	mutular
archlet	cipolin	gateway	narthex
archway	cistern	godroon	necking
areaway	citadel	gradine	newtown
armoury	cloison	granary	nursery
arsenal	cobwall	granite	obelisk
asphalt	concave	grating	offices
astylar	conduit	grounds	ossuary
balcony	console	hallway	outlook
barmkin	contour	hiproof	outwork
baroque	cornice	hospice	palazzo
barrack	cottage	housing	pannier
beading	crocket	hydrant	pantile
bearing	cubicle	keyhole	parapet
bedroom	culvert	kitchen	parlour
boudoir	cushion	klinker	parquet
boxroom	derrick	lagging	passage
bracing	dinette	landing	pendant
bracket	doorway	lantern	pension
bulwark	dungeon	larmier	pergola
cabaret	echinus	lattice	plafond
canteen	edifice	library	plaster
cantina	entasis	lodging	ponceau

portico	terrace	banister	curb|roof
postern	theatre	bannerol	cymatium
purlieu	tie,beam	barbican	dark,room
pyramid	tracery	bartisan	dead,wall
railing	transom	base|line	detached
rampart	trefoil	basement	diggings
Rathaus	trellis	basilica	domicile
reredos	tribune	bathroom	doorhead
roofage	tumulus	bell|tent	doorjamb
roofing	upright	best|room	doorpost
rooftop	veranda	blinding	doorsill
roomlet	viaduct	brattice	downpipe
rosette	vitrail	building	driveway
rostrum	abamurus	bulkhead	dwelling
rotunda	abatjour	bull's,eye	ebenezer
sanctum	abatvoix	bungalow	entrance
Schloss	abbatoir	buttress	entresol
sea|wall	abutment	canephor	epistyle
shebeen	acanthus	cantoned	erection
shelter	acrolith	capstone	espalier
shelter	air,drain	caracole	estancia
shingle	anteroom	caryatid	exterior
shore|up	aperture	casement	extrados
shoring	apophyge	catacomb	fanlight
shutter	aqueduct	chapiter	farmyard
sinkage	arcature	chaptrel	fastness
skew|put	archives	chez,nous	faubourg
skid|row	artefact	cincture	fire|plug
slating	astragal	clithral	fireside
station	Atlantes	cloister	fire|stop
steeple	aularian	colossus	flat|arch
storied	back,door	concrete	flat|roof
subbase	baguette	corridor	flooring
sundial	baluster	cross,tie	fortress
surbase	bandelet	cul,de,sac	fossette
Telamon	banderol	cupboard	fountain

funkhole	outhouse	subtopia
fusarole	palisade	suburbia
gableend	palmette	sunporch
gameroom	Pantheon	tectonic
gargoyle	parabema	tenement
gatepost	parclose	teocalli
hacienda	parterre	terraced
handrail	pavilion	thalamus
headpost	peakarch	tileroof
headsill	pedestal	tolbooth
highrise	pediment	topfloor
hospital	pilaster	townhall
hothouse	pinnacle	transept
housetop	platform	trapdoor
interior	playroom	traverse
intrados	pointing	triglyph
isodomon	property	triptych
keystone	prospect	tympanum
kingpost	quarters	underpin
lavatory	rocaille	upstairs
lichgate	sacristy	verandah
lodgings	scaffold	voussoir
lodgment	scullery	wainscot
logcabin	semidome	walltent
lotusbud	shoulder	windmill
lovenest	shutters	woodworm
magazine	sidedoor	ziggurat
martello	skewback	acoustics
messhall	skylight	acropolis
messuage	slumarea	alignment
monolith	snackbar	almshouse
monrepos	solarium	angleiron
monument	spandril	anthemion
ogeearch	stairway	apartment
openplan	stockade	architect
ornament	storeyed	archivolt

Attic|base	converted	framework
banderole	courtyard	front|door
banquette	cross|beam	front|room
bas|relief	crossette	fundament
bay|window	crown|post	gable|roof
bead|house	cubby|hole	garderobe
bell|tower	cubiculum	glory|hole
belvedere	curtilage	green|belt
blueprint	curvature	guildhall
bolection	cyma|recta	guttering
bottoming	decastyle	gymnasium
bow|window	door|frame	headboard
box|girder	door|panel	headmould
breezeway	doorstone	headpiece
brickwork	dormitory	hexastyle
bunkhouse	doss|house	homecroft
butt|joint	drainpipe	homestall
cafeteria	dripstone	homestead
campanile	dry|fresco	hoodmould
cartouche	earthwork	houseboat
cartulary	edificial	house|plan
cathedral	elevation	impromptu
cauliculi	esplanade	inglenook
chophouse	estaminet	ingleside
clapboard	extension	inner|city
classical	fan|window	landscape
cleithral	farmhouse	low|relief
cloakroom	fastigium	marquetry
clubhouse	fireplace	masonwork
coal|house	fixed|arch	mausoleum
coffer|dam	flagstone	mezzanine
coffering	flathouse	mock|Tudor
colonnade	floor|plan	modillion
Colosseum	flophouse	mouldings
columella	footstone	neo|Gothic
composite	forecourt	Nissen|hut

octastyle	stateroom	battlement
open|floor	still,room	bedchamber
outskirts	stonewall	bidonville
paintwork	stormdoor	blind|alley
panelling	structure	breakwater
Parthenon	stylobate	bressumer
partition	sunk|fence	canephorus
pedentive	sun|lounge	cantilever
penthouse	swingdoor	cauliculus
peridrome	synagogue	cellar|door
peristyle	telamones	chimney,pot
pontlevis	threshold	cinquefoil
proseuche	tierceron	clearstory
prothesis	tollbooth	clerestory
reception	tollhouse	clock|tower
refectory	town|house	coffee|shop
reservoir	tree,house	common|room
residence	triforium	compluvium
revetment	truss|beam	conversion
ridgepole	Tudor|arch	Corinthian
rigid|arch	vallation	covered|way
ring|fence	vestibule	crosswalls
roadhouse	wallboard	damp|course
rough|arch	warehouse	denticular
roughcast	whitewash	diaconicon
round|arch	window|bay	dining|hall
rus|in|urbe	window|box	dining|room
sally|port	acroterion	doll's|house
scagliola	arched|door	Doric|order
scantling	arched|roof	downstairs
shopfront	architrave	drawbridge
skew,table	art|gallery	earthworks
slate|roof	auditorium	excavation
staircase	balustrade	family|seat
stairhead	barge,board	fan,tracery
stanchion	base|course	fire|escape

27

first|floor	pied|à|terre	structural
first|story	pigeonhole	sun|parlour
foot|bridge	pile|bridge	terra|cotta
French|roof	portcullis	trust|house
garden|wall	priest|hole	tumbledown
glass|house	projection	turret|room
glebe|house	proportion	undercroft
Greek|Ionic	propylaeum	university
greenhouse	proscenium	ventilator
ground|plan	quadrangle	watch|tower
groundsill	quatrefoil	wicket|door
groundwork	Quonset|hut	wicket|gate
habitation	ranch|house	antechamber
hammer|beam	real|estate	atmospheric
hipped|roof	repository	barge|couple
Ionic|order	restaurant	barge|stones
ivory|tower	retrochoir	barrel|vault
jerry|built	ribbed|arch	buttressing
lancet|arch	ridge|strut	campaniform
Lebensraum	rising|arch	caravansary
lighthouse	rising|damp	chimney|tops
living|room	road|bridge	coffee|house
luxury|flat	Roman|Doric	common|stair
maisonette	Romanesque	compartment
manor|house	rose|window	concert|hall
mantel|tree	rumpus|room	coping|stone
masonry|pin	Saxon|tower	cornerstone
mitre|joint	screenings	country|seat
monolithic	scrollhead	crazy|paving
opera|house	sewing|room	crenellated
orthograph	skew|bridge	cyma|reversa
orthostyle	skew|corbel	drawing|room
passageway	skyscraper	duplex|house
paving|flag	split|level	eating|house
pebble|dash	storehouse	entablature
pentastyle	stronghold	fan|vaulting

foundations	roofing tile	buttress pier
gambrel roof	room divider	caravanserai
ground floor	scaffolding	chapter house
ground table	service lane	charnel house
hanging post	service lift	chimney shaft
hearthstone	shingle roof	chimney stack
ichnography	sitting room	city planning
inhabitancy	smoking room	common bricks
kitchenette	stately home	conservatory
lancet style	step terrace	construction
latticework	street floor	country house
laundry room	summerhouse	dividing wall
leaded glass	sunken fence	Dormer window
lecture hall	trefoil arch	double glazed
linen closet	Tuscan order	double scroll
little boxes	urban sprawl	entrance hall
mansard roof	utility room	espagnolette
mantelpiece	ventilation	false ceiling
mantelshelf	wainscoting	fluted column
masonry arch	waiting room	French Gothic
mews cottage	water closet	french window
morning room	weathercock	frontispiece
Norman tower	willow cabin	galilee porch
oeil de boeuf	window frame	garden suburb
oriel window	window glass	head moulding
outbuilding	wrought iron	hitching post
pantile roof	amphitheatre	hotel de ville
paving stone	architecture	hunting lodge
pendant post	assembly hall	inner sanctum
picket fence	audience hall	lake dwelling
pitched roof	Bailey bridge	lancet window
plasterwork	balustrading	lodging place
pointed arch	bead moulding	machicolated
public house	billiard room	Maiden Castle
rampant arch	breastsummer	main entrance
restoration	building line	mansion house

29

meeting|house	dormitory|town
Nelson|column	doubleg|lazing
phrontistery	dwelling|house
pier|buttress	dwelling|place
plaster|board	emergency|exit
porte|cochere	ferroconcrete
prefabricate	fire|resisting
privy|chamber	floodlighting
rooming|house	furnished|flat
salle|à|manger	Gothic|revival
semi|detached	housing|estate
shutting|post	jerry|building
smallholding	lattice|girder
snubbing|post	master|builder
stained|glass	open|plan|house
string|course	owner|occupied
substructure	palais|de|danse
swinging|post	partition|wall
thatched|roof	picture|window
town|planning	prefabricated
underpinning	public|gallery
urban|renewal	public|library
weatherboard	retaining|wall
accommodation	revolving|door
architectonic	shooting|lodge
architectural	sound|proofing
assembly|rooms	triumpha|l|arch
boarding|house	wattle|and|daub
building|block	apartment|house
building|board	apartment|toilet
butler's|pantry	banqueting|hall
chimney|corner	bed|sitting|room
community|home	consulting|room
council|estate	country|cottage
county|council	funeral|parlour
cross|vaulting	housing|problem

14/15 LETTERS

housing project	banqueting house
interior design	clustered column
listed building	community centre
office building	discharging arch
picture gallery	dormitory suburb
pleasure ground	foundation stone
prefabrication	married quarters
slaughterhouse	owner occupation
superstructure	reception centre
system building	spiral staircase
air conditioning	state apartments
architectonical	unfurnished flat

Artists

Arp	Wren	Monet	Duccio
Low	Bacon	Orpen	Giotto
Adam	Berry	Piper	Ingres
Cuyp	Blake	Pugin	Knight
Dali	Bosch	Rodin	Laszlo
Etty	Clark	Scott	Lavery
Eyck	Corot	Smith	Ledoux
Gill	Crome	Soane	Mabuse
Gogh	David	Steer	Millet
Goya	Degas	Watts	Morris
Hals	Dürer	Wyatt	Panini
Hunt	Frith	Bewick	Pisano
John	Giles	Braque	Renoir
Klee	Kelly	Casson	Romney
Lely	Lippi	Claude	Rubens
Nash	Lowry	Corbet	Ruskin
Opie	Manet	Cotman	Seurat

ARTISTS

Sisley	Phidias
Spence	Picasso
Stubbs	Poussin
Tadema	Raeburn
Titian	Raphael
Turner	Sargent
Van Ryn	Sickert
Warhol	Spencer
Bassano	Tenniel
Bellini	Tiepolo
Bernini	Uccello
Boucher	Utrillo
Cellini	Van Dyck
Cézanne	Van Eyck
Chagall	Van Gogh
Chardin	Vermeer
Cimabue	Watteau
Courbet	Zoffany
Daumier	Angelico
Da Vinci	Brancusi
De Hooch	Brangwyn
El Greco	Brueghel
Epstein	Hepworth
Gauguin	Landseer
Gibbons	Leonardo
Gillray	Mantegna
Gropius	Montegna
Hobbema	Munnings
Hockney	Perugino
Hogarth	Pissarro
Holbein	Rossetti
Matisse	Rousseau
Memlinc	Vanbrugh
Millais	Veronese
Murillo	Vlaminck
Pasmore	Whistler

Beardsley	Mackintosh
Canaletto	Praxiteles
Constable	Rowlandson
Correggio	Sutherland
Delacroix	Tintoretto
Donatello	Fra Angelico
Fragonard	Ghirlandaio
Giorgione	Le Corbusier
Hawksmoor	Gainsborough
Rembrandt	Michelangelo
Velásquez	Winterhalter
Botticelli	Leonardo da Vinci
Caravaggio	Toulouse Lautrec

Astronomy

sky	apsis	Orion	Auriga	Hyades
sun	Ariel	phase	bolide	Hydrus
Argo	Cetus	Pluto	Boötes	meteor
Bora	comet	Rigel	Caelum	Nereid
Hebe	Dione	saros	Castor	Oberon
Juno	Draco	solar	Caurus	Octans
Lynx	Hydra	Spica	corona	Pictor
lyra	Indus	stars	Corvus	planet
Mars	Lepus	Titan	cosmic	Pollux
moon	lunar	umbra	cosmos	quasar
nova	Lupus	Venus	Cygnus	Saturn
Pavo	Mensa	albedo	dipper	Selene
Rhea	Musca	Antlia	Dorado	Sirius
star	nadir	apogee	galaxy	starry
Vega	Norma	Aquila	gnomon	syzygy
Algol	orbit	astral	heaven	Tethys

Triton	transit	red dwarf
Tucana	Achernar	red giant
Uranus	aerolite	Sculptor
Vulcan	Almagest	sidereal
zodiac	aphelion	solarium
Antares	Arcturus	sunspots
appulse	asteroid	universe
apsides	Canicula	upper air
azimuth	Cepheids	Aldebaran
Canopus	Circinus	Andromeda
Cepheus	Cynosure	anthelion
Columba	ecliptic	astrolabe
day star	empyrean	astrology
dog star	Erodanus	astronomy
eclipse	evection	celestial
equinox	fenestra	Centaurus
faculae	flocculi	coelostat
gibbous	full moon	corposant
heavens	galactic	cosmogony
Jupiter	ganymede	cosmology
Lacerta	half moon	Delphinus
Neptune	heavenly	ephemeris
new moon	Hercules	fenestral
Pegasus	hyperion	firmament
perigee	isochasm	fixed star
Perseus	luminary	flocculus
Phoenix	Milky Way	giant star
Polaris	mock moon	Great Bear
Procyon	moonbeam	heliostat
Regulus	night sky	light year
Sagitta	nutation	lunar halo
Serpens	parallax	lunar rays
sextile	penumbra	meteorite
stellar	Pleiades	meteoroid
sunspot	Pointers	Monoceros
Titania	pole star	moonlight

moonshine	perihelion
Ophiuchus	phenomenon
parhelion	precession
planetary	quadrature
planetoid	selenology
polar|star	solar|cycle
quasi,star	solar|flare
radio|star	star|stream
refractor	terminator
satellite	tropopause
scintilla	waning|moon
solar|wind	waxing|moon
starlight	Andromedids
super.nova	Baily's|beads
telescope	coronagraph
uranology	cosmography
Ursa|Major	cosmosphere
Ursa|Minor	evening|star
Vulpecula	falling|star
almacantar	Gegenschein
Canis|major	Kelper's|laws
Canis|minor	league|table
Cassiopeia	lunar|crater
Chamaeleon	major|planet
collimator	midnight|sun
double|star	minor|planet
geocentric	morning|star
green|flash	observatory
Horologium	occultation
ionosphere	Orion's|sword
Lesser|Bear	photosphere
light,curve	planetarium
luminosity	planisphere
Orion's|belt	polar|aurora
outer|space	polar|lights
paraselene	radio,source

ASTRONOMY

solar|corona
solar|energy
solar|system
star|cluster
stella|maris
stratopause
tail|of|comet
Telescopium
translunary
astronomical
astrophysics
Canis|majoris
Charles's|wain
chromosphere
crescent|moon
Halley's|comet
heavenly|body
man|in|the|moon
meteor|crater
meteorograph
selenography
shooting|star
space|station
spectrograph

spectroscope
spectroscopy
star|spangled
stratosphere
variable|star
vertical|rays
constellation
extra|galactic
printed|matter
Southern|Cross
annular|eclipse
astrogeologist
heavenly|bodies
northern|lights
partial|eclipse
radioastronomy
radio|telescope
southern|lights
St|Anthony's|fire
Astronomer|Royal
Hubble's|constant
Nautical|Almanac
sun,|moon|and|stars

Biblical Names

Ur	Ham	Abel	Amon	Cana	Gath
Dan	Job	Adam	Amos	Eden	Gaza
Eli	Lot	Agag	Baal	Edom	Jael
Eve	Nod	Ahab	Boaz	Esau	Jehu
Gad	Abba	Ahaz	Cain	Ezra	Joel

John	Hosea	Dorcas	Pilate
Jude	Isaac	Elijah	Rachel
Leah	Jonah	Elisha	Reuben
Levi	Jacob	Emmaus	Romans
Luke	James	Esther	Salome
Magi	Jesse	Eunice	Samson
Mark	Joppa	Exodus	Samuel
Mary	Jubal	Festus	Simeon
Moab	Judah	Gehazi	Sisera
Noah	Judas	Gibeon	Thomas
Omri	Laban	Gideon	Abaddon
Paul	Micah	Gilboa	Abigail
Ruth	Moses	Gilead	Abilene
Saul	Nahum	Gilgal	Abraham
Seth	Naomi	Goshen	Absalom
Shem	Peter	Haggai	Adullam
Aaron	Sarah	Hannah	Ananias
Abihu	Sheba	Hebron	Antioch
Abner	Silas	Isaiah	Antipas
Abram	Simon	Israel	Azariah
Annas	Sinai	Jairus	Babylon
Asher	Sodom	Jethro	Calvary
Babel	Titus	Jordan	Cherith
Barak	Uriah	Joseph	Cleopas
Caleb	Zadok	Joshua	Corinth
Cyrus	Zimri	Josiah	Deborah
Dagon	Amalek	Judaea	Delilah
David	Andrew	Kishon	Didymus
Dinah	Ararat	Martha	Eleazar
Elias	Balaam	Miriam	Elkanah
Elihu	Belial	Mizpah	Ephesus
Endor	Bethel	Naaman	Ephraim
Enoch	Canaan	Naboth	Ezekiel
Haman	Carmel	Nathan	Gabriel
Herod	Daniel	Nimrod	Galilee
Hiram	Darius	Patmos	Genesis

BIBLICAL NAMES

Gentile	Caiaphas
Goliath	Chorazin
Hebrews	Damascus
Ichabod	Ebenezer
Ishmael	Gadarene
Japheth	Gamaliel
Jericho	Gehennah
Jezebel	Golgotha
Jezreel	Gomorrah
Lazarus	Habakkuk
Malachi	Herodias
Matthew	Hezekiah
Meshach	Immanuel
Messiah	Iscariot
Michael	Issachar
Nineveh	Jephthah
Obadiah	Jeremiah
Pharaoh	Jeroboam
Rebekah	Jonathan
Solomon	Manasseh
Stephen	Matthias
Timothy	Naphtali
Zebedee	Nazareth
Abednego	Nehemiah
Abinadab	Potiphar
Adonijah	Abimelech
Akeldama	Ahasuerus
Amorites	Arimathea
Appelles	Bathsheba
Ashkelon	Beelzebub
Barabbas	Beer,sheba
Barnabas	Bethlehem
Behemoth	Bethphage
Benjamin	Bethsaida
Bethesda	Boanerges
Caesarea	Capernaum

Elimelech	Armageddon
Elisabeth	Bartimaeus
Esdraelon	Belshazzar
Galatians	Colossians
Jerusalem	Gethsemane
Magdalene	Methuselah
Nicodemus	Shibboleth
Pharisees	Bartholomew
Sadducees	Jehoshaphat
Samaritan	Philippians
Zacchaeus	Philistines
Zachariah	Sennacherib
Zechariah	Thessalonians
Zephaniah	Nebuchadnezzar

Biological Sciences

lab	bursa	order	bionic
ova	class	ovate	biotin
sac	clone	ovoid	botany
alar	cyton	ovule	coccus
axil	fauna	petri	cohort
cell	fibre	slide	colony
cone	flora	spore	cytode
cyte	gemma	still	embryo
gene	genes	taxis	enzyme
germ	genus	virus	fibrin
ovum	group	zooid	foetus
talc	hypha	aerobe	foment
tank	linin	agamic	gamete
algae	lymph	amoeba	gas|jar
bifid	lysin	biogen	hybrid

BIOLOGICAL SCIENCES

lacuna	ecology	section	entozoon
lamina	egg|cell	shellac	epiblast
lanate	enation	stimuli	eugenics
lipase	fertile	synapse	feedback
nekton	fistula	synergy	fistular
ovisac	flaccid	syringe	follicle
phylum	forceps	trypsin	genetics
plasma	gametes	vaccine	geotaxis
staple	genesis	vascula	homogamy
system	gliadin	vitamin	inositol
theory	habitat	yolk|sac	involute
tissue	haploid	zoology	isotropy
zymase	histoid	zootomy	lenticel
acyclic	lactase	adhesion	meniscus
aerobic	lamella	adhesive	mutation
albumen	lateral	amitosis	mycology
albumin	microbe	aquarium	nucleole
amylase	mitosis	autology	organism
anatomy	monitor	basidium	plankton
anomaly	myology	bioblast	prophase
aquaria	nascent	biometer	rudiment
atavism	network	biophore	sex|ratio
benthos	obovate	blastema	sitology
biology	obovoid	body|cell	specimen
blubber	oxidase	carotene	sphenoid
booster	paracme	cell|wall	stimulus
breeder	pedicel	co|enzyme	sub|order
calorie	pigment	cohesion	synapsis
cell|sap	plastid	conchate	syndesis
congeal	primary	cyclosis	taxonomy
cordate	primate	cytology	thiamine
culture	protein	demersal	transect
deltoid	radicle	diastase	trencher
dentine	saltant	diatomic	unciform
diploid	scanner	ectogeny	vascular
dissect	science	effluent	virology

vitamin|A	gestation	telophase
vitamin|B	halophily	threshold
vitamin|C	herbarium	toast,rack
vitamin|D	heterosis	vitelline
vitamin|E	histology	yolk|stalk
vitellus	incubator	zoobiotic
xenogamy	initiator	zoogamete
zoospore	injection	achromatin
ambergris	isotropic	albuminoid
anabolism	klinostat	anisotropy
anaerobic	lactation	antecedent
archetype	life,cycle	antibodies
atavistic	limnology	antitoxins
attenuate	luciferin	biochemics
bifarious	metaplasm	biochemist
bigeneric	microsome	biogenesis
bilateral	microtome	biometrics
bionomics	morphosis	biophysics
bisulcate	myography	biorhythms
body|clock	nutrition	blastoderm
chromatin	occlusion	blastomere
coenobium	ovulation	cacogenics
conjugate	paralyser	carcinogen
convolute	petri|dish	catabolism
cytoplasm	phenology	cell|tissue
dichotomy	phenotype	centrosome
dimorphic	phycology	chromosome
duplicate	phytotron	consequent
ectoplasm	potometer	culture|jar
effluvium	processed	deep|freeze
endoplasm	protogyny	depilatory
endosperm	prototype	dissection
endospore	pyrogenic	egg,albumen
evolution	scientist	embryology
folic|acid	subdivide	entomology
geobiotic	symbiosis	enzymology

ephemerist	agglutinate	Y₁chromosome
etiolation	attenuation	zoochemical
exobiology	auxanometer	zooplankton
formic|acid	benthoscope	acceleration
generation	bioengineer	anthropogeny
growth|ring	bipartition	anthropology
homochromy	cellulation	anthropotomy
incubation	chlorophyll	antithrombin
involution	chloroplast	astrobiology
katabolism	chromoplast	bacteriology
laboratory	coagulation	biochemistry
maturation	cod|liver|oil	biosatellite
metabolism	culture|tube	biosynthesis
microscope	eccrinology	carbohydrate
microscopy	elimination	cell|division
morphology	environment	cross|section
mother|cell	generic|name	cryoplankton
odontogeny	heterotopes	culture|flask
organology	homogenizer	dietotherapy
osteoblast	hygroscopic	disinfectant
pasteurise	insecticide	essential|oil
petri|plate	lactalbumin	eurythermous
physiology	lactoflavin	experimental
primordial	lipoprotein	fermentation
protogenic	microscopic	formaldehyde
protoplasm	monomorphic	immune|bodies
riboflavin	pure|culture	keratogenous
scientific	sensitivity	microspecies
sensitizer	somatic|cell	mitotic|index
somatology	stimulation	monomorphous
spirometer	synoecology	palaeobotany
sterilizer	systematics	pyridoxamine
vital|stain	thermolysis	radiobiology
viviparous	thermolytic	reflex|action
zoophysics	unicellular	regeneration
accelerator	X₁chromosome	serum|albumin

```
simple|tissue        sterilisation
specific|name        aerobiological
trace|element        anthropologist
ultramicrobe         bacteriologist
vitaminology         biodegradation
water|culture        bioengineering
zoochemistry         breeding|ground
zoogeography         electrobiology
acotyledonous        microbiologist
biodegradable        natural|history
biogeographer        natural|science
blastogenesis        photosynthesis
crossbreeding        plant|formation
fertilisation        anthropological
hermaphrodite        bacteriological
heterogenesis        biological|clock
heterogenetic        dissecting|table
micro,organism
```

Birds

```
auk    owl    chat   eyry   kiwi   rail
caw    pen    claw   fowl   kora   rhea
coo    pet    coop   game   lark   rook
cry    pie    coot   guan   loon   ruff
daw    roc    crow   gull   lory   skua
emu    tit    dodo   hawk   mina   smew
fly    tui    dove   honk   mute   sord
hen    zoo    down   hoot   nest   swan
jay    bevy   duck   ibis   nide   tail
kea    bill   erne   kaka   pavo   tern
moa    bird   eyas   kite   pern   weka
```

BIRDS

wing	hobby	serin	darter
wisp	homer	skart	dipper
wren	jenny	skein	drongo
aerie	junco	snipe	dunlin
agami	larus	solan	eaglet
argus	macaw	squab	elanet
avian	madge	stilt	falcon
booby	mavis	stork	flight
brace	merle	torsk	fulmar
brant	moray	trill	gaggle
capon	moult	tweet	gambet
cavie	murre	veery	gander
charm	nandu	vireo	gannet
cheep	nidus	wader	garrot
chick	ornis	aquila	garuda
chirp	ousel	argala	godwit
cluck	ouzel	auklet	gooney
covey	owlet	aviary	grouse
crake	oxeye	avocet	henrun
crane	peggy	bantam	herald
crest	pekan	barbet	honker
diver	pewit	blenny	hooper
drake	picus	bonito	hoopoe
eagle	pipit	bulbul	howlet
egret	pitta	canary	jabiru
eider	poker	chough	jacana
eyrie	Polly	clutch	kakapo
finch	poult	condor	lanner
geese	quack	corbie	linnet
genus	quail	coucal	magpie
glede	raven	covert	martin
goose	reeve	cuckoo	mopoke
grebe	robin	culver	motmot
harpy	roost	curlew	nandoo
hatch	rotch	cushat	oriole
heron	saker	cygnet	oscine

44

osprey	willet	goldeye	peafowl
ox̧bird	ynambu	gorcock	pelican
palama	antbird	goŗcrow	penguin
parrot	barņowl	goshawk	phoenix
passer	bittern	gosling	pinnock
pavone	bluȩeye	grackle	pinnock
peahen	bluȩjay	grey̧hen	pintado
peewee	bluȩtit	greylag	pintail
peewit	brooder	grey̧owl	plumage
petrel	bunting	haggard	pochard
phoebe	busḩtit	halcyon	pollack
pigeon	bustard	hawķowl	poulard
plover	buzzard	heņcoop	poultry
pouter	cariama	hennery	puttock
puffin	catbird	hoatzin	quetzal
pullet	chewink	hooţowl	redbird
rallus	chicken	hornowl	redwing
redcap	chirrup	icȩbird	rookery
roller	coaļtit	jacamar	rooster
scoter	colibri	jackdaw	rosella
sea̧cob	cotinga	kestrel	ruddock
sea̧mew	cowbird	killdee	sagȩhen
sea̧owl	creeper	lapwing	sea̧bird
shrike	dopping	licḩowl	sea̧dove
simurg	doŗhawk	mallard	sea̧duck
siskin	dovecot	manakin	seagull
thrush	dunnock	marabou	sea̧hawk
toucan	egģbird	martlet	sea̧lark
towhee	emu̧wren	migrant	seriema
trogon	fantail	mooŗhen	simurgh
turdus	feather	muḑlark	sirgang
turkey	ferņowl	oilbird	skimmer
volary	flapper	ortolan	skylark
warble	flicker	ostrich	sparrow
weaver	gadwall	Partlet	staniel
wigeon	gobbler	peacock	striges

45

sturnus	bellbird	flamingo	philomel
sunbird	berghaan	forewing	podargus
swallow	birdbath	gamecock	poorwill
tattler	birdcage	garefowl	popinjay
tiercel	birdcall	garganey	puffbird
tinamou	bird'segg	greatauk	raraavis
titlark	blackcap	grosbeak	rarebird
titling	bluebill	guacharo	redshank
tumbler	bluebird	hangbird	redstart
twitter	bluewing	hawfinch	reedbird
vulture	boatbill	henhouse	ricebird
wagtail	boattail	hernshaw	ringdove
warbler	bobolink	hindwing	ringtail
waxwing	bobwhite	hornbill	rockbird
webfoot	brownowl	killdeer	rockdove
widgeon	bushwren	kingbird	rocklark
woodowl	caracara	kingcrow	sagecock
wrentit	cardinal	kiwikiwi	sandlark
wryneck	cargoose	lameduck	sandpeep
aasvogel	cockatoo	landrail	screamer
accentor	cockerel	lanneret	seasnipe
adjutant	curassow	laverock	shelduck
aigrette	dabchick	lovebird	shoebill
albacore	deadduck	megapode	skuagull
alcatras	didapper	moorcock	snowbird
amadavat	dobchick	moorfowl	songbird
anserine	dotterel	muskduck	starling
anserous	dovecote	muteswan	sungrebe
antpipit	duckhawk	nightjar	surfbird
apterous	duckling	nightowl	swiftlet
aquiline	duckmole	nuthatch	tapaculo
arapunga	duckpond	ovenbird	tawnyowl
avifauna	eagleowl	oxpecker	tealduck
baldpate	fauvette	parakeet	thrasher
barnacle	feathers	pavonian	throstle
beeeater	fishhawk	pheasant	titmouse

tragopan	bottle|tit	heath,cock
trembler	bower|bird	heronshaw
troupial	brambling	horned|owl
waterhen	bull|finch	jacksnipe
wheatear	campanero	Jenny|wren
whimbrel	cedarbird	king,eider
whinchat	chaffinch	kittiwake
white|cap	chickadee	little|auk
wild|duck	cockatiel	merganser
wildfowl	cock,robin	migration
wingspan	cocks,comb	migratory
woodchat	columbary	mound,bird
woodcock	columbine	nightbird
wood,duck	crossbill	night,crow
wood|ibis	currawong	night,fowl
woodlark	dicky,bird	nighthawk
wood,wren	eagle,eyed	nocturnal
yoke,toed	eider|duck	on|the|wing
yoldring	fieldfare	ossifrage
aepyornis	field|lark	owl,parrot
albatross	firecrest	parrakeet
ant,thrush	flute|bird	partridge
bald|eagle	frogmouth	passerine
beaf,eater	gallinazo	peregrine
bean,goose	gallinule	phalarope
beccafico	gerfalcon	pine,finch
birdhouse	gier,eagle	ptarmigan
bird's,nest	goldcrest	quail,dove
bird,table	goldeneye	razorbill
blackbird	goldfinch	redbreast
blackcock	goldspink	redbreast
blackgame	goosander	red,grouse
blackhead	grey,goose	rifle,bird
black|swan	guillemot	ringouzel
black|tern	guinea,hen	rock,pipit
blue|heron	gyrfalcon	salangane

47

sanctuary	aberdevine	hen‚harrier
sandpiper	aviculture	herald‚duck
sapsucker	battery|hen	honey‚eater
scamp|duck	bird|of|prey	honey‚guide
scrubbird	bluebreast	hooded‚crow
sea‚dragon	blue|pigeon	hoodie‚crow
sea‚parrot	bluethroat	house|finch
sedge‚bird	brent|goose	Indian|kite
sedge‚wren	budgerigar	indigo‚bird
seed|snipe	burrow‚duck	jungle|fowl
sheldrake	bush‚shrike	kingfisher
shore|bird	butter‚bird	meadow‚lark
snake‚bird	canvas‚back	missel|bird
snow‚fleck	Cape|pigeon	mutton‚bird
snowgoose	cheep|cheep	night‚churr
solitaire	chiff‚chaff	night|heron
sooty|tern	chittagong	night‚raven
spoonbill	cow‚bunting	nutcracker
stilt‚bird	crab|plover	parrotbill
stock‚dove	crested‚jay	parson‚bird
stonechat	deep|litter	pigeon|hawk
stone‚hawk	demoiselle	pigeon|loft
talegalla	dickeybird	poll|parrot
tom|turkey	didunculus	pratincole
trumpeter	ember‚goose	quack‚quack
turnstone	fallow‚chat	Quaker|bird
water‚bird	flying|fish	ring|plover
water‚cock	get|the|bird	road‚runner
water‚fowl	goatsucker	rock‚hopper
water‚rail	greenfinch	rock|pigeon
web‚footed	green‚goose	sage‚grouse
wheatbird	greenshank	sailorbird
whitehead	grey|parrot	sanderling
whitewing	guinea‚cock	sandgrouse
wild‚goose	guinea‚fowl	sand‚martin
windhover	harpy|eagle	screech‚owl

sea swallow	butcher bird	singing bird
sea vampire	Canada goose	sitting duck
setting hen	carrion crow	snow bunting
shearwater	Chanticleer	song sparrow
sheathbill	Cochin china	Spanish fowl
sickle bill	cock a doodle	sparrowhawk
solan goose	cock sparrow	stilt plover
song thrush	columbarium	stone curlew
stone snipe	dead as a dodo	stone falcon
summer duck	fallow finch	stone plover
summer teal	fan tail dove	swallowtail
sun bittern	gnatcatcher	tree swallow
tailor bird	golden eagle	Vanga shrike
talk turkey	green linnet	wattled crow
tawny eagle	ground robin	weaver finch
thick knees	honey sucker	whitethroat
tropic bird	king penguin	wood swallow
turkey cock	king vulture	wood warbler
turtle dove	lammergeier	adjutant bird
wading bird	man o war bird	barndoor fowl
water ousel	meadow pipit	barnyard fowl
weaver bird	muscovy duck	bird's eye view
willow wren	nightingale	bramble finch
wood grouse	pied wagtail	brown pelican
woodpecker	pigeon house	burrowing owl
wood pigeon	pigeon's milk	bustard quail
wood shrike	Pretty Polly	capercaillie
wood thrush	pterodactyl	capercailzie
wren thrush	purple finch	cardinal bird
yellow bird	reed bunting	chicken house
zebra finch	reed sparrow	chimney swift
accipitrine	reed warbler	cliff swallow
bastard wing	rock sparrow	crested swift
black grouse	rooster fish	crowned eagle
black martin	scissorbill	cuckoo roller
brush turkey	sea dotterel	cuckoo shrike

BIRDS

diving petrel	stubble goose
domestic fowl	tropical bird
elephant bird	ugly duckling
falcon gentil	umbrella bird
fighting cock	velvet scoter
flower pecker	water wagtail
fully fledged	whip poor will
galli naceous	wingless bird
golden oriole	wood pheasant
golden plover	yellow hammer
ground cuckoo	barnacle goose
hedge sparrow	bird of passage
hedge warbler	carrier pigeon
hermit thrush	ornithologist
homing pigeon	oyster catcher
honey buzzard	spring chicken
mandarin duck	trumpeter swan
marsh harrier	turkey buzzard
merry thought	willow warbler
missel thrush	yellow bunting
mistle thrush	bird of paradise
mourning dove	bird of paradise
painted snipe	ornithological
rifleman bird	Rhode Island Red
ring dotterel	robin redbreast
sedge warbler	wild goose chase
serpent eater	birds of a feather
stone chatter	peregrine falcon
stormy petrel	

Capacity

cran	dry quart
gill	hogshead
peck	spoonful
pint	teaspoon
homer	decalitre
litre	decilitre
pinta	fluid dram
quart	kilolitre
barrel	centilitre
bushel	millilitre
chopin	tablespoon
cupful	thimbleful
gallon	teaspoonful
magnum	imperial pint
dry pint	cubic capacity

Cereals

awn	corn	durra	pulse
ear	crop	field	spear
lea	husk	flour	spike
oat	oats	glean	straw
rye	reap	grain	wheat
sow	rice	maize	barley
soy	soya	paddy	cereal

51

farina	soy flour	ground rice
groats	wild oats	Indian corn
hominy	broomcorn	kaffir corn
lentil	buckwheat	paddy field
mealie	corn bread	rolled oats
millet	corn field	wheat field
corncob	cornflour	whole wheat
harvest	corn salad	corn in Egypt
oatmeal	ear of corn	corn in Israel
tapioca	rice paddy	corn on the cob
wildoat	sweetcorn	decorticated
ripe corn	barley corn	
semolina	brome grass	

Character Types

ass	doll	rake	puppy	Amazon	
cad	dolt	scab	rogue	apache	
fop	drip	snob	saint	beauty	
hag	dude	thug	scamp	bibber	
ham	dupe	toff	scold	cadger	
hex	fool	twit	shrew	canter	
oaf	gull	wimp	siren	carper	
pal	guru	joker	sneak	codger	
rat	heel	Judas	spark	con man	
rip	hick	knave	sport	coward	
sot	hype	macho	stoic	dodger	
wit	liar	miser	toady	dotard	
bore	lout	moron	toper	duffer	
brat	minx	mouse	trier	egoist	
chum	ogre	nomad	vixen	faggot	
cove	prig	prude	wally	fantod	

fawner	sinner	dilutee	kingpin
fellow	square	doubter	knowall
fibber	stooge	dreamer	liberal
gasbag	vandal	drifter	lieabed
gaydog	virago	dropout	lounger
genius	voyeur	dullard	lowbrow
gossip	Watson	egghead	Luddite
grouch	worthy	egotist	lunatic
hassle	wretch	epicure	man'sman
hepcat	zealot	eremite	marxist
hippie	zombie	faddist	meddler
humbug	abadegg	fallguy	MrRight
jetset	alsoran	fanatic	niggard
junkie	ancient	fathead	nutcase
layman	ascetic	flaneur	oddball
leader	avenger	gabbler	oldfogy
loafer	babbler	gallant	oldmaid
madman	beatnik	glutton	outcast
martyr	bonkers	gourmet	paragon
nobody	bounder	groupie	parvenu
nutter	bucolic	haggler	patriot
ogress	buffoon	halfwit	PaulPry
oldboy	bumpkin	hangdog	peasant
pariah	charmer	hardman	playboy
pedant	chauvin	hasbeen	prodigy
pundit	cheater	hellcat	puritan
puppet	copycat	hellier	radical
purist	coxcomb	heretic	recluse
rabbit	crybaby	hoodlum	ruffian
rascal	cuckold	hothead	runaway
roamer	culprit	hotspur	sadsack
Romany	dabbler	hustler	saviour
rotter	dallier	hypedup	sceptic
rustic	darling	infidel	Scrooge
sadist	devotee	Jezebel	showman
sexist	diehard	JoeSoap	showoff

shyster	blighter	imbecile
slacker	bluenose	impostor
sponger	Bohemian	innocent
suspect	braggart	intruder
swinger	busybody	jabberer
thinker	carouser	jailbird
tippler	cenobite	jawsmith
tosspot	crackpot	John Bull
traitor	criminal	laidback
trueman	deceiver	lameduck
twister	defector	layabout
upstart	derelict	livewire
villain	dirtydog	lonewolf
vulture	dogooder	lowlifer
wastrel	drunkard	machismo
welcher	everyman	manhater
welsher	evildoer	martinet
whipcat	feminist	Napoleon
windbag	finelady	nepotist
wiseguy	folkhero	nihilist
workshy	follower	nuisance
wrecker	frontman	numskull
absentee	funnyman	objector
aesthete	gadabout	offender
agitator	gamester	optimist
agnostic	gaolbird	outsider
alarmist	gourmand	pacifist
alterego	greatman	paleface
altruist	groupnik	paramour
antihero	hangeron	parasite
antipope	hectorer	partisan
apostate	hedonist	penitent
banterer	highbrow	perjurer
beginner	hooligan	plebeian
betrayer	humorist	poltroon
bignoise	idolater	poorsoul

54

popinjay	battle|axe	good|mixer
prattler	Bluebeard	gradgrind
quackery	blusterer	greenhorn
quisling	boy|wonder	harebrain
rakehell	careerist	Hellenist
renegade	career|man	honest|man
romancer	character	honour|man
romantic	charlatan	hypocrite
saucebox	chatterer	ignoramus
scalawag	chiseller	inamorata
skinhead	churchman	inebriate
slattern	comforter	introvert
somebody	consenter	jet,setter
sorehead	coughdrop	ladies|man
spitfire	dark|horse	late|riser
stranger	defeatist	lazybones
swindler	defrauder	libertine
sybarite	demagogue	log,roller
tell,tale	desperado	lost|sheep
theorist	dignitary	loudmouth
tightwad	dissenter	man|of|mark
truckler	dogmatist	man|of|note
turncoat	dolly|bird	masochist
two,timer	early|bird	nonentity
underdog	eccentric	non,smoker
vagabond	Edwardian	odd|man|out
whizz|kid	exploiter	pacemaker
wiseacre	extravert	patrician
wise|fool	extrovert	Pecksniff
accessory	family|man	peculator
adulterer	favourite	persuader
adversary	fire,eater	pessimist
alcoholic	flag|waver	plutocrat
aunt|sally	fossicker	poetaster
bacchanal	free|agent	poison|pen
barbarian	gentleman	pothunter

CHARACTER TYPES

pretender	aficionado	lawbreaker
queer|fish	anglophile	left,winger
racketeer	anglophobe	lotus,eater
reprobate	antagonist	malefactor
roisterer	aristocrat	malingerer
roughneck	benefactor	man|of|straw
Samaritan	best|friend	mastermind
sassenach	Big|Brother	matchmaker
scapegoat	blackguard	merrymaker
scoundrel	black|sheep	Methuselah
screwball	bobbysoxer	middlebrow
simpleton	bootlicker	militarist
skylarker	career|girl	misogynist
slowcoach	chatterbox	mountebank
sob,sister	chauvinist	ne'er,do,well
socialist	church,goer	non,starter
socialite	Cinderella	old|soldier
star|pupil	confidante	past,master
strongman	daydreamer	peeping|Tom
sundowner	delinquent	philistine
suppliant	Don|Quixote	pragmatist
swaggerer	drug|addict	prima|donna
swellhead	Dutch|uncle	psychopath
sycophant	enthusiast	recidivist
tactician	fly,by,night	ringleader
termagant	fuddy,duddy	secularist
terrorist	gastronome	shoplifter
underling	gentlefolk	smart|aleck
visionary	girl|Friday	sneak|thief
warmonger	girl|friend	socia|l|lion
womanizer	gold,digger	spoilsport
womenfolk	goody,goody	squanderer
wrongdoer	human|wreck	street|arab
xenophobe	jackanapes	sugar,daddy
young|fogy	Jesus|freak	taskmaster
adventurer	lady,killer	time,server

troglodyte	gate,crasher	soliloquist
tub,thumper	grave|robber	spendthrift
upper|crust	guttersnipe	stool|pigeon
utopianist	hard,drinker	suffragette
vacillator	helping|hand	sympathiser
vegetarian	homo,sapiens	teacher's|pet
wallflower	human,nature	teeny,bopper
well,wisher	imperialist	town,dweller
wine,bibber	licks,pittle	Walter|Mitty
woman,hater	lifemanship	artful|dodger
young|blood	line,shooter	awkward|squad
Young|Fogey	living|image	babysnatcher
adventuress	man,of|genius	backwoodsman
animal|lover	materialist	bible,thumper
beachcomber	mental|giant	blue|stocking
Bible|reader	merry,andrew	bobby,dazzler
blackmailer	misanthrope	carpet,knight
blue,eyed|boy	named,ropper	collaborator
braggadocio	nationalist	Colonel|Blimp
cattle|thief	nosey,parker	conservative
centenarian	opportunist	cosmopolitan
chain|smoker	personality	doppelganger
cheese,parer	pettifogger	eavesdropper
Cinemascope	philanderer	featherbrain
close|friend	prodigal|son	flittermouse
common|scold	quacksalver	flower|people
connoisseur	rapscallion	grey|eminence
country|girl	rationalist	hair,splitter
deadly|enemy	reactionary	headshrinker
dipsomaniac	reparteeist	humanitarian
eager|beaver	right,winger	kleptomaniac
femme|fatale	Sabbatarian	lounge,lizard
francophile	scaremonger	mad,as|a|hatter
francophobe	self,made|man	man,about,town
freethinker	simple|Simon	modest|violet
gallows|bird	sleep,walker	moneygrubber

one:upmanship	compassionate
poor relation	conceitedness
prevaricator	condescending
right hand man	condescension
rolling stone	conscientious
rough diamond	consternation
salvationist	controversial
scatterbrain	country cousin
single person	courteousness
somnambulist	deserving poor
street urchin	determination
stuffed shirt	dishonourable
swashbuckler	dispassionate
transgressor	distinguished
transvestite	double crosser
troublemaker	double dealing
truce breaker	dyed in the wool
ugly customer	egocentricity
ugly duckling	egotistically
woolgatherer	excitableness
absence of mind	exhibitionism
accident prone	exhibitionist
Anglo American	foolhardiness
angry young man	fool's paradise
anthropomorph	forgetfulness
anthropophagi	fortune hunter
antichristian	fresh air fiend
anythingarian	frivolousness
apple pie order	gentle hearted
barbarousness	gentlemanlike
bare faced liar	gentlewomanly
bargain hunter	go as you please
best of friends	good influence
clapperclawer	good Samaritan
clishmaclaver	go the whole hog
companionship	grandiloquent

58

hair splitting	overexcitable
half heartedly	overindulgent
heartlessness	pain in the neck
hole and corner	panic stricken
hunger marcher	penny pinching
hypercritical	perspicacious
hypochondriac	plain speaking
idiosyncratic	procrastinate
impassiveness	prophet of doom
imperturbable	pusillanimous
impetuousness	quiet as a mouse
impulsiveness	ray of sunshine
inconsiderate	remittance man
inconsistency	riotous living
incorruptible	rough and ready
indefatigable	rough customer
individualist	round the twist
infant prodigy	sanctimonious
in honour bound	scandalmonger
insignificant	self appointed
insubordinate	self approving
intransigence	self assertive
introspective	self conceited
irrepressible	self conscious
irresponsible	self deceitful
lackadaisical	self important
Lady Bountiful	self indulgent
latchkey child	self satisfied
laughing stock	sense of humour
long suffering	sense of values
lunatic fringe	sharp practice
misadventurer	short tempered
misanthropist	sign the pledge
mischief maker	sit on the fence
over confident	smooth tongued
overcredulous	soapbox orator

sober as a judge
social climber
social outcast
sophisticated
soul searching
stick in the mud
stiff upper lip
supercritical
superstitious
sweet tempered
swelled headed
swollen headed
sycophantical
temperamental
tender hearted
tongue in cheek
unadventurous
uncomplaining
uncooperative
undisciplined
unenlightened
ungentlemanly
unimaginative
unintelligent
unsympathetic
untrustworthy
unworkmanlike
well respected
well thought of
wheeler dealer
willing helper
willing worker
auto suggestion
back scratching
back seat driver
beat generation

changeableness
characteristic
class conscious
claustrophobia
common or garden
credibility gap
crocodile tears
culture vulture
disciplinarian
dog in the manger
doubting Thomas
easy come, easy go
factitiousness
fastidiousness
fish out of water
flower children
formidableness
free spokenness
frolicsomeness
full of mischief
glutton for work
good for nothing
gracious living
hell for leather
high handedness
high mindedness
high principled
holier than thou
hot air merchant
hypersensitive
impressionable
inveterate liar
jealous husband
larger than life
Macchiavellian
male chauvinist

man|in|the|street
man,in,the,street
man|of|many|parts
man|of|substance
man|of|the|moment
mods|and|rockers
nasty|bit|of|work
nimble,fingered
obstructionist
overscrupulous
petit|bourgeois
philanthropist
pleased|as|Punch
pleasure,seeker
pluck|up|courage
practical|joker
presence|of|mind
public|nuisance
public,spirited
rich|as|a|Croesus
salt|of|the|earth
scatter,brained
self,advertiser
self,controlled
self,interested
self,sufficient
sensationalist
sentimentalist
someone|or|other
straight|as|a|die
supersensitive
tail,end|Charlie
terror,stricken
three|bottle|man
total|abstainer
traditionalist

troubleshooter
unconventional
unenterprising
universal|aunts
unostentatious
unprofessional
ambulance,chaser
ancestor,worship
antivivisection
awkward|customer
bats|in|the|belfry
birds|of|a|feather
connoisseurship
conservationist
conventionalist
conversationist
cool|as|a|cucumber
cryptocommunist
cuckoo|in|the|nest
dual|personality
eternal|triangle
flibbertigibbet
good,naturedness
half,heartedness
hope|against|hope
humanitarianism
little|Englander
middle,of,the,raod
model|of|industry
non,professional
paragon|of|virtue
philanthropical
pillar|of|society
platitudinarian
quite|a|character
ready|and|willing

CHARACTER TYPES

second|childhood
self,considering
self,destructive
self,opinionated
sensation,monger
snake|in|the|grass
stable|companion
stage|door|Johnny
stand|on|ceremony
stark,|staring|mad
strong,|silent|man
thorn|in|the|flesh
too|clever|by|half
to|the|manner|born

tower|of|strength
unaccommodating
uncommunicative
undemonstrative
under|privileged
undistinguished
unprepossessing
unsportsmanlike
unstatesmanlike
well,intentioned
whited|sepulchre
with|bated|breath
yours|faithfully

Chemical Sciences

pH	muon	borax	oxide	action
dye	neon	boron	ozone	air|gas
gas	norm	dregs	poise	alkali
gel	otto	ester	radon	amylum
ion	rust	ether	resin	anneal
lab	soda	ethyl	rosin	atomic
sol	zein	flask	salts	barite
acid	agene	fluid	toxin	barium
alum	agent	hexad	uredo	baryta
amyl	alkyl	inert	U,tube	beaker
atom	amide	latex	vinyl	boffin
buna	amine	leach	xenon	borate
calx	argon	monad	xylem	bunsen
dyad	assay	nitre	yeast	calcar
etna	basic	nylon	acetic	calxes

62

carbon	octane	alembic	dioxide
carboy	osmium	amalgam	element
casein	oxygen	ammonia	essence
cerate	pectin	ampoule	eutropy
cerium	pepsin	aniline	exhaust
citric	petrol	antacid	ferment
cobalt	phenol	arsenic	formula
curium	poison	atrazin	gallium
decane	potash	balance	geogony
dilute	radium	bell|jar	geology
diplon	reflux	benzene	glucose
dry|ice	retort	bismuth	hafnium
erbium	ribose	bitumen	halogen
ethane	saline	boiling	holmium
filter	silica	bromide	hydrate
funnel	sinter	bromine	hydride
fusion	sodium	burette	hyperon
galena	spirit	cadmium	iridium
gas|jar	stable	caesium	isotope
gluten	starch	calomel	isotopy
halide	symbol	capsule	isotron
helium	theory	carbide	keratin
indium	thoron	chemism	krypton
inulin	toxoid	chemist	lacquer
iodide	tripod	citrate	lactate
iodine	vapour	coal|tar	lactose
isomer	xylose	colloid	lanolin
ketone	acetate	corrode	leucine
labile	acetone	crystal	lipoids
litmus	acetose	cuprite	lithium
lutein	acid|dye	cyanide	matrass
lysine	acidity	deposit	melanin
matter	acyclic	dextrin	mercury
methyl	aerosol	dialyse	metamer
natron	alchemy	dibasic	methane
niacin	alcohol	diluent	micelle

CHEMICAL SCIENCES

mixture	titrate	Bakelite	equation
muonium	toluene	basicity	ethylene
niobium	tritium	benzoate	europium
nitrate	uranide	biochemy	exhalant
nitride	uranium	bivalent	filtrate
nitrite	valence	carbonyl	fluoride
nonacid	valency	catalyst	fluorine
nuclide	vinegar	catalyse	formulae
osmosis	vitriol	charcoal	francium
oxalate	yttrium	chemical	gasoline
oxidant	zymurgy	chemurgy	gelatine
oxidase	acid|bath	chlorate	globulin
oxonium	acid|salt	chloride	glutelin
oxyacid	acid|test	chlorine	glutenin
pentose	actinism	chlorite	glycogen
peptide	actinium	chromate	honeydew
reagent	actinoid	chromium	hydrogen
rhenium	activate	cleveite	isomeric
rhodium	activity	cobalite	isoteric
science	additive	cohesion	isotopic
sebacic	agar|agar	collagen	kerosene
silicon	alcahest	compound	leaching
solvent	aldehyde	copperas	lecithin
spatula	alkahest	crucible	levulose
spireme	alkaline	cucurbit	litharge
spirits	amandine	cyanogen	lutetium
subacid	ammonium	dendrite	magnesia
sucrose	analogue	dextrose	marshgas
sulphur	analyser	dialysis	melamine
tarnish	analysis	dialytic	mercuric
terbium	analytic	dilution	miscible
terpene	antimony	diplogen	molecule
thermal	arsenate	divalent	monoxide
thorium	arsenide	docimasy	nicotine
thulium	asbestos	dye|stuff	nitrogen
tinfoil	astatine	emulsion	nobelium

nonmetal	titanium	chemurgic
oxidizer	tribasic	colloidal
pedology	trioxide	copolymer
pentosan	tungsten	cork|borer
peroxide	unstable	corrosion
phenolic	uric|acid	covalence
phosgene	vanadium	covalency
plastics	volatile	desiccant
platinum	absorbent	detergent
polonium	actinides	detonator
polyacid	alchemist	deuterium
quantity	allotropy	developer
reactant	americium	dimorphic
reaction	amino|acid	dispenser
reactive	anglesite	distiller
research	anhydride	elastomer
resinoid	apparatus	elemental
rheology	aqua|regia	emanation
rubidium	aspirator	erythrite
samarium	atmolysis	erythrose
scandium	atmometer	fulminate
sediment	autoclave	fungicide
selenium	barricade	galactose
silicate	basic|salt	germanium
silicone	berkelium	glucoside
solation	beryllium	glutinous
solution	bivalence	glycerine
spagyric	bivariant	histidine
sulphate	boric|acid	homocycle
sulphide	carbonate	hydrazine
sulphite	carbonize	hydrolist
tantalum	catalysis	hydrolyte
tartrate	catalytic	hydroxide
test|tube	celluloid	inhibitor
thallium	cellulose	isinglass
tincture	chemiatry	isocyclic

65

isomerism	synthetic	disulphide
lanthanum	teleology	dysprosium
magnesium	tellurite	elementary
malic acid	tellurium	emulsifier
manganese	tetroxide	equivalent
metalloid	titration	estimation
metameric	univalent	eudiometer
neodymium	verdigris	experiment
neptunium	virginium	fibrinogen
nitration	viscosity	fluorotype
oxidation	ytterbium	formic acid
palladium	zirconium	gadolinium
petroleum	alkalinity	gallic acid
phosphate	alpha helix	heavy water
phosphide	amylaceous	high octane
phosphite	antifreeze	homocyclic
photogene	antimatter	hydrolysis
plutonium	aqua fortis	hydrolytic
polybasic	ballistite	hypothesis
polyester	biochemics	immiscible
polythene	biochemist	ion counter
potassium	bisulphate	ionization
prolamine	bisulphide	laboratory
protamine	calcareous	lactic acid
pyrolysis	calciferol	lead glance
pyrometer	cellophane	metamerism
raffinose	chloroform	molybdenum
reservoir	chrome alum	monovalent
ruthenium	citric acid	neutralize
saccharin	coalescent	nitric acid
saltpetre	cyanic acid	nucleonium
scientist	decinormal	octavalent
still room	decompound	oxalic acid
strontium	denaturant	phlogiston
sulphacid	dichromate	phosphorus
synthesis	disulphate	photolysis

picric|acid	butyric|acid	niacinamide
promethium	calcination	opalescence
rare|earths	calibration	oxidization
reactivity	californium	oxygen|meter
resolution	calorimeter	pectization
saccharate	calorimetry	pentavalent
saccharose	carbonation	peptization
scientific	chloric|acid	phosphorous
sodium|lamp	chromic|acid	pitchblende
solubility	closed|chain	plasmolysis
sorbic|acid	cobalt|bloom	polymorphic
sulphation	constituent	polyvalence
suspension	contaminate	proteolysis
technetium	dehydration	prussic|acid
technology	dissolution	quantometer
trivalence	double|helix	quicksilver
tryptophan	endothermal	radiocarbon
univalence	evaporation	retort|stand
viscometer	filter|paper	rule|of|thumb
wash|bottle	fume|cabinet	sal|ammoniac
water|still	gas|detector	sal|volatile
Winchester	haloid|acids	sub|critical
yield|point	heptavalent	technocracy
zero|valent	heterocycle	tetravalent
accelerator	hydrocarbon	transuranic
acidulation	hydrogen|ion	tripod|stand
acrylic|acid	hydrogenoid	volatile|oil
agglomerate	impermeable	xanthophyll
arsenic|acid	interaction	acceleration
atomic|table	lanthanides	acid|solution
atomologist	lipoprotein	aspartic|acid
beaker|flask	litmus|paper	atomic|theory
benzene|ring	mendelevium	atomic|weight
benzoic|acid	mensuration	Avogadro's|law
bicarbonate	monovalence	barrier|cream
brittleness	neutralizer	bicarbonates

biochemistry	liquid|oxygen
breathalyzer	lysergic|acid
bunsen|burner	melting|point
burette|stand	mesomorphous
carbolic|acid	microbalance
carbonic|acid	microburette
chemical|bond	microelement
chemical|pump	minor|element
chlorination	multivalence
chlorous|acid	muriatic|acid
cobalt|glance	nicotinamide
constituents	nitromethane
deactivation	oil|of|vitriol
deionization	oxycellulose
deliquescent	oxychromatin
dissociation	pangamic|acid
distillation	permanganate
effervescent	permeability
experimental	photochemist
ferrous|oxide	praseodymium
flocculation	quadrivalent
fluorocarbon	radiochemist
fluorography	radioelement
fume|cupboard	radioisotope
geochemistry	radionuclide
glutamic|acid	reactivation
glycoprotein	spark|chamber
gram|molecule	thermocouple
heterocyclic	transuranian
hydrocarbons	zoochemistry
hydrogen|atom	carbon|dioxide
hydrostatics	carbonisation
iatrochemist	chain|reaction
inactivation	compatibility
ion|exchanger	corrosiveness
liquefaction	decomposition

demonstration	distilled water
diffusion tube	electrochemist
dissolubility	microchemistry
hydrochloride	nitroglycerine
hydrosulphide	petroleum jelly
hydrosulphite	phosphorescent
hydroxylamine	photochemistry
nitro compound	photosynthesis
nitrogen cycle	surgical spirit
periodic table	biogeochemistry
petrochemical	decarbonisation
precipitation	electrochemical
radioactivity	molecular weight
reducing agent	nitro derivative
sulphuric acid	phosphorescence
carbon monoxide	trinitrotoluene

Cinema and Television

TV	play	movie	movies
act	plot	odeon	rushes
BBC	role	oscar	screen
cue	shot	radio	script
fan	show	scene	serial
ITV	star	telly	series
set	unit	video	sit com
cast	actor	camera	studio
crew	cable	Ceefax	talkie
film	drama	cinema	TV show
hero	enact	comedy	actress
mike	extra	critic	cartoon
part	flick	make up	compere

feature	cameraman
film|set	character
flicker	direction
heroine	entertain
musical	exhibitor
network	film|actor
perform	film|extra
phone¡in	film|strip
pop|star	flash¡back
portray	goggle¡box
present	guest|star
produce	interview
sponsor	movie¡goer
tragedy	movie|show
trailer	movie|star
audience	performer
bioscope	photoplay
chat|show	programme
Cinerama	projector
comedian	recording
director	rehearsal
festival	soap¡opera
film|club	spectacle
film|crew	title|role
film|star	voice¡over
fruit¡pie	commercial
newsreel	crowd|scene
pictures	home¡movies
premiere	horror|film
producer	horse¡opera
quiz|show	microphone
tape¡deck	movie|actor
telecast	needle|time
telefilm	newscaster
blue¡movie	newsreader
broadcast	on|location

performing	global village
production	motion picture
screenplay	motion picture
silent film	Nouvelle Vague
television	picture palace
the critics	tape recording
broadcaster	telerecording
credit title	television set
documentary	videocassette
echo chamber	video recorder
entertainer	book at bedtime, a
feature film	cinematography
performance	continuity girl
picture show	feature picture
radio caster	features editor
sound effect	moving pictures
talking film	question master
academy award	supporting cast
cinéma vérité	supporting film
clapperboard	supporting part
film festival	supporting role
picture house	television play
scriptwriter	Third Programme
show business	animated cartoon
silver screen	cable television
sound effects	cinematographer
technicolour	cinematographic
Chinese puzzle	documentary film
cinematograph	French subtitles
cine projector	peak viewing time
clapperboards	situation comedy
closed circuit	slapstick comedy
continuity man	spot advertising
entertainment	

Cities

Baku	Berne	Paris	Boston	Madras
Bari	Bursa	Patna	Bremen	Madrid
Bonn	Cairo	Perth	Cracow	Málaga
Brno	Chiba	Poona	Dallas	Małang
Cork	Dacca	Quito	Dayton	Manila
Gifu	Davao	Rabat	Denver	Moscow
Giza	Delhi	Sakai	Dublin	Multan
Graz	Essen	Seoul	Dundee	Munich
Homs	Genoa	Sofia	Durban	Mysore
Hull	Gorky	Surat	El Paso	Nagpur
Ipoh	Haifa	Tampa	Frunze	Nantes
Kano	Halle	Tokyo	Fukoka	Naples
Kiel	Hanoi	Tomsk	Fushun	Newark
Kiev	Izmir	Tunis	Gdansk	Odessa
Kobe	Kabul	Turin	Geneva	Oporto
Lima	Kazan	Aachen	Harbin	Ottawa
Lodz	Kyoto	Abadan	Havana	Oxford
Nice	Lagos	Aleppo	Ibadan	Peking
Omsk	La Paz	Ankara	Indore	Penang
Oran	Leeds	Asmara	Jaipur	Poznan
Oslo	Lyons	Athens	Kanpur	Prague
Riga	Malmo	Austin	Khulna	Puebla
Rome	Mecca	Baroda	Kumasi	Quebec
Accra	Miami	Beirut	Lahore	Santos
Adana	Milan	Berlin	Lisbon	Shiraz
Amman	Mosul	Bilbao	London	St Paul
Basle	Omaha	Bochum	Luanda	Sydney
Basra	Osaka	Bogota	Lübeck	Tabriz
Belem	Padua	Bombay	Lusaka	Taipei

Talinn	Hanover	Teheran
Toledo	Houston	Tel Aviv
Venice	Irkutsk	Toronto
Verona	Isfahan	Trieste
Vienna	Jakarta	Tripoli
Warsaw	Kalinin	Utrecht
Zagreb	Karachi	Aberdeen
Zürich	Kharkov	Adelaide
Abidjan	Kowloon	Amritsar
Algiers	Kwangju	Auckland
Antwerp	La Plata	Augsburg
Atlanta	Leipzig	Belgrade
Baghdad	Lucknow	Bordeaux
Bangkok	Managua	Bradford
Barnaul	Memphis	Brasilia
Belfast	Messina	Brisbane
Bologna	Mombasa	Brussels
Brescia	Nairobi	Budapest
Bristol	Nanking	Bulawayo
Buffalo	Oakland	Cagliari
Caracas	Palermo	Calcutta
Cardiff	Phoenix	Campinas
Chengtu	Rangoon	Canberra
Chicago	Rosario	Capetown
Cologne	San Jose	Columbus
Colombo	San Juan	Coventry
Córdoba	Santa Fe	Curitiba
Corunna	Sapporo	Damascus
Detroit	Saratov	Dortmund
Donetsk	Seattle	Duisburg
Dresden	Seville	Edmonton
Firenze	Soochow	Florence
Foochow	Stettin	Gorlovka
Glasgow	St Louis	Hague, The
Gwalior	Taranto	Haiphong
Hamburg	Tbilisi	Hamilton

CITIES

Hangchow	Ahmedabad	Marrakesh
Helsinki	Allahabad	Melbourne
Honolulu	Amagasaki	Milwaukee
Istanbul	Amsterdam	Nuremberg
Katmandu	Archangel	Reykjavik
Katowice	Asahikawa	Rotterdam
Khartoum	Astrakhan	Salisbury
Kingston	Baltimore	Samarkand
Kinshasa	Bangalore	Saragossa
Kumamoto	Barcelona	Sheffield
Kweiyang	Brunswick	Singapore
Mandalay	Bucharest	Stockholm
Mannheim	Cambridge	Stuttgart
Montreal	Cartagena	Vancouver
Murmansk	Chengchow	Volgograd
Nagasaki	Chihuahua	Wuppertal
Peshawar	Cleveland	Addis Ababa
Plymouth	DesMoines	Alexandria
Portland	Edinburgh	Baton Rouge
Port Said	Fort Worth	Birmingham
Pretoria	Frankfurt	Bratislava
Pyongang	Guayaquil	Canterbury
Richmond	Hamamatsu	Casablanca
Salonika	Hiroshima	Chittagong
San Diego	Hyderabad	Cincinnati
Santiago	Jerusalem	Coimbatore
Sao Paulo	Karlsruhe	Copenhagen
Sarajevo	Krasnodar	Düsseldorf
Shanghai	Kuibyshev	Gothenburg
Sholapur	Kwangchow	Jamshedpur
Srinagar	Las Palmas	Kansas City
Tashkent	Leicester	Krivoi Roig
Tientsin	Leningrad	Los Angeles
Toulouse	Liverpool	Louisville
Winnipeg	Magdeburg	Manchester
Yokohama	Maracaibo	Marseilles

74

MexicoｷCity	RostovｷonｷDon
Montevideo	SanｷSalvador
NewｷOrleans	Southampton
Nottingham	Vladivostok
PanamaｷCity	Barquisimeto
Pittsburgh	Bloemfontein
Portsmouth	Braunschweig
Rawalpindi	Indianapolis
Sacramento	Jacksonville
SanｷAntonio	Johannesburg
Strasbourg	Magnitogorsk
Sunderland	OklahomaｷCity
Sverdlovsk	Philadelphia
Tananarive	PortｷauｷPrince
Valparaiso	RioｷdeｷJaneiro
Washington	SaltｷLakeｷCity
Wellington	SanｷFrancisco
Baranquilla	SantoｷDomingo
BuenosｷAires	StokeｷonｷTrent
Chelyabinsk	Gelsenkirchen
DarｷesｷSalaam	GuatemalaｷCity
Guadalajara	KarlｷMarxｷStadt
KualaｷLumpur	PortｷElizabeth
MarｷdelｷPlata	Shihkiachwang
NewｷYorkｷCity	Wolverhampton
Novosibirsk	Dnepropetrovsk
Pondicherry	

Clothes

alb	bib	bob	bun	fez	fop
bag	boa	bra	cap	fob	fur

hat	drag	muff	warp	cymar	moire
hem	duck	mule	wear	dandy	motif
kid	elan	peak	weft	denim	mufti
mac	felt	poke	welt	derby	mules
nap	fold	pump	woof	dhoti	nappy
net	frog	rags	wool	drape	ninon
pin	gamp	ring	wrap	dress	nylon
rag	garb	robe	yarn	drill	Orlon
rig	gear	ruff	yoke	ducks	paint
sox	gilt	sack	A line	ephod	pants
tab	gore	saga	amice	fanon	parka
tag	gown	sari	ao dai	fichu	patch
tie	haik	sark	apron	flare	patte
wig	heel	sash	array	flash	pique
zip	hood	seal	badge	frill	pixie
Afro	hoop	seam	baize	frock	plaid
alba	hose	shoe	bands	gauze	plait
bags	hyke	silk	bangs	get up	pleat
band	hype	skip	batik	glove	plume
bang	jean	slip	beard	grego	plush
bead	jupe	sock	beret	guimp	point
belt	kepi	sole	blond	guise	print
bias	kilt	stud	blues	gunny	pumps
boot	knot	suit	boots	habit	purse
brim	lace	talc	braid	jabot	queue
cape	lame	tick	busby	jeans	rayon
clog	lawn	tile	chain	jupon	robes
coat	list	toga	chaps	lapel	romal
coif	lock	togs	check	Levis	rumal
comb	mask	torc	cloak	linen	sable
cope	maud	tuck	clogs	lisle	sabot
cord	maxi	tutu	cotta	lungi	sagum
cowl	mini	vamp	crape	lurex	satin
cuff	mink	veil	crash	manta	scarf
curl	mitt	vent	crepe	manto	scrim
dart	mode	vest	crown	model	serge

shako	v̩neck	brogan	denier	infula
shawl	voile	brogue	diaper	insole
sheer	waist	brolly	dickey	jacket
shift	wamus	buckle	dimity	jemima
shirt	watch	burlap	dirndl	jerkin
shoes	weave	buskin	dittos	jersey
simar	wigan	bustle	dolman	jumper
skein	woven	button	duffel	kaftan
skirt	achkan	byssus	ermine	kagool
smock	afghan	caftan	fabric	kimono
snood	alnage	calash	facial	kirtle
spats	alpaca	calico	facing	lappet
specs	angora	camise	faille	lining
stays	anklet	canvas	fallal	livery
stock	anorak	capote	fannel	locket
stole	armlet	casque	fascia	madras
stuff	attire	castor	fedora	magyar
style	basque	cestus	feeder	make̩up
suede	bauble	chimer	fillet	mantle
tabby	beaver	chintz	finery	mantua
tails	bertha	chiton	fox̩fur	marcel
talma	biggin	choker	frills	melton
tammy	bikini	chopin	fringe	minium
terry	blazer	cilice	gaiter	mitten
thrum	blouse	cloche	galosh	mob̩cap
tiara	boater	coatee	gamash	mohair
topee	bodice	collar	garter	moreen
toque	bodkin	collet	girdle	muslin
train	bolero	corset	goatee	nankin
tress	bonnet	cotton	greave	needle
trews	bootee	cravat	gusset	nylons
tulle	bouclé	crewel	hankie	outfit
tunic	bowler	curler	hairdo	panama
tweed	bow̩tie	Dacron	hat̩box	parure
twill	braces	damask	hatpin	patent
upper	briefs	dapper	helmet	peplos

CLOTHES

peplum	tabard	wimple	chaplet
peruke	talcum	woolly	chechia
pocket	tartan	zoster	chemise
pomade	tassle	Acrilan	cheviot
pompom	tettix	àl1a|mode	chevron
poncho	thread	alamode	chiffon
pongee	tiepin	apparel	chignon
poplin	tights	armband	chimere
powder	tin|hat	armhole	chlamys
raglan	tippet	baboosh	chopine
rebato	tissue	baldric	civvies
reefer	toecap	bandana	clobber
revers	tongue	bandbox	clothes
ribbon	top|hat	bandeau	cockade
rigout	topper	bath|oil	compact
rochet	torque	batiste	corsage
roller	toupee	beading	costume
ruffle	tricot	belcher	couture
sacque	trilby	biretta	coxcomb
samite	trunks	bombast	crewcut
sandal	T,shirt	brocade	crochet
sarong	tucker	buckram	cuculla
sateen	turban	bunting	culotte
scarab	tussah	burdash	doeskin
semmit	tusser	burnous	doublet
serape	tuxedo	bycoket	drawers
sheath	tweeds	cagoule	dress|up
shoddy	ulster	calotte	droguet
shorts	unisex	cambric	drugget
shroud	uppers	capuche	elastic
ski|cap	velure	cassock	falsies
slacks	velvet	casuals	fashion
sleeve	waders	cat's|eye	feather
slip,on	wallet	cat|suit	felt|hat
sun|hat	wampus	chamois	ferrule
switch	whites	chapeau	fig|leaf

78

filibeg	leghorn	panache	singlet
fitting	leotard	pannier	skimmer
flannel	loafers	panties	slicker
flounce	long|bob	parasol	soft|hat
foulard	Mae|West	partlet	soutane
freckle	malines	pattern	spencer
frocked	maniple	pegtops	sporran
frogged	manteau	pelisse	stammel
fur|coat	manteel	pendant	stetson
fustian	mascara	percale	sun|suit
gaiters	Mechlin	perfume	surcoat
garment	modesty	peridot	surtout
gingham	modiste	periwig	swaddle
girasol	monocle	petasus	sweater
glasses	mozetta	pigskin	tabaret
grogram	mudpack	pigtail	taffeta
G,string	muffler	pillbox	taffety
guipure	nankeen	pin|curl	tarbush
gumboot	necktie	pith|hat	tatters
gym|slip	New|Look	porkpie	tatting
haircut	nightie	puttees	tea|gown
hairnet	oil|silk	pyjamas	textile
hairpin	oilskin	raiment	texture
handbag	organdy	ringlet	ticking
hatband	organza	rompers	tiffany
hemline	orphrey	rosette	tile|hat
hessian	outsize	rubbers	tonsure
high|hat	overall	rug|gown	top|boot
hip|boot	Oxfords	sacking	topcoat
homburg	padding	sagathy	top|hose
hosiery	paenula	sandals	topknot
jaconet	page|boy	sarafan	torchon
jaegers	paisley	selvage	tricorn
kilt|pin	pajamas	shampoo	trinket
layette	paletot	shingle	tunicle
leather	pallium	silk|hat	turn,ups

twinset	calyptra	elflocks	hairline
undress	camisole	ensemble	half‚boot
uniform	capeline	Eton|crop	half‚hose
veiling	capuchin	Eton|suit	hand‚knit
velours	cardigan	eyeshade	hatguard
webbing	cashmere	face‚lift	headband
wellies	Celanese	face|pack	headgear
worsted	chaperon	fair|isle	headwear
yashmak	chasuble	fastener	high|heel
aigrette	chenille	fatigues	himation
appliqué	cheverel	fillibeg	hipsters
Ascot|tie	ciclaton	fish‚tail	homespun
babouche	cincture	flannels	hot|pants
Balmoral	cingulum	fob|watch	inch|tape
barathea	cloth|cap	fontange	jackboot
basquine	clothing	fool's|cap	Jacquard
bath|cube	coiffure	footwear	jodhpurs
bathrobe	cold|wave	frippery	kerchief
bearskin	corduroy	froufrou	kiss|curl
bedsocks	corselet	furbelow	knickers
birretta	cosmetic	fur|stole	knitwear
black|tie	creepers	galoshes	leggings
bloomers	cretonne	gamashes	leotards
boat|neck	crew|neck	gambados	lingerie
bobbinet	crush|hat	gambeson	lip|brush
body|suit	culottes	gauntlet	lip|rouge
bongrace	dalmatic	glad|rags	lip|salve
boot‚lace	day|dress	gold|lamé	lipstick
bouffant	disguise	gossamer	mackinaw
braiding	dress‚tie	grey|hair	manicure
brass‚hat	drilling	gridelin	mantelet
breeches	drop|curl	guernsey	mantilla
brocatel	dunce|cap	gym|pants	material
buckskin	dust|coat	gym|shoes	moccasin
burberry	Dutch|cap	gym|tunic	moleskin
bustline	ear‚muffs	hair|band	mourning

muscadin	raincoat	surplice
mustache	red|sable	swaddled
nail|file	reticule	swim|suit
nainsook	sandshoe	taglioni
near,silk	scanties	tail|coat
neckband	scapular	tapestry
neckline	sealskin	tarboosh
negligee	seamless	tarlatan
nightcap	Shantung	Terylene
nose,ring	shirring	Thai|silk
oilcloth	shirting	toilette
oilskins	shirt|pin	top|boots
opera|hat	shoehorn	trimming
overalls	shoelace	trot,cozy
overcoat	shoe|tree	trousers
pabouche	short|bob	tweezers
paduasoy	shot|silk	two,piece
pedicure	sideburn	umbrella
peignoir	side|vent	vestment
pelerine	siege|cap	wardrobe
perruque	ski,boots	war|paint
philabeg	ski,pants	whiskers
pinafore	skullcap	white|tie
play|suit	slipover	wig|block
plimsoll	slippers	woollens
pochette	smocking	wristlet
polka|dot	snap|brim	zoot|suit
polo|neck	snubnose	Alice|band
pomander	sombrero	astrakhan
ponyskin	spit|curl	baby|linen
pony|tail	stickpin	balaclava
postiche	stocking	baldachin
pullover	straw|hat	ball|dress
pure|silk	streamer	bath|salts
quilting	subucula	bed|jacket
rag|trade		billycock

blue|jeans	drape|suit	hoop|skirt
bobbin|net	dress|coat	horsehair
bombasine	dress|ring	housecoat
bowler|hat	dress|suit	huckaback
brassiere	duffel|bag	in|fashion
breast|pin	dungarees	Inverness
Breton|hat	epaulette	jockey|cap
broadloom	eye|shadow	Juliet|cap
bush|shirt	face|cream	kick|pleat
calamanco	false|face	kid|gloves
camel|coat	false,face	kirby|grip
camel|hair	farandine	knee,socks
caparison	filoselle	lambswool
cap|in|hand	fingering	linenette
cap|sleeve	floss|silk	loincloth
cassimere	forage|cap	longcloth
chantilly	frock|coat	longcoats
chevelure	full|dress	lorgnette
China|silk	full|skirt	millinery
chinstrap	gabardine	miniskirt
coat,frock	gaberdine	model|gown
coat,tails	georgette	moustache
cocked|hat	girandole	muckender
cold|cream	gold|watch	mustachio
comforter	great|coat	nauticals
corduroys	Greek|lace	neckcloth
cosmetics	grenadine	neckpiece
crinoline	grosgrain	nightgown
Cuban|heel	hairbrush	nightwear
cuff,links	hair|cloth	nun's|habit
décolleté	hairpiece	off|the|peg
demob|suit	hair|shirt	overdress
deodorant	hand|cream	overshoes
djellabah	headdress	overskirt
dog,collar	headpiece	Panama|hat
drainpipe	high|stock	pantalets
	hip|pocket	

82

Paris doll	ski jacket	whalebone
pea jacket	ski jumper	wrap round
peaked cap	skin tight	wristband
percaline	sloppy Joe	zucchetto
petersham	slouch hat	after shave
petticoat	snowshoes	all the rage
phillibeg	solitaire	ankle socks
pinstripe	souwester	astringent
pixie hood	sphendone	Balbriggan
plus fours	spun rayon	ballet shoe
point lace	steenkirk	bathing cap
polo shirt	stitching	beauty spot
pompadour	stockinet	Berlin wool
pourpoint	stomacher	black dress
press stud	strapless	bobbed hair
ready made	sun bonnet	bobbin lace
redingote	sun helmet	bobby socks
Roman lace	swansdown	boiler suit
round neck	sweatband	boudoir cap
sack dress	swing curl	bovver boot
safety pin	tarpaulin	broadcloth
sailcloth	toilet bag	bubble bath
sailor hat	towelling	bush jacket
school cap	track suit	buttonhole
school hat	trousseau	button hook
scoop neck	tube dress	camel's hair
separates	undervest	cap and gown
sharkskin	underwear	chaparajos
sheepskin	urchin cut	chatelaine
shirt band	velveteen	chevesaile
shirt stud	victor'ine	chinchilla
shirt tail	waistband	claw hammer
shovel hat	waistcoat	coat hanger
shower cap	waistline	coat of mail
sideburns	war bonnet	collarette
siren suit	wedge heel	collar stud

83

college cap	Geneva gown	persiennes
cossack hat	grass skirt	picture hat
cotton wool	habit cloth	pillow lace
court dress	hair ribbon	pin cushion
court shoes	half kirtle	pith helmet
covert coat	halter neck	plastic mac
cummerbund	hand lotion	poke bonnet
curling pin	headsquare	powder puff
dentifrice	hook and eye	print dress
deshabille	hop sacking	puff sleeve
dinner gown	hugmetight	rabbitskin
dishabille	jersey silk	riding hood
double chin	jersey wool	romper suit
drainpipes	lappet head	roquelaure
dressing up	life jacket	rubber sole
dressmaker	lounge suit	sailor suit
dress shirt	lover's knot	scalloping
duster coat	mackintosh	scatter pin
embroidery	maquillage	scratch wig
emery board	marcel wave	seersucker
empire line	masquerade	shaving kit
Eton collar	mess jacket	shirtdress
Eton jacket	monk's cloth	shirt frill
evening bag	monk's habit	shirtfront
eyeglasses	mousseline	shoe buckle
face powder	nail polish	silhouette
false teeth	needlecord	silver lamé
fancy dress	nightdress	ski sweater
fascinator	nightshirt	sleeveless
fearnought	old clothes	smock frock
feather boa	overblouse	smoking cap
fitted coat	Oxford bags	solar topee
flak jacket	Oxford ties	spectacles
foundation	pantaloons	sports coat
fourchette	Paris model	sport shirt
fustanella	party dress	sports suit

sportswear	aiguillette	farthingale
square,neck	alexandrite	fine|feather
suede|shoes	barrel|dress	flannelette
Sunday|best	bathing|suit	flared|skirt
sunglasses	beauty|sleep	flying|panel
suspenders	bellbottoms	formal|dress
sweat|shirt	best|clothes	granny|dress
tailor,made	black|patent	grease|paint
terry|cloth	black|velvet	guipure|lace
the|cap|fits	Blucher|boot	hand|me|downs
threadbare	blue|clothes	Harris|tweed
tight|skirt	boiled|shirt	herringbone
toiletries	boutonniere	high|fashion
toilet|soap	boxer|shorts	hobble|skirt
toothbrush	button|shoes	Indian|shawl
toothpaste	campaign|hat	kilted|skirt
trench|coat	candy|stripe	lacing|shoes
turtle|neck	canvas|shoes	lawn|sleeves
under|linen	cap|and|bells	leatherette
underpants	casual|shoes	leg|of|mutton
undershirt	cheesecloth	leopardskin
underskirt	Chinese|silk	marquisette
upper,stock	clodhoppers	matinee|coat
vanity|case	cloth|of|gold	Mechlin|lace
virgin|knot	contact|lens	middy|blouse
wampum|belt	crash|helmet	morning|coat
watch,chain	cutaway|coat	morning|gown
watchstrap	dark|glasses	mortarboard
waterproof	décolletage	mutton|chops
Wellington	deerstalker	nail|varnish
widow's|peak	dinner|dress	neckerchief
Windsor|tie	dreadnought	needle|point
wing|collar	dress|length	orangestick
wrap,around	dressmaking	overgarment
wrap|rascal	dress,shield	Oxford|shoes
wrist|watch	evening|gown	panty|girdle

Persian|lamb	white|collar	divided|skirt
Phrygian|cap	widow's|weeds	donkey|jacket
pilot|jacket	windbreaker	double|jersey
ready|to|wear	windcheater	dressing|case
regimentals	Windsor|knot	dressing|gown
riding|habit	wooden|shoes	dressing|room
school|dress	work|clothes	dress|uniform
set|in|sleeve	woven|fabric	dropped|waist
shaving|soap	antigropelos	duchesse|lace
shawl|collar	apron|strings	duffel|jacket
shell|jacket	bathing|dress	Easter|bonnet
shirt|button	bespectacled	evening|cloak
shock|headed	bib|and|tucker	evening|dress
shoe|leather	bicycle|clips	evening|shoes
shoulder|bag	birthday|suit	fashion|house
Spanish|comb	blue|stocking	fashion|plate
spatterdash	body|stocking	fatigue|dress
stiff|collar	brass|buttons	flaxen|haired
subcingulum	breast|pocket	football|boot
suede|gloves	brilliantine	full|mourning
Sunday|black	business|suit	galligaskins
swagger|coat	cap|of|liberty	glass|slipper
swallowtail	cardinal's|hat	golden|haired
tailor|tacks	cavalry|twill	haberdashery
tam|o|shanter	chastity|belt	hair|dressing
tennis|dress	chesterfield	hair|restorer
tennis|shoes	chin|whiskers	half|mourning
toilet|water	clothes|brush	handkerchief
tooth|powder	clothes|horse	haute|couture
torchon|lace	collar|and|tie	Hessian|boots
trencher|cap	college|scarf	hummel|bonnet
trouser|suit	combinations	if|the|cap|fits
walking|shoe	crepe|de|Chine	knee|breeches
wash|leather	crewel|needle	knitting|wool
watch|pocket	curling|tongs	lightning|zip
watered|silk	dinner|jacket	

lumber jacket	shoulder strap
magyar sleeve	smoking jacket
monkey jacket	sock suspender
morning dress	suspender belt
mousquetaire	underclothing
nail clippers	unfashionable
nail scissors	anti perspirant
night clothes	artificial silk
old fashioned	chest protector
out of fashion	cleansing cream
Paisley shawl	clerical collar
Paris fashion	collar attached
pedal pushers	double breasted
Penang lawyer	evening clothes
plain clothes	fireman's helmet
pressure suit	fully fashioned
Prince Albert	hobnailed boots
Princess line	mandarin collar
raglan sleeve	off the shoulder
set one's cap at	ostrich feather
beauty parlour	pair of slippers
camel hair coat	pair of trousers
carpet slipper	pyjama trousers
casual clothes	riding breeches
cocktail dress	shooting jacket
fashion parade	single breasted
hacking jacket	stocking stitch
Highland dress	tartan trousers
Inverness cape	top hat and tails
lavender water	vanishing cream
leather jacket	wedding garment
made to measure	winter woollies
matinee jacket	working clothes
patent leather	Balaclava helmet
period costume	civilian clothes
quizzing glass	crease resistant

foundation|cream	sheepskin|jacket
full,bottomed|wig	shrink,resistant
highland|costume	swallow,tail|coat
outdoor|clothing	swimming|costume
pair|of|stockings	wellington|boots
regulation|dress	

Colours

dun	flame	cerise	emerald
red	green	cobalt	filemot
tan	helio	copper	gamboge
blue	henna	indigo	iron|red
buff	ivory	lustre	magenta
fawn	khaki	madder	new|blue
flam	lemon	maroon	old|blue
gold	lilac	modena	old|gold
grey	mauve	murrey	ruby|red
lake	ochre	orange	saffron
navy	peach	pastel	scarlet
pink	perse	purple	sea|blue
puce	rouge	reseda	sky|blue
rose	sepia	russet	tile|red
rust	taupe	sienna	ash,blond
sage	tawny	silver	baby|blue
saxe	umber	titian	blood|red
wine	white	violet	brunette
azure	albert	yellow	Burgundy
beige	annato	apricot	chestnut
black	auburn	carmine	dark|blue
brown	blonde	citrine	dove|grey
cream	bronze	crimson	dyestuff

eau de nil	madder red	Irish green
iron grey	moss green	madder blue
lavender	mouse grey	madder lake
mulberry	Naples red	madder pink
navy blue	Nile green	marine blue
off white	olive drab	olive brown
pea green	opera pink	olive green
poppy red	pearl grey	Oxford grey
primrose	raw sienna	Paris green
raw umber	royal blue	Persian red
red ochre	smoke grey	powder blue
sanguine	solferino	raven black
sap green	soot black	rose madder
sapphire	steel blue	salmon pink
saxe blue	steel grey	silver grey
sea green	tangerine	terra cotta
tincture	Turkey red	trypan blue
viridian	turquoise	bottle green
xanthein	vermilion	brown madder
azure blue	acid yellow	burnt orange
blue black	apple green	burnt sienna
burnt lake	aquamarine	cardinal red
burnt rose	Berlin blue	carmine lake
cameo pink	beryl green	chrome green
champagne	brown ochre	chrome lemon
cherry red	burnt umber	cobalt green
chrome red	Chinese red	crimson lake
claret red	cobalt blue	cyanine blue
duck green	direct blue	Dresden blue
Dutch pink	fast yellow	English pink
Indian red	flake white	flesh colour
jade green	French blue	hunting pink
leaf green	French grey	incarnadine
light blue	grass green	Italian blue
lime green	green ochre	Italian pink
livid pink	heliotrope	Japanese red

COLOURS

king's|yellow
lemon|yellow
Paris|yellow
Persian|blue
Persian|blue
Prussian|red
Russian|jade
terra|sienna
ultramarine
Venetian|red
Vienna|green
yellow|ochre
air|force|blue
burnt|carmine
canary|yellow
cerulean|blue
Chinese|white
chrome|orange
chrome|yellow
electric|blue
emerald|green
golden|yellow
gun|metal|grey
hyacinth|blue
lavender|blue
Lincoln|green
madder|orange
madder|violet
madder|yellow
midnight|blue
orange|madder
pastel|colour
pillar|box|red
Prussian|blue
quince|yellow

sapphire|blue
scarlet|ochre
black|and|white
Cambridge|blue
flame|coloured
kaleidoscopic
lemon|coloured
monochromatic
multicoloured
particoloured
peach|coloured
pepper|and|salt
slate|coloured
stone|coloured
straw|coloured
sulphur|yellow
tortoise|shell
cornflower|blue
glowing|colours
heather|mixture
imperial|purple
livery|coloured
orange|coloured
platinum|blonde
primary|colours
salmon|coloured
strawberry|roan
swaddling|cloth
turquoise|green
colour|blindness
colouring|matter
greenery|yallery
rainbow|coloured
secondary|colour

90

Composers

Bax	Dukas	Bartók	Rubbra
Gay	Elgar	Brahms	Schutz
Suk	Fauré	Bridge	Searle
Adam	Field	Busoni	Tallis
Arne	Finzi	Coates	Varese
Bach	Gluck	Czerny	Wagner
Berg	Grieg	Daquin	Walton
Blow	Haydn	Delius	Webern
Byrd	Henze	Duparc	Wilbye
Cage	Holst	Dvořák	Albeniz
Ives	Ibert	Flotow	Allegri
Lalo	Lehár	Franck	Bellini
Nono	Liszt	Gliere	Bennett
Orff	Locke	Glinka	Berlioz
Wolf	Lully	Gounod	Borodin
Alwyn	Parry	Gretry	Britten
Auber	Ravel	Handel	Copland
Auric	Reger	Herold	Corelli
Balfe	Satie	Hummel	Creston
Berio	Sousa	Joplin	Debussy
Bizet	Spohr	Kodaly	Delibes
Bliss	Suppé	Lassus	Dowland
Bloch	Verdi	Ligeti	Duruflé
Boito	Weber	Mahler	Falla, de
Boyce	Weill	Moeran	Gibbons
Brian	Widor	Morley	Howells
Bruch	Alfven	Mozart	Ireland
Cilea	Arnold	Piston	Janáček
d'Indy	Barber	Rameau	Lambert

COMPOSERS

Litolff	Cimarosa	MacDowell
MacCunn	Clementi	Meyerbeer
Martinu	Couperin	Offenbach
Mathias	Gabrieli	Pachelbel
Medtner	Gershwin	Pergolesi
Menotti	Giordano	Prokoviev
Milhaud	Grainger	Scarlatti
Nielsen	Granados	Birtwistle
Poulenc	Honegger	Boccherini
Puccini	Ketelbey	Kabalevsky
Purcell	Korngold	Monteverdi
Quilter	Kriesler	Mussorgsky
Rodrigo	Mascagni	Palestrina
Rossini	Massenet	Penderecki
Roussel	Messiaen	Ponchielli
Salieri	Paganini	Praetorius
Schuman	Panufnik	Rawsthorne
Shankar	Respighi	Rubinstein
Smetana	Sarasate	SaintSaens
Stainer	Schubert	Schoenberg
Stamitz	Schumann	Stravinsky
Strauss	Scriabin	VillaLobos
Tartini	Sibelius	Waldteufel
Thomson	Stanford	Wieniawski
Tippett	Sullivan	Williamson
Vivaldi	Taverner	Butterworth
Warlock	Telemann	Charpentier
Weelkes	Beethoven	Dittersdorf
Albinoni	Bernstein	Humperdinck
Benedict	Boellmann	Leoncavallo
Benjamin	Buxtehude	LloydWebber
Berkeley	Cherubini	Lutoslawski
Boughton	Donizetti	Mendelssohn
Bruckner	Glazounov	Rachmaninov
Chabrier	Hindemith	Stockhausen
Chausson	Hoddinott	Szymanowski

Tchaikovsky	Rimsky-Korsakov
Khachaturian	Coleridge-Taylor
Shostakovich	Vaughan-Williams
Maxwell-Davies	

Computing

baud	deprogram
byte	mainframe
chip	programme
read	slide-rule
Algol	alphameric
Basic	memory-bank
Cobol	peripheral
input	throughput
micro	binary-digit
adding	binary-scale
binary	multi-access
hacker	punched-card
on-line	punched-tape
Fortran	programmable
gigabit	random-access
off-line	adding-machine
program	microcomputer
bistable	shift-register
computer	word-processor
data-bank	analog-computer
database	data-processing
hardware	microprocessor
print-out	systems-analyst
software	computerisation
terminal	computer-science

COMPUTING

digital|computer   storage|capacity
electronic|brain   systems|analysis

Deadly Sins

envy	pride	accidie
lust	sloth	gluttony
anger	wrath	covetousness

Drink

ale	sake	bisque	shandy
bin	soup	borsch	sherry
gin	Toby	bottle	spirit
jug	wine	brandy	squash
nip	wino	carafe	tea bag
pop	booze	cassis	teacup
rum	broth	cellar	tipple
tea	cider	claret	whisky
tot	cocoa	coffee	absinth
tyg	cream	cognac	alcohol
urn	drain	eggnog	aniseed
vat	dregs	goblet	Bacardi
beer	drink	imbibe	beef tea
brew	gumbo	kirsch	beer mug
cafe	jorum	kumiss	bitters
cask	julep	kummel	borscht
coke	lager	liquid	bouquet
dram	Médoc	liquor	bourbon
flip	mocha	magnum	carouse
grog	punch	muscat	chianti
hock	quaff	nectar	cobbler
kola	stock	noggin	cordial
lees	stout	oxtail	curacao
mead	syrup	Pernod	custard
milk	toddy	porter	draught
must	treat	posset	dry wine
ouzo	vodka	potage	egg flip
port	water	rummer	gin fizz
sack	bibber	Scotch	iced tea

limeade	Dubonnet	black drop
liqueur	fruit cup	cappucino
Madeira	gin and it	champagne
malmsey	gin sling	clear soup
martini	green tea	Cointreau
Moselle	hangover	cold drink
new wine	highball	dishwater
philtre	hot drink	doorframe
potable	hot toddy	dry sherry
red wine	hydromel	firewater
sherbet	ice water	ginger ale
shoe box	infusion	ginger pop
sloe gin	julienne	heavy wine
spirits	lemonade	light wine
spritza	libation	metheglin
tea leaf	muscatel	milk shake
tequila	nightcap	mint julep
vintage	pink lady	muscadine
wassail	port wine	neat drink
whiskey	potation	onion soup
absinthe	rice beer	orangeade
Adam's ale	rice soup	Rhine wine
anisette	Riesling	rye whisky
aperitif	root beer	small beer
armagnac	ruby port	soda water
audit ale	rum punch	soft drink
beverage	Sauterne	still wine
Bordeaux	schnapps	sweet wine
bouillon	schooner	tawny port
Burgundy	tantalus	tea leaves
China tea	tea caddy	tiger milk
cocktail	verjuice	white wine
consommé	vermouth	yard of ale
daiquiri	Adam's wine	Beaujolais
demijohn	appetiser	Bloody Mary
Drambuie	aqua vitae	buttermilk

café au lait	whisky sour
cappuccino	amontillado
Chambertin	apple brandy
Chartreuse	barley broth
fruit juice	barley water
ginger beer	beef extract
grape juice	Benedictine
half bottle	black coffee
Holland gin	brandy smash
iced coffee	chicken soup
intoxicant	coffee break
Jamaica rum	cooking wine
lemon juice	cowslip wine
liquid diet	draught beer
love potion	French wines
malt whisky	ginger punch
malted milk	Irish coffee
manzanilla	orange juice
maraschino	peach brandy
minestrone	Scotch broth
mixed drink	strong drink
mock turtle	sweet sherry
Mulled wine	tomato juice
Munich beer	vintage wine
on the rocks	white coffee
Russian tea	breathalyser
slivowitza	café espresso
soda syphon	Danzig brandy
stiff drink	hot chocolate
stirrup cup	ice cream soda
Tom Collins	Irish whiskey
tomato soup	mineral water
tonic water	non alcoholic
turtle soup	Pilsener beer
usquebaugh	sarsaparilla
Vichy water	spirit of wine

DRINK

supernaculum
apricot|brandy
brandy|and|soda
coffee|grounds
condensed|milk
cooking|sherry
creme|de|menthe
dandelion|wine
deoch|an|doruis
estate|bottled
gin|and|bitters
instant|coffee
liqueur|brandy
liquid|measure
mild|and|bitter
morning|coffee
prairie|oyster
round|of|drinks
Scotch|and|soda
sparkling|wine
whisky|and|soda
as|drunk|as|a|lord
bottle|of|brandy
bottle|of|claret

bottle|of|Scotch
bottle|of|whisky
champagne|lunch
cocktail|shaker
coffee|strainer
elderberry|wine
espresso|coffee
evaporated|milk
French|vermouth
John|barleycorn
lemonade|shandy
little|brown|jug
Napoleon|brandy
pineapple|juice
Scotch|and|water
beer|and|skittles
drop|of|good|stuff
gin|and|angostura
grapefruit|juice
green|Chartreuse
Italian|vermouth
one|over|the|eight
wines|and|spirits

Education

BA	ABC	ink	book	dean	fail
Dr	con	jot	co-ed	demy	form
go	den	pen	copy	desk	gown
IQ	dux	ambo	cram	exam	grad
MA	fag	blot	crib	fact	guru

head	flunk	browse	old|boy
lore	forum	bursar	optime
mark	fresh	campus	pandit
mode	gaudy	course	pedant
mods	gloss	creche	pencil
note	grade	debate	period
nous	grind	degree	peruse
oral	guide	docent	preach
pass	hadji	doctor	primer
prep	house	duenna	pundit
prof	imbue	eraser	reader
quad	khoja	examen	recite
quiz	kudos	fellow	rector
read	learn	finals	regius
roll	lines	genius	remove
sage	loach	grader	report
seat	lycee	grades	rubber
soph	major	gradus	savant
swat	merit	greats	school
swot	minor	ground	scroll
talk	paper	homily	senior
tech	poser	infant	sermon
term	prime	infuse	smalls
test	prize	inkpot	syndic
tyro	quill	jotter	taught
atlas	sizar	junior	teaser
board	slate	lector	theory
chair	spell	lesson	tripos
chalk	staff	lyceum	truant
class	study	manual	vellum
coach	teach	master	academy
dunce	tutor	matron	alumnus
ecole	usher	mentor	amateur
edify	alumna	mullah	boarder
essay	brains	munshi	bookish
final	brainy	novice	bookman

Braille	maestro	written	highbrow
brush|up	major|in	academic	homework
bursary	minor|in	aegrotat	humanism
coacher	monitor	agitprop	inceptor
college	nursery	aularian	informed
crammer	old|girl	beginner	inkstand
culture	oppidan	book|lore	instruct
dabbler	pandect	bookworm	Latinist
degrees	papyrus	classman	learning
diploma	passman	coaching	lecturer
dominie	pointer	commoner	lettered
Dunciad	precept	copybook	liripipe
egghead	prefect	cramming	liripoop
entrant	primary	cultural	literacy
erudite	problem	cultured	literate
examine	proctor	didactic	little|go
explain	qualify	disciple	memorize
expound	read|for	division	mistress
faculty	reading	dry|nurse	moralize
failure	satchel	educable	neophyte
fresher	scholar	educated	note|book
grammar	schools	educator	Oxbridge
great|go	seminar	elective	pansophy
grinder	student	emeritus	pass|mark
hearing	studier	examiner	pedagogy
honours	studies	exercise	pedantic
inkhorn	teacher	foolscap	pedantry
inkwell	teach,in	freshman	playtime
instill	the|arts	Gamaliel	polemics
learned	theatre	glossary	polyglot
learner	thinker	gownsman	pore|over
lectern	three|R's	graduand	postgrad
lecture	trainee	graduate	preacher
letters	tuition	guidance	punditry
lexicon	varsity	half,term	question
lowbrow	writing	harangue	read|up|on

redbrick	chalkdust	institute
research	chalk|talk	knowledge
revision	champaign	law|school
roll|cast	classmate	lucubrate
sciolist	classroom	masterate
semester	collegian	note|paper
seminary	cosmogony	novitiate
servitor	day|school	orography
spelling	dean|of|men	palaestra
studious	desk|bound	parchment
studying	didactics	pedagogic
teaching	diligence	pedagogue
textbook	direction	pensioner
training	discourse	play|group
treatise	doctorate	portioner
tutoring	dunce's|cap	precentor
tutelate	education	preceptor
tutorage	enlighten	prelector
tutoress	erudition	pre|school
tutorial	extempore	principal
vacation	fifth|form	professor
versed|in	final|year	proselyte
well|read	first|form	qualified
wordbook	first|year	receptive
wrangler	formalist	refresher
absey|book	gaudeamus	rough|note
alma|mater	gazetteer	scholarch
art|school	governess	scholarly
assistant	greenhorn	schoolboy
associate	Gymnasium	schooling
Athenaeum	homiletic	schoolish
booklover	honour|man	school|kid
brainwave	hortatory	school|lad
brainwork	ignoramus	schoolman
catechism	ingestion	sermonize
catechize	inspector	sixth|form

smatterer	curricular	memorandum
sophister	curriculum	middle｜brow
sophomore	dame｜school	Nobel｜prize
staffroom	dictionary	past｜master
star｜pupil	dilettante	pedagogics
streaming	discipline	pedagogist
supplicat	dual｜school	pensionnat
syndicate	educatress	Philistine
take｜notes	eleven｜plus	playground
teachable	escritoire	playschool
thesaurus	exposition	postmaster
third｜form	extramural	preceptive
third｜year	fellowship	prep｜school
timetable	form｜master	prize｜idiot
tuitional	fourth｜form	prolocutor
tutorhood	fraternity	propaganda
tutorship	free｜period	quadrangle
undergrad	free｜school	quadrivium
abiturient	graduation	quiz｜master
academical	hard｜lesson	readership
arithmetic	headmaster	report｜card
bibliology	high｜school	Sabbatical
bibliomane	humanities	scholastic
bibliosoph	illiterate	schoolbook
blackboard	illuminate	school｜chum
brainchild	illuminati	schooldame
brain｜storm	imposition	schoolgirl
cap｜and｜gown	inquisitor	school｜ma'am
catechumen	instructed	schoolmaid
chautauqua	instructor	schoolmarm
classicism	intramural	schoolmate
classicist	junior｜high	school｜meal
college｜boy	lead｜pencil	school｜miss
collegiate	lower｜fifth	schoolroom
common｜room	lower｜sixth	scrutinize
coryphaeus	lower｜third	second｜form

second|head	college|girl	preparation
second|year	collegianer	prizegiving
self,taught	crash|course	prizewinner
senior|high	enlightened	probationer
shibboleth	examination	questionist
smattering	fellow|pupil	read|a|lesson
specialist	former|pupil	reading|desk
specialize	give|a|lesson	re|education
sub,culture	grade|school	researchist
supervisor	head|teacher	responsions
tenderfoot	house|master	scholarship
university	inculcation	School|Board
upper|fifth	information	sharp|lesson
upper|sixth	informative	spelling|bee
upper|third	institution	student|body
vocabulary	instruction	teachership
well,versed	instructive	teacher's|pet
widely|read	intelligent	teaching|aid
abecedarian	invigilator	trade|school
abecedarium	lecture|hall	upper|fourth
academician	lecture|room	wide|reading
arts|college	lectureship	writing|desk
attainments	liberal|arts	amphitheatre
Bible|school	literary|man	aptitude|test
bibliolatry	litterateur	assimilation
bibliomania	moral|lesson	baccalaureus
bibliophile	mortarboard	battle|of|wits
board|school	music|lesson	bibliomaniac
bookishness	music|school	blue|stocking
brain|teaser	naval|school	book|learning
bright|pupil	night|school	brain|twister
certificate	omniscience	church|school
charm|school	point|a|moral	classicalist
class|fellow	polytechnic	College|Board
coeducation	preceptress	conservatory
college,bred	preparation	disciplinary

disquisition	roll|of|honour
encyclopedia	school|dinner
exercise|book	schoolfellow
exhibitioner	schoolkeeper
form|mistress	schoolmaster
French|lesson	self,educated
ground|school	senior|school
headmistress	spelling|book
indoctrinate	summer|school
infant|school	Sunday|school
instructress	teach|a|lesson
intellectual	training|slip
intelligence	underteacher
junior|school	writing|table
kindergarten	academic|dress
learn|by|heart	advanced|level
make|the|grade	baccalaureate
man|of|letters	Berkeleianism
master|of|arts	careers|master
matter|of|fact	charity|school
memorization	coeducational
menta|l|labour	comprehension
middle|school	comprehensive
nava|l|academy	concentration
norma|l|school	conceptualism
painting|book	conceptualist
parish|school	contemplation
perscrutator	contemplative
phrontistery	contradiction
postgraduate	educationally
preselection	encyclopaedia
professorate	enlightenment
professorial	faculty|of|arts
psychometric	grammar|school
pupil|teacher	home|economics
riding|school	honours|degree

infant|prodigy	existentialist
learning|curve	high|technology
matriculation	honorary|degree
metaphysician	honorary|fellow
misunderstand	intelligentsia
moment|of|truth	lending|library
non,collegiate	loaded|question
nursery|school	metempsychosis
ordinary|level	misinstruction
parrot|fashion	moral|certainty
philosophical	multiple,choice
primary|school	multiracialism
private|school	Open|University
professorship	parapsychology
psychoanalyst	postmastership
Rhodes|scholar	predestination
scholasticism	psychoanalysis
school,leaving	sandwich|course
school|prefect	schoolmistress
schoolteacher	senior|wrangler
social|science	speech|training
speech|therapy	vice,chancellor
undergraduate	a|little|learning
understanding	analytical|logic
vice,president	Aristotelianism
vice|principal	audio,visual|aids
vicious|circle	careers|mistress
word|blindness	combination|room
approved|school	domestic|economy
beg|the|question	domestic|science
boarding|school	epistemological
Cuisenaire|rods	extra,curricular
educationalist	finishing|school
encyclopaedist	first|principles
epistemologist	higher|education
existentialism	horns|of|a|dilemma

EDUCATION

lateral|thinking	regius|professor
logical|analysis	schoolboy|howler
moral|philosophy	school|inspector
open|scholarship	secondary|modern
oral|examination	secondary|school
pathetic|fallacy	tertiary|college
psychometrician	training|college
refresher|course	

First Names

Abe	Guy	Net	Tim	Bart	Elma
Ada	Ian	Nye	Tom	Bert	Elsa
Alf	Ina	Pam	Una	Bess	Emma
Amy	Isa	Pat	Val	Beth	Enid
Ann	Jan	Peg	Vic	Bill	Eric
Bab	Jim	Pen	Viv	Cara	Evan
Bea	Joe	Pip	Wal	Carl	Ewan
Bel	Joy	Pru	Zoe	Chad	Fred
Ben	Kay	Rab	Abel	Ciss	Gail
Bob	Kim	Rae	Abie	Clem	Gene
Dan	Kit	Ray	Adam	Cleo	Gill
Don	Len	Reg	Alan	Dave	Gina
Dot	Leo	Rex	Aldo	Dawn	Gwen
Ena	Liz	Roy	Ally	Dick	Gwyn
Eva	Lyn	Sal	Alma	Dirk	Hope
Eve	Max	Sam	Amos	Dora	Hugh
Fay	May	Sid	Andy	Drew	Hugo
Flo	Meg	Sis	Anna	Duke	Iain
Gay	Nan	Sue	Anne	Earl	Iona
Ger	Nat	Tam	Avis	Edna	Iris
Gus	Ned	Ted	Babs	Ella	Ivan

Ivor	Nell	Aaron	Cecil	Effie	Hetty
Jack	Nick	Abbie	Celia	Elias	Hilda
Jake	Nina	Adele	Chloe	Eliot	Hiram
Jane	Nita	Aggie	Chris	Elise	Honor
Jean	Noel	Agnes	Clara	Eliza	Inigo
Jeff	Olaf	Aidan	Clare	Ellen	Irene
Jess	Olga	Ailie	Cliff	Ellis	Isaac
Jill	Oona	Ailsa	Clive	Elmer	Jacky
Joan	Owen	Alfie	Colin	Elsie	Jacob
Jock	Paul	Algie	Coral	Emily	James
John	Pete	Alice	Corin	Enoch	Jamie
Josh	Phil	Aline	Cyril	Ernie	Janet
Judy	Rene	Alvin	Cyrus	Errol	Janey
June	Rhys	Angus	Daisy	Ethel	Jason
Karl	Rick	Anita	Danny	Faith	Jayne
Kate	Rita	Annie	Darby	Fanny	Jenny
Leah	Rolf	April	D'Arcy	Felix	Jerry
Lena	Rory	Avril	David	Fiona	Jesse
Leon	Rosa	Barry	Davie	Fleur	Jimmy
Lily	Rose	Basil	Delia	Flora	Josie
Lisa	Ross	Becca	Denis	Frank	Joyce
Lois	Ruby	Bella	Derek	Freda	Julie
Lola	Ruth	Benny	Diana	Garry	Karen
Lucy	Ryan	Berry	Diane	Garth	Keith
Luke	Sara	Beryl	Dilys	Gavin	Kevin
Lynn	Saul	Betsy	Dinah	Geoff	Kitty
Mark	Sean	Betty	Dodie	Gerda	Lance
Mary	Stan	Biddy	Dolly	Giles	Laura
Matt	Tess	Boris	Donna	Ginny	Leila
Maud	Theo	Brian	Doris	Grace	Lenny
Mick	Toby	Bruce	Dylan	Greta	Leona
Mike	Tony	Bruno	Eamon	Harry	Lewis
Muir	Vera	Caleb	Eddie	Hazel	Libby
Myra	Walt	Carla	Edgar	Helen	Linda
Neal	Will	Carol	Edith	Helga	Lindy
Neil	Yves	Cathy	Edwin	Henry	Lloyd

FIRST NAMES

Lorna	Niall	Tania	Audrey	Dugald
Louis	Nicky	Tanya	Aurora	Dulcie
Lucia	Nicol	Tatum	Austin	Duncan
Lydia	Nigel	Terry	Aylwin	Dustin
Lynne	Norma	Tilly	Barney	Dwight
Mabel	Orson	Tracy	Bertha	Easter
Madge	Oscar	Vicky	Billie	Edmund
Maeve	Paddy	Vince	Blaise	Edward
Magda	Patty	Viola	Bobbie	Edwina
Mamie	Paula	Wanda	Brenda	Egbert
Manny	Pearl	Wayne	Bryony	Eileen
Marge	Peggy	Wendy	Calvin	Eilidh
Margo	Penny	Adrian	Carmen	Elaine
Maria	Perce	Agatha	Carole	Elinor
Marie	Percy	Aileen	Carrie	Elisha
Mario	Perry	Albert	Caspar	Elvira
Marty	Peter	Aldous	Cedric	Emilia
Maude	Polly	Alexis	Cherry	Ernest
Mavis	Ralph	Alfred	Cheryl	Esmond
Merle	Rhoda	Alicia	Claire	Esther
Miles	Rhona	Alison	Claude	Eugene
Milly	Robin	Althea	Connor	Eunice
Mitzi	Rodge	Amanda	Conrad	Evadne
Moira	Roger	Amelia	Damian	Evelyn
Molly	Rufus	Andrea	Daniel	Fergus
Morag	Sadie	Andrew	Daphne	Gareth
Moray	Sally	Angela	Darsey	Gaston
Morna	Sandy	Antony	Davina	George
Moses	Sarah	Arabel	Debbie	Gerald
Myles	Sarah	Archie	Denise	Gerard
Myrna	Simon	Arline	Dermot	Gertie
Nancy	Sonia	Arnold	Dianne	Gideon
Nanny	Steve	Arthur	Donald	Gladys
Naomi	Susan	Astrid	Doreen	Gloria
Nelly	Susie	Athene	Dougal	Gordon
Netty	Sybil	Aubrey	Dudley	Graham

108

6 LETTERS

Gregor	Judith	Mervyn	Robert
Gretel	Julian	Michel	Robina
Gwenda	Juliet	Mickey	Rodney
Hamish	Julius	Minnie	Roland
Hannah	Justin	Miriam	Ronald
Harold	Kenelm	Monica	Rowena
Harvey	Kirsty	Morgan	Roxana
Hattie	Larrie	Morrie	Rupert
Hector	Laurie	Morris	Sabina
Hester	Lesley	Morven	Salome
Hilary	Leslie	Muriel	Samuel
Horace	Lester	Murray	Sandra
Howard	Lilian	Myrtle	Selina
Hubert	Lionel	Nadine	Selwyn
Hunter	Lolita	Nathan	Serena
Imogen	Lottie	Nessie	Sharon
Ingram	Louisa	Nettie	Sheena
Ingrid	Louise	Nicola	Sheila
Irving	Lucius	Nicole	Sidney
Isabel	Luther	Noelle	Silvia
Isaiah	Maggie	Norman	Sophia
Isobel	Magnus	Norris	Sophie
Isolde	Maisie	Odette	Stella
Israel	Manuel	Oliver	Steven
Jackie	Marcia	Oonagh	Stuart
Janice	Marcus	Oriana	Sydney
Jasper	Margie	Osbert	Sylvia
Jemima	Marian	Oswald	Tamsin
Jeremy	Marion	Pamela	Thelma
Jerome	Marius	Petrus	Thomas
Jessie	Martha	Petula	Trevor
Joanna	Martin	Philip	Tricia
Joanne	Maxine	Phoebe	Trixie
Joseph	Melvin	Rachel	Trudie
Joshua	Melvyn	Regina	Ursula
Josiah	Merlin	Reuben	Verity

FIRST NAMES

Victor	Brendan	Fenella	Lucinda
Violet	Bridget	Florrie	Malcolm
Vivian	Bronwen	Flossie	Margery
Vivien	Cameron	Frances	Marilyn
Wallis	Camilla	Francis	Martina
Walter	Candida	Gabriel	Martine
Warner	Carlton	Geordie	Matilda
Warren	Carolyn	Geraint	Matthew
Wesley	Cecilia	Gilbert	Maureen
Wilbur	Celeste	Gillian	Maurice
Willie	Charity	Giselle	Maxwell
Willis	Charles	Godfrey	Melanie
Winnie	Charlie	Gregory	Melissa
Yehudi	Chrissy	Gwyneth	Michael
Yvette	Christy	Harriet	Mildred
Yvonne	Clarice	Heather	Mirabel
Abigail	Claudia	Herbert	Miranda
Abraham	Clement	Horatio	Modesty
Adriana	Clemmie	Jeffrey	Montagu
Alfreda	Corinna	Jessica	Murdoch
Alister	Cynthia	Jocelyn	Myfanwy
Ambrose	Deborah	Juliana	Natalie
Annabel	Deirdre	Justine	Natasha
Annette	Desmond	Katrina	Neville
Anthony	Diarmid	Kenneth	Nicolas
Antonia	Dolores	Kirstie	Obadiah
Ariadne	Dominic	Lachlan	Ophelia
Aurelia	Dorothy	Lavinia	Ottilie
Baldwin	Douglas	Leonard	Patrick
Barbara	Eleanor	Leonora	Pauline
Barnaby	Elspeth	Leopold	Perdita
Belinda	Emanuel	Letitia	Petrina
Bernard	Erasmus	Lillian	Phyllis
Bernice	Estella	Lindsey	Queenie
Bertram	Eugenia	Linette	Quentin
Blanche	Ezekiel	Lucille	Raphael

Raymond	Alastair	Florence
Rebecca	Aloysius	Francine
Richard	Angeline	Geoffrey
Roberta	Arabella	Georgina
Rosalie	Augustus	Gertrude
Rudolph	Barnabas	Hercules
Rudyard	Beatrice	Hermione
Russell	Benedict	Humphrey
Sabrina	Benjamin	Iseabail
Shelagh	Bertrand	Jeanette
Shelley	Beverley	Jennifer
Shirley	Carlotta	Jonathan
Siobhan	Carolina	Kathleen
Solomon	Caroline	Lancelot
Spencer	Cathleen	Laurence
Stanley	Catriona	Lawrence
Stephen	Charlton	Llewelyn
Stewart	Charmian	Lorraine
Susanna	Clarence	Madeline
Suzanne	Claribel	Magdalen
Terence	Clarissa	Margaret
Theresa	Claudius	Marianne
Timothy	Clemence	Marigold
Valerie	Clifford	Marjorie
Vanessa	Collette	Matthias
Vaughan	Cordelia	Meredith
Vincent	Cressida	Michelle
Wallace	Cuthbert	Montague
Wilfred	Danielle	Morrison
William	Dominica	Mortimer
Windsor	Dorothea	Nicholas
Winston	Drusilla	Octavius
Wyndham	Ebenezer	Odysseus
Yolande	Euphemia	Patience
Adrienne	Farquhar	Patricia
Alasdair	Felicity	Penelope

FIRST NAMES

Percival	Christine
Perpetua	Constance
Philippa	Cornelius
Primrose	Elizabeth
Prudence	Esmeralda
Prunella	Ethelbert
Reginald	Ferdinand
Roderick	Francesca
Rosalind	Frederica
Rosamund	Frederick
Rosemary	Genevieve
Samantha	Geraldine
Scarlett	Gwendolyn
Sherlock	Henrietta
Silvanus	Jacquetta
Sinclair	Josephine
Somerset	Katharine
Theodora	Madeleine
Theodore	Magdalene
Veronica	Marmaduke
Victoria	Millicent
Violette	Mirabelle
Virginia	Nathaniel
Winifred	Nicolette
Alexander	Peregrine
Alexandra	Priscilla
Alphonsus	Rosabella
Anastasia	Sebastian
Annabella	Sempronia
Archibald	Seraphina
Augustine	Siegfried
Cassandra	Stephanie
Catherine	Sylvester
Charlotte	Veronique
Christian	Antoinette
Christina	Bernadette

Christabel	Marguerite	Wilhelmina
Christiana	Maximilian	Bartholomew
Clementine	Montgomery	Christopher
Jacqueline	Petronella	Constantine

Fish

bib	goby	cohog	skate	cockle
cod	hake	dorse	smelt	comber
dab	huso	fluke	smolt	conger
eel	kelt	gaper	snook	cottus
fin	keta	gaper	spawn	cuttle
gar	luce	genus	sprat	darter
hag	opah	guppy	squid	dorado
ide	parr	hydra	sting	ellops
ray	pike	lance	tench	fogash
roe	pout	murex	trout	garvie
barb	rudd	murry	tunny	grilse
bass	scad	ormer	umber	groper
blay	scup	perch	whelk	gurnet
carp	shad	pinna	alevin	kipper
char	sole	pogge	angler	launce
chub	tail	polyp	barbel	limpet
chum	tope	porgy	beluga	maigre
clam	tuna	prawn	bester	marlin
claw	basse	roach	bowfin	meagre
coho	blain	roker	burbot	medusa
crab	bleak	saury	Cancer	megrim
dace	bream	scale	caplin	merman
dory	brill	shark	caribe	milter
fish	cobia	shell	cheven	minnow
gill	cohoe	shoal	chevin	mudeel

FISH

mullet	tarpon	herring	sea,cock
murena	tautog	hogfish	sea,dace
murine	triton	homelyn	sea,hare
murray	turbot	jawfish	sea,pike
murrey	twaite	jewfish	sea,slug
mussel	urchin	lamprey	sea,star
nekton	weever	lobster	sea,wife
ostrea	wrasse	mahseer	sea,wolf
oyster	abalone	merling	sea,worm
partan	abalone	mermaid	sockeye
pholas	acaleph	mollusc	spawner
pirana	alewife	mollusk	sun,fish
pisces	anchovy	mudfish	tiddler
plaice	aquatic	muraena	titling
pollan	benthos	mytilus	toheroa
puffer	bergylt	oarfish	torpedo
quahog	bivalve	octopod	trepang
redeye	bluecap	octopus	whiting
redfin	bummalo	osseter	anguilla
remora	capelin	pellock	band|fish
robalo	catfish	piddock	blue,back
salmon	cichlid	piranha	bluefish
sea,bat	codfish	piscine	bonefish
sea,cat	codling	pomfret	brisling
sea,ear	cyclops	pompano	bullhead
sea,eel	dogfish	redfish	calamary
sea,fox	eel,pout	rock,cod	carapace
sea,hog	finnock	sand,eel	coalfish
sea,pen	flipper	sardine	congo,eel
sea,pig	garfish	sawfish	crawfish
serran	gar,pike	scallop	crayfish
shiner	grouper	scomber	deal|fish
shrimp	gudgeon	sculpin	dragonet
sponge	gurnard	sea,bass	eagle,ray
squama	haddock	sea,bear	earshell
sucker	halibut	sea,calf	filefish

firebird	sailfish	conger|eel
fishpond	salmonid	crossfish
fish|tank	sandling	devil,fish
flatfish	sand,sole	dog,salmon
flounder	sea,acorn	dorsal,fin
fox,shark	sea,adder	Dover|sole
frog,fish	sea,beast	fish,garth
game|fish	sea,bream	fish,louse
goatfish	sea,devil	gaspereau
goldfish	sea,eagle	gastropod
grayling	sea,hound	ghost|crab
hornbeak	sea,lemon	globe|fish
John|Dory	sea,lungs	goldfinny
king,crab	sea,perch	goldsinny
kingfish	sea,robin	green,bone
land,crab	sea,snail	horny,head
lemon|dab	sea,trout	ichthyoid
lion|fish	sparling	jellyfish
lump,fish	spawning	lake|trout
lungfish	starfish	langouste
mackerel	sting,ray	lemon|sole
man,eater	sturgeon	pike,perch
man,of,war	tentacle	pilot|fish
menhaden	tuna|fish	porbeagle
monkfish	univalve	razorfish
nauplius	wallfish	red,mullet
physalia	weakfish	rock,perch
pickerel	wolf,fish	round|clam
pilchard	angel|fish	royal,fish
pipefish	barracuda	sandpride
plankton	black|bass	scaldfish
red,belly	blackfish	schnapper
rock,cook	blindfish	sea,nettle
rock,fish	blue|shark	sea,salmon
rockling	brandling	sea,sleeve
rose,fish	bull,trout	sea,urchin

FISH

selachian	lumpsucker	lantern,fish
shellfish	mossbunker	laterigrade
solenette	mud,skipper	lophobranch
stonefish	paddlefish	muskellunge
surmullet	parrot,fish	pearl,oyster
swordfish	periwinkle	pelican,fish
sword,tail	purple,fish	piranha,fish
thornback	rabbit,fish	piscatorial
trachinus	red,herring	salmon,trout
troutling	ribbon,fish	sea,cucumber
trunkfish	rock,salmon	sea,hedgehog
water,flea	rock,turbot	sea,scorpion
whitebait	salamander	soldier,crab
white,bass	sand,dollar	spawning,bed
whitefish	sand,launce	stickleback
widow,bird	sand,sucker	striped,bass
acorn,shell	sea,poacher	sucking,fish
archer,fish	sea,surgeon	trumpet,fish
bêche,de,mer	shovelhead	whiting,pout
bitterling	silverfish	basking,shark
Bombay,duck	spider,crab	branchiopoda
bottle,fish	spotted,ray	fighting,fish
brook,trout	squeteague	golden,salmon
brown,trout	tiger,shark	goldfish,bowl
butterfish	vinegar,eel	ground,feeder
candlefish	whale,shark	ichthyopsida
coelacanth	bellows,fish	kettle,of,fish
crustacean	brine,shrimp	man,of,war,fish
cuttle,fish	calling,crab	mantis,shrimp
demoiselle	channel,bass	miller's,thumb
fish,ladder	Dolly,Varden	paradise,fish
hammer,fish	electric,eel	rainbow,trout
hellbender	flying,squid	scorpion,fish
hermit,crab	golden,trout	sea,butterfly
kabeljauer	heart,urchin	sea,porcupine
lancet,fish	hippocampus	sentinel,crab

sergeant‚fish
silver|salmon
spring|keeper
swimming|crab
trachypterus
tropical|fish
trout|nursery

white|herring
findon|haddock
finnan|haddock
horse|mackerel
ichthyologist
spermaceti|whale

Flowers

bed	aster	sprig	florid
bud	bloom	stalk	flower
lei	calyx	stock	garden
sow	clump	style	growth
arum	daisy	thorn	hen‚bit
bulb	dwale	tulip	hybrid
corm	flora	viola	lupine
cyme	graft	yulan	maguey
flag	hardy	althea	mallow
geum	lotus	annual	mimosa
irid	malva	anther	nectar
iris	mould	azalea	orchid
lily	ocrea	border	orchis
pink	oxlip	carpel	pistil
poke	pansy	cistus	pollen
posy	peony	corona	raceme
rosa	petal	corymb	rosery
seed	phlox	cosmos	runner
spur	poppy	crocus	salvia
stem	sepal	dahlia	scilla
wort	shoot	exotic	silene
agave	spray	floret	smilax

FLOWERS

spadix	kingcup	verbena
spathe	leafage	verdant
stamen	leaflet	verdure
stigma	lily|pad	weed|out
sucker	lobelia	amaranth
violet	may,lily	anthesis
wreath	mimulus	arum|lily
yarrow	mullein	auricula
zinnia	nemesia	bear's|ear
aconite	nigella	biennial
althaea	nosegay	bird's,eye
alyssum	panicle	bluebell
anemone	papaver	buddleia
begonia	pedicel	camellia
blawort	petiole	camomile
blossom	petunia	catchfly
bouquet	primula	chinampa
burgeon	pruning	clematis
campion	ragweed	corn,flag
chaplet	ragwort	cyclamen
clarkia	rambler	daffodil
climber	rampion	dianthus
corolla	red|rose	dog,daisy
corsage	rockery	epicalyx
cowslip	rosebay	feverfew
cutting	rosebud	floweret
day|lily	roselle	foxglove
dog,rose	saffron	gardenia
erodium	sea,pink	geranium
figwort	seed|pod	gladioli
fuchsia	setwall	gloxinia
garland	spiraea	goat's,rue
gentian	sub|rosa	greenery
godetia	tagetes	harebell
jasmine	tea|rose	hawkweed
jonquil	thyrsus	henequen

118

hot,house	wood,sage	full|bloom
hyacinth	Aaron's|rod	gelsemium
japonica	amarantus	gladiolus
larkspur	amaryllis	golden|rod
lily|pond	aquilegia	gynophore
marigold	bear's,foot	half,hardy
maybloom	bedded|out	hellebore
moss|rose	bulb|field	herb|Paris
musk,rose	buttercup	hollyhock
myosotis	calendula	home,grown
offshoot	campanula	lady,smock
peduncle	candytuft	mayflower
perianth	capitulum	moon,daisy
petalody	carnation	naked|lady
pond|lily	celandine	narcissus
primrose	China,rose	nelumbium
red|poppy	cineraria	perennial
rock|rose	clove,pink	perpetual
rose|bush	colchicum	pimpernel
roseroot	coltsfoot	pollen,sac
scabiosa	columbine	pollinate
scabious	composite	poppy,head
sea,heath	coreopsis	pyrethrum
seedcase	cotyledon	remontant
seedling	culver,key	richardia
seminary	dandelion	root,prune
snowdrop	digitalis	rootstock
stapelia	dog,violet	rose,elder
sundrops	dry,garden	saxifrage
sweetpea	duck's|foot	seed|plant
trillium	edelweiss	snowflake
veronica	eglantine	speedwell
wild|rose	flowerage	sunflower
wistaria	flower|bed	tiger|lily
woodbind	flowering	wake,robin
woodbine	flower,pot	water,flag

water lily	goldilocks	stavesacre
wax flower	gypsophila	stork's bill
white wood	heart's ease	sweet briar
window box	helianthus	sweet brier
wolf's bane	heliotrope	wallflower
amaranthus	herbaceous	water elder
anthophore	Indian pink	water lemon
belladonna	Indian poke	wild flower
bellflower	Indian shot	willow herb
bluebottle	king's spear	wood sorrel
burnet rose	lady's smock	yellow root
buttonhole	maiden pink	yellow weed
carpophore	marguerite	yellow wort
China aster	marshlocks	Aaron's beard
cinquefoil	mayblossom	antirrhinum
compositae	mignonette	bear's breech
corncockle	mock orange	boutonniere
cornflower	nasturtium	cabbage rose
crane's bill	nightshade	calceolaria
cuckoo pint	opium poppy	convallaria
cut flowers	orange lily	convolvulus
daisy chain	ox eye daisy	dusty miller
damask rose	passiflora	everlasting
delphinium	periwinkle	forget me not
Dutch tulip	pillar rose	garden glass
field poppy	poinsettia	gillyflower
fleur de lis	polyanthus	guelder rose
floral leaf	ranunculus	hardy annual
floribunda	red jasmine	honeysuckle
flower head	rock garden	Indian cress
flower show	rock violet	lady's mantle
frangipani	roof garden	London pride
fritillary	rose mallow	loosestrife
garden city	sarracenia	love in a mist
gelder rose	Scotch rose	Madonna lily
German iris	snapdragon	meadow sweet

Nancy|pretty	fresh|flowers
night|flower	Iceland|poppy
orange|grass	lady's|slipper
Parma|violet	monkey|flower
phyllomania	morning|glory
plum|blossom	old|man's|beard
pollen|grain	orange|flower
pollination	pasque|flower
propagation	peach|blossom
ragged|robin	rambling|rose
rambler|rose	rhododendron
red|hot|poker	rose|of|Sharon
rose|campion	Shirley|poppy
stephanotis	snow|in|summer
St|John's|wort	Solomon's|seal
tiger|flower	St|Peter's|wort
water|garden	sunken|garden
white|bottle	sweet|alyssum
wild|flowers	sweet|William
wood|anemone	virgin's|bower
Adam's|flannel	water|flowers
alpine|flower	wild|hyacinth
apple|blossom	bougainvillea
autumn|crocus	cherry|blossom
bog|pimpernel	Christmas|rose
bridal|wreath	chrysanthemum
Carolina|pink	eschscholtzia
century|plant	Flanders|poppy
corn|marigold	floricultural
cuckoo|flower	marsh|marigold
fennel|flower	meadow|saffron
flower|border	orange|blossom
flower|delice	passion|flower
flower|de|luce	traveller's|joy
flower|garden	bladder|campion
flower|of|Jove	bunch|of|flowers

FLOWERS

Canterbury|bell   shepherd's|purse
floriculturist   butterfly|orchis
lords|and|ladies   evening|primrose
love|in|idleness   lily|of|the|valley
love|in|idleness   Michaelmas|daisy
night|flowering   woody|nightshade
shepherd's|glass

Food

bin	cafe	lamb	stew	crust	lunch
bun	cake	lard	suet	curds	manna
can	chop	loaf	tart	curry	mince
egg	chow	loin	tuck	dicer	offal
fry	curd	malt	tuna	dough	pasta
ham	deli	mash	veal	feast	pasty
ice	diet	meal	whet	flank	patty
jam	dine	meat	whey	fudge	pecan
leg	dish	menu	wing	gigot	pilaf
nut	duck	nosh	yolk	goody	pilaw
oil	duff	olio	zest	goose	pizza
ort	eats	olla	àdemi	gorge	poach
pie	Edam	pate	aspic	Gouda	purée
poi	fare	peel	bacon	gravy	quail
roe	feed	pork	bread	grill	roast
sup	flan	puff	bully	gruel	round
wok	food	rare	candy	honey	salmi
beef	fool	rock	capon	icing	sauce
bite	fowl	roll	cheer	jelly	sauté
boil	game	rump	chips	joint	scone
bolt	grub	rusk	chuck	kebab	scrag
bran	hash	salt	crumb	liver	shank

slops	course	mutton	trifle
snack	croute	noodle	tucker
spice	cutlet	nougat	tuck,in
steak	dainty	nutmeg	turbot
sugar	dining	omelet	turkey
sweet	dinner	oxtail	umbles
swill	dragee	paella	viande
table	eat,out	panada	viands
T,bone	eclair	parkin	waffle
toast	edible	pastry	walnut
torte	egg,box	peanut	albumen
treat	entree	pepper	aliment
tripe	flitch	pickle	anchovy
vegan	fodder	picnic	bannock
wafer	fondue	pilaff	banquet
addled	forage	quiche	banting
almond	frappe	ragout	Bath,bun
banger	fridge	rasher	biscuit
batter	gammon	ration	boiling
blintz	gateau	recipe	brisket
bonbon	giblet	relish	brittle
breast	grouse	repast	broiler
brunch	hot,dog	saddle	cake,mix
buffet	hot,pot	salami	calorie
butter	humbug	salmon	candies
cachou	jam,jar	sponge	caramel
canape	jam,pot	spread	catchup
cashew	jujube	sundae	caviare
catsup	junket	supper	cayenne
caviar	kernel	sweets	charqui
cheese	kidney	tamale	chicken
cockle	kipper	tamara	chowder
collop	leaven	tiffin	chutney
comfit	morsel	titbit	commons
cookie	mousse	toffee	compote
cornet	muffin	tongue	cookery

cooking	matzoth	strudel	date|roll
cracker	meat|pie	tabasco	déjeuner
crumpet	mustard	teacake	delicacy
cuisine	nurture	treacle	doggy|bag
cupcake	oatcake	truffle	doughnut
deep|fry	pabulum	vanilla	dressing
dine|out	pancake	venison	dried|egg
edibles	paprika	vinegar	dripping
egg|yolk	parfait	vitamin	duckling
epicure	pikelet	wine|gum	dumpling
essence	pimento	yoghurt	egg|shell
fig|roll	poisson	acid|drop	egg|white
fondant	popcorn	a|la|carte	Emmental
fritter	popover	allspice	escalope
game|pie	pork|pie	ambrosia	escargot
gelatin	pottage	angelica	flan|case
giblets	poultry	antepast	flapjack
glucose	praline	ante|room	flesh|pot
glutton	pretzel	appetite	fried|egg
gnocchi	protein	apple|pie	frosting
goulash	pudding	baked|egg	fruit|gum
gourmet	ratafia	barbecue	gelatine
granish	rations	betel|nut	grilling
grocery	ravioli	bull's|eye	hard|tack
Gruyère	risotto	caneloni	hazelnut
gumdrop	rissole	chapatty	ice|cream
helping	rum|baba	chop|suey	kedgeree
hot|cake	sardine	chow|mein	licorice
ice|cube	sausage	cinnamon	loin|chop
ingesta	saveloy	clambake	lollipop
jam|roll	savoury	cold|meat	luncheon
jam|tart	seafood	conserve	macaroni
ketchup	seltzer	coq|au|vin	macaroon
knuckle	sirloin	cross|bun	main|dish
lardoon	soufflé	croutons	marinade
lozenge	soupçon	crudités	marinate

124

marzipan	soy|sauce	butter|pat
meat|ball	stockpot	calf's|head
meat|loaf	stuffing	Camembert
meat|roll	supplies	cashew|nut
meat|stew	syllabub	charlotte
meringue	take|away	club|steak
mince|pie	tamarind	cochineal
molasses	tarragon	colcannon
moussaka	teabread	collation
mushroom	tea|break	condiment
olive|oil	tortilla	confiture
omelette	trotters	cough|drop
pastille	turnover	crackling
pastrami	viaticum	cream|cake
pemmican	victuals	cream|horn
pheasant	water|ice	cream|puff
pig's|feet	wishbone	croissant
pig's|will	yoghourt	croquette
plum|cake	zwieback	croustade
pope's|eye	acid|drops	dark|bread
pork|chop	addled|egg	dried|eggs
porridge	aitchbone	drop|scone
pot|roast	angel|cake	drumstick
preserve	antipasto	egg|powder
quenelle	arrowroot	elevenses
rock|cake	banquette	entremets
rock|salt	barmbrack	epicurean
roly|poly	bean|feast	epulation
rye|bread	beefsteak	foodstuff
salt|beef	beer|glass	forcemeat
salt|pork	bite|to|eat	foretaste
sandwich	boiled|egg	fricassee
scrag|end	Brazil|nut	fried|rice
scramble	breakfast	fried|sole
shoulder	bubble|gum	fruit|cake
side|dish	bully|beef	galantine

gravy|soup	provender	blue|cheese
groceries	provision	boiled|fish
groundnut	rabbit|pie	boiled|meat
guest|room	red|pepper	Bombay|duck
half|a|loaf	rice|paper	bon|appetit
hamburger	roast|beef	brandy|snap
humble|pie	rock|candy	breadcrumb
Irish|stew	Roquefort	bread|sauce
jelly|baby	rump|steak	bread|stick
lamb|chops	Scotch|egg	Brie|cheese
lamb|fries	seasoning	brown|sugar
layer|cake	shortcake	calf's|brain
left|overs	short|ribs	candy|floss
leg|of|lamb	soda|bread	caper|sauce
liquorice	soda|scone	cooking|fat
loaf|sugar	spaghetti	cooking|oil
lump|sugar	spareribs	corned|beef
macedoine	spearmint	corned|meat
marchpane	spun|sugar	cornflakes
margarine	sugar|lump	custard|pie
marmalade	sweet|corn	daily|bread
meat|paste	sweetmeat	Danish|blue
mincemeat	Swiss|roll	devil's|food
mint|sauce	tasty|dish	dill|pickle
monkey|nut	tipsy|cake	dinner|roll
nutriment	vol|au|vent	dog|biscuit
patty|cake	wheat|germ	double|loin
peanut|bar	white|meat	dropped|egg
petit|four	wild|honey	Edam|cheese
phosphate	apple|cover	fatted|calf
picnic|ham	apple|sauce	flank|steak
piping|hot	aristology	food|supply
pistachio	baked|beans	fork|supper
pot|pourri	Bath|oliver	frangipane
pound|cake	bill|of|fare	French|cake
preserves	blancmange	fresh|cream

126

fricandeau	provisions	Vienna|loaf
frozen|food	puff|pastry	Vienna|roll
garlic|salt	regalement	water|icing
ginger|snap	rolled|lamb	white|bread
Gorgonzola	rolled|pork	white|sauce
ham|and|eggs	round|steak	zabaglione
hearty|meal	royal|icing	almond|icing
hickory|nut	saccharine	almond|paste
honey|crisp	salmagundi	banana|split
hot|and|cold	sea|biscuit	barley|sugar
icing|sugar	shallow|fry	beef|sausage
ingredient	sheep's|head	black|butter
jardinière	shirred|egg	black|pepper
jugged|hare	shish|kebab	bonne|bouche
lamb|cutlet	shortbread	brandy|sauce
light|lunch	shortcrust	breadcrumbs
liverwurst	silverside	burnt|almond
maple|syrup	Simnel|cake	caster|sugar
marble|cake	sour|pickle	Castile|soap
marrow|bone	spatchcock	chicken|feed
mayonnaise	sponge|cake	chilli|sauce
meal|ticket	spotted|dog	clam|chowder
Melba|toast	square|meal	clove|pepper
mint|humbug	staple|diet	comestibles
mortadella	stroganoff	cottage|loaf
mozzarella	stuffed|egg	cover|charge
mutton|chop	sucking|pig	cream|cheese
pastry|case	sugar|candy	curry|powder
pâtisserie	sugar|mouse	custard|tart
peach|melba	sweetbread	devilled|egg
peppermint	sweet|stuff	devilled|ham
piccalilli	table|d'hôte	dinner|party
pickled|egg	tea|biscuit	double|cream
plat|du|jour	tenderloin	dressed|crab
poached|egg	veal|cutlet	Dutch|cheese
potted|meat	vermicelli	Eve's|pudding

festal|board	poached|fish	afternoon|tea
fillet|steak	pork|sausage	apple|fritter
flank|mutton	potato|crisp	apple|strudel
frankfurter	potato|salad	bacon|and|eggs
French|bread	preparation	bakewell|tart
French|toast	pressed|beef	birthday|cake
fresh|butter	refreshment	bitter|almond
gammon|steak	rice|pudding	black|pudding
gingerbread	roast|grouse	blood|pudding
Gouda|cheese	roast|potato	bouquet|garni
green|pepper	room|service	breast|of|lamb
griddlecake	sausage|roll	breast|of|veal
ground|spice	self|service	brewer's|yeast
health|foods	ship|biscuit	butcher's|meat
Hollandaise	side|of|bacon	butterscotch
hors|d'oeuvre	single|cream	caraway|seeds
hot|cross|bun	sliced|bread	cheeseburger
hot|luncheon	smörgasbord	chilli|pepper
ice|lollipop	spotted|Dick	chitterlings
invalid|fare	staff|of|life	chocolate|box
iron|rations	suet|pudding	choice|morsel
jam|turnover	sweet|almond	cinnamon|ball
jellied|eels	sweet|pepper	clotted|cream
leg|of|mutton	sweet|pickle	club|sandwich
light|repast	Swiss|cheese	Cornish|pasty
link|sausage	tagliatelle	coupe|Jacques
loaf|of|bread	toffee|apple	crust|of|bread
Madeira|cake	tomato|sauce	curds|and|whey
marshmallow	tossed|salad	custard|sauce
milk|pudding	treacle|tart	Danish|pastry
morning|roll	Vienna|steak	delicatessen
olla|podrida	wedding|cake	fillet|of|sole
parson's|nose	Welsh|rabbit	finnan|haddie
petits|fours	wheaten|loaf	fish|and|chips
pig's|trotter	white|pepper	fish|dressing
plum|pudding	white|potato	Forfar|bridie

French|pastry	Waldorf|salad
grated|cheese	water|biscuit
grilled|steak	Welsh|rarebit
ground|almond	whipped|cream
ground|ginger	apple|crumble
ground|pepper	apple|dumpling
Hamburg|steak	apple|fritters
hasty|pudding	apple|turnover
haute|cuisine	barbecue|sauce
ice,cream|cone	bouillabaisse
Leyden|cheese	bread|and|water
luncheon|meat	breakfast|food
mulligan|stew	burnt,offering
peanut|butter	buttered|toast
pease|pudding	cayenne|pepper
pickled|onion	chateaubriand
pig's|knuckles	cheddar|cheese
pistachio|nut	cheese|biscuit
planked|steak	Christmas|cake
pork|and|beans	confectionery
potato|crisps	contamination
pumpernickel	cottage|cheese
Russian|salad	custard,powder
sage|and|onion	Edinburgh|rock
salted|peanut	finnan,haddock
scrambled|egg	food|poisoning
sherry|trifle	French|mustard
short|commons	fruit|cocktail
sirloin|steak	lemon|meringue
smoked|salmon	meals,on,wheels
sponge|finger	meat|and|two|veg
streaky|bacon	mess|of|pottage
sweet|and|sour	milk,chocolate
tabasco|sauce	minced|collops
tartare|sauce	Neapolitan|ice
vegetable|oil	pease,porridge

pickled|walnut	mock|turtle|soup
rasher|of|bacon	nutritiousness
roll|and|butter	Parmesan|cheese
salad|dressing	pate|de|fois|gras
scrambled|eggs	peppermint|drop
smoked|sausage	pickled|herring
soused|herring	plaice|and|chips
starch,reduced	plain|chocolate
stilton|cheese	polyunsaturate
strawberry|ice	pontefract,cake
strawberry|jam	saddle|of|mutton
sugar|and|spice	sausage|and|mash
summer|pudding	Scotch|woodcock
toad|in,the,hole	steak|and|kidney
transport|cafe	tapioca|pudding
veal|and|ham|pie	tea|and|biscuits
vegetable|dish	treacle|pudding
apple|charlotte	tripe|and|onions
banana|fritters	Turkish|delight
bangers|and|mash	vegetable|curry
bar|of|chocolate	vegetable|salad
bread|and|butter	vegetarian|dish
bread|and|cheese	Worcester|sauce
bread|and|scrape	box|of|chocolates
cabinet,pudding	breakfast|cereal
Canterbury|lamb	bubble,and,squeak
charlotte|russe	Camembert|cheese
cheese|sandwich	chicken|Maryland
Cheshire|cheese	chocolate|eclair
college|pudding	chocolate|sundae
curried|chicken	convenience|food
French|dressing	cooked|breakfast
gooseberry,fool	Devonshire|cream
hearty|appetite	French|breakfast
ice,cream|sundae	fricassee|of|veal
macaroni|cheese	grilled|sausages

grilled|tomatoes   redcurrant|jelly
orange|marmalade   roly|poly|pudding
peaches|and|cream   sausage|and|chips
peppermint|cream   sausages|and|mash
ploughman's|lunch   Wiener|schnitzel

Foreign Words and Phrases

ami	ca|ira	tutti	emptor
jeu	canto	usine	en|fête
mot	corno	abattu	fi|donc
à|bas	desto	abrege	flèche
abbé	dolce	agrege	giusto
doge	domus	allons	grazia
gene	école	aperçu	ibidem
in|re	étude	à|terre	in|vivo
lied	grave	aubade	legato
vivo	largo	au|fait	Lieder
ab|ovo	lento	au|fond	maison
addio	lycée	avanti	mañana
à|deux	mores	avenir	nobile
ad|hoc	obiit	bel|air	ottava
adios	per|se	bêtise	palais
ad|lib	plaza	bon|mot	posada
ad|rem	pleno	bon|ton	presto
adsum	Reich	Cortes	rubato
à|gogo	salle	crible	sempre
aidos	segno	da|capo	subito
apage	segue	dégagé	tenuto
arras	sordo	déja|vu	torero
assai	tacet	de|jure	troppo
buffo	torte	der|Tag	vivace

acharne	chanson	peccavi	au|revoir
ad|astra	château	pension	autobahn
ad|finem	chez|moi	pesante	aux|armes
ad|litem	clavier	piacere	à|volonté
à|droite	codetta	plafond	banlieue
ad|vivum	comedia	pomposo	bel|canto
affaire	con|brio	pro|rata	bien|être
affiche	con|moto	qui|vive	bona|fide
agaçant	couloir	ragazza	bout|rime
à|gauche	cui|bono	Rathaus	chez|nous
agitato	d'accord	Rigsdag	col|legno
à|jamais	danseur	Riksdag	con|amore
à|la|mode	ébauche	ripieno	con|fuoco
alcaide	en|prise	rondeau	coryphée
alcalde	en|route	rondino	cum|laude
al|conto	ex|aequo	rosalia	dal|segno
altesse	fagotto	roulade	danseuse
animato	farceur	Schloss	déjeuner
a|priori	fermata	sine|die	démarche
à|quatre	friture	sordino	Deus|vult
attacca	furioso	sub|rosa	dies|irae
au|mieux	Gestalt	tant|pis	distrait
Aus|lese	giocoso	vibrato	doloroso
bas|bleu	gouache	abat|jour	duettino
battuta	haut|ton	abat|voix	enceinte
berceau	ich|dien	abat|voix	entresol
bonjour	in|utero	ad|summum	estancia
bonsoir	in|vacuo	agacerie	et|cetera
bourrée	in|vitro	agrément	excerpta
bravura	Ländler	à|la|carte	ex|gratia
calando	laus|Deo	alta|moda	faubourg
cantina	Märchen	apéritif	Fine|Gael
canzona	morceau	a|piacere	gendarme
canzone	morendo	après|ski	grand|mal
caramba	palazzo	à|quoi|bon	hacienda
chambre	pas|seul	au|gratin	hic|jacet

idée|fixe	ad|valorem	coup|d'état
leggiero	a|fortiori	das|heisst
maestoso	alla|breve	dei|gratia
maggiore	alma|mater	de|rigueur
mala|fide	âme|perdue	dolce|vita
mal|de|mer	Anschluss	en|famille
mandamus	antipasto	en|passant
mea|culpa	à|outrance	et|tu,|Brute
moderato	arc|en|ciel	flute|a|bec
mon|repos	aria|buffa	Folketing
mot|juste	assez|bien	gemütlich
ostinato	au|courant	glissando
par|avion	au|naturel	grandioso
parlando	au|secours	grand|prix
parlante	Ausgleich	haut|monde
pro|forma	autopista	inter|alia
raisonné	autoroute	ipse|dixit
rara|avis	bal|masque	ipso|facto
ritenuto	beaux|arts	Landsting
sayonara	beaux|yeux	Leitmotiv
scordato	bel|esprit	Mardi|Gras
semplice	belle|amie	meden|agan
serenata	ben|venuto	mezza|voce
Sobranje	bête|noire	nisi|prius
spianato	bon|marché	obbligato
staccato	bon|vivant	objet|d'art
sub|poena	bon|viveur	pari|passu
trouvère	bon|voyage	pas|de|deux
una|corda	Bundesrat	passepied
Vorspiel	Bundestag	per|capita
à|bon|droit	buona|sera	per|contra
ab|origine	cantabile	petit|four
a|cappella	carpe|diem	piacevole
ad|hominem	cauchemar	piangendo
ad|libitum	cave|canem	Politburo
ad|nauseam	centumvir	pro|patria

pro|re|nata	bêche|de|mer	perdendosi
ricercare	ben|trovato	pied|à|terre
rus|in|urbe	billet|doux	plat|du|jour
scherzoso	bon|appetit	ponticello
sforzando	buon|giorno	prima|facie
siciliana	café|au|lait	Prix|unique
sine|prole	camino|real	pro|hac|vice
smerzando	canto|fermo	quid|pro|quo
solfeggio	canzonetta	recitativo
sostenuto	certiorari	ritardando
sotto|voce	cinquepace	ritornelle
spiritoso	confiserie	ritornello
sub|judice	con|sordini	scherzando
sub|specie	con|spirito	scordatura
succès|fou	cordon|bleu	seguidilla
tant|mieux	danke|schön	semper|idem
taoiseach	Deo|gratias	sens|unique
tête|à|tête	Deo|volente	sine|qua|non
tout|à|fait	dernier|cri	stringendo
tout|court	Eisteddfod	sui|generis
vers|libre	feuilleton	table|d'hôte
Volkslied	Fianna|Fáil	terra|firma
vox|humana	fortepiano	thé|dansant
à|bon|marché	Gesundheit	Tiergarten
absente|reo	in|excelsis	tout|de|même
ad|absurdum	in|extremis	tremolando
affettuoso	jardinière	ultra|vires
aficionado	jus|commune	urbi|et|orbi
alla|Franca	jus|gentium	villanella
allargando	Lebensraum	accelerando
anno|Domini	magnum|opus	ad|avizandum
art|nouveau	mezzo|forte	ad|infinitum
au|pis|aller	mezzo|piano	aetatis|suae
autostrada	nom|de|plume	aide|mémoire
avant|garde	opera|buffa	alla|tedesca
bar|mitzvah	ottava|rima	allez|vous|en

alto|relievo	hors|d'oeuvre	ante|meridiem
amor|patriae	in|medias|res	appassionata
amour|propre	in|principio	appoggiatura
à|nos|moutons	lèse|majesté	à|quatre|mains
a|posteriori	lignum|vitae	arrière|garde
Arcades|ambo	litterateur	ave|atque|vale
arrivederci	mise|en|scène	ballon|d'essai
au|contraire	motu|proprio	basso|relievo
avec|plaisir	musica|ficta	basso|rilievo
à|votre|santé	ne|plus|ultra	buenas|noches
belle|époque	nihil|obstat	carte|blanche
bien|entendu	nom|de|guerre	cause|célèbre
bonne|bouche	nous|verrons	caveat|emptor
boutonnière	obiter|dicta	compos|mentis
capriccioso	objet|trouvé	Concertstück
carte|du|jour	opera|bouffe	conseil|d'état
cavo|relievo	papier|mâché	contra|mundum
che|sera|sera	pas|de|quatre	crème|caramel
comme|il|faut	pax|vobiscum	degringolade
concertante	polit|bureau	Donnerwetter
contrapunto	raison|d'être	doppelganger
contredanse	rallentando	eppur|si|muove
coram|populo	savoir|faire	experto|crede
crème|brûlée	Schottische	fait|accompli
Dáil|Éireann	smörgasbord	ferae|naturae
decrescendo	summum|bonum	feu|d'artifice
degringoler	tempo|giusto	force|majeure
de|haut|en|bas	tempus|fugit	Gesellschaft
de|profundis	tempus|fugit	glockenspiel
ex|hypothesi	tertium|quid	Habeas|corpus
ex|post|facto	tout|le|monde	hasta|la|vista
femme|fatale	und|so|weiter	haute|couture
fieri|facias	vivacissimo	haute|cuisine
fin|de|siècle	acciaccatura	homme|du|monde
fritto|misto	amicus|curiae	honoris|causa
hasta|mañana	ancien|régime	hors|concours

hors de combat	crème de menthe
hotel de ville	croix de guerre
laissez faire	cum grano salis
lapsus calami	deux ex machina
lite pendente	éminence grise
mezzo relievo	exempli gratia
modus vivendi	ex proprio motu
nolens volens	faites vos jeux
obiter dictum	fête champêtre
opéra comique	force de frappe
piobaireachd	in vino veritas
pollice verso	laissez passer
pons asinorum	lapsus linguae
porte cochère	magna cum laude
porte monnaie	mirabile dictu
quelque chose	modus operandi
rien ne va plus	multum in parvo
salle à manger	noli me tangere
sauve qui peut	nolle prosequi
s'il vous plaît	Nouvelle Vague
terminus a quo	nulli secundus
Zigeunerlied	palais de danse
ab urbe condita	poisson d'avril
aggiornamento	quartier latin
à la bonne heure	Schadenfreude
à propos de rien	succès d'estime
ariston metron	summa cum laude
arrière pensée	très au sérieux
avant gardiste	a minori ad majus
avis au lecteur	annus mirabilis
basso profondo	auf Wiedersehen
Champs Élysées	bureau de change
cogito ergo sum	ceteris paribus
corps de ballet	crème de la crème
corpus delicti	Deuxième Bureau
couleur de rose	dis aliter visum

divide|et|impera
dolce|far|niente
double|entendre
ejusdem|generis
enfant|terrible
et|in|Arcadia|ego
facile|princeps
hapax|legomenon
homme|d'affaires
in|loco|parentis
ipsissima|verba
maxima|cum|laude
ne|obliviscaris
obiit|sine|prole
petit|bourgeois

terminus|ad|quem
terra|incognita
tertius|gaudens
valet|de|chambre
ad|misericordiam
amende|honorable
à|propos|de|bottes
argumentum|ad|rem
cherchez|la|femme
cordon|sanitaire
crime|passionnel
gaudeamus|igitur
mutatis|mutandis
persona|non|grata
rem|acu|tetigisti

French Revolutionary Calendar

Nivose	Frimaire	Fructidor
Floreal	Germinal	Thermidor
Ventose	Messidor	Vendémiaire
Brumaire	Pluviose	
Fervidor	Prairial	

Fruit

cob	anise	achene	pomelo
fig	apple	acinus	punica
fir	areca	almond	quince
haw	berry	ananas	raisin
hip	cacao	banana	rennet
hop	cocoa	cashew	rocket
nut	drupe	cherry	russet
pip	fruit	citron	savory
uva	gourd	citrus	squash
yam	graft	cobnut	tomato
aloe	grape	damson	unripe
core	guava	doghip	vinery
crab	gumbo	durian	apricot
date	hazel	kernel	avocado
gean	lemon	litchi	blossom
hull	mango	locust	bramble
lime	melon	lovage	brinjal
okra	olive	lychee	buckeye
pear	orris	mammee	capsule
peel	papaw	medlar	catawba
pepo	peach	muscat	coconut
pina	pecan	nutmeg	colanut
pith	pinon	orange	cumquat
plum	prune	papaya	currant
pome	shell	pawpaw	dessert
rind	shoot	peanut	dikanut
ripe	stalk	pippin	eggplum
seed	stipe	pollen	filbert
sloe	stone	pomato	grapery

138

harvest	chestnut	vine|leaf
kola|nut	citrange	vineyard
kumquat	cocoanut	alligator
lettuce	coco|palm	apple|tree
malmsey	cow|berry	baneberry
morello	date|plum	blaeberry
orchard	dewberry	blueberry
palm|nut	dogberry	Brazil|nut
pimento	earthnut	candle|nut
plumcot	endocarp	cashew|nut
putamen	follicle	cherimoya
rhubarb	fructose	coco|de|mer
rose|hip	hagberry	corozo|nut
ruddock	hazelnut	crab|apple
ruellia	hot|house	cranberry
salsify	locoweed	fruit|tree
sea|kale	mad|apple	grapevine
seed|pod	mandarin	greengage
sorosis	May|apple	groundnut
soursop	mulberry	grugru|nut
succory	muscatel	home|grown
sultana	musk|pear	in|blossom
tangelo	musk|plum	Indian|fig
vintage	nutshell	jackfruit
aesculus	oak|apple	jenneting
apple|pip	oleaster	jequirity
autocarp	orangery	Juneberry
beechnut	peachery	king|apple
beetroot	pericarp	kiwi|fruit
bergamot	pimiento	lemon|peel
betel|nut	prunello	love|apple
bilberry	sainfoin	manzanita
bromelia	self|heal	melocoton
calabash	shaddock	monkey|nut
capparis	sloebush	muscadine
caprifig	tiger|nut	muskmelon

nectarine	orange|peel
nux|vomica	peach|bloom
orange|pip	peppercorn
persimmon	prayer|bead
physic|nut	Punic|apple
pineapple	red|currant
pistachio	rowan|berry
poison|nut	sand|cherry
raspberry	strawberry
salad|herb	sugar|apple
sapodilla	watermelon
succulent	wild|cherry
sugar|plum	an|apple|a|day
tangerine	anchovy|pear
wild|grape	avocado|pear
wild|olive	bittersweet
banana|skin	boysenberry
bird|cherry	bramble|bush
blackberry	candleberry
blackheart	chokecherry
breadfruit	citrus|fruit
cantaloupe	eating|apple
chokeberry	goldenberry
conference	hesperidium
dried|fruit	huckleberry
elderberry	Indian|berry
French|plum	Jaffa|orange
fruit|salad	mammee|apple
gooseberry	navel|orange
granadilla	phyllomania
grapefruit	pomegranate
hickory|nut	pompelmoose
holly|berry	prickly|pear
Idaean|vine	quince|jelly
loganberry	suwarrow|nut
mangosteen	sweet|cherry

tutti,frutti	sassafras nut
American aloe	seaside grape
apple of Sodom	service berry
blackcurrant	Victoria plum
bottled fruit	white currant
cherry laurel	whortleberry
cooking apple	alligator pear
custard apple	bunch of grapes
Dead Sea apple	honeydew melon
Dead Sea fruit	raspberry cane
ground cherry	Ribston pippin
mulberry bush	Seville orange
passion fruit	conference pear
Persian berry	gooseberry bush
Persian melon	mandarin orange
pistachio nut	

Furniture

bar	door	chair	shelf	galley
bed	hall	chest	stool	garage
cot	loft	couch	study	garret
den	nook	decor	suite	larder
mat	oven	diner	table	lounge
pad	rack	divan	tapis	lowboy
pew	safe	duvet	alcove	luxury
rug	seat	lobby	bureau	mirror
ambo	sofa	piano	carpet	pantry
bath	ambry	porch	carver	remove
bunk	arras	press	castor	rocker
crib	attic	quilt	closet	ruelle
desk	blind	salon	daybed	screen

FURNITURE

serdab	ballroom	club|chair
settee	banister	cookhouse
settle	barstool	cubby|hole
teapoy	basement	davenport
veneer	bedstead	deck|chair
almirah	bookcase	double|bed
antique	chair|bed	drum|table
armoire	chair|leg	easy|chair
bedroom	corridor	footstool
bibelot	hatstand	furniture
boudoir	jalousie	garden|hut
boxroom	love|seat	glory|hole
bunk|bed	mess|hall	grillroom
buttery	outhouse	guest|room
canteen	pembroke	hallstand
car|port	playroom	high|chair
chamber	scullery	household
charpoy	stairway	house|room
commode	table|leg	inglenook
curtain	table|top	leaf|table
dinette	tea|table	lunchroom
dresser	upstairs	maid's|room
epergne	vargueno	marquetry
furnish	wall|safe	mezzanine
kitchen	wardrobe	music|room
landing	woodshed	parquetry
library	apartment	pierglass
nursery	bed|settee	pier|table
ottoman	bookshelf	refectory
parlour	brasserie	rice|paper
picture	bric|a|brac	sideboard
tallboy	cane|chair	side|table
tearoom	card|table	spare|room
whatnot	carpeting	sun|lounge
armchair	carpet|rod	top|drawer
back|door	cloakroom	washstand

wing|chair	fireside|rug
balustrade	fold₄away|bed
bucket|seat	furnishings
chiffonier	garden|chair
coal₁cellar	Heppelwhite
dining|hall	kitchenette
dining|room	laundry|room
downstairs	morning|room
dumb|waiter	player|piano
escritoire	reading|lamp
featherbed	roll₁top|desk
folding|bed	sitting|room
four₁poster	studio|couch
garden|shed	summer|house
lumber|room	swivel|chair
music|stool	utility|room
passageway	wicker|chair
piano|stool	writing|desk
public|room	bedside|table
rumpus|room	chaise|longue
scatter|rug	chesterfield
secretaire	console₁table
sun|parlour	contour|chair
swing|chair	dressing|room
upholstery	Dutch|dresser
Victoriana	emergency|bed
wicker|work	fitted|carpet
wine|cellar	gate₁leg|table
basket|chair	inner|sanctum
below|stairs	ironing|table
bookshelves	kitchen|table
cabriole|leg	kneehold|desk
Chippendale	library|table
coffee|table	nest|of|tables
dining|table	regency|chair
drawing|room	reproduction

143

FURNITURE

<table>
<tr><td>rocking|chair</td><td>airing|cupboard</td></tr>
<tr><td>sheepskin|rug</td><td>breakfast|table</td></tr>
<tr><td>spare|bedroom</td><td>central|heating</td></tr>
<tr><td>trestle|table</td><td>chest|of|drawers</td></tr>
<tr><td>upright|piano</td><td>French|polisher</td></tr>
<tr><td>Welsh|dresser</td><td>kitchen|cabinet</td></tr>
<tr><td>writing|table</td><td>kitchen|dresser</td></tr>
<tr><td>dressing|table</td><td>venetian|carpet</td></tr>
<tr><td>Louis|quatorze</td><td>Axminster|carpet</td></tr>
<tr><td>Persian|carpet</td><td>cocktail|cabinet</td></tr>
<tr><td>reception|room</td><td>dining|room|table</td></tr>
<tr><td>revolving|door</td><td>furniture|polish</td></tr>
<tr><td>room|with|a|view</td><td>gate|legged|table</td></tr>
<tr><td>skirting|board</td><td>occasional|table</td></tr>
<tr><td>umbrella|stand</td><td>soft|furnishings</td></tr>
<tr><td>wash|hand|basin</td><td>tables|and|chairs</td></tr>
</table>

Geography

air	fen	pap	arid	calm	duct
ait	fog	pit	bank	cape	dune
alp	gap	ria	beck	cave	dust
bed	gas	rip	belt	city	dyke
ben	GMT	sea	berg	clay	east
bog	har	sod	bill	crag	eyot
cay	jet	wad	bolt	dale	fall
col	jut	wax	bomb	damp	fell
cwm	map	wet	bore	dawn	firn
dam	mud	adit	brae	deep	floe
dew	nip	apex	burn	dell	flow
dip	oil	arch	bush	dirt	flux
eye	orb	area	calf	down	fold

fork	moss	spot	bourn	dunes	joint
foss	mull	spur	brash	dwarf	karoo
gang	naze	tarn	broad	eagre	knoll
gill	neck	till	broch	earth	kopje
glen	ness	tilt	brogh	emery	kraal
grit	neve	town	brook	erode	lapse
hade	node	trap	brush	esker	layer
hail	ooze	vale	burgh	ether	levee
halo	park	vane	butte	falls	level
haze	pass	veld	campo	fault	llano
head	peak	void	canal	fauna	local
high	peat	wadi	canon	fiord	locus
hill	plat	wane	chain	firth	loess
holm	pole	ward	chalk	fjord	lough
home	pond	warm	chart	flats	magma
hook	pool	wash	chase	flint	marge
isle	purl	weir	chasm	flood	marly
kame	race	well	chine	flora	marsh
khor	rack	west	cliff	fluor	mould
lake	rias	wold	clime	focus	mount
land	rift	zoic	close	frith	mouth
lias	rill	zone	coast	froth	nodes
lieu	ring	abysm	coomb	gelid	north
limb	sand	abyss	crack	geode	Notus
lime	scar	adobe	craig	geoid	oasis
linn	scud	amber	creek	ghyll	ox.bow
loam	seam	ambit	crust	glare	ozone
loch	seat	argil	cycle	globe	place
lord	sial	atlas	deeps	gorge	plain
mere	sill	azure	delta	grail	plash
mesa	silt	bayou	ditch	grove	playa
midi	sima	beach	downs	gully	plaza
mild	site	bedew	drift	heath	point
mire	slag	bleak	drink	humus	polar
mist	soil	bluff	dross	inlet	range
moor	spit	boggy	druse	islet	rapid

145

reach	urban	deluge	lagoon	runlet
realm	vault	depths	layers	runnel
Reich	veldt	desert	levant	rustic
ridge	waste	dewbow	locale	saddle
right	weald	dingle	lochan	salina
river	wilds	dolmen	lunate	sarsen
rural	wilds	domain	maplout	schist
salse	world	efflux	margin	season
sault	alpine	Empire	marshy	sector
scale	arctic	Eocene	massif	shadow
scarp	autumn	eothen	menhir	sierra
scaur	barrow	ethnic	mirage	sinter
scree	border	Europa	morass	skerry
serac	bottom	facies	nation	slough
shade	branch	famine	native	slurry
shaft	broads	feeder	nebula	solano
sheer	brough	flurry	Orient	source
shelf	burrow	geodes	outlet	sphere
shire	canopy	geyser	pampas	splash
slope	canton	gravel	parish	spring
slush	canyon	groove	pebble	steppe
smoke	cavern	grotto	period	strata
solum	circle	ground	placer	strath
sough	cirque	gulley	plains	stream
south	clayey	hamlet	plasma	strial
spate	clunch	hiatus	plenum	suburb
stack	colony	hiemal	polder	summer
state	colure	hollow	puddle	summit
stria	common	Icelage	quaggy	sunldog
surge	corral	icecap	rapids	swampy
swale	corrie	icicle	ravine	tremor
swamp	coulee	influx	region	trench
swirl	county	inland	riding	tropic
table	course	island	rillet	trough
talus	crater	jungle	ripple	tundra
tract	defile	karroo	rubble	tunnel

146

turnip	crevice	meander	tideway
upland	crystal	mill|run	topical
valley	culvert	Miocene	topsoil
vernal	debacle	mofette	torrent
vortex	demesne	mundane	trickle
welkin	diurnal	Neogene	tropics
wester	dog|days	pot|hole	uplands
window	freshet	prairie	village
winter	full|sun	proctor	volcano
zenith	geodesy	profile	West|end
zephyr	geogony	quarter	worldly
alluvia	geology	quietus	affluent
almanac	glacial	radiant	alluvial
azimuth	glacier	rivulet	alluvion
barrens	habitat	road|map	alluvium
bedding	hachure	salband	altitude
bone|bed	harbour	salt|pan	anabatic
bottoms	hillock	savanna	autumnal
boulder	hilltop	section	bearings
breaker	horizon	settled	bone|cave
caldera	hummock	shingle	boom|town
capture	iceberg	sky|line	boondock
cascade	ice|cave	snow|bed	borehole
chimney	icefall	snow|cap	boundary
clachan	ice|floe	souther	brooklet
cluster	ice|pack	station	calciole
commune	ice|raft	stratum	Cambrian
compass	incline	stretch	catacomb
conduit	insular	subsoil	cataract
conflux	isobase	suburbs	causeway
contour	isthmus	sunbeam	cleavage
corcass	kingdom	sundown	coal|mine
couloir	lakelet	surface	confines
country	land|ice	terrain	corridor
country	lowland	the|line	crevasse
crannog	machair	thermal	darkling

darkness	indigent	overhang
date|line	interior	photomap
detritus	irrigate	pinnacle
diluvium	isostasy	plateaux
district	Jurassic	Pliocene
dominion	lakeland	polar|cap
downtown	land|form	position
drainage	land|mass	precinct
dustbowl	landslip	prospect
easterly	latitude	province
effluent	lava|flow	purlieus
Eolithic	left|bank	quagmire
epifocal	lenticle	ring|dyke
eruption	levanter	riparian
exposure	Lewisian	river|bed
fold|axis	littoral	riverine
foreland	location	rotation
fountain	lodestar	sabulose
fracture	lowlands	salt|lake
frontier	mainland	sandbank
fumarole	Menevian	sand|dune
granules	Mesozoic	sandhill
headland	millpool	sandspit
headrace	millrace	seaboard
hibernal	monolith	sea|level
hick|town	monticle	seashore
highland	moorland	sediment
hillside	mountain	seedtime
homeland	Nearctic	shallows
Huronian	Near|East	Silurian
hypogene	New|World	snowball
hypogeum	Occident	snowland
ice|blink	Old|World	snow|line
ice|field	on|the|map	spectrum
ice|sheet	ordnance	stagnant
indented	overfold	Stone|Age

suburban	cisalpine	intrusion
syncline	city,state	isoclinal
tailrace	cliff,face	Kainozoic
telluric	coalfield	lake basin
Tertiary	coastland	landscape
tide gate	coastline	landslide
tide race	concourse	loadstone
time zone	continent	longitude
township	cornbrash	low ground
Triassic	cosmology	macrocosm
undertow	curvature	maelstrom
undulate	dead water	magnitude
upheaval	detrition	mare's,tail
vicinity	down under	marshland
warm cell	earth,wave	mattamore
warm wave	epicentre	midstream
water gap	esplanade	Neolithic
westerly	estuaries	north east
Wild West	estuarine	northerly
workings	everglade	north pole
zastruga	evolution	North star
adumbrate	exosphere	north west
affluence	foliation	obsequent
anabranch	foothills	off the map
antarctic	foreshore	Oligocene
anticline	geography	parallels
antipodes	ghost town	peneplain
Armorican	glacieret	peninsula
avalanche	green belt	phacolith
backwater	highlands	phenomena
backwoods	Holarctic	polar axis
billabong	homotaxis	pozzolana
Bronze Age	hour angle	precipice
brushland	hypogaeum	quicklime
canicular	ice action	rainwater
catchment	inner city	refluence

149

relief map	tidal flow	campestral
reservoir	tidal flux	chalk downs
right bank	tide gauge	chersonese
riverhead	tidewater	cismontane
riverside	tornadoes	colatitude
rock basis	tributary	confluence
salt marsh	underfoot	consequent
sand dunes	unsettled	contortion
satellite	upcountry	contour map
Secondary	volcanoes	cordillera
sheer drop	vulcanism	cosmic dust
shoreline	wasteland	demography
situation	waterfall	denudation
snowdrift	water flow	deposition
snow field	water hole	depression
snowfield	watershed	dreikanter
snowscape	waterside	drosometer
solfatara	whirlpool	druid stone
solstices	wide world	earthlight
south east	wind blown	earthquake
southerly	aerography	earthshine
south land	aerosphere	embankment
south pole	air current	ephemerist
south west	arable land	equatorial
statehood	arid desert	escarpment
streamlet	atmosphere	excavation
streamway	barysphere	fatherland
subregion	bathometer	fieldstone
summer day	body of land	floatstone
surveying	borderland	fore shocks
survey map	borderline	fossilized
tableland	Boreal zone	foundation
tectonics	bottom land	freshwater
temperate	bradyseism	geographer
territory	breakwater	geophysics
tidal bore	Caledonian	groundmass

hard|winter	oppressive	subtropics
headstream	Ordovician	summertide
headwaters	orogenesis	summertime
hemisphere	outline|map	terra|firma
high|ground	overshadow	theodolite
hinterland	overthrust	topography
homosphere	Palaeogene	torrid|zone
hot|springs	Palaeozoic	trade|route
hour|circle	phenomenon	tramontana
hypocentre	plot|of|land	undercliff
ice|crystal	population	undulation
insularity	potamology	vegetation
inundation	promontory	visibility
irrigation	rain|forest	waterflood
jet|streams	rift|valley	water|front
lacustrine	river|basin	water|gauge
landlocked	rock|bottom	waterspout
large|scale	rock|desert	water|table
latent|heat	rock|pillar	weathering
mappemonde	rock|series	wilderness
map|reading	rupestrian	wintertide
market|town	seismic|map	wintertime
meteor|dust	seismology	archipelago
metropolis	serpentine	back|country
micrometer	settlement	barrier|lake
midchannel	small|scale	bathysphere
Middle|East	spring|slope	bottom|glade
millstream	stalactite	boulder|clay
morphology	stalagmite	buffer|state
motherland	steep|slope	capital|city
narrow|seas	still|water	cartography
native|land	stratiform	cataclastic
native|soil	subsequent	chorography
natural|gas	subsidence	circumpolar
no|man's|land	substratum	climate|zone
old|country	subterrene	

climatology	land|surface	troposphere
colorimetry	lone|prairie	true|horizon
Continental	monticolous	ultra|violet
convergence	mountaintop	underground
coral|island	mural|circle	under|the|sun
counterflux	nationality	universally
counter|glow	native|heath	vulcanicity
countryside	native|lands	vulcanology
country|town	open|country	warm|springs
crag|and|tail	Palaearctic	watercourse
drusy|cavity	passage|beds	water|pocket
dust|counter	pile|dweller	whereabouts
earth|pillar	polar|circle	white|cliffs
earth's|crust	polar|region	wind|erosion
earth|tremor	PreCambrian	alluvial|flat
environment	prominences	arctic|circle
equinoctial	raised|beach	artesian|well
exploration	raw|material	barren|ground
fata|Morgana	reclamation	biogeography
frontal|wave	rising|coast	Black|country
frozen|north	river|course	cartographer
fulmination	river|system	commonwealth
grain|of|sand	river|valley	compass|point
great|circle	seismic|zone	conglomerate
harvest|time	seismograph	cross|bedding
ice|movement	spelaeology	elevated|area
ichnography	stony|ground	evaporimeter
ignis|fatuus	submergence	false|bedding
impermeable	subtropical	false|horizon
indentation	swallow|hole	field|of|force
isogeotherm	terrestrial	fountainhead
katabothron	thrust|plane	frozen|tundra
Kelvin|scale	torridonian	geanticlinal
lake|dweller	transalpine	geochemistry
land|feature	transandine	geographical
land|measure	transmarine	geomagnetism

geosynclinal	subterranean
geotectonics	transleithan
glacial|drift	transmundane
glacial|epoch	transoceanic
glaciologist	tropical|heat
granular|snow	tropical|zone
jack|o'|lantern	unconformity
Lake|District	undercurrent
lake|dwelling	variable|zone
law|of|gravity	volcanic|cone
magnetic|axis	volcanic|rock
magnetic|pole	will|o'|the|wisp
main|sequence	zoogeography
marginal|land	above|sea|level
mean|sea|level	active|volcano
metamorphism	cardinal|point
metasomatism	cardinal|point
midcontinent	catchment|area
mountain|pass	drainage|basin
mountain|peak	east,north,east
municipality	east,south,east
neighbouring	Latin|American
oceanography	Mediterranean
one|horse|town	mountain|chain
otherworldly	North|Atlantic
palaeobotany	north|easterly
Palaeolithic	north|eastward
parcel|of|land	north|westerly
polarization	north|westward
principality	seismographer
rising|ground	seismological
running|water	south|easterly
semi|diameter	south|eastward
sinking|coast	south|westerly
stratigraphy	south|westward
subcontinent	temperate|zone

GEOGRAPHY

transatlantic	south‸eastwards
arrondissement	south‸south‸east
cartographical	south‸south‸west
compass|bearing	south‸westwards
compass|reading	Antarctic|Circle
ethnologically	biogeographical
geographically	north‸eastwardly
north‸eastwards	north‸westwardly
north‸north‸east	south‸eastwardly
north‸north‸west	south‸westwardly
north‸westwards	topographically
Ordnance|Survey	

Government

CD	HMS	brig	imam	poll	tana
MP	nob	bull	Inca	pomp	toft
PC	red	camp	jack	rack	Tory
PM	rex	clan	king	raja	tsar
UN	rod	czar	lady	rani	visa
act	SOS	dame	left	rank	vote
aga	tax	deed	levy	rent	ward
beg	UDI	demo	mace	rota	Whig
bey	UNO	diet	memo	rule	whip
bug	wet	dove	mute	sack	aegis
CID	ally	duke	nick	seal	agent
con	alod	duty	OHMS	seat	agora
dip	axis	earl	oyes	serf	alias
don	beat	emir	oyez	shah	amban
dot	bill	fief	pact	soke	baron
FBI	bloc	file	peer	sway	begum
Fed	bond	hawk	pink	tail	blimp

154

5/6 LETTERS

board	junto	sheik	debate	nonage
bonds	laird	slate	depute	notice
booty	liege	staff	deputy	nuncio
boule	lobby	thane	despot	office
bulla	major	tribe	digest	orator
burgh	manor	truce	domain	ordeal
cabal	mayor	trust	durbar	papacy
caste	minor	usurp	dynast	parage
cause	Mogul	voter	empire	patrol
chair	nabob	Whigs	eparch	patron
chief	nawab	agenda	exarch	pledge
civic	Neddy	aristo	Fabian	pogrom
class	negus	asylum	faggot	policy
co,opt	noble	ballot	fasces	polity
corps	noose	bandit	Fuhrer	pow,wow
count	panel	barony	gentry	prince
crown	party	brevet	holder	puisne
curia	pasha	bureau	homage	puppet
deeds	plebs	Caesar	induna	quorum
divan	poach	caliph	junker	ransom
doyen	polls	caliph	Kaiser	rapine
draft	Porte	caucus	keeper	rating
duchy	posse	censor	knight	recess
edict	power	census	leader	record
elder	proof	clause	legate	reform
elect	proxy	clique	Majlis	regent
elite	queen	coheir	master	regime
fence	rajah	colony	mayhem	reward
filch	rally	con,man	mikado	sachem
forum	realm	consul	milady	satrap
frame	rebel	copper	milord	sconce
front	regal	cordon	moiety	senate
graft	reign	Cortes	motion	shogun
guard	royal	county	mutiny	sircar
guild	ruler	curfew	Nazism	sirdar
junta	ruler	daimio	NIBMAR	socage

155

soviet	cacique	enclave	neutral
speech	canvass	esquire	NewDeal
squire	capital	faction	officer
status	Capitol	Fascism	pageant
sultan	captain	Fascist	patriot
summit	captive	federal	peerage
syndic	Chamber	general	peeress
throne	charter	Gestapo	pension
ticket	closure	grandee	Pharaoh
tocsin	colonel	harmost	pillage
Tories	command	hidalgo	plunder
treaty	Commons	his|nibs	poacher
truant	compact	hot|seat	podesta
Tyburn	con|game	infanta	politic
tyrant	consort	khedive	praetor
umpire	coronet	Knesset	precept
vassal	corsair	Kremlin	prefect
vizier	council	land|tax	Premier
voting	counsel	leftist	primary
warden	czarina	libelee	process
yeoman	deed|box	Liberal	protest
abstain	diarchy	lording	proviso
adjourn	dictate	majesty	purview
admiral	D|notice	mandate	radical
adviser	dowager	marquis	reality
Aga|Khan	duarchy	Marxism	recount
amnesty	duchess	Marxist	red|tape
anarchy	dukedom	measure	referee
annuity	dyarchy	mediate	refugee
armiger	dynasty	militia	regency
autarky	earldom	minutes	regimen
band|aid	elector	mob|rule	returns
baronet	embargo	mobsman	Rigsdag
biparty	embassy	mobster	Riksdag
borough	emperor	monarch	royal|et
cabinet	empress	mormaor	royalty

sacking	argument	diadochi	kingship
samurai	arrogate	dictator	ladyship
sceptre	aspirant	diplomat	left|wing
senator	assassin	division	legation
settler	Assembly	doctrine	lobbying
shyster	assessor	dominion	lobbyist
soapbox	atheling	don't|know	lordship
Speaker	autarchy	election	loyalist
spy|ring	autonomy	embezzle	maharani
station	averment	Fine|Gael	majority
statist	balloter	flatfoot	mandarin
steward	bankrupt	freehold	marauder
sultana	baronage	free|vote	margrave
Sun|King	baroness	fugitive	martinet
support	Bastille	Gaullist	mayoress
supremo	bicamera	gendarme	mem|sahib
swear|in	Black|Rod	genocide	Minister
sworn|in	brass|hat	governor	ministry
tallage	campaign	grilling	minority
Templar	caudillo	guardian	monarchy
toisech	ceremony	gynarchy	monition
torture	chairman	hanger|on	movement
Tory|ism	chambers	heckling	narratio
tsarina	champion	hegemony	navicert
uniform	chartism	heirloom	nihilism
Vatican	citation	henchman	nobility
viceroy	civilian	heritage	nobleman
villain	claw|back	highness	nonvoter
villein	Conclave	home|rule	official
abdicate	congress	hustings	oligarch
abrogate	countess	imperial	overlord
accolade	danegeld	in|camera	overrule
activism	dead|hand	incivism	pacifism
alienate	delegate	Jingoism	palatine
alliance	demagogy	John|Bull	partisan
archduke	Democrat	jointure	party|man

passport	thearchy	bodyguard
patentee	thechair	bolshevik
Pentagon	topbrass	bourgeois
platform	townhall	brainwash
politico	treasury	buccaneer
politics	triarchy	Bundesrat
polygamy	ultraist	Bundestag
preamble	UncleSam	caliphate
princess	upperten	candidate
protocol	vendetta	capitular
puissant	verbatim	captaincy
putupjob	viceking	catchpole
question	viscount	centumvir
quisling	wardmote	chaingang
reformer	Whiggism	chieftain
regicide	WoolSack	ChiefWhip
regnancy	abduction	classrule
reigning	absconder	coalition
republic	accession	collegian
royalist	accessory	colonelcy
sabotage	actionist	Cominform
saboteur	Admiralty	Comintern
Saliclaw	alarmbell	commander
sanction	amendment	committee
security	anarchist	communism
seigneur	annulment	communist
shanghai	apartheid	complaint
Sobranje	Areopagus	concordat
solatium	authority	constable
splinter	autocracy	consulate
Stormont	backbench	cosmocrat
suffrage	bailiwick	coupdetat
summitry	ballotbox	custodian
suzerain	blackbook	DalaiLama
tanaiste	bloodfeud	deathblow
taxation	blueblood	demagogue

democracy	Landsting	presidium
desertion	lend₁lease	pretender
desperado	liege‖lord	princedom
diplomacy	life‖owner	princelet
dogmatist	logroller	privateer
enactment	LordⅯayor	procedure
espionage	maharajah	programme
exchequer	maharanee	protector
exciseman	majordomo	publicist
executive	majorship	put‖in‖suit
ex‖officio	manifesto	queenship
extremist	mayoralty	quittance
feudalism	menshevik	red₁tapism
feudatory	mobocracy	registrar
fire‖alarm	moral‖code	remainder
first‖lady	next‖of‖kin	represent
first‖lord	oligarchy	right‖wing
Folketing	Ombudsman	sanctions
formality	pageantry	sanhedrin
franchise	palsgrave	secretary
frithgild	paramount	selectman
generalcy	party‖line	seneschal
grand‖duke	party‖whip	sheriffry
GrandⅯTurk	patriarch	socialism
high‖birth	patrician	socialist
impartial	patronage	sovereign
imperator	pendragon	statement
incognito	plutocrat	statesman
incumbent	Politburo	straw‖poll
influence	political	straw‖vote
IronⅯGuard	portfolio	supporter
kingcraft	potentate	synedrion
kingmaker	power‖game	taoiseach
Labourite	precedent	terrorism
landgrave	prescript	tetrarchy
landslide	president	theocracy

think|tank	Chauvinism	grass|roots
tidal|wave	chrematist	Green|Paper
top|secret	city|father	handshaker
treasurer	civil|death	harman|beck
viscounty	classified	hatchet|man
waldgrave	commandant	heteronomy
walkabout	commissary	hold|office
abdication	commission	Home|Office
absolutism	common|weal	imposition
aggression	communiqué	inducement
allegiance	conversion	in|jeopardy
ambassador	coronation	Inner|House
annexation	corruption	invocation
arbitrator	councillor	king's|peace
aristarchy	councilman	knighthood
aristocrat	counsellor	land|pirate
autonomous	department	leadership
bureaucrat	dispatches	left|winger
Big|Brother	dotted|line	legitimacy
bill|of|sale	doubletalk	Liberalism
birthright	duumvirate	lieutenant
Black|Shirt	electorate	logrolling
blood|royal	encyclical	lower|house
blue|murder	Falangists	mace|bearer
brevet|rank	federation	machinator
by|election	Fianna|Fáil	Magna|Carta
Caesarism	figurehead	maiden|name
campaigner	filibuster	major|party
canvassing	fiscal|year	man|of|straw
capitalist	forfeiture	margravine
capitulary	front|bench	marquisate
cashiering	full|pardon	matriarchy
casual|ward	Gallup|poll	memorandum
censorship	gas|chamber	metrocracy
centralism	government	metropolis
chancellor	Grand|Mufti	militarism

minor|party	queencraft	trade|union
mitigation	ransacking	underworld
morganatic	ration|book	upper|class
mouthpiece	real|estate	upper|crust
muckraking	referendum	upper|house
mugwumpery	reform|bill	vigilantes
neutralism	refutation	voters|roll
neutrality	regulation	White|House
noble|birth	reparation	White|Paper
noblewoman	Republican	adjournment
no|man's|land	resolution	agrarianism
nomination	revolution	appointment
ochlocracy	right|of|way	archduchess
on|the|fence	ringleader	aristocracy
Ostpolitik	sanctioned	authorities
Outer|House	search|form	backbencher
palatinate	separation	black|and|tan
parliament	settlement	body|politic
party|liner	single|vote	buffer|state
patriarchy	speed|limit	bureaucracy
plebiscite	Square|Deal	burgomaster
plundering	stadholder	Butskellism
plural|vote	statecraft	candidature
pocket|veto	Statehouse	capital|city
politician	statistics	casting|vote
Post|Office	statute|cap	chairperson
power|happy	strategist	chamberlain
pray|a|tales	straw|voter	civil|rights
presidency	succession	civvy|street
princeling	suffragist	co|existence
procession	suspension	colonelship
protection	suzerainty	colonialism
proveditor	the|Commons	condominium
pursuivant	the|Royal|we	confederate
quarantine	third|reich	congressman
quarter|day	throne|room	constituent

161

corporation	investiture	public|enemy
crowned|head	Iron|Curtain	public|works
crown|prince	Kellogg|pact	queen|mother
Dail|Eireann	king's|speech	rate|capping
declaration	Labour|party	reactionary
diplomatics	lieutenancy	rear|admiral
disarmament	limited|veto	right|to|vote
dissolution	Machiavelli	right|winger
divine|right	maintenance	Royal|Assent
doctrinaire	marchioness	royal|family
duty|officer	meritocracy	royal|palace
electioneer	ministerial	royal|pardon
empanelment	mudslinging	royal|person
ergatocracy	nationalism	rubber|stamp
fifth|column	National|rat	rule|of|thumb
functionary	negotiation	ruling|class
generalship	nonpartisan	safe|conduct
gentlewoman	null|and|void	sansculotte
geopolitics	officialdom	secretariat
gerrymander	officialism	senatorship
good|offices	Papal|Nuncio	ship|of|state
grand|vizier	partisanism	shore|patrol
gynecocracy	partnership	show|of|hands
head|of|state	party|member	sovereignty
heir|general	peace|treaty	speech|maker
high|sheriff	policy|maker	squirearchy
high|society	politbureau	stateswoman
high|steward	powermonger	statute|book
House|of|Keys	power|of|veto	stratocracy
hunger|march	prerogative	suffragette
imperialist	proceedings	summit|talks
independent	procuration	sympathizer
in|duplicate	progressive	syndicalism
inner|circle	Prohibition	Tammany|Hall
institution	proletariat	technocracy
intercessor	protest|vote	traffic|duty

triumvirate	grand duchess
undersigned	guardianship
vice admiral	heir apparent
vindication	House of Lords
viscountess	House of Peers
voting paper	Imperial Diet
Westminster	independence
wirepulling	in triplicate
absolute veto	isolationism
administrate	Jack in office
after the fact	knight errant
ancien regime	laissez faire
Board of Trade	landed gentry
civil defence	leading light
civil service	left of centre
collectivism	Liberal party
Colonel Blimp	lord temporal
commissariat	lower chamber
commissioner	lying in state
commonwealth	maiden speech
compensation	majority rule
conscription	majority vote
conservatism	metropolitan
Conservative	modus vivendi
constituency	municipality
constitution	office bearer
customs union	officeholder
dictatorship	pantisocracy
dominion rule	party machine
domino theory	peace officer
Federal Union	people's front
feudal estate	plural voting
feudal system	point of order
First Chamber	politicaster
floating vote	polling booth
gerontocracy	popular front

powers|that|be
prescription
Prince|Regent
Privy|council
protectorate
protest|march
puppet|regime
queen|dowager
queen's|speech
question|time
registration
royal|charter
royal|command
run|for|office
security|risk
seignioralty
self|governed
split|the|vote
standing|army
status|symbol
stuffed|shirt
subcommittee
totalitarian
Traitor's|gate
upper|chamber
viscountship
welfare|state
worldly|goods
absolute|power
absolute|ruler
administrator
anti|marketeer
antisocialism
appropriation
associateship
authorisation

authoritarian
authoritative
branch|officer
British|Consul
bureaucratist
ceremonialism
chain|of|office
class|struggle
committee|room
committeeship
communist|bloc
confrontation
congressional
congresswoman
consideration
consul|general
contentiously
contravention
county|borough
court|circular
courtesy|title
cross|the|floor
crown|imperial
crown|princess
demonstration
devolutionist
diplomatic|bag
division|lobby
Downing|Street
election|fever
electoral|roll
establishment
fellow|citizen
filibustering
floating|voter
Foreign|Office

foreign policy	quadrumvirate
founder member	questionnaire
franchisement	royal standard
governing body	second chamber
Home Secretary	second reading
incomes policy	Secret Service
Inland Revenue	secret session
international	self governing
letters patent	shadow cabinet
London Gazette	smear campaign
Lord President	snap judgement
Lord Privy Seal	splinter group
minority group	splinter party
misgovernment	standing order
mismanagement	statesmanlike
mother country	statesmanship
nationalistic	straight fight
order of the day	supranational
parish council	Supreme Soviet
parliamentary	ten minute rule
parliament man	three line whip
party politics	Treasury bench
peace and quiet	Triple Entente
peacock throne	United Kingdom
plenary powers	United Nations
pocket borough	urban district
power politics	valuation roll
pressure group	War Department
prime minister	accountability
prince consort	administration
Prince of Wales	administrative
Princess Royal	affairs of state
proconsulship	ambassadorship
protectorship	antimonarchist
public records	balance of power
Public Trustee	banana republic

165

British|embassy	Primrose|League
chancellorship	read|the|riot|act
committee|stage	registry|office
communist|party	security|police
constitutional	self|government
controllership	shadow|minister
corporate|state	silent|majority
council,chamber	social|contract
credibility|gap	Social|Democrat
current|affairs	social|security
democratically	standing|orders
disenfranchise	state|ownership
early|day|motion	town|councillor
elder|statesman	Triple|Alliance
electioneering	trust|territory
firm|government	under|secretary
foreign|affairs	vice,presidency
general|council	watch,committee
go|to|the|country	works|committee
government|whip	Young|Pretender
grace,and,favour	absolute|monarch
grace,and,favour	Act|of|Parliament
High|Commission	antimonarchical
Home|Department	birthday|honours
House|of|Commons	cabinet|minister
labour|movement	chamberlainship
local|authority	charged,affaires
Lords|spiritual	clerk|of|the|house
matters|of|state	Council|of|Europe
multiracialism	counter,movement
national|anthem	democratic|party
New|Year|honours	diplomatic|corps
non,involvement	director,general
official|secret	district|council
order|in|council	dollar|diplomacy
polling|station	emergency|powers

enfranchisement
equalitarianism
fellow traveller
full dress debate
General Assembly
general election
governor general
heir presumptive
Independence Day
insubordination
local government
Lord High Steward
mass observation
Minister of State
Ministry of Works
nationalisation
non intervention
opposition bench
overflow meeting
parliamentarian
parliament house
party government
peace conference
personality cult

Petition of Right
plenipotentiary
political asylum
political career
political office
political theory
Privy Councillor
public ownership
quarter sessions
regional council
republican party
Right Honourable
royal commission
Security Council
select committee
standing ovation
Stars and Stripes
State Department
the powers that be
vice chamberlain
white man's burden
working majority
world government

Heraldry

or	arms	coif	fret	lion	paly
bar	bard	Cork	gamb	lure	pean
orb	bend	coup	helm	Lyon	pile
rod	boss	flag	jack	orle	ring
ankh	coat	foot	jamb	pale	rose

HERALDRY

Ross	pales	dexter	sallet
seal	pheon	diadem	scutum
sign	plain	dragon	shield
sown	plate	Dublin	signet
spur	razed	emblem	sleeve
toga	rebus	ensign	spread
umbo	rowel	ermine	symbol
undy	sable	fillet	tabard
vair	scion	fitche	Ulster
vert	staff	fitchy	uraeus
wavy	stake	flanch	voided
York	tenne	fretty	wreath
aegis	tiara	fylfot	wyvern
azure	torse	garter	armiger
badge	visor	gemels	armoury
cadet	Albany	gobony	attired
chief	argent	gorget	basinet
crest	armour	guidon	bearing
crook	banner	heaume	bezants
cross	beaver	helmet	bordure
crown	bezant	herald	buckler
dance	billet	livery	bunting
dwale	blazon	lodged	Carrick
fesse	border	lorica	chaplet
field	braced	mantle	charged
fusil	burgee	mascle	checker
giron	camail	morion	Chester
gules	canton	mullet	chevron
gyron	casque	Norroy	cockade
label	charge	patent	college
luces	cheeky	pellet	colours
March	cleche	pennon	coronet
mitre	collar	potent	corslet
motto	couped	raguly	crozier
order	cuisse	rustre	cuirass
paled	device	salade	dolphin

dormant	statant	herisson
engrail	surcoat	indented
estoile	trefoil	insignia
flanche	unguled	invected
gardant	unicorn	Lord|Lyon
garland	uniform	mill,rind
grafted	vermeil	ordinary
greaves	Windsor	powdered
griffon	accolade	Richmond
gyronny	ancestor	Rothesay
hauberk	armorial	sanguine
heralds	banneret	scallops
impaled	bearings	segreant
labarum	blazoner	siege|cap
leopard	blazonry	sinister
lozenge	brassard	Somerset
martlet	caduceus	standard
nombril	cantoned	streamer
oak|leaf	chamfron	swastika
pageant	cheveron	tau|cross
panoply	cinqfoil	tincture
parting	corselet	tressure
passant	couchant	trippant
pendant	crescent	vambrace
pennant	crosslet	vexillum
pierced	dancetty	armorials
quarter	demi,lion	assigning
rampant	erminees	assurgent
regalia	erminois	backplate
roundel	fan,crest	banderole
salient	fountain	blackjack
saltant	gauntlet	blue|peter
saltier	gonfalon	cadet|line
Saltire	half,mast	embattled
sceptre	heraldic	epaulette
sixfoil	heraldry	face|guard

flaunches	cap|and|gown	supporters
genealogy	cinquefoil	wavy|border
gonfannon	Clarenceux	achievement
Great|Arms	coat|armour	ancient|coat
great|seal	coat|of|arms	assignments
habergeon	cockatrice	bar|sinister
hatchment	decrescent	bishop's|lawn
head|piece	dexter|half	breastplate
Lancaster	dexter|side	counterseal
nose|guard	difference	countervair
nose|piece	dovetailed	crested|helm
oriflamme	eagle|crest	demi|leopard
pageantry	escutcheon	differenced
powdering	family|tree	dimidiation
prick|spur	figurehead	display|arms
privy|seal	fleur|de|lis	distaff|side
quarterly	fleur|de|lys	dormant|lion
red|ensign	gimmal|ring	engrailment
regardant	increscent	flag|officer
rerebrace	Jolly|Roger	fleurs|de|lys
royal|coat	King|of|Arms	gilded|spurs
royal|seal	Lyon|depute	grant|of|arms
scutcheon	ordinaries	lion|passant
sollerets	parted|arms	lion|rampant
spear|side	parted|coat	lion|salient
spur|rowel	plain|cross	marshalling
trappings	plain|field	mortarboard
tricolour	portcullis	pickelhaube
Union|Jack	pursuivant	privy|signet
assign|arms	quartering	rampant|lion
assignment	quatrefoil	robe|of|state
at|half|mast	roll|of|arms	rod|of|empire
blue|ensign	Rouge|Croix	Rouge|Dragon
Blue|Mantle	royal|crown	spindle|side
brigandine	signal|flag	spread|eagle
broad|arrow	stall|plate	subordinary

triple|crown   ine|scutcheon
triple|plume   laurel|wreath
true|colours   office|of|arms
voided|cross   parted|shield
white|ensign   paternal|arms
armorial|seal   purple|ermine
bend|sinister   rowelled|spur
bishop's|apron   sinister|half
border|gobony   sinister|side
cadet's|shield   tabard|of|arms
cardinal's|hat   College|of|Arms
charged|field   unscutcheoned
couchant|lion   counter|passant
cross|botonny   heraldic|colour
differencing   heraldic|device
false|colours   heraldic|shield
grand|quarter   herald's|college
granting|arms   Lyon|King|at|Arms
grants|of|arms   St|Andrew's|cross
heraldic|seal   St|George's|cross
imperial|seal   St|Anthony's|cross

Household Items

bib	log	tin	door	iron	plug
box	mop	beam	ewer	jamb	safe
cup	mug	bell	flue	lamp	sash
fan	pan	bowl	fork	lift	seat
gas	peg	bulb	fuel	lock	sink
hob	pot	case	gong	oven	soap
jar	rug	coal	hi,fi	pail	soda
key	tap	dish	hose	pipe	sofa

spit	ladle	candle	louvre
tank	latch	caster	mangle
tidy	linen	coffer	menage
tile	mixer	colmar	mincer
tray	mural	cooker	mobile
vase	paint	cradle	napkin
zarf	panel	damper	patina
apron	plate	dishes	pelmet
ashet	poker	dolium	pillow
basin	quilt	drawer	plaque
bench	radio	duster	polish
besom	sheet	eggcup	pouffe
bidet	shelf	fender	pulley
blind	sieve	fiasco	rhyton
board	spoon	fingan	salver
broil	stove	flacon	saucer
brush	straw	flagon	scales
caddy	timer	fridge	sconce
chore	tongs	frieze	shovel
cigar	torch	gasjet	shower
clock	towel	gastap	skewer
cloth	trunk	geyser	sponge
cover	whisk	grater	starch
crock	aerial	hamper	string
cruet	ashbin	handle	switch
cruse	ashcan	hearth	teapot
diota	awning	heater	teaset
doily	basket	icebox	teaurn
duvet	beaker	jumble	toybox
flask	biggin	kaross	trivet
frame	bleach	kettle	tureen
glass	bluing	ladder	vessel
grate	boiler	lagena	washer
hinge	bucket	lintel	window
juice	bunker	locker	wiring
knife	burner	logbin	adaptor

172

amphora	hickory	tea,cosy	colander
ashtray	high|tea	tea|tray	coverlet
bath|tub	hip|bath	thermos	cream|jug
bedding	holdall	thimble	crockery
blanket	keyhole	ticking	cupboard
bolster	lacquer	toaster	cuspidor
bouquet	lagging	Toby|jug	cut|glass
cake|tin	lantern	tool|kit	decanter
canteen	lattice	transom	doorbell
ceiling	matches	trellis	doorknob
chalice	oil|lamp	trolley	doorpost
chamois	overall	tumbler	doorstep
chimney	padella	utensil	doorstop
chopper	parquet	valance	driptray
cistern	pass,key	varnish	eggslice
cleaver	pie,dish	washday	eggspoon
coaster	pitcher	washtub	eggtimer
coconut	platter	worktop	eggwhisk
crystal	play|pen	wringer	emulsion
cushion	pottery	atomiser	fanlight
cutlery	ramekin	ballcock	filament
deed|box	roaster	barbecue	fireside
dish|mop	samovar	bassinet	firewood
doorway	sanctum	bath|cube	fixtures
dustbin	service	bath|soap	flat|iron
dust,pan	serving	bed|cover	flour|bin
faience	shelves	bed|linen	fly|paper
fitting	skillet	bell|pull	food,mill
fixture	spatula	billy|can	fuse,wire
furbish	spy,hole	bird|bath	gallipot
furnace	stamnos	bookends	gas,meter
fuse|box	steamer	cache,pot	handbell
gas,ring	stewpot	canister	handrail
griddle	sundial	casement	hangings
hammock	sweeper	cauldron	hip|flask
heating	tankard	cigar|box	Hollands

homespun	sitz|bath	beer|glass
hot|plate	skylight	blank|door
immerser	slop|bowl	cakestand
jelly|bag	slop|pail	cantharus
jewel|box	snuff|box	casserole
kickshaw	soap|dish	chinaware
kindling	soapsuds	cigarette
linoleum	soft|soap	clepsydra
matchbox	solarium	coffee|cup
mattress	spice|jar	container
meatsafe	spittoon	corkscrew
monogram	squeezer	crossbeam
moth|ball	strainer	cullender
moulding	sunblind	demitasse
new|broom	surround	desk|light
ornament	tablemat	detergent
ovenware	tapestry	directory
painting	tea|chest	dishcloth
pannakin	tea|cloth	dish|towel
paraffin	teaspoon	distemper
patty|pan	trapdoor	dog|basket
pendulum	underlay	doorplate
pipe|rack	wainscot	drainpipe
polisher	water|jug	dust|sheet
portrait	water|tap	Dutch|oven
pot|plant	wig|block	Dutch|wife
radiator	wireless	egg|beater
rosebowl	Yale|lock	egg|slicer
saucepan	Ansaphone	eiderdown
scissors	auto|timer	facecloth
scrubber	baking|tin	face|towel
shoehorn	barometer	fire|alarm
shredder	bath|salts	fireguard
shutters	bath|towel	fire|irons
side|door	bay|window	firelight
sink|unit	bedspread	fireplace

fish knife	place card	toilet bag
fish slice	porcelain	underfelt
flower pot	porringer	wall clock
foodmixer	punchbowl	wall light
front door	radiogram	wallpaper
fruit bowl	safety pin	washbasin
fruit dish	salad bowl	washboard
frying pan	sauceboat	water butt
gas burner	serviette	water cock
gas cooker	shakedown	water pipe
girandole	shoeblack	water tank
glass door	shower cap	wax polish
gold plate	side light	whitewash
gravy boat	slop basin	window box
hand towel	soup plate	wine glass
hourglass	soup spoon	abstergent
housewife	spin drier	alarm clock
housework	sponge bag	anthracite
japanning	staircase	apple cover
jewel case	statuette	baking bowl
joss stick	steam iron	baking tray
lamplight	steel wool	bedclothes
lampshade	storm door	bedsprings
lampstand	stovepipe	bellarmine
letterbox	sugar bowl	boot polish
light bulb	swing door	bread board
log basket	table lamp	breadknife
loving cup	tableware	butter dish
master key	tea kettle	candelabra
mousetrap	tea waggon	cassolette
objet d'art	telephone	chafing pan
panelling	threshold	chandelier
partition	timepiece	chopsticks
patchwork	tinder box	clothes peg
phone book	tin opener	clothes pin
pie funnel	toast rack	coal bucket

coal bunker	paint brush	time switch
coat hanger	paper knife	tobacco jar
coffee mill	pepper mill	toilet roll
curtain rod	percolator	toilet soap
deep freeze	Persian rug	toothbrush
dinner gong	persiennes	toothpaste
dishwasher	photograph	transistor
doorhandle	pillowcase	trinket box
drawing pin	pillow slip	vanity lamp
Dutch clock	pilot light	ventilator
featherbed	pin cushion	waffle iron
finger bowl	plate glass	wall socket
fire basket	plate piece	warming pan
fire escape	pot scourer	washbasket
firescreen	pot scraper	watch glass
fish kettle	power point	water clock
floor cloth	rain barrel	whisk broom
forcing bag	ration book	window pane
fruit knife	rolling pin	window sash
glass cloth	rose window	window seat
gramophone	salt cellar	window sill
grand piano	sealing wax	wine basket
hollow ware	silverware	wine cooler
knickknack	soap flakes	wine bottle
lamp socket	soap powder	wooden ware
letter rack	spirit lamp	work basket
loose cover	step ladder	worry beads
matchstick	storage jar	airtight jar
milk bottle	strip light	baking sheet
mixing bowl	tablecloth	bead curtain
musical box	table knife	broom handle
mustard pot	table linen	butter knife
napkin ring	tablespoon	candelabrum
night light	tea service	candlestick
nutcracker	television	centrepiece
oven gloves	thermostat	chafing dish

cheese|board
china|figure
Chinoiserie
clothes|line
clothes|pole
coal|scuttle
cookery|book
cooling|tray
counterpane
cuckoo|clock
curtain|hook
curtain|rail
curtain|ring
dessert|fork
door|knocker
earthenware
eating|irons
elbow|grease
family|album
firelighter
first|aid|box
floor|polish
French|chalk
garden|party
garden|swing
hearth|brush
kitchen|sink
kitchen|unit
laundry|room
light|switch
linen|basket
loving|spoon
mantelpiece
meat|chopper
meat|cleaver
metal|polish

non|stick|pan
oil|painting
Oriental|rug
paperweight
picture|rail
plant|holder
pocket|flask
primus|stove
pudding|bowl
pumice|stone
record|album
roasting|tin
rotary|whisk
sauce|bottle
scouring|pad
serving|dish
shopping|bag
shower|cloth
silver|plate
silver|spoon
skeleton|key
sliding|door
spring|clean
storm|window
table|napkin
tape|measure
tea|strainer
thermometer
vacuum|flask
vinaigrette
washing|line
washing|soap
washing|soda
wassail|bowl
water|closet
water|heater

window|blind
window|frame
window|light
wintergreen
wooden|spoon
work|surface
wrought|iron
adhesive|tape
antimacassar
apron|strings
ball|of|string
bedside|light
bottle|opener
bottom|drawer
candleholder
candle|sconce
carpet|beater
carriage|lamp
carving|knife
cheesegrater
chiming|clock
chimney|piece
chimney|stack
cigarette|box
clothes|brush
clothes|drier
clothes|horse
companion|set
convex|mirror
cooking|range
dessert|spoon
disinfectant
double|boiler
electric|fire
electric|iron
electric|lamp

extractor|fan	table|service
firelighters	talcum|powder
fireside|seat	tape|recorder
flower|holder	thermos|flask
French|polish	toasting|fork
hot|water|tank	turkish|towel
ironing|board	user|friendly
kettle|holder	visiting|card
labour|saving	washing|board
light|fitting	washing|cloth
looking|glass	backscratcher
lunch|counter	blanket|stitch
magazine|rack	blotting|paper
mulligatawny	candle|snuffer
paraffin|lamp	carpet|sweeper
passe|partout	carriage|clock
perambulator	chopping|block
picnic|basket	chopping|board
picnic|hamper	clothes|basket
picture|frame	cocktail|stick
place|setting	darning|needle
pudding|basin	dinner|service
radiant|plate	draught|screen
record|player	electric|mixer
reel|of|cotton	electric|razor
reel|of|thread	emulsion|paint
refrigerator	feather|duster
serving|hatch	fire|resistant
serving|spoon	food|processor
sewing|needle	household|gods
shopping|list	hurricane|lamp
silver|polish	lawn|sprinkler
stain|remover	microwave|oven
standard|lamp	mowing|machine
swizzle|stick	petrol|lighter
table|lighter	pinking|shears

preserving|pan
Saratoga|trunk
sewing|machine
smoothing|iron
soldering|iron
storage|heater
vacuum|cleaner
venetian|blind
washing|powder
water|softener
cartridge|paper
casement|window
central|heating
Chinese|lantern
cocktail|shaker
coconut|matting
corrugated|iron
cut|throat|razor
electric|cooker
electric|kettle
electric|shaver
hot|water|bottle
hot|water|system
household|goods

household|linen
insulating|tape
kitchen|utensil
knitting|needle
knives|and|forks
luncheon|basket
pair|of|scissors
patchwork|quilt
pressure|cooker
scrubbing|brush
spring|cleaning
spring|mattress
washing|machine
cigarette|holder
combination|lock
corrugated|paper
electric|blanket
electric|toaster
immersion|heater
knitting|machine
pencil|sharpener
photograph|album
weighing|machine

Insects

ant	eft	bley	gila	mite	slug
asp	fly	cleg	gnat	moth	tick
bee	nit	comb	grig	newt	wasp
bug	web	croc	grub	pest	wing
dor	bike	flea	lice	pupa	worm

INSECTS

adder	apiary	nereid	cricket
agama	aranea	palolo	cutworm
aphid	bedbug	python	deer₁fly
aphis	bee|fly·	red|ant	earworm
aweto	beetle	sawfly	echidna
brize	botfly	scarab	emperor
chirp	breeze	slough	firefly
cobra	burnet	sow\bug	flyblow
croak	chafer	sphinx	frog₁fly
culex	chigoe	spider	gallfly
drone	chinch	teredo	glowfly
emmet	cicada	thrips	goldbug
fluke	cicala	tipula	hive₁bee
gecko	cocoon	tsetse	hop|flea
genus	dayfly	tunnel	hornbug
guana	dipsas	turtle	hornfly
imago	dorfly	weevil	ice\worm
krait	earwig	anguine	June\bug
larva	ellops	annelid	June|fly
leech	gadfly	antenna	katydid
limax	gavial	antheap	lacerta
louse	hop₁fly	ant\hill	ladybug
mamba	hornet	ant|lion	lady₁cow
midge	iguana	army\ant	ladyfly
nymph	insect	axolotl	lampfly
sedge	jigger	bat|tick	lobworm
skink	lizard	bean₁fly	lugworm
snail	locust	bee\hive	mawworm
snake	looper	beeline	monitor
sting	maggot	bee\moth	ophidia
swarm	mantid	blowfly	papilio
vespa	mantis	boat|fly	phasmid
viper	maybug	carabus	pill\bug
acarus	mayfly	cat|flea	pinworm
anguis	motuka	cestoid	pismire
ant\cow	mugger	chigger	prepupa

180

pyralis	flatworm	ophidian
rat flea	flesh fly	parasite
reptile	froth fly	pit viper
rose bug	fruit fly	puss moth
sand fly	gall gnat	queen ant
saurian	gall wasp	queen bee
serpent	glow worm	sand dart
shad fly	goat moth	sand flea
strigil	gold wasp	sand wasp
syrphus	greenfly	scarabee
termite	hair worm	scorpion
tuatara	hawk moth	sea snake
vespoid	helminth	shipworm
wax moth	honey bee	silkworm
webworm	hookworm	slave ant
wood ant	horntail	slow worm
yard ant	hornworm	stone fly
anaconda	horse fly	subimago
antennae	house ant	tapeworm
apterous	housebug	tubeworm
arachnid	house fly	vespiary
army worm	inchworm	viperish
avicular	itch mite	viperous
basilisk	lacewing	wall newt
black ant	ladybird	water boa
black fly	linkworm	waterbug
bollworm	matamata	water fly
book lice	meal worm	wheat eel
bookworm	mealy bug	wheatfly
caseworm	moccasin	white ant
cerastes	mosquito	white fly
crane fly	mud puppy	wireworm
curculio	myriapod	woodlice
ephemera	night fly	woodmite
firebrat	nurse ant	wood tick
fireworm	oak eggar	wood wasp

INSECTS

woodworm	ephemerid	sea‚turtle
alligator	flour‚moth	sheep‖tick
amazon‖ant	forest‚fly	snakelike
angleworm	fruit‖moth	spillworm
ant‖patrol	gall‖midge	spinneret
aphid‖pest	gipsy‖moth	squash‖bug
arachnoid	grain‖moth	swift‖moth
bee‚beetle	gregarine	tiger‖moth
berg‚adder	gypsy‖moth	tree‖snake
birdlouse	hawksbill	trematode
blindworm	hemiptera	tsetse‖fly
book‖louse	hodmandod	tumblebug
brandling	horned‖bug	turnip‖fly
breeze‖fly	hornet‖fly	velvet‖ant
brimstone	humble‖bee	wasp's‖nest
bull‖snake	king‖cobra	wheatmoth
bumble‖bee	king‖snake	wheatworm
butterfly	milk‖snake	wood‚borer
caddis‖fly	millepede	woodlouse
candle‖fly	millipede	worker‚ant
canker‚fly	orange‚tip	worker‖bee
cantharis	paper‖wasp	worm‚eaten
centipede	peripatus	anguifauna
chaetopod	plume‖moth	bird‚spider
chameleon	potato‖bug	black‖snake
cheesefly	pterosaur	black‖widow
chinch‖bug	puff‖adder	blister‖fly
chrysalis	red‖spider	bluebottle
cicindela	reptilian	boll‚weevil
clavicorn	rhynchota	buffalo‖bug
cochineal	ring‖snake	burnetmoth
coffee‚bug	robber‖fly	bushmaster
corn‖borer	rock‖snake	cabbage‚fly
corncrake	roundworm	caddice‚fly
cuckoo‚fly	sand‖mason	caddis‖worm
earthworm	satin‖moth	canker‖worm

182

carpetmoth	lanternfly	webspinner
clamshrimp	lappetmoth	wheatmidge
cockatrice	leafcutter	wintermoth
cockchafer	leafhopper	wolfspider
codlinmoth	leafinsect	assassinbug
coleoptera	muskbeetle	beehawkmoth
congosnake	palmerworm	blackbeetle
copperhead	phylloxera	bloodsucker
copperworm	pinebeauty	bristletail
coralsnake	pinebeetle	cabbagemoth
cornbeetle	pinechafer	cabbageworm
deathwatch	redadmiral	caterpillar
diggerwasp	ribbonworm	clothesmoth
drosophila	Romansnail	coconutmoth
dungbeetle	rosebeetle	codlingmoth
firebeetle	rosechafer	constrictor
fleabeetle	rovebeetle	cornearworm
flycatcher	sandlizard	cottonmouth
fritillary	scarabaeus	crocodilian
froghopper	serpentine	desertsnail
galleyworm	sheeplouse	drinkermoth
gasteropod	sidewinder	emperormoth
glasssnake	socialwasp	fencelizard
grasssnake	soldierant	flourweevil
greendrake	soldierfly	Gilamonster
greensnake	Spanishfly	grainbeetle
guineaworm	sphinxmoth	grasshopper
hairstreak	spidersweb	greenbottle
hangingfly	stagbeetle	hornedsnake
harvestbug	Syrphusfly	insectarium
hessianfly	tigersnake	leatherback
horseleech	tomatoworm	lepidoptera
jiggerflea	turnturtle	meadowbrown
Junebeetle	vinegarfly	paintedlady
kittenmoth	walllizard	phantomgnat
ladybeetle	watersnake	rattlesnake

rhopalocera
ringed|snake
scale|insect
scissor|tail
scolopendra
scorpion|fly
sea|longworm
Skye|terrier
snout|beetle
stick|insect
tiger|beetle
tobacco|worm
tussock|moth
vine|fretter
water|beetle
wood|fretter
xylophagous
beaded|lizard
book|scorpion
buzzard|clock
cabbage|white
carpenter|ant
carpenter|bee
carpet|python
cecropia|moth
cinnabar|moth
cucumber|flea
December|moth
diving|beetle
dragon|lizard
flying|lizard
garden|spider
ground|beetle

hellgrammite
horned|lizard
lightning|bug
limnophilous
marbled|white
mosquito|hawk
queen|termite
radish|maggot
salamandrian
serpentiform
social|insect
spring|beetle
Suffolk|punch
tropical|moth
vapourer|moth
walking|stick
water|boatman
water|strider
white|admiral
winged|insect
worm's|eye|view
arachnologist
daddy|longlegs
entomological
harvest|spider
herpetologist
leather|jacket
praying|mantis
boa|constrictor
Colorado|beetle
herpetological
entomologically

184

Islands

Als	Haiti	Hainan	Curacao
Cos	Ibiza	Hawaii	Cythera
Vis	Islay	Honshu	Formosa
Aran	Lewis	Ischia	Gotland
Bali	Leyte	Ithaca	Grenada
Cebu	Luzon	Jersey	Iceland
Coll	Malta	Kyushu	Ireland
Cuba	Naxos	Lemnos	IwoJima
Eigg	Nevis	Lesbos	Jamaica
Elba	Panay	Midway	Lismore
Gozo	Rugen	Quemoy	Madeira
Guam	Samar	Rhodes	Majorca
Iona	Samoa	Saipan	Mindoro
Java	Samos	Sicily	Molokai
Jura	Samso	Skyros	Oceania
Muck	Sumba	Staffa	Okinawa
Mull	Texel	Tahiti	Orkneys
Oahu	Timor	Taiwan	Palawan
Rhum	Tiree	Thasos	Rathlin
Sark	Tonga	Tobago	Re,Ⅰlede
Skye	Aegina	Ushant	Reunion
Unst	Amager	Amboina	Salamis
Arran	Andros	Andaman	Shikoku
Barra	Azores	Antigua	Socotra
Capri	Bangka	Bahamas	StKilda
Chios	Bikini	Bahrein	StKitts
Corfu	Borneo	Bermuda	StLucia
Crete	Cyprus	Celebes	Sumatra
Delos	Euboea	Corsica	Sumbawa

Surtsey	St|Pierre	Heligoland
Tenedos	Tasmania	Hispaniola
Zealand	Tenerife	Holy|Island
Zeeland	Trinidad	Long|Island
Abu|Dhabi	Zanzibar	Madagascar
Akimiski	Aleutians	Martinique
Alcatraz	Ascension	Montserrat
Alderney	Balearics	New|Zealand
Anglesey	Benbecula	Puerto|Rico
Anguilla	Ely,|Isle|of	Samothrace
Antilles	Falklands	Seychelles
Barbados	Greenland	Wake|Island
Belitung	Innisfree	Yap|Islands
Beveland	Manhattan	Fiji|Islands
Bornholm	Man,|Isle|of	Florida|Keys
Canaries	Mauritius	Grand|Canary
Colonsay	Melanesia	Guadalcanal
Cyclades	Nantucket	Lindisfarne
Dominica	New|Guinea	New|Hebrides
Fair|Isle	Polynesia	Philippines
Foulness	Rarotonga	Rhode|Island
Guernsey	Runnymede	San|Salvador
Hebrides	Shetlands	Spitzbergen
Hokkaido	Singapore	Wight,|Isle|of
Hong|Kong	St|Vincent	Baffin|Island
Jan|Mayen	Uist,|North	Bougainville
Malagasy	Uist,|South	British|Isles
Mindanao	Vanua|Levi	Canvey|Island
Moluccas	Walcheren	Cocos|Islands
Sakhalin	Ailsa|Craig	Devil's|Island
Sardinia	Cephalonia	Easter|Island
Scillies	Dodecanese	Farne|Islands
Sporades	Dogs,|Isle|of	Faroe|Islands
Sri|Lanka	East|Indies	Great|Britain
St|Helena	Fernando|Po	Mont|St|Michel
St|Martin	Grenadines	New|Caledonia

Newfoundland	Gilbert Islands
South Georgia	Leeward Islands
Spice Islands	Lofoten Islands
Staten Island	Maldive Islands
Thanet, Isle of	Nicobar Islands
Cayman Islands	Pitcairn Island
Ellice Islands	Solomon Islands
Ionian Islands	Tierra del Fuego
Kurile Islands	Tristan da Cunha
Lipari Islands	Christmas Island
New Providence	Falkland Islands
Purbeck, Isle of	Friendly Islands
Sheppey, Isle of	Marshall Islands
Virgin Islands	Severnaya Zemlya
Channel Islands	Vancouver Island
Frisian Islands	Windward Islands

Jewellery

gem	carat	fibula	coronet
gold	charm	garnet	diamond
jade	clasp	gewgaw	earring
onyx	coral	jargon	emerald
opal	ivory	jasper	jacinth
ruby	jewel	pearls	jargoon
sard	lapis	plasma	olivine
agate	paste	sequin	sautoir
amber	pearl	silver	spangle
beads	topaz	spinel	aigrette
beryl	bangle	zircon	amethyst
bijou	brooch	abraxas	bracelet
cameo	diadem	adamant	carcanet

churinga	lucky charm
crucifix	paste jewel
diamante	rhinestone
filigree	ring brooch
fire opal	rose quartz
gemstone	signet ring
girasole	spinel ruby
necklace	tourmaline
platinum	bishop's ring
sapphire	chrysoberyl
sardonyx	chrysoprase
sunstone	lapis lazuli
black onyx	slave bangle
black opal	wedding ring
brilliant	eternity ring
cairngorm	link bracelet
carbuncle	mourning ring
carnelian	semi precious
cornelian	charm bracelet
gemmology	cultured pearl
guard ring	diamond brooch
jadestone	mother of pearl
jewellery	precious stone
moonstone	cairngorm stone
morganite	diamantiferous
moss agate	engagement ring
seed pearl	precious metals
tremblant	string of pearls
turquoise	cultivated pearl
water opal	diamond merchant
adder stone	diamond necklace
black pearl	emerald bracelet
bloodstone	emerald necklace
chalcedony	imitation pearls
chrysolite	

Lakes

Bala	Taupo, Lake
Kyoga	Thirlmere
Aral Sea	Ullswater
Dead Sea	Wastwater
Dead Sea	Albert, Lake
Tuz, Lake	Baikal, Lake
Van, Lake	Brienz, Lake
Chad, Lake	Caspian Sea
Como, Lake	Geneva, Lake
Earn, Loch	Great Lakes
Erie, Lake	Kariba, Lake
Eyre, Lake	Ladoga, Lake
Fyne, Loch	Linnhe, Loch
Grasmere	Lomond, Loch
Holy Loch	Lugano, Lake
Kivu, Lake	Malawi, Lake
Long, Loch	Peipus, Lake
Ness, Loch	Windermere
Tana, Lake	Corrib, Lough
Tonle Sap	Katrine, Loch
Azov, Sea of	Lucerne, Lake
Derg, Lough	Nipigon, Lake
Erne, Lough	Ontario, Lake
Garda, Lake	Rannoch, Loch
Huron, Lake	Balkhash, Lake
Leven, Loch	Derwentwater
Maree, Loch	Galilee, Sea of
Mweru, Lake	Maggiore, Lake
Nyasa, Lake	Manitoba, Lake

LAKES

Michigan,Lake	ConistonWater
Superior,Lake	Constance,Lake
Tiberias,Lake	Great Bear Lake
Titicaca,Lake	Great Salt Lake
Victoria,Lake	Maracaibo,Lake
Wakatipu,Lake	Trasimene,Lake
Winnipeg,Lake	Great Slave Lake
Champlain,Lake	Tanganyika,Lake

Law

JP	case	nick	bribe	judge
KC	cell	oath	brief	jurat
QC	code	oyer	by|law	juror
act	dent	plea	canon	lease
bar	dock	rape	choky	legal
cop	doge	silk	claim	libel
feu	eyre	stir	clink	licit
jug	feod	suit	court	Mafia
jus	feud	swag	crime	mores
lag	fiat	thug	crook	mufti
law	fine	tort	dower	mulct
lex	gaol	veto	dowry	pinch
rob	gyve	will	ephor	plead
soc	hang	writ	felon	Provo
sue	heir	aggro	feoff	quash
try	jail	alibi	fraud	reeve
wig	jury	annat	garda	reset
bail	just	arson	gavel	rider
beak	kadi	bench	guilt	right
bill	lien	birch	hakim	screw
cadi	lord	bobby	in|law	Solon

190

swear	fetter	pardon	autopsy
theft	fiscal	parole	bailiff
thief	forger	peeler	Beltane
trial	gaoler	piracy	bencher
trust	guilty	pirate	bequest
ulema	gunman	police	binding
usher	harman	prison	borstal
vakil	heriot	remand	bribery
visne	holdup	report	burglar
abjure	honour	rip¡off	case¡law
action	indict	robber	cashier
appeal	infamy	rozzer	caution
archon	jailer	rubric	charter
arrest	junior	ruling	chattel
asylum	jurant	search	circuit
bailie	jurist	simony	codicil
bigamy	kidnap	speech	cojuror
breach	laches	stocks	convict
bye¡law	Lammas	suitor	coroner
caveat	lawful	sultan	counsel
censor	lawman	tenant	custody
charge	lawyer	tenure	damages
clause	leaser	tie¡wig	defence
cooler	legacy	warder	delator
decree	legist	abscond	demesne
delate	lessee	accused	deodand
delict	lessor	accuser	deposit
denial	lethal	adjourn	divorce
dharma	lictor	alcalde	dossier
dictum	mollah	alimony	dragnet
dogate	motive	alodium	dungeon
emptor	murder	amnesty	enfeoff
entail	octroi	arbiter	escheat
equity	old¦lag	arraign	estover
estate	on¦oath	assault	estreat
felony	outlaw	assizes	fair¦cop

fee|tail	looting	treason	deponent
felonry	mafioso	tribune	detainee
feoffee	manacle	trustee	distrain
feu|duty	marshal	turnkey	distress
footpad	nonsuit	Tynwald	domicile
foreman	offence	verdict	embracer
forfeit	on|trial	warrant	eviction
forgery	parolee	witness	evidence
frame|up	penalty	abductor	executor
gallows	perjury	accusant	findings
garotte	pillory	adultery	forensic
grassum	pinched	advocate	foul|play
hanging	pleader	amortise	game|laws
hangman	probate	articled	gangster
harbour	proctor	articles	garrotte
hearing	provost	attorney	gravemen
hearsay	purloin	backlash	Gray's|Inn
heiress	questor	bastardy	green|bag
heritor	Riot|Act	black|cap	homicide
illicit	robbery	burglary	hung|jury
impeach	shackle	calendar	informer
inquest	sheriff	canon|law	innocent
inquiry	slander	chancery	Interpol
jeofail	soccage	chantage	jailbird
John|Doe	statute	civil|law	judgment
jury|box	stick|up	claimant	judicial
juryman	stretch	contempt	law|agent
justice	summons	contract	law|court
ladrone	suspect	copyhold	lawgiver
larceny	swear|in	criminal	lawmaker
latitat	swindle	crown|law	lay|judge
law|list	sworn|in	cursitor	legal|aid
law|lord	tenancy	deedpoll	legalism
lawsuit	testate	defender	legality
legatee	testify	delictum	libelant
legator	traitor	demurrer	litigant

litigate	sergeant	barrister
loophole	sessions	blackmail
lynching	Sing|Sing	body|of|law
lynch|law	smuggler	bound|over
mandamus	speed|cop	bridewell
messuage	squad|car	brief|case
mistrial	stealage	bring|suit
mittimus	stealing	Bumbledom
mortgage	subpoena	case|lists
mortmain	sub|poena	cassation
mortuary	swindler	cell|block
Mounties	take|silk	champerty
nomology	talesman	civil|case
offender	tenement	civil|list
on|the|run	tenendum	civil|suit
outlawry	testamur	common|law
panda|car	test|case	coparceny
peculate	the|Bench	copyright
penal|law	thievery	court|list
penology	thirlage	court|roll
petition	tipstaff	courtroom
picaroon	trespass	cracksman
pleading	tribunal	death|duty
porridge	true|bill	defendant
precinct	vice|ring	detective
prisoner	Wool|Sack	detention
promisor	acquittal	direct|tax
quaestor	ademption	discharge
rebuttal	affidavit	disseisin
receiver	appellant	disseizin
recorder	appellate	distraint
reprieve	Areopagus	doing|time
Roman|law	attainder	drug|squad
scaffold	attestant	embezzler
scot|free	avizandum	embracery
sentence	barmaster	enactment

193

equity|bar	law|report	pilfering
ex,convict	law|school	plaintiff
execution	leasehold	pleadings
exonerate	legal|heir	police|car
extortion	legal|term	police|dog
fair|trial	legal|year	policeman
fee|simple	licitness	police|van
felonious	litigator	polyandry
feudal|law	litigious	portreeve
feudal|tax	matricide	probation
frithborh	mercy|seat	prolicide
grand|jury	miscreant	pronounce
Great|Seal	moot|court	prosecute
guardroom	moot|point	public|law
handcuffs	mortgagee	racketeer
heir,at,law	mortgager	recaption
High|Court	Mosaic|Law	receiving
hit,and,run	Mr|Justice	red,handed
Identi,kit	nisi|prius	registrar
income|tax	not|guilty	remission
indemnity	not|proven	represent
injustice	novo|damus	reprimand
inspector	objection	resetting
intestate	Old|Bailey	riot|squad
inventory	ombudsman	Royal|seal
Jack|Ketch	open|court	rule|of|law
jailbreak	ordinance	sanctions
judge|made	oubliette	smuggling
judgement	parricide	solicitor
judicator	patrimony	stamp|duty
judiciary	patrol|car	statement
jungle|law	patrolman	stuff|gown
jury|woman	peculator	sub|judice
justiciar	penal|code	suit|at|law
kidnapper	petit|jury	suit|in|law
law|reform	petty|jury	summing,up

testament	corregidor	justiciary
testatrix	courthouse	King's|bench
testifier	court|of|law	land,tenure
testimony	court|order	law,abiding
title|deed	court|usher	lawbreaker
trial|jury	crime|sheet	lawfulness
truncheon	crime|squad	law|officer
uxoricide	death|chair	Law|Society
vice|squad	decree|nisi	legal|right
vigilante	delinquent	legislator
violation	deposition	litigation
wanted|man	disherison	magistracy
witch|hunt	entailment	magistrate
accomplice	estate|tail	Magna|Carta
accusation	eye|witness	mail|robber
aid|and|abet	find|guilty	martial|law
allegation	fratricide	mass|murder
amercement	fraud|squad	Murphy's|law
arbitrator	freebooter	nomography
bank|robber	free|pardon	out|of|court
Black|Maria	glasshouse	palliation
Black|Power	grand|juror	papal|brief
breath,test	guardhouse	Papal|Court
certiorari	guillotine	peccadillo
chancellor	gunrunning	petitioner
circuiteer	hamesucken	petty|juror
code|of|laws	hard|labour	petty|theft
confession	highwayman	pickpocket
confiscate	hold|a|brief	point|of|law
conspiracy	illegality	postliminy
constraint	impediment	post|mortem
contraband	in|articles	praesidium
contravene	in|chancery	prefecture
conveyance	indictment	private|law
conviction	injunction	prize|court
coparcener	jus|commune	procurator

195

prosecutor	black|market	false|arrest
punishment	breatha|lyse	fieri|facias
purloining	burglarious	fingerprint
put|on|trial	cattle|thief	firing|squad
recidivist	civil|arrest	flying|squad
recognizer	civil|rights	foreclosure
regulation	Common|Pleas	found|guilty
remand|home	complainant	gallows|bird
respondent	compurgator	garnishment
Richard|Roe	confinement	grave|robber
sergeantcy	contract|law	guilty|party
serve|a|writ	contractual	higher|court
shoplifter	conveyancer	high|treason
sneak|thief	coparcenary	house|arrest
state|trial	corroborate	impeachment
statute|law	county|court	impoundment
stillicide	criminal|law	incarcerate
third|party	criminology	incriminate
title|deeds	delinquency	inculpation
trafficker	diet|of|proof	indirect|tax
undress|wig	digest|of|law	infanticide
usurpation	double|cross	inheritance
witness|box	embracement	Inner|Temple
written|law	enfeoffment	Inns|of|Court
your|honour	engrossment	inquisition
appeal|court	equity|court	insufflator
arbitration	escheatment	jury|process
arm|of|the|law	estate|in|fee	last|request
arraignment	examination	law|and|order
assumed|name	exculpation	law|breaking
attestation	executioner	lawlessness
bag|snatcher	exoneration	law|merchant
bank|robbery	extenuation	legal|action
bear|witness	extradition	legal|battle
bill|chamber	factory|acts	legal|estate
blackmailer	fair|hearing	legal|record

legal reform	questioning	Chief Justice
legal remedy	ransom money	circuit court
legal tender	reformatory	circuit judge
legislation	safecracker	codification
legislative	shanghaiing	common lawyer
legislature	sheriffwick	compurgation
lese majeste	shoplifting	condemnation
libel action	Star Chamber	condemned man
lie detector	statute book	confiscation
Lincoln's Inn	stolen goods	constabulary
long stretch	stool pigeon	conveyancing
Lord Justice	take to court	coroner's jury
magisterial	tenant right	court martial
malpractice	testamental	court of wards
man on the run	third degree	criminal code
military law	train robber	criminal suit
mosstrooper	trial by jury	cross examine
murder squad	under arrest	death penalty
omnibus bill	ward of court	death warrant
open verdict	writ of error	debtor's court
patent right	your worship	den of thieves
patent rolls	adjudication	dispensation
pathologist	amicus curiae	divorce court
penal reform	amortisement	dressing down
pettifogger	appeal motion	ducking stool
police court	apprehension	embezzlement
police force	bar of justice	estate at will
police judge	bench warrant	estate in tail
police squad	Bill of Rights	false witness
police state	breathalyser	first offence
policewoman	bring charges	frankalmoign
prosecution	burglar alarm	grand juryman
Provisional	carpet bagger	grand larceny
puisne judge	cause celebre	Habeas corpus
Queen's bench	cause in court	hanging judge
Queen's peace	chattels real	hereditament

197

housebreaker
House|of|Lords
imprisonment
incriminator
in|litigation
intromission
investigator
jail|sentence
judge|and|jury
judge|made|law
judgment|debt
judgment|hall
judgment|seat
judicial|oath
jurisdiction
jurisprudent
Justice|clerk
King's|counsel
King's|Proctor
Land|Registry
law|of|the|land
legal|adviser
legal|aid|fund
legal|fiction
legal|history
legally|bound
legal|redress
legal|science
life|sentence
Lord|Advocate
magistrature
maiden|assize
manslaughter
mercy|killing
misdemeanour
pass|sentence

Patent|Office
penitentiary
petty|juryman
petty|larceny
plain|clothes
plea|for|mercy
police|cordon
police|office
police|patrol
prison|warder
probate|court
probate|judge
reform|school
rent|tribunal
resist|arrest
rest|one's|case
right|of|entry
rough|justice
safe|breaking
safe|cracking
scene|of|crime
Scotland|Yard
secret|police
sergeantship
sheriff|court
silk|gownsman
smash|and|grab
strait|jacket
summary|trial
supreme|court
tenant|at|will
third|borough
unwritten|law
violent|death
whipping|post
witness|stand

word|of|honour	hunger|marcher
against|the|law	hunger|striker
articled|clerk	impersonation
assassination	incarceration
break|the|peace	interrogation
break|the|rules	investigation
burden|of|proof	investigative
call|the|police	jiggery|pokery
cast|iron|alibi	judge|advocate
cat|o|nine|tails	jurisprudence
chief|of|police	juvenile|court
code|of|conduct	kangaroo|court
common|assault	King's|evidence
company|lawyer	knuckleduster
condemned|cell	licensing|laws
coroner's|court	litigiousness
corroboration	mental|cruelty
corroborative	moonlight|flit
countercharge	mounted|police
counterfeiter	non|appearance
Court|of|Appeal	non|attendance
courts|martial	non|compliance
criminal|trial	non|fulfilment
criminologist	non|observance
cross|question	parking|ticket
Dean|of|Faculty	Petty|Sessions
electric|chair	poetic|justice
expert|witness	police|officer
expropriation	police|station
extra|judicial	Queen's|counsel
false|evidence	race|relations
first|offender	read|for|the|bar
flying|pickets	reinstatement
funny|business	rightful|owner
High|Constable	right|of|appeal
house|breaking	rogues|gallery

search|warrant
seat|of|justice
security|check
sharp|practice
sheep|stealing
sheriff|depute
sitting|tenant
Special|Branch
the|law|is|an|ass
under|sentence
unlawful|entry
watching|brief
absolute|decree
according|to|law
action|for|libel
Act|of|Indemnity
aggressiveness
bring|to|justice
Chancery|Office
Chief|Constable
Children's|Panel
citizen's|arrest
civil|liberties
code|of|practice
commit|for|trial
commit|to|prison
Common|Sergeant
conjugal|rights
court|of|inquiry
court|of|justice
Court|of|Session
court|procedure
crime|of|passion
crime|passionel
criminal|charge
criminal|lawyer

criminal|record
customs|barrier
customs|officer
decree|absolute
defence|counsel
defence|witness
detention|order
devil's|advocate
disinheritance
driving|licence
false|pretences
finders|keepers
finger|printing
forbidden|fruit
general|amnesty
general|damages
guilty|of|murder
habit|and|repute
high|court|judge
highway|robbery
hostile|witness
identification
identity|parade
incident|centre
Inns|of|Chancery
lack|of|evidence
lawful|occasion
law|of|the|jungle
learned|counsel
legal|liability
legally|binding
legal|ownership
legal|procedure
letter|of|the|law
licensing|court
loaded|question

Lord|Chancellor
McNaghten|rules
member|of|the|bar
military|police
monkey|business
naturalisation
non,cooperation
parish|register
partner|in|crime
penal|servitude
pillar|of|the|law
plead|not|guilty
presiding|judge
prohibitionism
prohibitionist
provost|marshal
Queen's|evidence
question|of|fact
read|the|riot|act
receiving|order
registry|office
sheriff|officer
silence|in|court
special|damages
special|licence
sworn|statement
thick|as|thieves
verbal|evidence
ward|in|chancery
ward|of|the|court
Attorney,General
bankruptcy|court
barrister's|clerk
blunt|instrument
breach|of|promise
bring|in|a|verdict

capital|sentence
clerk|of|the|court
commit|an|offence
confidence|trick
conscience|money
contempt|of|court
coroner's|inquest
coroner's|verdict
counsel's|opinion
counter,evidence
decree|of|nullity
detention|centre
disorderly|house
false|accusation
full,bottomed|wig
inadmissibility
indecent|assault
insurrectionist
judgment|summons
judicial|trustee
laughter|in|court
legal|department
legal|profession
legal|settlement
long|arm|of|the|law
majority|verdict
my|learned|friend
Newgate|calendar
performing|right
plain,clothes|man
police|constable
police|inspector
positive|vetting
power|of|attorney
protection|money
provost,sergeant

reinterrogation   sentence|to|death
rent|restriction   shotgun|marriage
scales|of|justice   statement|on|oath
scene|of|the|crime   stay|of|execution
sentence|of|death   under|lock|and|key

Length, Area, Volume, Speed

are	gauge	coulomb
ell	metre	deciare
mph	perch	furlong
rod	ruler	granule
acre	stere	hectare
area	toise	virgate
foot	ton|up	calipers
hand	arpent	carucate
inch	bovate	centiare
knot	decare	distance
link	fathom	dividers
mile	finger	inchmeal
pace	height	inch|tape
pole	league	land|mile
rood	length	quadrant
rule	linear	board,foot
step	micron	callipers
tape	oxgang	cubic|foot
yard	oxgate	cubic|inch
broad	oxland	cubic|mile
chain	parsec	cubic|yard
cubit	sector	decametre
depth	square	decastere
folio	volume	decimetre

dekametre	square|yard
kilometre	tachometer
light|year	cable|length
milestone	square|metre
size|stick	statute|mile
thickness	tape|measure
try|square	hairsbreadth
yardstick	measured|mile
centimetre	miles|per|hour
centistere	nautical|mile
planimeter	cruising|speed
square|feet	full|speed|ahead
square|foot	middle|distance
square|inch	rod,|pole|or|perch
square|mile	

Literary Characters

Eva	Smee	Taper	Figaro	Piglet
Rat	Alice	Tessa	Gretel	Pinkie
Aida	Baloo	Tosca	Hansel	Pogner
Dido	David	Venus	Hassan	Rabbit
Elsa	Fagin	Wotan	Isolde	Rosina
Iago	Gilda	Abessa	Jeeves	Salome
Ilia	Mabel	Aeneas	Jenufa	Sophie
Ko,Ko	Marco	Ayesha	Kundry	Stalky
Loge	Norma	Barkis	Lenski	Tamino
Lulu	Oscar	Bumble	Merlin	Thisbe
Mime	Osmin	Carmen	Mole,Mr	Toad,Mr
Mimi	Senta	Cassio	Mowgli	Turnus
Pooh	Smike	Daland	Otello	Ulrica
Puff	Sneer	Eeyore	Pamina	Yum,Yum

LITERARY CHARACTERS

Absalom	Abanazar	Nanki‚Poo
Aladdin	Alberich	Octavian
Amneris	Amfortas	Papagena
Ariadne	Amonasro	Papageno
Azucena	Anchises	Parsifal
Belinda	Apollyon	Patience
Colline	Badger‚Mr	Pervaneh
Dandini	Bede‚Adam	Peter Pan
Darcy‚Mr	Belmonte	Pinch‚Tom
Despina	Bly‚Nelly	Ridd‚John
Don José	Brangane	Sarastro
Faninal	Claggart	Slightly
Gunn‚Ben	Clorinda	Strephon
Kai Lung	Dangle‚Mr	Svengali
Kala Nag	Dixon‚Jim	Tom‚Uncle
Leonora	Eyre‚Jane	Turandot
Manrico	Falstaff	Violetta
Masetto	Ferrando	Wardle‚Mr
Musetta	Flashman	Water Rat
Peachum	Frederic	Watson‚Dr
Pelleas	Gianetta	Battle‚Ben
Phyllis	Giuseppe	Budd‚Billy
Pooh Bah	Grose‚Mrs	Cherubino
Radames	Gunga Din	Cio Cio San
Raffles	Hiawatha	Constanze
Rodolfo	Idomeneo	Desdemona
Salieri	Iolanthe	Don Carlos
Scarpia	Jekyll‚Dr	Donna Anna
Susanna	Jokanaan	Dorabella
Tadpole	Jones‚Tom	Elisabeth
Tatiana	Klingsor	Escamillo
Tristan	Kurwenal	Gamp‚Sarah
Walther	Lucretia	Grundy‚Mrs
Wolfram	Macavity	Guglielmo
Wozzeck	MacHeath	Guinevere
Zerlina	Marcello	Gurnemanz

Hieronimo	Clare, Angel	Willy Nilly
Janos, Hary	Collatinus	Zerbinetta
Josephine	Dartle, Rosa	Ahab, Captain
Leporello	Dombey, Paul	Bedivere, Sir
Lohengrin	Don Alfonso	Billows, Lady
Manette, Dr	Don Basilio	Brown, Father
Marke, King	Doone, Lorna	Butler, Rhett
Melisande	Drood, Edwin	Cavaradossi
Minnehaha	Eliot, Lewis	Charles, Nick
Ochs, Baron	Fiordiligi	Cratchit, Bob
Paget, Jean	Gargery, Joe	Dawkins, Jack
Pinkerton	Gilpin, John	Don Giovanni
Podsnap, Mr	Gray, Dorian	Donna Elvira
Point, Jack	Hawkins, Jim	Don Pasquale
Pross, Miss	Holy Willie	Doone, Carver
Proudie, Dr	Jellyby, Mrs	Dormouse, The
Rigoletto	Jessel, Miss	Finn, Phineas
Sachs, Hans	Lampton, Joe	Garter, Polly
Sawyer, Tom	Leigh, Amyas	Grimes, Peter
Schaunard	Magnus, King	Hook, Captain
Siegfried	Marguerite	Kipps, Arthur
Sieglinde	McGregor, Mr	Lancelot, Sir
Sikes, Bill	Miniver, Mrs	Legree, Simon
Wegg, Silas	Monostatos	Linton, Edgar
Weller, Sam	Mulliner, Mr	Machin, Denry
Zenocrate	Nogood Boyo	Mad Margaret
Achitophel	Pangloss, Dr	Malaprop, Mrs
Allan a Dale	Poste, Flora	Malatesta, Dr
Aram, Eugene	Quint, Peter	Marner, Silas
Arrowsmith	Rabbit, Brer	Miller, Luisa
Aschenbach	Remus, Uncle	Mitty, Walter
Aylmer, Rose	Robin, Fanny	Morgan, Organ
Bardell, Mrs	Sharp, Becky	Mudjekeewis
Bard of Avon	Tannhauser	Noggs, Newman
Beckmesser	Tapley, Mark	Oakroyd, Jess
Brunnhilde	Tinker Bell	Orford, Ellen

Paris, Judith	Humpty Dumpty
Pecksniff, Mr	Jarndyce, John
Polly, Alfred	Jimson, Gulley
Pooter, Lupin	Jingle, Alfred
Porter, Jimmy	Jorrocks, John
Quilp, Daniel	LaCreevy, Miss
Rabbit, Peter	Magwitch, Abel
Rochester, Mr	Manette, Lucie
Scobie, Henry	March Hare, The
Sparafucile	Merrilies, Meg
Spenlow, Dora	Millamant, Mrs
Stone, Rodney	M'Turk, William
Tamburlaine	Norris, Arthur
Tam o' Shanter	Omnium, Duke of
Traddles, Tom	Peachum, Polly
Tulliver, Tom	Pooter, Carrie
Tupman, Tracy	Probert, Rosie
Twist, Oliver	Reece, Captain
Varden, Dolly	Rudge, Barnaby
Vere, Captain	Smith, Winston
Absolute, Jack	Traill, Archie
Baggins, Bilbo	Troy, Sergeant
Bland, Pigling	Waters, Esther
Bloom, Leopold	Wilkes, Ashley
Borgia, Caesar	Willcox, Henry
Carton, Sydney	Worthing, John
Cheeryble, Ned	Almaviva, Count
Claypole, Noah	Bartolo, Doctor
Cuff, Sergeant	Benyon, Butcher
Datchery, Dick	Blake, Franklin
Despair, Giant	Bountiful, Lady
Dracula, Count	Bracknell, Lady
Flanders, Moll	Bultitude, Paul
Green, Verdant	Cruncher, Jerry
Havisham, Miss	Darnay, Charles
Higgins, Henry	Dashwood, Henry

Defarge, Madame	Dingo, Yellow Dog
Dobson, Zuleika	Doolittle, Eliza
Forsyte, Jolyon	Fairfax, Colonel
Forsyte, Soames	Flyte, Sebastian
Greystoke, Lord	Germont, Alfredo
Grimes, Captain	Holmes, Sherlock
Hannay, Richard	Hunter Dunn, Joan
Herring, Albert	Jollifant, Inigo
Holmes, Mycroft	Madam Butterfly
Honeycomb, Will	Marschallin, The
Jenkins, Rev Eli	Mephistopheles
Languish, Lydia	Nutkin, Squirrel
Mock Turtle, The	Prince Charming
Nickleby, Ralph	Rabbit, The White
Oakapple, Robin	Rackstraw, Ralph
O'Hara, Scarlett	Rikki tikki tavi
Peggotty, Clara	Salteena, Alfred
Perrin, Vincent	Shandy, Tristram
Pirate King, The	Silver, Long John
Poirot, Hercule	Teazle, Sir Peter
Pooter, Charles	Tiggy Winkle, Mrs
Skimbleshanks	Trotwood, Betsey
Sneerwell, Lady	Tulliver, Edward
Tolloller, Earl	Tulliver, Maggie
Winnie the Pooh	Wickfield, Agnes
Winslow, Ronnie	Absolute, Anthony
Woffington, Peg	Bennet, Catherine
Wooster, Bertie	Bennet, Elizabeth
Allnutt, Charlie	Commendatore, The
Battle, Mrs Sarah	Corcoran, Captain
Beynon, Gossamer	Cratchit, Tiny Tim
Borgia, Lucretia	Crummles, Vincent
Buzfuz, Sergeant	Doolittle, Alfred
Collins, William	Earnshaw, Hindley
Crusoe, Robinson	Finn, Huckleberry
Dedalus, Stephen	Harlowe, Clarissa

LITERARY CHARACTERS

Hawk, Sir Mulberry	Queen of the Night
Hentzau, Rupert of	Scrooge, Ebenezer
Knightley, George	Smollett, Captain
Little Buttercup	Squeers, Wackford
Micawber, Wilkins	Steerforth, James
Mountararat, Earl	Tarzan of the Apes
Murdstone, Edward	Trelawney, Squire
Plaza Toro, Duke of	Valiant for Truth
Porter, Sir Joseph	Wimsey, Lord Peter
Prufrock, J Alfred	Wotton, Lord Henry

Literature

Ed	pen	copy	mora	root	yarn
em	pie	dash	muse	ruby	acute
en	pun	dele	myth	rune	adage
MS	rag	demy	note	saga	affix
op	saw	edit	noun	scan	album
ps	set	epic	opus	slip	annal
ABC	anas	epos	page	slug	argot
act	anon	font	part	song	arsis
ana	bard	foot	past	star	atlas
bar	beat	gest	pica	stem	axiom
cap	bold	hack	plan	stet	bible
dot	book	hero	play	tale	blurb
gem	bull	iamb	plot	term	books
ink	cant	idea	poem	text	brace
lay	card	joke	poet	tome	breve
log	case	leaf	puff	type	brief
mot	Clio	line	pull	verb	canon
ode	code	mode	quad	word	canto
pad	coin	mood	read	work	caret

5/6 LETTERS

codex	Ionic	runes	abrege	digest
colon	irony	runic	accent	dipody
comic	issue	scald	action	doodle
comma	lingo	scene	adverb	editor
cover	lyric	sci,fi	Alcaic	emquad
daily	maxim	scrip	Aldine	ending
devil	metre	serif	annals	eponym
diary	moral	setup	annual	epopee
ditto	motto	sheet	aorist	errata
divan	Muses	skald	apercu	etymon
draft	novel	slang	Apollo	eulogy
drama	odist	slant	author	expose
dummy	organ	slate	ballad	fabler
elegy	paean	space	bathos	favour
envoi	paper	spell	binder	figure
envoy	parse	stamp	bonmot	flimsy
epode	pearl	story	browse	folder
essay	phone	study	burden	future
extra	piece	style	byword	galley
fable	plume	summa	chorus	gender
farce	poesy	tense	clause	gerund
final	point	thema	cliche	gnomic
folio	press	theme	climax	Gothic
forel	prime	tilde	colour	gradus
fount	print	title	column	heroic
genre	proem	topic	comedy	hiatus
geste	proof	tract	copula	homily
ghost	prose	trope	crambo	hybrid
gloss	prosy	twist	critic	hyphen
gnome	quill	usage	dactyl	iambic
grave	quote	verse	dagger	iambus
heads	rebus	verso	dative	impose
ictus	recto	voice	delete	italic
idiom	reply	vowel	depict	jacket
idyll	rhyme	words	dictum	jargon
index	Roman	works	diesis	jingle

209

leader	postil	series	antique
legend	potted	seriph	antonym
letter	praxis	sermon	apostil
lyrist	precis	sestet	article
mackle	prefix	sextet	autonym
macron	primer	simile	ballade
macule	prolix	sketch	binding
make｟up	pundit	sonnet	bookery
manual	purist	spread	book｟fed
margin	quarto	stanza	bookish
matter	quotes	strain	booklet
memoir	reader	stress	Boswell
metric	recant	Strine	brevier
minion	record	stylus	bucolic
monody	relate	suffix	caconym
morgue	remark	syntax	caesura
neuter	report	tablet	calamus
notice	resume	tercet	capital
number	Reuter	theory	capsule
obelus	review	thesis	cedilla
object	revise	tongue	chapter
octave	rhymer	truism	classic
octavo	rhymic	umlaut	codices
offcut	rondel	uncial	coinage
offset	run｟off	vellum	comment
old｟saw	satire	verbal	compend
pathos	saying	volume	compose
patois	scheme	weekly	context
pencil	scrawl	writer	copyman
penman	screed	zeugma	coterie
penned	scribe	abridge	couplet
pen｟pal	script	account	creator
period	scrive	acronym	dash｟off
person	scroll	addenda	daybook
phrase	sequel	adjunct	decline
poetry	serial	anagram	delenda

demotic	heading	missive	portray
descant	Helicon	monthly	preface
dialect	heroine	morceau	prelims
diamond	history	mystery	present
dimeter	Homeric	narrate	printed
distich	homonym	neology	printer
eclogue	huitain	newsman	profile
edition	idyllic	newword	pronoun
elegiac	imagery	nominal	proofer
English	impress	nookman	prosaic
enstamp	imprint	notepad	prosody
epigram	initial	novella	proverb
episode	in|print	obelisk	publish
epistle	insight	octapla	quadrat
epitaph	italics	old|joke	recount
epithet	journal	omnibus	refrain
epitome	jussive	on|paper	reissue
eponymy	justify	opuscle	release
erratum	laconic	outline	reprint
excerpt	lampoon	overrun	reverso
extract	leaders	oxytone	reviser
fabliau	leaflet	pandect	rewrite
factual	Leonine	papyrus	rhyming
fad|word	letters	parable	romance
fantasy	lexicon	paradox	rondeau
feature	library	paragon	roundel
fiction	literal	parsing	sagaman
flowers	litotes	passage	Sapphic
fluency	log|book	pen|name	sarcasm
flyleaf	lyrical	perfect	scaldic
garland	Marchen	phoneme	scholia
gazette	meaning	playlet	section
georgic	measure	Pléiade	sestina
grammar	memoirs	poetess	shocker
graphic	message	poetics	sorites
handout	metonym	poetise	special

spondee	alphabet	bookworm	dramatic
storied	analecta	bout‚rime	elegiast
strophe	analects	brackets	ellipsis
subject	analogue	brochure	enallage
summary	analysis	bulletin	end|paper
synesis	anapaest	buzz|word	end|rhyme
synonym	anaphora	cacology	epanodos
tabloid	anecdote	calendar	epic|poet
telling	annalist	Calliope	epigraph
textual	annotate	causerie	epilogue
themata	antihero	chapbook	epitasis
theNine	aphorism	chestnut	epopoeia
tragedy	apodosis	chiasmus	essayist
treat|of	apologia	choliamb	eulogium
trilogy	apologue	circular	euphuism
triolet	apothegm	city|desk	excerpta
triplet	appendix	city|room	excursus
tripody	archaism	classics	exegesis
triseme	archives	clerihew	extracts
trochee	asterisk	co‚author	eye|rhyme
typeset	Atticism	colophon	fabulist
verbose	autotype	compiler	fabulous
versify	ballader	composer	fair|copy
virelay	banality	construe	fascicle
virgule	biweekly	contents	feminine
vocable	boldface	copybook	folk|tale
western	bold|hand	copy|desk	foolscap
wordage	bookcase	creative	footnote
write|up	book|club	critique	fragment
writing	book|ends	cuttings	fullface
written	book|mark	dactylic	full|stop
ablative	bookrack	describe	genitive
abstract	book‚read	despatch	glossary
acrostic	bookrest	dispatch	Good|Book
allegory	bookroom	document	graffiti
allusion	bookshop	doggerel	graffito

212

handbook	metrical	pleonasm	scholium
headline	minstrel	poethood	scribble
hexapody	misnomer	poetizer	sentence
hieratic	misprint	poet|king	skeleton
historic	misusage	poetling	slip|case
hornbook	modifier	poetship	slipslop
humorist	molossus	polyglot	solecism
ideogram	monotype	post|card	spelling
idyllist	morpheme	pressman	spondaic
inkstand	mot|juste	printers	subtitle
inscribe	mythical	printery	syllable
inscroll	narrator	printing	syllabus
Irishism	notation	prologue	symploce
jongleur	notebook	prosaism	synopsis
kyrielle	novelist	protasis	synoptic
laconics	obituary	put|to|bed	textbook
language	octapody	quatrain	thematic
laureate	offprint	rare|book	the|Press
libretto	old|story	read|copy	thriller
ligature	open|book	ready|pen	toponymy
limerick	opuscule	relation	tractate
link|verb	original	reporter	treasury
linotype	oxymoron	rescript	treatise
lipogram	palinode	reviewer	tribrach
literacy	pamphlet	revision	trigraph
literate	parabole	rhapsode	trimeter
logogram	paradigm	rhapsody	tristich
logotype	paragoge	rhetoric	trochaic
longhand	paragram	romancer	trouvere
love|poem	particle	romantic	trouveur
madrigal	password	root|word	type|face
magazine	pastoral	ruby|type	type|page
malaprop	pencraft	satirist	type|size
measured	Pierides	scanning	verbatim
metaphor	Pindaric	scansion	verbiage
metonymy	playbook	scholion	verselet

verseman	blackface	consonant
versicle	bold‚faced	conundrum
vignette	bookboard	copy|chief
vocative	book|cloth	copy|paper
web|press	book|cover	copyright
whodunit	bookcraft	criticism
wordbook	booklover	crossword
word|form	bookmaker	cuneiform
yearbook	bookshelf	Decameron
accidence	bookstall	depiction
acrostics	bookstand	depictive
adjective	bookstore	descanter
adventure	book|token	diaeresis
adverbial	book|trade	diphthong
allograph	bourgeois	directory
amoebaean	brilliant	discourse
ampersand	bucoliast	dithyramb
amphigory	cap|rhymes	dramatist
anacrusis	cap|verses	editorial
anecdotal	catalogue	emphasize
annotator	catch|line	end‚reader
anonymous	catchword	ephemeris
anthology	character	epic|verse
anti‚novel	chronicle	epithesis
antispast	clarendon	epizeuxis
apostille	classical	eponymism
assonance	clippings	epopoeist
Athenaeum	coin|a|word	etymology
Attic|salt	collector	euphemism
attribute	collotype	exegetics
authoress	columnist	expositor
autograph	comic|book	expounder
ballpoint	commenter	extrabold
battology	composing	fairy|tale
bimonthly	condensed	fictional
biography	conjugate	folk|story

fragments	lightface	paper,back
free|lance	limp,cover	parabolic
free|verse	lithotype	paragraph
full,faced	livraison	parchment
gazetteer	local|room	Parnassus
gerundive	logogriph	partitive
ghost|word	logomachy	past|tense
gleanings	love|story	pen|and|ink
go|to|press	lower|case	penscript
great|work	macaronic	pentapody
guidebook	major|poet	personify
hair|space	majuscule	philology
half,title	masculine	phonemics
hard|cover	Meliboean	phonetics
headlines	melodrama	phonology
heptapody	Menippean	phototypy
heteronym	minor|poet	pictorial
hexameter	minuscule	platitude
hexastich	monograph	poetaster
historian	monostich	poetastry
historify	mythmaker	poetcraft
holograph	narration	poeticule
hypallage	narrative	Poet's|Poet
hyperbole	necrology	portrayal
idiomatic	neologism	potboiler
idioticon	neoterism	potential
Indian|Ink	newspaper	predicate
in|measure	newsprint	pressroom
intensive	nonce|word	presswork
Irish|bull	nonpareil	preterite
late|extra	note|paper	print|shop
Leavisite	novelette	prolative
legendary	octastich	prolepsis
lettering	onomastic	prolixity
librarian	page|proof	proofread
life|story	palillogy	proofroom

pseudonym
publicist
punch|line
punctuate
qualifier
quarterly
quodlibet
quotation
raconteur
rationale
recountal
recounter
reference
reflexive
represent
retelling
rhymester
rigmarole
romancist
rotograph
roundelay
round|hand
runesmith
sans|serif
satirical
scholiast
scribbler
scription
scrivener
scrivenry
secretary
secret|ink
selection
semanteme
semantics
semicolon

semiotics
sgraffito
sheetwork
shorthand
signature
slip|cover
small|pica
soft|cover
songsmith
sonneteer
spin|a|yarn
statement
stenotype
storiette
story|book
story|line
strike|off
subeditor
substance
summarize
sumpsimus
syllabary
syllepsis
symbolism
symposium
tail|rhyme
tall|story
tetrapody
tetraseme
thesaurus
thin|space
title|page
treatment
triticism
true|story
type|mould

upper|case
vade|mecum
verbalism
verbarian
verbosity
verse|form
versifier
vers|libre
vocabular
vogue|word
vulgarism
witticism
wordiness
write|upon
zincotype
abridgment
accusative
active|verb
adaptation
adjectival
adversaria
alliterate
amanuensis
amphibrach
amphimacer
anapaestic
anastrophe
anecdotage
anecdotist
Anglo|Saxon
annotation
antecedent
anticlimax
antithesis
apocalypse
apostrophe

atmosphere	classicism	exposition
authorship	collection	expression
background	colloquial	fairy|story
back|number	colportage	feuilleton
bad|grammar	colporteur	fictionist
battledore	comic|strip	figurative
best|seller	commentary	filing|room
bibliology	common|noun	finite|verb
bibliomane	compendium	funeral|ode
bibliopegy	compositor	ghost|story
bibliopole	conspectus	glossarist
bibliosoph	continuity	glossology
bibliothec	copulative	glottology
billet|doux	copyholder	grammarian
biographer	copying|ink	hack|writer
blank|verse	copyreader	Heptameron
Bloomsbury	corruption	heptameter
bookbinder	cradle|book	heptastich
bookdealer	cryptogram	historical
bookholder	curate's|egg	house|organ
book|jacket	cyclopedia	hybrid|word
book|loving	dead|letter	hyperbaton
bookmaking	dead|matter	imperative
bookmonger	declension	imposition
book|review	dedication	impression
bookseller	definition	incunabula
bookwright	denotation	indicative
brain|child	derivation	infinitive
broadsheet	diaskeuast	inflection
bucket|seat	dictionary	ink|slinger
cacography	discourser	job|printer
catalectic	dissertate	journalese
chapel|text	dust|jacket	journalism
chromotypy	embroidery	journalist
chronicler	epanaphora	lame|verses
circumflex	epic|poetry	lead|pencil

217

letter|card
lexicology
lexiconist
librettist
light,faced
light|verse
literature
live|matter
logorrhoea
long|accent
long|primer
love|letter
macaronics
magazinist
magnum|opus
make|a|proof
make,up|room
manuscript
metalepsis
metaphrase
metathesis
metrically
miscellany
mock,heroic
morphology
neuter|verb
news|editor
newsletter
news|writer
nom,de,plume
nominative
non,fiction
noun|clause
obligative
obsoletism
open|letter

orismology
ottava|rima
palaeotype
palimpsest
palindrome
palinodist
paper|tiger
paraphrase
Parnassian
participle
pen|pushing
pentameter
pentastich
periodical
permissive
plate|proof
playwright
pleonastic
pluperfect
poet,artist
poetastery
poet,farmer
poet,priest
possessive
prenominal
press|proof
production
proof|sheet
proper|noun
prosaicism
prospectus
publishers
publishing
put|to|press
recounting
rhapsodist

rhyme|royal
round|robin
runic|verse
schoolbook
scratch|pad
scribbling
scriptural
scrivening
sealed|book
set|in|print
shibboleth
short|story
slim|volume
socio,drama
soubriquet
spoonerism
stereotype
storiology
storymaker
subheading
Swan|of|Avon
synecdoche
syntactics
taleteller
tell|a|story
tetrameter
tetrastich
thick|space
transitive
troubadour
true|to|life
type|matter
typescript
typesetter
typewriter
typography

218

verbal|note	bookbinding	dissyllable
verbal|noun	bookishness	dithyrambic
vernacular	book|learned	dithyrambus
versecraft	Book|of|books	dittography
versemaker	book|of|verse	electrotype
versesmith	book|printer	Elzevir|book
villanelle	book|selling	enchiridion
vocabulary	book|support	engrossment
word|coiner	bring|to|book	exclamation
word|seller	catachresis	festschrift
writership	catch|phrase	first|person
abecedarian	circulation	Fleet|Street
active|voice	cliff|hanger	flow|of|words
acute|accent	collectanea	fortnightly
adversative	commentator	fountain|pen
alexandrine	compendious	future|tense
alphabetics	compilation	galley|proof
anachronism	composition	ghostwriter
anacoluthia	concordance	glottal|stop
Anacreontic	conditional	grammatical
antiphrasis	confessions	grave|accent
antispastic	conjugation	great|primer
antistrophe	conjunction	gutter|press
antonomasia	conjunctive	·handwriting
attributive	connotation	happy|ending
authorcraft	contributor	heroic|verse
author's|copy	correlative	incunabulum
ballad|maker	corrigendum	inscription
bastard|type	counterterm	inspiration
bibliolater	crabbed|hand	interviewer
bibliophage	crambo|clink	letter|paper
bibliophile	cub|reporter	letter|press
bibliotheca	description	library|book
biographist	descriptive	linguistics
black|comedy	disjunctive	literary|man
black|letter	dissertator	litterateur

219

local|colour	poet|pilgrim	tragi|comedy
logographer	poet|thinker	transcriber
lucubration	poet|warrior	translation
lyric|poetry	point|tenses	true|meaning
malapropism	preposition	type|foundry
memorabilia	press|revise	typesetting
memorialist	printed|word	typographer
miracle|play	printer's|ink	typographic
miscellanea	proofreader	unfold|a|tale
monographer	psychodrama	verbigerate
Mrs|Malaprop	publication	versemaking
Mrs|Slipslop	public|press	vers|librist
nom|de|guerre	punctuation	war|reporter
novelettist	reading|room	word|history
nursery|tale	real|meaning	word|painter
onomasticon	retold|story	word|picture
onomatology	rhyme|scheme	written|word
orthography	rotary|press	yarn|spinner
pamphleteer	rotogravure	Yellow|press
paragrapher	sad|to|relate	abbreviation
parenthesis	scriptorial	abbreviature
participial	semantology	abstract|noun
Passion|play	semasiology	adherent|noun
passive|verb	short|accent	advance|proof
past|perfect	solid|matter	alliteration
patent|space	stenography	author's|proof
penny|a|liner	storyteller	balladmonger
perissology	story|writer	ballpoint|pen
phrasemaker	subjunctive	bedtime|story
phraseology	substantive	bibliography
picture|book	superscribe	bibliologist
Pindaric|ode	tachygraphy	bibliomaniac
play|on|words	taletelling	bibliopegist
poetic|prose	terminology	bibliopolist
poetic|works	the|Good|Book	bibliotheque
poet|patriot	third|person	binder's|title

block|capital
book|learning
book|reviewer
bookstitcher
brachygraphy
calligrapher
chrestomathy
chronography
classicalism
collaborator
collectarium
commentation
complete|work
complication
condensation
construction
dead|language
deponent|verb
direct|object
direct|speech
disquisition
dissertation
double|dagger
early|edition
elegiac|verse
encyclopedia
epigrammatic
fat,faced|type
first|edition
foundry|proof
fourth|estate
frontispiece
gnomic|aorist
gobbledegook
gossip|column
halting|rhyme

hermeneutics
hieroglyphic
Hudibrastics
indelible|ink
initial|rhyme
instrumental
interjection
intransitive
introduction
invisible|ink
king's|English
leader|writer
letter|writer
lexicography
literary|hack
literary|lion
logodaedalus
man|of|letters
metaphorical
metrical|foot
metrical|unit
monkish|Latin
monosyllable
morality|play
mother|tongue
newspaperman
nomenclature
nursery|rhyme
onomatopoeia
palaeography
paragraphist
part|of|speech
passive|voice
pastoral|poet
perfect|rhyme
perfect|tense

plain|English	bibliographer
poetastering	bibliophilist
poetic|genius	book|of|the|film
poet|laureate	book|of|the|play
poet,novelist	border|ballads
poet|satirist	boustrophedon
polysyllable	colloquialism
present|tense	conquistadors
press|release	correspondent
question|mark	double|meaning
quill|driving	epigrammatist
rhyming|slang	gerund|grinder
Rosetta|stone	Homeric|simile
second|person	internal|rhyme
slanting|hand	lexicographer
slip|of|the|pen	literary|agent
society|verse	mixed|metaphor
space|fiction	nonsense|verse
speed|writing	palaeographer
spelling|book	palaeontology
stock|of|words	penny|dreadful
story|telling	pidgin|English
strip|cartoon	pocket|edition
turn|of|phrase	poetical|works
type|printing	poetic|licence
uncial|letter	poetry|reading
versemongery	polysyllabism
word|painting	prehistorical
writer's|cramp	purple|passage
writing|paper	put|pen|to|paper
yarn|spinning	reading|matter
alpha|and|omega	reference|book
anagrammatist	romantic|novel
autobiography	Shakespearean
back,formation	spring,cleaner
belles,lettres	structuralism

subject matter	living language
subject,object	locus classicus
tongue,twister	masculine rhyme
versification	mistranslation
work of fiction	Norman Conquest
ancient history	past participle
archaeological	Pilgrim Fathers
apple of discord	pre,reformation
autobiographer	principal parts
bowdlerisation	relative clause
circumlocution	rhyming couplet
circumlocutory	science fiction
collected poems	shaggy dog story
concrete poetry	Shakespeareana
correspondence	sonnet,sequence
covering letter	subject heading
cross,reference	transitive verb
Dear John letter	ancient monument
detective novel	bibliographical
detective story	Bloomsbury group
early Victorian	character sketch
epigrammatical	cloud,cuckoo,land
etymologically	coffee,table book
figure of speech	complex sentence
four,letter word	creative writing
glossy magazine	definite article
grammaticaster	exclamation mark
imperative mood	higher criticism
imperfect tense	historical novel
indicative mood	Hundred Years War
indirect object	naughty nineties
indirect speech	palaeontologist
interpretation	personal pronoun
inverted commas	portmanteau word
Kailyard school	proof correcting
limited edition	punctuation mark

relative|pronoun   standard|English
shilling|shocker   subjunctive|mood
spelling|mistake   thumbnail|sketch
split|infinitive

Machinery

bar	case	lock	vice	drain	panel
cam	cell	loom	wire	drier	pedal
car	cock	luff	yale	earth	pivot
cog	coil	mast	yoke	edges	plant
fan	cowl	mike	anode	Ernie	plate
gin	dial	mill	anvil	fence	press
gun	drum	mine	Asdic	fiche	prong
hub	duct	mule	baler	flare	pylon
jet	flex	nail	bevel	forge	quill
jib	flue	pile	block	frame	quoin
key	fuse	pipe	brake	gauge	radar
nut	gear	plug	brush	gland	radio
ram	grab	pump	cable	guide	razor
rig	grid	rack	chain	hoist	relay
tap	hasp	reel	chase	inlet	rifle
vat	hi-fi	rule	choke	jenny	rivet
bank	horn	seal	clamp	ladle	robot
bolt	iron	shoe	clock	lance	rotor
bomb	kiln	skip	crane	laser	screw
boom	knob	slur	crank	lathe	shaft
bore	last	sump	crate	litho	shank
boss	lead	tank	davit	meter	shunt
buff	lens	till	diode	mixer	sieve
bush	lift	tube	dolly	motor	spool
butt	link	vane	dowel	mould	spray

stick	clutch	needle	ticker
still	collar	nipple	torque
stove	conrod	nozzle	trepan
strut	cooker	oilrig	triode
thole	cooler	outlet	tripod
timer	cutout	pharos	trivet
tooth	device	pickup	turret
torch	diesel	pinion	tympan
tower	dredge	pintle	volery
train	dynamo	pistol	washer
truck	engine	piston	woofer
TVset	etcher	platen	airlock
valve	faggot	pulley	airpump
wheel	filter	ramjet	antenna
winch	flange	reglet	arclamp
xerox	galley	riddle	arsenal
abacus	gantry	rocket	balance
aerial	garnet	rounce	ballast
baffle	gasket	rudder	battery
barrel	Gclamp	runner	bearing
barrow	grader	saddle	bellows
beacon	ground	scales	bindery
bigend	gutter	seeder	blanket
binder	handle	siphon	blender
blower	heater	sleeve	booster
bobbin	hopper	sluice	caisson
boiler	jumper	smithy	cannery
brayer	keyway	socket	capstan
breech	klaxon	spring	cathode
broach	leader	square	chamber
buffer	magnet	stator	charger
burton	matrix	stroke	chassis
busbar	mincer	switch	chatter
camera	monkey	tackle	circuit
caster	mortar	Tannoy	combine
castor	muzzle	tappet	compass

MACHINERY

control	pottery	armament	hardware
decoder	push|rod	armature	hemostat
derrick	ratchet	backlash	hose|pipe
dredger	reactor	ballista	hotplate
dry|cell	sawmill	bearings	ignition
ejector	scanner	bloomery	impeller
encoder	shackle	blowpipe	intercom
exciter	shutter	bosshead	iron|lung
exhaust	sleeper	camshaft	isolator
factory	smelter	cogwheel	laser|gun
fanbelt	speaker	cold|weld	lift|pump
ferrule	spindle	colliery	linotype
flare|up	starter	computer	lock|gate
foghorn	stirrer	controls	lock|weir
foundry	sweeper	conveyor	logotype
frisket	tannery	coupling	manifold
fulcrum	televox	crucible	monotype
furnace	terebra	cylinder	neon|tube
fuse|box	toaster	Davy|lamp	outboard
gearbox	tracker	demister	pendulum
grommet	tractor	detector	pinwheel
hydrant	treadle	dip|stick	pipeline
lighter	trigger	dynamite	pulse|jet
limiter	trolley	earphone	radiator
locknut	turbine	elevator	radio|set
magneto	tweeter	fail|safe	receiver
measure	utensil	filament	recorder
monitor	welding	fly|press	refinery
muffler	wet|cell	flywheel	register
network	winding	fork|lift	repeater
overlay	wing|nut	fuse|wire	resistor
padlock	wringer	gadgetry	rheostat
palette	absorber	garrotte	scaffold
pattern	actuator	gaslight	selector
pentode	air|brake	governor	shredder
planter	air|motor	gyrostat	silencer

slip ring	bevel gear	force pump
smithery	bilge pump	fumigator
software	booby trap	fuseboard
sprocket	brake drum	fuse links
spurgear	brake shoe	gas engine
teetotum	bulldozer	gas holder
teletype	burnisher	gasometer
template	capacitor	gear lever
terminal	clockwork	gear train
thole pin	component	gearwheel
thresher	condenser	generator
throttle	contactor	gyroplane
time bomb	converter	gyroscope
track rod	cotton gin	half shaft
turbofan	crankcase	hand brake
turbojet	crosshead	harvester
underlay	diaphragm	headlight
vibrator	disc brake	hydrofoil
web press	disc valve	incubator
windlass	disc wheel	indicator
windmill	drop forge	inlet port
wind pump	drop press	insulator
wireless	electrode	interlock
X ray tube	escalator	jackscrew
Yale lock	explosive	jet engine
zoom lens	face lathe	land rover
air engine	fire alarm	light bulb
alarm bell	flash bulb	limelight
altimeter	flash lamp	liquefier
amplifier	floodgate	lithotype
apparatus	flour mill	loadstone
aspirator	flow valve	mechanism
automatic	focus lamp	milk churn
automaton	food mixer	mill wheel
autopilot	foot brake	milometer
bar magnet	footstick	monoscope

227

neon light	stop light	check valve
oiling can	strip mill	cine camera
overdrive	sump guard	cobalt bomb
page gauge	tabulator	coffee mill
periscope	tail light	commutator
piston rod	telephone	compressor
plug point	thyristor	controller
pneumatic	tool chest	corking pin
power line	top burton	cotton mill
power pack	treadmill	crankshaft
preheater	turbopump	crown wheel
projector	turntable	crystal set
propeller	type mould	depth gauge
propshaft	water cock	dictaphone
prototype	watermill	dishwasher
punch card	wattmeter	diving bell
punch tape	wood screw	donkey pump
pyrometer	worm wheel	drum sander
radiogram	yardstick	dry battery
rectifier	zincotype	duplicator
reflector	aero engine	earth mover
regulator	alarm clock	economiser
rotary gap	alternator	emery board
sandpaper	angle block	emery wheel
separator	angle board	escapement
sidelight	angle brace	explosives
skyrocket	angle plate	filter pump
small bore	arc welding	fire engine
solar cell	attachment	flare light
sound unit	automation	flashlight
spin drier	automobile	floodlight
spotlight	bench drill	gas turbine
stamp mill	calculator	grindstone
star drill	centrifuge	gudgeon pin
steel mill	chain block	guillotine
stink bomb	chain drive	hearing aid

heat|engine	power|brake	transducer
hectograph	power|drill	twin|triode
hovercraft	power|press	typewriter
humidifier	push|button	vacuum|pump
hydroplane	quartz|lamp	vacuum|tube
incendiary	respirator	vapour|lamp
inductance	road|roller	ventilator
laundromat	robot|pilot	water|clock
lighthouse	rose|engine	water|gauge
lock|washer	rotary|pump	water|tower
locomotive	sack|barrow	water|wheel
luff|tackle	safety|fuse	wind|tunnel
Machine|Age	safety|lamp	yard|tackle
magnet|core	serve|valve	zircon|lamp
marker|buoy	servomotor	accelerator
masonry|pin	shunt|motor	accumulator
microfiche	silk|screen	afterburner
micrometer	slide|valve	aftercooler
microphone	sluice|gate	anchor|light
mimeograph	snowplough	atomic|power
miner's|lamp	spring|lock	autostarter
motorcycle	stay|tackle	ball|bearing
oil|derrick	stenograph	barrel|scale
oscillator	stereotype	battery|lamp
osmium|lamp	strip|light	beam|antenna
oxygen|tent	sunray|lamp	beam|balance
paramagnet	suppressor	bevel|square
pari|mutuel	suspension	bicycle|pump
percolator	switchgear	brake|lining
petrol|pump	tachometer	cam|follower
photoflash	television	carbon|light
photoflood	thermistor	carburettor
piledriver	thermostat	caterpillar
pilot|light	ticker|tape	choking|coil
piston|pump	time|switch	cold|welding
piston|ring	timing|gear	compensator

comptometer	offshore|rig	totalisator
cooling|coil	oil|refinery	track|rod|end
dark|lantern	on|off|switch	transceiver
depth|charge	platen|press	transformer
distributor	pop|rivet|gun	transmitter
dolly|camera	preselector	tumbler|drier
dynamometer	pulley|block	type|foundry
echo|sounder	radio|beacon	weighbridge
electric|arc	range|finder	X|ray|machine
electric|eye	relief|valve	aerial|camera
electrotype	road|scraper	arithmometer
engine|block	rocket|motor	assembly|line
engine|of|war	rolling|mill	balance|wheel
exhaust|pipe	rotary|press	barrel|plater
exhaust|port	safety|valve	battery|plate
feeler|gauge	scaffolding	binding|screw
Ferris|wheel	searchlight	blast|furnace
field|magnet	self|starter	blinker|light
filing|block	series|motor	burglar|alarm
hair|trigger	signal|light	capstan|lathe
interrupter	slot|machine	cash|register
ironmongery	snatch|block	control|panel
jumper|cable	solar|engine	control|valve
junction|box	speedometer	conveyor|belt
letterpress	spirit|level	cooling|tower
lie|detector	steam|engine	copying|press
limit|switch	steam|roller	cylinder|head
loud|speaker	stirrup|pump	depth|sounder
machine|made	stock|ticker	diesel|engine
machine|shop	storage|cell	differential
machine|work	stuffing|box	donkey|engine
memory|tubes	suction|pump	driving|force
mercury|lamp	switchboard	electric|cord
microswitch	synchromesh	electric|fire
mortice|lock	tackle|block	electric|wire
offset|litho	teleprinter	filament|lamp

flame,thrower	signal|rocket
flashing|lamp	single|tackle
forge|foundry	solar|battery
fruit|machine	sound|limiter
grease|nipple	sparking|plug
grinding|mill	spring|washer
high|fidelity	steam|turbine
landing|light	steering|gear
lightning|rod	supercharger
machine|ruler	tantalum|lamp
magic|lantern	tape|recorder
magnetic|tape	telecomputer
marine|engine	transmission
micro|circuit	tungsten|lamp
mine|detector	walkie,talkie
mobile|camera	wheel|bearing
monkey|wrench	aerodynamical
national|grid	air|compressor
nuclear|power	box|the|compass
pair|of|scales	concrete|mixer
petrol|engine	connecting,rod
photocathode	counter|motion
piston|engine	cylinder|block
potter's|wheel	electric|drill
power|station	electric|motor
pressure|mine	engine|failure
pulley|tackle	fuel|injection
radial|engine	Heath|Robinson
radio|compass	hydraulic|jack
record|player	jet|propulsion
refrigerator	manufacturing
resuscitator	mechanisation
rocket|engine	mowing|machine
rubber|hammer	oceanographer
short|circuit	power,assisted
signal|beacon	printing,press

rack|and|pinion
remote|control
sewing|machine
spinning|jenny
spinning|wheel
admiralty|chart
butterfly|screw
compound|engine
Davis|apparatus
design|engineer
hydraulic|brake
pneumatic|drill

production|line
propeller|shaft
starting|handle
three|speed|gear
universal|joint
companion|ladder
drilling|machine
knitting|machine
perpetual|motion
printing|machine
weighing|machine

Marine

bay	bight	benthos	sea|loch
ebb	briny	breaker	sea|mist
sea	ocean	catspaw	shingle
cove	shoal	channel	straits
eddy	shore	coastal	wavelet
foam	sound	current	becalmed
gulf	spume	deepsea	cerulean
kyle	swell	ebb|tide	doldrums
main	eddies	euripus	full|tide
neap	marine	harbour	heavy|sea
reef	roller	high|sea	high|seas
surf	sea|air	low|tide	high|tide
tide	sea|bed	narrows	littoral
wave	sea|fog	oceanic	low|water
atoll	seaway	pelagic	mainsail
basin	strait	riptide	mainsail
beach	strand	sandbar	maritime

mean|tide
mill|pond
neap|tide
ocean|bed
offshore
rough|sea
sandbank
sand|reef
seaboard
sea|floor
seascape
seashore
sounding
tidal|rip
choppy|sea
coastline
coral|reef
flood|tide
high|water
marigraph
quicksand
salt|water
sea|breeze
sea|margin
seven|seas
tidal|wave
choppiness
ebb|and|flow
heavy|swell

sea|breezes
spring|tide
arm|of|the|sea
deep|blue|sea
echo|sounder
ground|swell
hydrography
hydrosphere
neritic|zone
ocean|depths
wave|erosion
white|horses
drift|current
oceanography
opposite|tide
the|seven|seas
tidal|current
fall|overboard
high|water|mark
master|mariner
ship's|register
starboard|side
circumnavigate
herring|fishery
starboard|watch
any|port|in|a|storm
circumnavigable
circumnavigator

Mathematics

pi	trig	prism	Euclid
add	unit	radii	eureka
arc	zero	radix	factor
cos	acute	ratio	figure
cot	angle	rhomb	finite
nil	bevel	rider	fluent
sec	chord	ruler	heptad
sin	conic	solid	loglog
sum	cosec	table	matrix
tan	count	tenth	minute
apex	cubed	tithe	moduli
axes	cubic	triad	nonary
axis	curve	value	nought
cone	datum	X rays	number
cosh	digit	abacus	oblong
cube	equal	adding	octant
cusp	field	alidad	pentad
data	graph	apogee	radian
half	helix	binary	radius
line	index	binate	secant
lune	lemma	bisect	sector
node	locus	circle	senary
plot	minus	cosine	series
plus	octad	cosinh	sphere
root	octet	cuboid	square
sine	plane	cyclic	tables
sinh	point	degree	tetrad
sums	power	denary	trigon
surd	prime	divide	ungula

vector	minuend	analogue
versin	modulus	argument
vertex	nonuple	binomial
volume	nothing	brackets
abaxial	null|set	calculus
algebra	numeral	cardinal
alidade	numeric	centrode
aliquot	oblique	centroid
analogy	octagon	centuple
angular	octuple	constant
bearing	ordinal	cosecant
bracket	per|cent	cube|root
compass	polygon	cubiform
complex	problem	cylinder
counter	product	decimate
cubical	pyramid	diagonal
cycloid	quinary	diameter
decagon	radiant	dihedral
decimal	rhombic	dividers
diagram	rhombus	division
digital	scalene	dynamics
divided	segment	empty|set
divisor	sextant	exponent
ellipse	squared	figurate
figures	tabular	fluxions
flexure	tangent	formulae
fluxion	ternary	fraction
formula	ternion	function
fulcrum	theorem	geometer
hexagon	totient	geometry
indices	trapeze	gradient
inertia	unitary	helicoid
integer	accuracy	heptagon
isochor	addition	hexagram
isotype	algorism	infinity
lattice	aliquant	integral

isogonic	velocity	octagonal
mantissa	vicenary	parameter
matrices	vinculum	perimeter
monomial	aggregate	polygonal
multiple	algebraic	pyramidal
multiply	algorithm	quadruple
negative	bipyramid	quintuple
nonenary	callipers	reckoning
numerary	chiliagon	rectangle
octonary	cochleate	reduction
one,sided	compasses	re,entrant
parabola	cotangent	rhombical
parallel	curvature	set|square
pentagon	decagonal	slide|rule
prismoid	dimension	summation
quadrant	directrix	tabulator
quadrate	duodenary	tetragram
quantity	eccentric	trapezium
quotient	ellipsoid	trapezoid
rational	equipoise	trinomial
repetend	Euclidean	algebraist
rhomboid	figure|out	arithmetic
septimal	fluxional	asymmetric
septuple	hemicycle	biquadrate
sequence	hexagonal	calculator
sextuple	histogram	cancellate
spheroid	hyperbola	centesimal
subtract	increment	complement
sum|total	inversion	concentric
tetragon	isosceles	co,ordinate
totitive	logarithm	cross,staff
triangle	mechanics	decahedron
trigonal	Newtonian	difference
trochoid	numbering	duodecimal
variable	numerator	elongation
variance	numerical	estimation

fractional	subtrahend	mirror|image
half|circle	tetragonal	mixed|number
hemisphere	triangular	Napier's|rods
heptagonal	trilateral	number|field
hexahedral	triplicate	obtuse|angle
hexahedron	unilateral	pentahedral
hexangular	versed|sine	pentahedron
holohedral	aliquot|part	permutation
hypotenuse	binary|digit	prime|factor
irrational	binary|scale	prime|number
mathematic	bipartition	progression
multiplier	biquadratic	proposition
numeration	calculation	rectangular
octahedral	coefficient	reflex|angle
octahedron	combination	right|angled
orthogonal	comptometer	right|angles
pantograph	computation	round|number
pentagonal	coördinates	rule|of|three
percentage	cubic|system	sesquialter
polyhedral	denominator	simple|curve
polyhedron	directrices	solution|set
protractor	dodecagonal	submultiple
quadrangle	enumeration	subtraction
quadratrix	equidistant	tetrahedron
quadrature	equilibrium	trapezoidal
quadricone	equilateral	whole|number
quadriform	heptahedron	arithmograph
quaternary	holohedrism	arithmometer
reciprocal	icosahedron	chiliahedron
relativity	integration	combinations
rhomboidal	latus|rectum	common|factor
right|angle	locus|vector	conic|section
semicircle	logarithmic	critical|path
square|root	mathematics	decimal|point
statistics	mensuration	differential
subalgebra	metaphysics	dodecahedron

eccentricity	complex number
geometrician	computational
hyperalgebra	concentricity
line geometry	corresponding
long division	differentiate
metric system	dihedral angle
mixed decimal	disproportion
multiangular	exponentially
multilateral	exterior angle
multiplicand	geometrically
Napier's bones	geometric mean
oblique angle	golden section
open sentence	hydrodynamics
orthorhombic	indeterminate
Platonic body	interior angle
pons asinorum	irrationality
quadrangular	mathematician
quadrinomial	parallelogram
rhombohedron	perfect number
serial number	perpendicular
straight line	Platonic solid
substitution	quadratic mean
tally counter	quadrilateral
tetrahedroid	quantum number
trigonometry	ready reckoner
vernier scale	short division
antilogarithm	standard error
apportionment	statistically
approximately	alphanumerical
approximation	arithmetically
arithmetician	asymmetrically
associativity	asymptotically
beyond measure	axis of symmetry
circumference	cardinal number
commutability	common multiple
complementary	decimalisation

head|for|figures	vulgar|fraction
infinite|number	decimal|notation
linear|equation	differentiation
mathematically	Fibonacci|series
miscalculation	golden|rectangle
multiplication	identity|element
multiplicative	imaginary|number
natural|numbers	proportionately
parallellopiped	pure|mathematics
proper|fraction	square|the|circle
rational|number	trigonometrical
transformation	unknown|quantity
two|dimensional	

Measurement

amp	volt	plumb	chiliad
BTU	watt	score	compass
cab	angle	therm	decibel
erg	curie	third	geodesy
ohm	cycle	ampere	gilbert
rad	dozen	armful	hundred
rem	farad	calory	kiloton
atom	fermi	degree	lambert
BThU	gauge	kilerg	maximum
dyne	gross	megohm	maxwell
iota	henry	minute	minimum
mole	hertz	myriad	modicum
norm	joule	photon	neutron
phon	level	proton	pelorus
phot	lumen	radian	poundal
size	meter	second	quarter

rontgen	kilocycle	hypsometer
sextant	manometer	micrometer
sixfold	megacurie	multicurie
tenfold	megacycle	nitrometer
twofold	minometer	odorimetry
umpteen	nonillion	ombrometer
vernier	osmometer	pantometer
zillion	pedometer	piezometer
angstrom	pinchbeck	planimeter
electron	potometer	planimetry
fivefold	pyrometer	protractor
fourfold	set|square	pyknometer'
fraction	sevenfold	radiometer
gas|meter	slide|rule	radiometry
kilovolt	surveying	Rutherford
kilowatt	telemeter	spirometer
magneton	telemetry	tachometer
megavolt	threefold	tachymetry
megawatt	umpteenth	theodolite
microbar	vicesimal	tintometer
milliard	vigesimal	twelvefold
molecule	anemometer	viscometer
ninefold	audiometer	voltameter
odometer	bathometer	volt|ampere
particle	brinometer	actinometer
roentgen	Centigrade	baker's|dozen
standard	clinometer	calibration
thousand	cyclometer	calorimeter
viameter	densimeter	calorimetry
watt|hour	depth|gauge	candle|power
astrolabe	Fahrenheit	chronometry
barometer	goniometer	dynamometer
eightfold	goniometry	gradiometer
geodesist	gravimeter	mensuration
graticule	heliometer	polarimeter
hodometer	hygrometer	polarimetry

quantometer	respirometer
salinometer	spectrometer
spirit|level	thousandfold
thermal|unit	alcoholometer
thermometer	alcoholometry
undecennary	anticlockwise
undecennial	common|measure
cathetometer	dead|reckoning
decimal|point	made|to|measure
declinometer	measuring|tape
electrometer	quadruplicate
electronvolt	tablespoonful
extensometer	as|the|crow|flies
golden|guinea	commensuration
inclinometer	counterbalance
kilowatt|hour	counter|measure
magnetometer	mismeasurement
metric|system	third|dimension
microohmeter	antepenultimate
millirontgen	drop|in|the|bucket
psychrometer	fourth|dimension

Medicine

Dr	bed	ENT	hip	oil	sty
GP	cup	eye	ill	pep	tea
MD	cut	fat	jaw	pox	tic
MO	doc	fit	lab	pus	toe
os	DTs	flu	LDS	rib	vet
TB	ear	gas	leg	rub	wan
ail	ECG	gum	lip	sac	wen
arm	EEG	gut	LSD	spa	abed

ache	face	lint	shin	aorta	croup
acne	fade	lips	shot	atomy	dagga
ague	flux	lisp	sick	aural	dandy
AIDS	flux	lobe	skin	bathe	death
back	foot	lung	slim	baths	decay
bald	gall	maim	sole	belch	digit
balm	game	malt	sore	birth	dizzy
band	gash	mask	spot	blain	donor
bile	germ	mole	stab	bleed	drain
body	gout	mute	stye	blind	drill
boil	grip	nail	swab	blood	drops
bone	guts	nape	tent	bolus	dying
bubo	hair	nape	turn	bomoh	edema
burn	halt	neck	ulna	borax	elbow
burp	hand	noma	umbo	botch	ether
calf	harm	nose	vein	bowel	faint
case	head	numb	vena	brace	femur
cast	heal	oral	wale	brain	fever
cell	heel	otic	wall	brash	fibre
chin	hemp	pain	ward	break	flesh
clot	hips	pale	wart	build	flush
cold	home	palm	weal	bulla	fossa
coma	hurt	pang	welt	bursa	frame
corn	hypo	pest	wilt	canal	fugue
cure	ilia	pill	wits	catch	Galen
cusp	iris	plug	womb	chafe	gauze
cyst	iron	pock	X,ray	cheek	gland
daze	itch	pons	yawn	chest	gonad
deaf	junk	pore	yaws	chest	gored
diet	kibe	rash	acute	clava	gouty
dope	kink	rest	agony	colic	graft
dose	knee	ribs	algid	colon	graze
drip	lame	roof	alive	conch	gripe
drug	lens	root	ancon	cough	gumma
duct	limb	scab	ankle	cramp	gyrus
dumb	limp	scar	anvil	crick	heart

helix	opium	sound	virus	binder
herbs	organ	spasm	vomer	biopsy
hilum	ovary	spine	vomit	blanch
hives	palsy	stall	waist	bowels
hyoid	panel	sting	wheal	bracer
ictus	pinna	stupe	whelk	breast
ileum	plate	sweat	wince	breath
ilium	polio	swoon	wound	bruise
incus	polyp	tabes	wreck	bulimy
inion	probe	tabid	wrist	bunion
inlay	psora	taint	aching	caecum
jerks	pulse	talus	addict	caligo
joint	pupil	teeth	ailing	callus
jowls	purge	thigh	albino	cancer
lance	quack	throb	alexia	canker
lazar	rabid	throe	amytal	caries
leech	ramus	thumb	anemia	carpus
leper	raphe	tibia	anemic	cavity
liver	renal	tired	angina	cervix
local	rheum	tonic	anoint	chafed
locum	salts	tooth	antrum	chiasm
lungs	salve	torso	apnoea	choler
lymph	scalp	trace	areola	chorea
lysis	seedy	tract	armpit	clavus
mamma	senna	treat	arnica	clinic
medic	serum	trunk	artery	clonus
medic	shell	tummy	asthma	coccyx
miasm	shock	ulcer	ataxia	codein
molar	sight	ulnar	atocia	coelom
mouth	sinew	uncus	attack	comedo
mumps	sinus	unfit	aurist	concha
nasal	skull	urine	axilla	corium
navel	sleep	uvula	balsam	cornea
nerve	sling	vagus	bedpan	corpse
nevus	smart	valve	benign	cortex
nurse	sopor	villi	biceps	coryza

costal	fungus	lotion	peptic	septic
cowpox	gargle	lumber	phlegm	serous
crisis	goitre	lunula	phobia	sicken
crusta	gripes	maimed	physic	sickly
crutch	grippe	malady	pimple	simple
cuboid	growth	marrow	plague	sister
cuneus	gullet	matron	plasma	slough
damage	hallux	measly	pleura	sneeze
dartre	hammer	meatus	plexus	spatum
deadly	healer	medico	poison	spinal
defect	health	medius	poorly	spleen
demise	hearty	megrim	potion	splint
dengue	hernia	member	ptisan	spotty
dental	heroin	meninx	puncta	sprain
dermis	humour	mentum	pyemia	squint
doctor	immune	miasma	queasy	stapes
dorsum	infirm	midrib	quinsy	stasis
dosage	injury	mongol	rabies	stigma
dossil	inpain	morbid	rachis	stitch
dropsy	instep	mucous	radial	strium
eczema	insula	muscle	ranula	stroke
elixir	intern	mutism	reflex	struma
embryo	iodine	myopic	relief	stupor
emetic	kidney	naevus	remedy	stylet
engram	labial	nasion	retina	suffer
eschar	labour	nausea	rhesus	suture
eyelid	laidup	needle	rictus	tablet
fascia	lambda	neuron	robust	tampon
fester	lancet	nipple	roller	tarsus
fibula	lappet	oculus	sacrum	temple
figure	larynx	opiate	saliva	tender
fillip	lavage	osteal	scrape	tendon
finger	lesion	palate	scurvy	tetter
foetus	lichen	pallor	seeing	thorax
fornix	lipoma	papule	senses	throat
fundus	lobule	pelvis	sepsis	throes

thrush	airsick	calcium	decease
thymus	alcohol	calomel	decline
ticker	allergy	camphor	deltoid
tingle	allheal	cannula	dentist
tisane	ampulla	capsule	derange
tissue	anaemia	carcass	disease
tongue	anaemic	cardiac	draught
tragus	analyst	carious	earache
tremor	anatomy	carrier	eardrum
trepan	anodyne	carsick	ear|lobe
trocar	antacid	cascara	earshot
troche	antigen	catarrh	epithem
tumour	aphasia	cautery	erosion
twinge	aphonia	chalone	ethmoid
unwell	apraxia	chancre	eyeball
ureter	arcanum	chemist	eyebrow
vector	aspirin	chiasma	eyewash
vesica	assuage	cholera	failing
vessel	atebrin	chorion	fantasy
villus	atrophy	choroid	fatigue
viscus	auricle	chronic	febrile
vitals	autopsy	ciliary	feel|ill
vomica	bacilli	cocaine	feeling
voyeur	bandage	cochlea	femoral
weaken	bedfast	colicky	fibroid
weakly	bedsore	colitis	fidgets
wrench	bilious	condyle	filling
writhe	bismuth	cordial	fimbria
xyster	bladder	coroner	fistula
zygoma	blister	cranium	flushed
abdomen	booster	cricoid	foramen
abscess	bow|legs	cripple	forceps
acidity	bromide	cupping	forearm
aconite	bubonic	cure|all	frailty
adrenal	bulimia	cuticle	freckle
ailment	cadaver	deathly	frontal

MEDICINE

game|leg	linctus	panacea	rubeola
gastric	lockjaw	papilla	run|down
glasses	lozenge	paresis	rupture
gumboil	lumbago	parotid	saccule
haggard	malaise	passage	sarcoma
hashish	malaria	pass|out	scabies
heal|all	malleus	patella	scalpel
healing	massage	patient	scapula
healthy	masseur	pessary	scratch
hearing	mastoid	phalanx	seasick
hipbone	maxilla	pharynx	seconal
history	measles	pigment	section
hormone	medical	pill|box	seizure
hospice	medulla	pinkeye	seltzer
hot|bath	menthol	placebo	sensory
humerus	microbe	plaster	sick|bay
hygiene	midwife	pledget	sickbed
icterus	milk|leg	podagra	sinking
illness	mixture	pterion	skin|man
incisor	myringa	punctum	soother
innards	nail|bed	pustule	spastic
insides	nervous	putamen	spitoon
insulin	nostril	pyaemia	springs
invalid	nostrum	pylorus	stammer
ischium	obesity	pyramid	sterile
jawbone	occiput	pyretic	sternum
jejunum	oculist	pyrexia	stirrup
jugular	omentum	quassia	stomach
kneecap	operate	quinine	stutter
kneepan	orbital	regimen	sublime
laid|low	orderly	relapse	sulphur
lanolin	organic	removal	sun|bath
lazaret	osseous	reviver	sun|lamp
lentigo	ossicle	ribcage	surgeon
leprosy	otology	rickets	symptom
leprous	ovaries	rubella	syncope

syntone	vitamin	backache	collapse
syntony	whitlow	backbone	comatose
syringe	witless	bacteria	compress
tactile	zymotic	baldness	confined
taenial	abnormal	barbital	contract
take|ill	abortion	beriberi	coronary
talipes	abrasion	bicuspid	critical
tampion	accident	bifocals	crutches
tapetum	acidosis	bile|duct	curative
tear|bag	acromion	bistoury	cyanosis
tetanus	adenoids	black|eye	cynanche
theatre	adhesion	black|out	dandruff
theriac	agar|agar	bleeding	deathbed
thermae	agraphia	blind|eye	debility
thyroid	albinism	blockage	decrepit
toenail	allergic	brachial	delicate
tonsils	allopath	break|out	delirium
tormina	alopecia	bulletin	delivery
toxemia	amputate	caffeine	dentures
trachea	analysis	cannabis	diabetes
travail	anatomic	carditis	diagnose
triceps	antibody	casualty	digestif
trional	antidote	cataract	diplegia
typhoid	aperient	catching	disabled
unction	apoplexy	catheter	diseased
unguent	aposteme	cathexis	disgorge
unsound	appendix	cephalic	disorder
urethra	appetite	cerebral	dispense
utricle	arteries	cervical	diuretic
vaccine	Asian|flu	choleric	dog|tired
vapours	asphyxia	cicatrix	dosology
variola	assuager	clavicle	dressing
veronal	asthenia	clinical	drop|dead
verruca	atropine	club|foot	druggist
vertigo	autacoid	cockeyed	drumhead
viscera	bacillus	cold|sore	ductless

duodenum	glycerin	lethargy	ointment
ecraseur	grand|mal	leukemia	olive|oil
edgebone	hair,ball	ligament	operator
embolism	handicap	ligature	otoscope
emulsion	hard|drug	lincture	overdose
enceinte	hay|fever	liniment	pancreas
engramma	headache	lip|salve	pandemia
entrails	heat|lamp	lobotomy	papillae
epidemic	heat|spot	lordosis	parasite
epilepsy	heel|bone	love|drug	parietal
epiploon	hemostat	malarial	paroxysm
eruption	hip|joint	mal|de|mer	pectoral
erythema	holotony	mandible	peduncle
etiology	homesick	marasmus	pellagra
excision	hospital	masseter	perspire
exit|dose	hot|flush	masseuse	petit|mal
exposure	houseman	maturant	phalange
eye|drops	immunity	medicate	pharmacy
eye|patch	impetigo	medicine	philtrum
eyesalve	impotent	membrane	phthisis
eyesight	incision	midbrain	physical
eye,tooth	infected	migraine	physique
face|lift	inflamed	morphine	pia|mater
first|aid	inhalant	muscular	pick,me,up
flat|feet	inner|ear	mycology	pisiform
follicle	insomnia	naked|eye	placenta
forehead	internal	narcosis	pleurisy
fracture	iron|lung	narcotic	podagric
freak|out	irritant	necrosis	podiatry
frenulum	jaundice	nembutal	posology
fumigant	languish	neoplasm	poultice
furuncle	laudanum	neuritis	practice
gallipot	laudanum	nosogeny	pregnant
ganglion	lavement	nosology	premolar
gangrene	laxative	novocain	prenatal
glaucoma	lenitive	numbness	procaine

prostate	skin|dose	trachoma
pulmonic	smallpox	traction
pump|room	smarting	trephine
purblind	soft|drug	true|skin
pus|basin	somatist	tubercle
pyorrhea	soothing	tumerous
reaction	soreness	tympanum
receptor	sore|spot	ulcerous
Red|Cross	specimen	unciform
remedial	speculum	uroscopy
resident	sphenoid	vaccinia
rest|cure	sphygmus	valerian
ringworm	splenium	variolar
roborant	stinging	vascular
salivary	stitches	vaseline
sanatory	striatum	vena|cava
scaphoid	subacute	venotomy
scarring	sudarium	vertebra
sciatica	sufferer	vesicant
scrofula	surgical	vitality
secretin	swelling	vomiting
sedation	take|sick	wall|eyed
sedative	tear|drop	wandered
senility	tear|duct	weakling
serology	teething	wet|nurse
shinbone	temporal	admission
shingles	teratoma	adrenalin
shoulder	thalamus	aitchbone
sick|abed	the|bends	alcoholic
sickling	thin|skin	alkalizer
sickness	thoracic	alleviate
sickroom	thyroxin	allopathy
sinapism	tingling	amaurosis
skeletal	tocogony	ambulance
skeleton	tocology	analeptic
skin|deep	toponymy	analgesia

analgesic	callipers	cough|drop
anamnesis	callosity	crash|diet
anklebone	calmative	cretinism
ankylosis	calvities	cross,eyed
antenatal	cankerous	cuneiform
antihelix	carbuncle	curvature
antiserum	carcinoma	dead|faint
antitoxin	cartilage	dead|tired
arthritis	caruncula	defective
aspirator	case|sheet	delirious
assuasive	castor|oil	demulcent
audiology	catalepsy	dentistry
auriscopy	cataplasm	depth|dose
bacterium	cataplexy	diagnosis
bandaging	catatonia	diaphragm
barbitone	catatonic	diarrhoea
bath|chair	catch|cold	diathermy
bedridden	catharsis	dichotomy
bellyache	cathartic	diet|sheet
birthmark	cauterize	digitalis
blackhead	cheekbone	discharge
blindness	chilblain	dispenser
blind|spot	chin|cough	distemper
blood|bank	chiropody	dizzy|turn
blood|bank	cicatrice	dosimeter
blood|test	cirrhosis	dosimetry
blue,blood	claustrum	drain|tube
body|odour	cleansing	dropsical
boric|acid	collyrium	dura|mater
bow,legged	complaint	dysentery
brain|cell	condition	dyspepsia
breakdown	conscious	dyspeptic
broken|arm	contagion	dystrophy
broken|leg	contusion	echolalia
Caesarean	corpuscle	electuary
calenture	cortisone	emaciated

embrocate	gladiolus	lazaretto
emergency	glandular	leucocyte
emollient	glycerine	life|force
endocrine	halitosis	long|sight
endolymph	hammer|toe	lymphatic
energumen	hamstring	malar|bone
ephedrine	heartbeat	malignant
epidermis	heartburn	malleolus
epileptic	histamine	manubrium
epiphyses	homeopath	marihuana
esotropia	horehound	marijuana
exotropia	hunchback	maternity
extremity	idiopathy	maxillary
eye|doctor	ill|health	medicated
eyelashes	impatient	medicinal
faith|cure	incubator	mesentery
fallopian	incurable	mesocolon
fallotomy	infection	middle|ear
false|ribs	infirmary	midwifery
febrifuge	infirmity	milk|teeth
febrility	influenza	mongolism
festering	ingestion	morbidity
fetishism	inhalator	mortified
fever|heat	injection	mouthwash
fever|ward	injection	nappy|rash
flatulent	inoculate	narcotics
fore|brain	in|plaster	nasal|duct
frostbite	invalided	nauseated
fumigator	iron|pills	near|sight
fungosity	iron|tonic	nebulizer
funny|bone	isolation	neophobia
gastritis	jail|fever	nephritis
gathering	king's|evil	nerve|cell
geriatric	knee|joi.nt	neuralgia
germicide	labyrinth	neurology
give|birth	lachrymal	neuropath

noncompos	prescribe	sudorific
nutrition	prognosis	suffering
nux|vomica	prophasis	sunstroke
nystagmus	psoriasis	suppurant
occipital	pulmonary	sweat|bath
off|colour	purgative	syntectic
officinal	purifying	taste|buds
olfactory	quadratus	tear|gland
on|the|mend	rachidial	tegmentum
operation	radiogram	thanatoid
optic|disc	radiology	therapist
optometry	resection	thighbone
osteology	sartorius	thyrotomy
osteopath	sassafras	toothache
otologist	sauna|bath	toothpick
pacemaker	sclerosis	trapezium
paralysis	sclerotic	trapezius
paregoric	sebaceous	treatment
parotitis	secretion	tricuspid
pathology	seediness	tummy|ache
perilymph	semi|lunar	umbilical
pertussis	sensorium	umbilicus
pesthouse	sinusitis	unguentum
phagocyte	skingraft	unhealthy
phalanges	soporific	urticaria
phlebitis	spare|part	vaccinate
phrenetic	splay|feet	varicella
physician	squeamish	varicosis
pin|and|web	squinting	venectomy
pituitary	sterilize	ventricle
pneumeter	stiff|dose	vermifuge
pneumonia	stiff|neck	vertibrae
poisoning	stillborn	vestibule
pollution	stimulant	vulnerary
precuneus	stretcher	washed|out
premature	subsultus	waste|away

water|cure	blood|group	cystectomy
wax|glands	bloodstain	cystoscope
wellbeing	bloody|flux	dandy|fever
wristbone	bonesetter	danger|list
xeroderma	brain|fever	deathwatch
X|ray|plate	breastbone	dentifrice
zoophobia	breathless	dermatitis
zooplasty	broken|bone	dim|sighted
abirritant	broken|dose	diphtheria
abreaction	broken|nose	dipsomania
acetabulum	bronchitis	dirty|nurse
acrophobia	buccinator	disability
Adam's|apple	canker|rash	discomfort
aerophobia	castration	disfigured
affliction	catalepsis	dispensary
afterbirth	catholicon	dizzy|spell
algophobia	cerebellum	doraphobia
alimentary	chickenpox	draw|breath
amputation	chloroform	drop|serene
anesthesia	chromosome	drug|addict
ankle|joint	cibophobia	ear|trumpet
antibiotic	collarbone	ectodermal
antipoison	commissure	elbow|joint
antisepsis	common|cold	emaciation
antiseptic	compulsion	embonpoint
antitragus	concussion	embryology
apoplectic	consultant	emplastrum
apothecary	contagious	enclampsia
applicator	convalesce	entodermal
astragalus	convulsion	epispastic
barium|meal	corn|doctor	epithelium
batophobia	corrective	Epsom|salts
belladonna	cotton|wool	ergophobia
Black|Death	cough|syrup	erotomania
blood|count	cyclothyme	eructation
blood|donor	cynophobia	euthanasia

extraction	indisposed	metatarsus
faith|curer	infectious	microscope
false|teeth	inhibition	monophobia
farsighted	insolation	mutilation
feebleness	inspirator	nail|matrix
fever|pitch	instrument	narcissist
fibrositis	interferon	nauseation
fine|fettle	internship	nerve|fibre
fingernail	intestines	nettle|rash
five|senses	invalidate	neuropathy
flatulence	invalidism	night|float
fonticulus	invalidity	night|nurse
foot|doctor	irritation	nosophobia
gallstones	kill|or|cure	obstetrics
gamophobia	kiss|of|life	odontogeny
gastrotomy	knock|knees	oesophagus
geriatrics	laboratory	optic|nerve
gripe|water	laceration	optic|tract
haunch|bone	laparotomy	orthopraxy
healing|art	laryngitis	orthoscope
health|farm	lassa|fever	ossiferous
hearing|aid	last|breath	osteoblast
heatstroke	lazar|house	osteoclast
hemaglobin	leechcraft	osteopathy
hematology	lethal|dose	out|of|sorts
hemiplegia	loss|of|life	outpatient
hemisphere	lymph|gland	overweight
hemophilia	main|stream	oxygen|mask
hemophobia	medical|man	oxygen|tank
homeopathy	medicament	oxygen|tent
hot|springs	medicaster	padded|cell
hypodermic	medication	paediatric
hypodermis	meningitis	painkiller
idiopathic	mesogaster	palliative
immunology	metabolism	paraphasia
Indian|hemp	metacarpus	paraplegia

paronychia	resistance	strychnine
pathognomy	respirator	sublingual
pediatrics	rheumatics	suprarenal
pediatrist	root,sheath	sweat gland
penicillin	rude health	teratology
periosteum	salivation	thrombosis
peritoneal	salt,cellar	tonic spasm
peritoneum	sanatorium	toothpaste
pestilence	sanitarian	toponymics
pharmacist	saucer eyes	tourniquet
phenacetin	scarlatina	toxicology
phlebotomy	scrofulous	transplant
physiology	semeiology	traumatism
pigeon,toed	semeiotics	trochanter
pineal body	sense organ	truth serum
plague spot	septicemia	tumescence
podiatrist	serologist	ulceration
polychrest	short sight	urinalysis
polyclinic	sick as a dog	varicotomy
poor health	sickliness	vesicotomy
post,mortem	sixth sense	veterinary
premaxilla	soft palate	Vichy water
presbyopia	somatology	vital force
prevention	sore throat	vital spark
preventive	specialist	vocal cords
prognostic	spectacles	wheel chair
protective	sphacelate	witch hazel
public ward	spinal cord	wonder drug
pyretology	spirograph	xenophobia
radiograph	spirometer	yellow jack
radiometer	splanchnic	yellow spot
radioscopy	squint eyes	abnormality
radium bath	staff nurse	abortionist
ray therapy	sterilizer	airsickness
recuperate	strabismus	amphetamine
regression	strict diet	anaesthesia

anaesthetic
an|apple|a|day
antifebrile
antipyretic
aphrodisiac
application
arteriotomy
astigmatism
auscultator
bactericide
barbiturate
basket|cells
blood|stream
blood|stroke
blood,vessel
booster|dose
breaking|out
caesarotomy
canine|tooth
cardiograph
carminative
car,sickness
case|history
cephalalgia
chemiatrist
chiroplasty
chiropodist
chiropraxis
choroid|coat
circulation
cleft|palate
coconscious
cod|liver|oil
cold|therapy
colour|blind
confinement

conjunctiva
consumption
consumptive
contact|lens
convolution
convulsions
corn|plaster
decrepitude
deep|therapy
deobstruent
dermaplasty
dermatology
diagnostics
diaphoretic
dislocation
dull,sighted
eccrinology
Elastoplast
elixir|vitae
embrocation
endocardium
examination
exoskeleton
expectorant
extremities
face|lifting
facial|nerve
famine|fever
fatty|tissue
fibre|optics
fingerstall
floating|rib
fluoroscope
fomentation
gall,bladder
gastrectomy

gerontology
gild|the|pill
gnawing|pain
gold|therapy
granule|cell
growing|pain
gynaecology
haemorrhage
handicapped
healthiness
health|salts
heart|attack
hebephrenia
hectic|fever
hectic|flush
heteropathy
Hippocratic
hormonology
horse|doctor
hospital|bed
hospitalize
hydrophobia
indigestion
inoculation
internal|ear
intravenous
ipecacuanha
irradiation
isodose|line
jugular|vein
kidney|basin
laparoscopy
laughing|gas
locum|tenens
long,sighted
lycanthropy

256

malfunction	physiognomy	temperature
median|nerve	plaster|cast	therapeutic
medicine|man	prickly|heat	thermometer
miracle|drug	private|ward	the|sniffles
miscarriage	probationer	tonsillitis
mitral|valve	prognostics	tooth|powder
mortal|wound	prophylaxis	transfusion
musculature	quack|remedy	trench|fever
nasopharynx	quacksalver	trench|mouth
naturopathy	rabbit|fever	tumefaction
nearsighted	radiography	Turkish|bath
nerve|ending	radiologist	unconscious
nerve|supply	radiopraxis	vaccination
neurologist	radiothermy	venesection
neuroplasty	respiration	warm|springs
neutralizer	restorative	water|canker
nursing|home	rheumaticky	wisdom|tooth
nyctophobia	rhinoplasty	X|ray|machine
observation	rigor|mortis	X|ray|therapy
obstruction	roentgen|ray	yellow|fever
obtometrist	running|nose	aero|embolism
orthodontia	sal|ammoniac	alexipharmic
orthopaedic	sal|volatile	alpha|blocker
orthopedics	schizoidism	anaesthetist
orthopedist	seasickness	anthropotomy
palpitation	senile|decay	appendectomy
Pandora's|box	skin|disease	appendicitis
parathyroid	solar|plexus	aquapuncture
parturition	stethoscope	at|death's|door
pathologist	stirrup|bone	athlete's|foot
pelvic|colon	stomach|ache	auscultation
peptic|ulcer	stomach|pump	bacteriology
pericardium	stomatology	balm|of|Gilead
peristaltic	sudden|death	bill|of|health
peritonitis	suppuration	bismuth|salts
pharyngitis	surgeon's|saw	black|and|blue

bloodletting	gastric|juice	neurasthenia
breath|of|life	gastroplasty	obstetrician
casualty|ward	geriatrician	optic|chiasma
central|canal	grinding|pain	orthodiagram
chemotherapy	gynecologist	orthodontics
chiropractic	hair|follicle	orthodontist
chiropractor	hair|restorer	orthopaedics
cold|compress	health|resort	orthopaedist
come|down|with	heart|disease	ossification
complication	heart|failure	palpitations
conditioning	hydropathist	parasitology
constipation	hydrotherapy	parietal|bone
consultation	hypertension	parotid|gland
convalescent	hysterectomy	pediatrician
coronary|vein	iatrochemist	pelvic|girdle
cough|mixture	iatrophysics	perspiration
countervenom	immunization	pestilential
court|plaster	immunologist	pharmaceutic
critical|list	inflammation	pharmacology
curietherapy	integral|dose	pharmacopeia
debilitation	intoxication	phlebotomist
dietotherapy	island|of|Reil	phototherapy
disinfectant	knock|out|drop	pigmentation
electrolysis	laser|surgery	prescription
elixir|of|life	light|therapy	preventative
emergency|bed	lock|hospital	prophylactic
encephalitis	lose|one's|head	psychrometer
endoskeleton	lose|strength	purblindness
faith|healing	loss|of|memory	radiosurgery
fallen|arches	major|surgery	radiotherapy
family|doctor	malnutrition	radiotherapy
felinophobia	mammary|gland	reflex|action
fever|blister	minor|surgery	rehabilitate
feverishness	morbid|growth	resectoscope
formaldehyde	muscle|fibres	respirometer
friar's|balsam	natural|death	resuscitator

robust|health
rubber|gloves
scarlet|fever
serum|therapy
sesamoid|bone
shaking|palsy
shock|therapy
shooting|pain
shortsighted
simple|reflex
sleep|inducer
sleeping|pill
sleepwalking
slimming|diet
solar|therapy
somnambulism
sphygmograph
sphygmometer
spinal|column
spotted|fever
stabbing|pain
straitjacket
streptomycin
student|nurse
St|Vitus|dance
subcutaneous
surgical|boot
suture|needle
therapeutics
therapeutist
thyroid|gland
tonsillotomy
trained|nurse
tranquillize
tuberculosis
turn|a|deaf|ear

varicose|vein
violent|death
vitreous|body
water|blister
word|deafness
zinc|ointment
actinotherapy
adenoidectomy
anaphrodisiac
anastigmatism
anticoagulant
antihistamine
antiscorbutic
bacteriolysin
bacteriolysis
bacteriolytic
bacteriophage
blood|pressure
brainsickness
bubonic|plague
cardiac|arrest
cardiographer
cauterisation
confined|to|bed
contraception
contraceptive
convalescence
dental|surgery
dentist's|chair
dermatologist
diagnostician
Down's|syndrome
encephalogram
endocrinology
fertility|drug
fever|hospital

259

field dressing
field hospital
food poisoning
gentian violet
German measles
group practice
gynaecologist
haematologist
healthfulness
health service
health visitor
heat treatment
homoeopathist
indisposition
intensive care
kidney machine
medicine chest
paediatrician
pharmaceutics
pharmaceutist
pharmacopoeia
physicianship
physiognomist
physiotherapy
poliomyelitis
psychotherapy
second opinion
smelling salts
styptic pencil
tonsillectomy
tranquilliser
whooping cough
X ray apparatus
antaphrodisiac
anticonvulsant
antilymphocyte

antiseptically
appendicectomy
blood poisoning
breathlessness
Bright's disease
carcinogenesis
carcinological
cardiovascular
conjunctivitis
consulting room
contagiousness
cross infection
cystic fibrosis
dangerously ill
encephalograph
family planning
hole in the heart
housemaid's knee
house physician
infectiousness
medical officer
medical student
medicine bottle
milk of magnesia
national health
night blindness
operating table
pasteurisation
pharmaceutical
pharmacologist
phenobarbitone
pins and needles
plastic surgeon
plastic surgery
pneumoconiosis
rheumatic fever

surgical|spirit
travel|sickness
ankylostomiasis
anorexia|nervosa
antenatal|clinic
aversion|therapy
blackwater|fever
cerebrovascular
clearing|station
cottage|hospital
counter|irritant
delirium|tremens
dental|treatment

dressing|station
falling|sickness
gastroenteritis
general|practice
Hippocratic|oath
manic|depressive
morning|sickness
physiotherapist
psychotherapist
sleeping|draught
sticking|plaster
third|degree|burn

Meteorology

ice	wind	rainy	dry|air
icy	blast	sleet	flatus
low	blowy	storm	fogbow
blow	chill	sunny	freeze
cold	clime	windy	haboob
gale	cloud	Aeolus	hot|air
gust	Eurus	aurora	hot|day
haar	foggy	boreal	isobar
heat	front	Boreas	isohel
hoar	frost	breeze	nimbus
rain	gusty	breezy	red|sky
rime	hoary	brumal	samiel
smog	humid	chilly	serein
snow	misty	cirrus	simoom
thaw	muggy	cloudy	squall
warm	rains	degree	stormy

stuffy	squally	fresh|air
sultry	subzero	haziness
trades	sweltry	head|wind
aeolian	tempest	heat|haze
air|mass	the|blue	heatwave
aureola	thunder	heavy|sky
backing	tornado	high|wind
blue|sky	typhoon	humidity
bluster	veering	ice|storm
chinook	warm|air	isobront
clement	washout	isocheim
climate	weather	isocryme
cold|air	Beaufort	isothere
cumulus	black|ice	isotherm
current	blizzard	libeccio
cyclone	blow|over	low|cloud
drizzle	clear|day	moderate
drought	clear|sky	occluded
element	climatic	overcast
freshen	cloud|cap	pressure
gregale	cold|snap	rain|belt
grey|sky	cold|wave	rain|drop
ice|cold	cold|wind	rainfall
icy|wind	cyclonic	rainy|day
ill|wind	dew|point	scorcher
isohyet	doldrums	snowfall
khamsin	downpour	sunburst
mistral	east|wind	sunlight
monsoon	elements	sunshine
nebulae	Favonius	west|wind
pea|soup	favonian	wind|belt
rainbow	fireball	wind|cock
raining	firebolt	wind|cone
showery	fohn|wind	wind|vane
sirocco	forecast	anemology
sizzler	freezing	anemostat

barometer	northwind	clearskies
baroscope	norwester	cloudatlas
belowzero	occlusion	cloudburst
blueskies	overcloud	cloudiness
bourasque	raincloud	coastalfog
brilliant	raingauge	coolbreeze
cloudbank	rainspout	drivensnow
cloudcover	rainstorm	dryingwind
coldfront	rimefrost	Euroclydon
coldspell	sandblast	frontallow
corposant	sanddevil	gentlewind
dustdevil	sandspout	glaciation
duststorm	sandstorm	hailstones
fogginess	snowflake	hotweather
frostbite	snowstorm	hyetograph
galeforce	snowunder	hyetometer
hailstone	soueaster	hygrometer
hailstorm	southwind	insolation
hardfrost	souwester	nebulosity
harmattan	tradewind	nubilation
heavyrain	turbulent	ombrometer
highcloud	warmfront	powdersnow
hoarfrost	weakfront	radiosonde
hurricane	whirlwind	sharpfrost
inclement	williwaws	snowflurry
JackFrost	windgauge	snowsquall
lapserate	windiness	stormblast
levinbolt	windscale	stormcloud
lightning	windspeed	stormtrack
Londonfog	windstorm	strongwind
middaysun	windswept	summerheat
mildspell	anemometer	turbulence
mistiness	antitrades	weathereye
nephology	atmosphere	weatherman
nimbosity	blackfrost	weathermap
noreaster	Capedoctor	wetweather

wind|sleeve
anticyclone
arctic|front
cats|and|dogs
cirrus|cloud
cold|weather
driving|rain
evening|mist
flaming|June
fresh|breeze
frigid|zones
frontal|zone
frozen|stiff
frozen|water
gale|warning
ground|frost
harvest|moon
hunter's|moon
hydrometeor
hyperborean
light|breeze
lowering|sky
low|pressure
mackerel|sky
meteorology
monsoon|wind
northeaster
northwester
pluviometer
pouring|rain
precipitate
rainy|season
sheet|of|rain
snow|blanket
snow|crystal
southeaster

southwester
spell|of|rain
storm|centre
temperature
tempestuous
thermograph
thermometer
thunderball
thunderbolt
thunderclap
thunderpeal
weathercock
weathervane
bitterly|cold
blow|up|a|storm
cirro|cumulus
cirro|stratus
cumulo|cirrus
cumulo|nimbus
cumulus|cloud
etesian|winds
freezing|cold
high|pressure
Indian|summer
keraunograph
macroclimate
meteorograph
microclimate
migratory|low
moderate|wind
nephelometer
offshore|wind
piercing|wind
pressure|belt
pressure|wave
rainy|weather

snow|blizzard
thundercloud
thunderstorm
volcanic|wind
weather|chart
weather|gauge
weatherglass
wind|velocity
Beaufort|scale
climatography
climatologist
cumulostratus
electric|storm
meteorologist
thunder|shower
weather|report

weather|symbol
aurora|borealis
further|outlook
meteorological
roaring|forties
sheet|lightning
weather|prophet
weather|station
bolt|from|the|blue
forked|lightning
prevailing|winds
rain|cats|and|dogs
summer|lightning
tropical|climate
weather|forecast

Military Leaders

Lee	Alfred	Patton	Fairfax
Byng	Attila	Petain	Raleigh
Foch	Balboa	Pompey	Saladin
Haig	Beatty	Raglan	Sherman
Slim	Caesar	Rodney	Tirpitz
Blake	Cortes	Rommel	Wallace
Clive	Franco	Rupert	Wingate
Dayan	Gordon	Wavell	Agricola
Drake	Halsey	Allenby	Aurelian
Keyes	Ireton	Blucher	Burgoyne
Moore	Jervis	Bradley	Cardigan
Tromp	Moltke	Doenitz	Crockett
Wolfe	Nelson	Dowding	Cromwell

265

MILITARY LEADERS

Hannibal	MacArthur
Jellicoe	Montezuma
Lawrence	Trenchard
Leonidas	Abercromby
Montcalm	Alanbrooke
Montrose	Belisarius
Napoleon	Caractacus
Pershing	Clausewitz
Potemkin	Cornwallis
Runstedt	Eisenhower
Stilwell	KublaiKhan
Woodward	Montgomery
Alexander	Wellington
Bonaparte	Charlemagne
Glendower	Collingwood
Grenville	GenghisKhan
Hasdrubal	Marlborough
JoanofArc	Mountbatten
Kitchener	ChiangkaiShek

Minerals

gem	lode	tufa	fluor	steel
ore	marl	tuff	gault	stone
tin	mica	vein	ingot	topaz
coal	onyx	zinc	magma	wacke
clay	opal	agate	metal	basalt
gold	rock	alloy	ochre	bronze
iron	ruby	beryl	shale	cerium
jade	salt	borax	slack	chrome
lava	spar	coral	slate	cobalt
lead	talc	flint	sleet	copper

erbium	azurite	mineral	diggings
flinty	bauxite	niobium	dolerite
Flysch	biotite	olivine	dolomite
gabbro	bornite	peridot	epsomite
galena	breccia	pigiron	europium
gangue	cadmium	pyrites	euxenite
garnet	calcite	realgar	feldspar
gneiss	calcium	rhenium	fineness
gypsum	cat'seye	sulphur	fireopal
indium	chuckie	terbium	fluorite
iolite	citrine	thorium	gemstone
jargon	diabase	thulium	girasole
jasper	diamond	tinmine	golddust
kaolin	diorite	tripoli	goldmine
maltha	emerald	uranium	goldrush
marble	epidote	wolfram	graphite
molten	felspar	yttrium	gritrock
morion	gallium	zeolite	hematite
nickel	girasol	zincite	idocrase
oroide	gothite	amethyst	ilmenite
osmium	granite	amygdule	inkstone
pewter	hafnium	antimony	ironclay
pumice	holmium	argonite	lazurite
pyrite	hyalite	asbestos	limonite
quarry	igneous	autunite	liparite
quartz	iridium	basanite	lutecium
radium	ironore	brookite	metallic
rutile	ironpan	castiron	monazite
scoria	jacinth	chlorite	mudstone
silica	jargoon	chromite	mylonite
silver	kerogen	chromium	nephrite
spinel	kyanite	cinnabar	obsidian
zircon	lignite	corundum	platinum
adamant	lithium	cryolite	plumbago
apatite	lithoid	dendrite	polonium
asphalt	mercury	dibstone	porphyry

MINERALS

pumicite	brimstone	marlstone
pyroxene	burrstone	metalloid
rhyolite	cairngorm	microlite
rock|salt	carbuncle	milkstone
rubidium	carnelian	mispickel
samarium	carnotite	moonstone
sapphire	china|clay	morganite
sardonyx	diatomite	neodymium
scandium	dripstone	ozocerite
selenite	elaterite	palladium
siderite	flagstone	pegmatite
smelting	fluorspar	periclase
steatite	fool's|gold	petroleum
stibnite	freestone	petrology
sunstone	gemmology	petrology
tantalum	germanium	phenolite
thallium	goldstone	plutonium
tinstone	granulite	quartzite
titanium	gritstone	rhodonite
trachyte	haematite	ruthenium
traprock	ironstone	sandstone
tungsten	jackstone	scheelite
vanadium	jadestone	semimetal
volcanic	kaolinite	slabstone
xenolith	laccolite	soapstone
alabaster	laccolith	spodumene
aluminium	lanthanum	strontium
americium	lapideous	tellurium
amphibole	limestone	turquoise
anglesite	lithology	uraninite
aragonite	magnesite	vulcanite
argentite	magnesium	wulfenite
base|metal	magnetite	ytterbium
beryllium	malachite	zirconium
blacklead	manganese	adamantine
brilliant	marcasite	adder|stone

268

aquamarine	raremetals
aventurine	rosequartz
bloodstone	sheetmetal
brownstone	silvermine
chalcedony	slingstone
chalkstone	smokestone
chessylite	snakestone
chrysolite	spinel|ruby
clinkstone	stinkstone
common|salt	technetium
copper|mine	touchstone
drakestone	tourmaline
dysprosium	wolframite
eaglestone	alexandrite
gadolinium	cassiterite
glauconite	chrysoberyl
globulites	chrysoprase
graptolite	clinochlore
greenstone	country|rock
heliotrope	earth|metals
hornblende	gravelstone
lead|glance	hatchettite
lithomarge	igneous|rock
meerschaum	iron|pyrites
metallurgy	lapis|lazuli
mica|schist	layer|of|rock
mineralogy	lithosphere
mineral|oil	Lydian|stone
molten|lava	mineral|coal
molybdenum	mineral|salt
noble|metal	mineral|vein
ore|deposit	molybdenite
orthoclase	native|stone
peacock|ore	peristalith
pitchstone	petrography
promethium	pissasphalt

pitchblende
potter's clay
quarrystone
quicksilver
rock crystal
sarsen stone
schistosity
stone circle
vermiculite
vesuvianite
volcanic ash
alkali metals
anthraconite
argillaceous
arsenopyrite
black diamond
chalcopyrite
coal measures
duraluminium
electroplate
fuller's earth
metal fatigue
mineral pitch
native metals
oriental opal
praesodymium
protactinium

red sandstone
residual clay
star sapphire
wollastonite
carboniferous
chrome plating
cinnamon stone
copper pyrites
metalliferous
metallurgical
millstone grit
mineralogocal
petrification
Portland stone
quartz crystal
smokeless fuel
copper bottomed
electroplating
metallographer
mineral deposit
mineral kingdom
open cast mining
plaster of Paris
Portland cement
quartz porphyry
stainless steel
Old Red Sandstone

Money

as   bob   mag   pie   sol   yen
bit   écu   mil   sen   sou   anna

270

bean	fiver	nickel
buck	franc	peseta
cash	grand	rouble
cent	groat	scudos
chip	krona	sequin
coin	krone	shekel
dime	louis	solidi
doit	mohur	specie
kyat	noble	stater
lira	obang	stiver
mark	paolo	tenner
merk	pence	tester
mill	penny	teston
mint	piece	thaler
mite	pound	cordoba
obol	rupee	crusado
peso	sceat	denarii
plum	semis	drachma
pony	soldo	exergue
quid	sucre	guilder
rand	toman	ha'penny
real	verso	milreis
reis	aureus	moidore
rial	bawbee	nummary
ryal	copeck	obverse
thou	copper	pfennig
angel	denier	piastre
asper	dollar	red|cent
belga	drachm	reverse
colon	escudo	sawbuck
conto	florin	sceatta
crown	guinea	sextans
daric	gulden	smacker
dinar	kopeck	solidus
ducat	lepton	ten|spot
eagle	monkey	testoon

two|bits	half‚noble
base|coin	halfpenny
cruzeiro	pistareen
denarius	rose‚noble
didrachm	schilling
doubloon	sovereign
farthing	tremissis
gold|coin	yellow|boy
groschen	zwanziger
louis|d'or	reichsmark
napoleon	sestertius
new|pence	threepence
new|penny	double|eagle
picayune	silver|penny
planchet	sixpenny|bit
quadrans	base|shilling
semissis	imperial|coin
semuncia	piece|of|eight
shilling	quarter‚noble
short|bit	silver|dollar
sixpence	brass|farthing
ten|cents	half|sovereign
tuppence	pieces|of|eight
twopence	ten‚dollar|bill
zecchino	almighty‚dollar
dupondius	coin|of|the|realm
fourpence	debased|coinage
fourpenny	decimal|coinage
gold|crown	half‚a‚sovereign
gold|penny	half‚pennyworth
gold|piece	fifty‚pence|piece
half‚crown	handful|of|silver
half‚eagle	

Mountains

K2	Dartmoor	Monte Rosa
Alps	Demavend	Nanda Devi
Jura	Hymettus	Pikes Peak
Altai	Ida, Mount	Puy de Dome
Andes	Jungfrau	Ras Dashan
Eiger	Krakatoa	Ruwenzori
Ghats	Nevis, Ben	Stromboli
Hekla	Pennines	Zugspitze
Urals	Pyrenees	Arakam Yoma
Ararat	Tien Shan	Cader Idris
Exmoor	Vesuvius	Cairngorms
Kunlun	Aconcagua	Chimborazo
Pamirs	Allegheny	Coast Range
Pindus	Apennines	Dent du Midi
Vosges	Catskills	Elgon, Mount
Brocken	Chilterns	Kenya, Mount
Helicon	Cook, Mount	Khyber Pass
Mendips	Cotswolds	Sinai, Mount
Nan Ling	Dolomites	St Gotthard
Nan Shan	Erzebirge	Adirondacks
Rockies	Etna, Mount	Brenner Pass
Skiddaw	Grampians	Brooks Range
Snowdon	Helvellyn	Carmel, Mount
Sudeten	Himalayas	Drakensberg
Caucasus	Hindu Kush	Elbert, Mount
Cevennes	Huascaran	Elbrus, Mount
Cheviots	Meru, Mount	Erebus, Mount
Chirripo	Mont Blanc	Hermon, Mount
Cotopaxi	Mont Cenis	Katmai, Mount

MOUNTAINS

Kazbek, Mount
Kilimanjaro
Koryak Range
Lammermuirs
Mendip Hills
Nanga Parbat
Scafell Pike
Sierra Madre
Simplon Pass
Appalachians
Cheviot Hills
Gran Paradiso
Illampu, Mount
Kanchenjunga
Monte Cassino
Olympus, Mount
Palomar, Mount
Peak District
Popocatépetl
Rainier, Mount
Roraima, Mount
Ruapehu, Mount
Schiehallion
Sierra Nevada
Triglav, Mount
Whitney, Mount
Blue Mountains
Brecon Beacons

Cameroun, Mount
Chiltern Hills
Cotswold Hills
Grossglockner
Harz Mountains
Kinabalu, Mount
Massif Central
McKinley, Mount
Mitchell, Mount
Mount of Olives
move mountains
Riesengebirge
Sierra Maestra
Stanovoi Range
Sulaiman Range
Table Mountain
Black Mountains
Cleveland Hills
Galty Mountains
Karakoram Range
Kosciusko, Mount
Ozark Mountains
Parnassus, Mount
Snowy Mountains
White Mountains
Mourne Mountains
Taurus Mountains
Zagros Mountains

Muses

Music

A	me	hay	sax	blow	harp
B	op	hey	ska	brio	hi,fi
C	pp	hit	soh	clef	horn
D	re	hum	sol	coda	hymn
E	sf	jig	tie	dash	jack
f	te	key	uke	disc	jazz
F	ut	kit	wax	disk	jive
G	act	lah	alap	diva	jota
p	air	lay	alto	drum	juba
DC	bar	lip	arco	duet	keen
do	bop	lur	aria	dump	lead
DS	bow	nut	ayre	fife	lied
EP	cat	ode	band	fine	lilt
fa	cue	ped	bard	flat	lira
ff	doh	pes	base	flue	lure
fp	dot	pop	bass	form	lute
gu	duo	rag	beat	fret	lyra
la	fah	ray	bell	glee	lyre
LP	gue	run	bind	gong	mass

275

MUSIC

mode	tune	corno	luter	proms
mood	turn	crook	lyric	psalm
mute	vamp	croon	major	pulse
neck	viol	dance	march	quint
node	wait	desto	melic	range
noel	wind	dirge	metre	rebec
note	wood	disco	mezzo	reeds
oboe	work	ditty	minim	regal
open	ad|lib	dolce	minor	resin
opus	album	drone	modal	rondo
part	A\side	drums	motet	rosin
peal	assai	elegy	motif	round
pick	atone	Erato	musak	rumba
port	banjo	etude	music	runic
Prom	basso	fancy	naker	scale
raga	baton	farce	nebel	scena
rank	bebop	fifer	neume	score
reed	bells	fifth	ninth	segno
reel	belly	final	nonet	segue
rest	blues	flute	notes	shake
rock	bones	forte	octet	sharp
roll	brass	fugue	odeon	shawm
root	brawl	galop	opera	siren
rote	breve	gamba	organ	sixth
scat	B\side	gamut	paean	slide
sing	bugle	gigue	pause	snare
slur	canon	grace	pavan	sol\fa
solo	canto	grave	pedal	sordo
song	carol	ictus	piano	sound
stop	cello	idyll	piece	space
time	chant	jazzy	piper	staff
tone	chime	jodel	pitch	stave
toot	choir	kyrie	pleno	Strad
trio	chord	large	pluck	strum
tuba	close	largo	point	study
tuck	comma	lento	polka	suite

276

swell	accent	damper	legato	rounds
swing	accord	decani	Lieder	rubato
tabla	adagio	diesis	lutist	scorer
table	almain	direct	lyrist	second
tabor	almand	do,re,mi	manual	sempre
tacet	answer	double	maxixe	septet
tambo	anthem	drones	medley	sestet
tango	Apollo	dulcet	melody	sextet
tempo	arioso	ecbole	minuet	shanty
tenor	a|tempo	eighth	monody	shofar
theme	atonal	encore	motion	singer
third	aubade	euphon	motive	snatch
throb	ballad	fading	musico	sonata
thrum	ballet	fiddle	needle	spinet
tonic	bolero	figure	nobile	stanza
touch	bowing	finale	nowell	strain
triad	bridge	firing	oboist	string
trill	bugler	fourth	octave	subito
troll	burden	fugato	off|key	syrinx
trope	cadent	giusto	ottava	tabret
tuned	can,can	graces	pavane	tampon
tutti	cantor	grazia	period	tam,tam
up|bow	cantus	great|C	phrase	tattoo
valse	catchy	guitar	pipe|up	temper
valve	catgut	hammer	piston	tenor|C
verse	chanty	harper	player	tenuto
vibes	chimes	hepcat	presto	tercet
viola	choral	horner	quaver	terzet
voice	chorus	hymnal	racket	timbal
volta	cither	hymner	rattle	timbre
volte	citole	in|tune	rebeck	tom,tom
waits	cornet	jingle	record	tooter
waltz	corona	keener	reggae	top|ten
winds	cue,ing	kettle	repeat	treble
woods	cymbal	lament	rhythm	tromba
yodel	da|capo	leader		troppo

tucket	bazooka	codetta	furlana
tune|up	bellows	compass	fuzzbox
tuning	bombard	compose	gavotte
tymbal	bourdon	con|brio	giocoso
tympan	bourrée	concert	gradual
unison	brasses	concord	G|string
up|beat	bravura	conduct	halling
vielle	buccina	con|moto	harmony
violin	cadence	consort	harpist
vivace	cadency	cornett	hautboy
voices	cadenza	cornist	hit|song
waxing	calando	coupler	hit|tune
zambra	calypso	Cremona	hornist
zither	cantata	crooner	hot|jazz
zufolo	canzona	curtall	humming
agitato	canzone	cymbals	hymnist
allegro	caprice	descant	hymnody
althorn	carioca	discord	intrada
andante	celesta	double|C	introit
animato	cellist	doubles	ivories
arietta	cembalo	down|bow	juke|box
arrange	chanson	drummer	keening
art|song	chanter	episode	key|note
attacca	chantry	euphony	Landler
attuned	chikara	Euterpe	lullaby
bagpipe	chiming	fagotto	maestro
ballade	chorale	fanfare	mandola
bandman	chorine	fermata	mandora
bandore	chorist	fiddle|G	marcato
bar|beat	cithara	fiddler	marimba
bar|line	cithern	flutina	mazurka
baryton	cittern	fluting	measure
bassist	clapper	flutist	mediant
bassoon	clarion	forlana	melisma
battery	classic	fox|trot	melodia
battuta	clavier	furioso	melodic

278

middle|C	refrain	taboret	a|piacere
mixture	reprise	tambura	archlute
mordent	requiem	tangent	arpeggio
morendo	respond	the|Nine	arranger
musette	ribible	theorbo	Ave|Maria
musical	ripieno	timbrel	bagpiper
natural	romance	timpani	bagpipes
ocarina	rondeau	tirasse	bandsman
octette	rondino	toccata	banjoist
offbeat	rosalia	top|note	baritone
one|step	roulade	tracker	barytone
organum	sackbut	treble|C	base|clef
Orpheus	salicet	tremolo	base|note
pandora	sambuca	triplet	base|viol
pandore	samisen	tritone	bass|drum
pandura	Sanctus	trumpet	bass|horn
Panpipe	saxhorn	tuneful	bass|oboe
partial	saxtuba	two|step	beat|time
passage	scherzo	ukelele	berceuse
pas|seul	scoring	ukulele	boat|song
pesante	septuor	upright	bouffons
piacere	serpent	vespers	Calliope
pianist	service	vibrato	canticle
pianola	seventh	vihuela	canticum
pibroch	singing	violist	cantoris
piccolo	skiffle	violone	canzonet
piffero	soloist	warbler	carillon
pomposo	song|hit	war|song	cavatina
pop|song	soprano	wassail	chaconne
potlids	sordino	whistle	chanting
prelude	stopped	ziganka	choirboy
Psalter	stretto	Agnus|Dei	choirman
quartet	strings	alto|clef	choragus
quintet	subject	alto|horn	choregus
ragtime	syncope	alto|viol	clappers
recital	taborer	antiphon	clarinet

col|legno	fantasie	leggiero	Panpipes
composer	flautist	libretto	parallel
con|amore	flip|side	ligature	parlando
concerto	flourish	love|song	parlante
continuo	flue|pipe	low|pitch	part|song
coronach	flue|work	lutanist	pastoral
courante	folderol	madrigal	phantasy
cromorna	folk|rock	maestoso	phrasing
cromorne	folk|song	maggiore	pianette
crooning	galliard	major|key	pianiste
crotchet	gemshorn	mazurka	Pierides
cylinder	glee|club	mean|tone	pipe|tune
dal|segno	habanera	measured	plangent
diapason	half|rest	melodeon	plectron
diapente	hand|bell	melodica	plectrum
diatonic	harmonic	melodics	pop|group
doh|rayme	harp|lute	melodist	pop|music
doloroso	hornpipe	minor|key	post|horn
dominant	humstrum	minstrel	postlude
downbeat	hymeneal	moderato	psalmody
doxology	hymn|tune	monotone	psaltery
drumbeat	in|accord	movement	raga|rock
drumhead	in|chorus	musicale	ragtimer
drumskin	interval	music|box	recorder
duettino	in|unison	musician	reed|pipe
duettist	jazz|band	nocturne	reed|stop
dulciana	jazzed|up	notation	register
dulcimer	jew's|harp	open|note	response
emphasis	jongleur	operatic	reveille
ensemble	Jubilate	operetta	rhapsody
entr'acte	keyboard	oratorio	rigadoon
faburden	key|bugle	organist	ritenuto
falderal	last|post	ornament	saraband
falsetto	lay|clerk	ostinato	scordato
fandango	lay|vicar	overtone	semitone
fantasia	left|hand	overture	semplice

septette	tone|down	antiphony
sequence	tone|poem	arabesque
serenade	tone|poet	archilute
serenata	tonguing	aria|buffa
sextette	tonic|key	baby|grand
sextolet	triangle	bagatelle
side|drum	trombone	balalaika
sing|song	trouvere	ballerina
sliphorn	tunester	band|major
sol|faist	tympanon	bandstand
solo|stop	una|corda	banjolele
sonatina	vamp|horn	barcarole
songbird	Victrola	blow|a|horn
song|book	virginal	blues|song
songplay	virtuosa	bombardon
songster	virtuosi	bow|fiddle
sour|note	virtuoso	brass|band
spianato	vocalion	bugle|call
spinette	vocalism	bugle|horn
squiffer	vocalist	cacophony
staccato	Vorspiel	cantabile
strike|up	warbling	cantilena
strummer	wind|band	capriccio
strummer	woodwind	carolling
swan|song	yodeller	castanets
swell|box	zambomba	celestina
symphony	zarzuela	chalumeau
tamboura	a|cappella	chantress
tenor|cor	accompany	charivari
tenoroon	accordion	choralist
terzetto	acoustics	chorister
the|Muses	adagietto	chromatic
threnody	ad|libitum	citharist
tonalist	alla|breve	clarionet
tonality	allemande	classical
tone|deaf	andantino	claviharp

concentus	folk|music	larghetto
conductor	fugue|form	leger|line
consonate	full|close	Leitmotiv
contralto	full|organ	lyric|bass
cornopean	full|score	lyrichord
crescendo	glissando	major|mode
croon|song	grace|note	malaguena
cymbalist	grandioso	mandoline
dance|band	Gregorian	mediation
dance|form	guitarist	melodious
dead|march	half|close	melodrama
death|song	hand|bells	melomania
diaphonia	hand|organ	metronome
dithyramb	harmonica	mezza|voce
double|bar	harmonics	minor|mode
drone|bass	harmonist	modulator
drum|corps	harmonium	monochord
drum|major	harmonize	monophony
drumstick	head|voice	music|hall
dulcitone	hexachord	music|roll
duple|time	high|pitch	music|room
echo|organ	hit|parade	music|wire
ecossaise	homophony	mute|pedal
entrechat	hymnology	obbligato
epicedium	imitation	octachord
epinicion	impromptu	offertory
euphonium	improvise	open|notes
execution	inflexion	open|score
extempore	interlude	orchestra
farandole	invention	organ|stop
figurante	inversion	orpharion
fine|toned	jazz|stick	out|of|tune
fingering	jitterbug	overtones
flageolet	kent|bugle	part|music
flute|a|bec	krummhorn	pas|de|deux
folk|dance	langspiel	passepied

pasticcio	right|hand	tabor|pipe
pastorale	rondo|form	tail|piece
pedal|note	roundelay	tambourin
performer	saxcornet	tempo|mark
piacevole	saxophone	tenor|clef
piangendo	scherzoso	tenor|drum
piano|keys	scrapegut	tenor|horn
pianolist	semibreve	tenor|tuba
piano|wire	semitonic	tenor|viol
pipe|organ	seraphine	tessitura
pitch|pipe	serenader	theme|song
pizzicato	sforzando	theorbist
plainsong	shantyman	time|value
play|by|ear	siciliana	timpanist
polonaise	signature	top|twenty
polychord	singspiel	torch|song
polyphony	sink|a|pace	transpose
pop|record	slow|march	tremulant
potpourri	smerzando	triangles
precentor	soap|opera	trumpeter
principal	soft|pedal	tuning|bar
programme	solfeggio	tympanist
prolation	solo|organ	tymp|stick
promenade	song|sheet	undertone
quadrille	sonometer	variation
quartette	sostenuto	viola|alto
quintette	sotto|voce	violin|bow
quodlibet	sound|hole	violinist
recording	sound|post	virginals
reed|organ	spiritoso	virtuosic
remote|key	spiritual	vocalizer
rendering	stockhorn	voice|part
rendition	succentor	Volkslied
resonance	swing|band	voluntary
rhythmics	symphonic	vox|humana
ricercare	tablature	waltz|time

whole|note	bull|fiddle	double|time
whole|rest	cancionero	drummer|boy
whole|step	cancrizans	dulcetness
whole,tone	canto|fermo	Eisteddfod
wind|chest	canzonetta	enharmonic
wind|music	chest|voice	euphonious
wind|trunk	chime,bells	exposition
woodwinds	chitarrone	expression
wrestpins	choir|organ	five,finger
wrong|note	chorus|girl	Flugelhorn
xylophone	cinquepace	folk|singer
zitherist	clavichord	fortepiano
accidental	coloratura	fortissimo
adaptation	comic|opera	French|harp
added|sixth	common|time	French|horn
affettuoso	concertina	golden|disc
allargando	concertino	grace|notes
allegretto	concertist	gramophone
alteration	concordant	grand|opera
antiphoner	conducting	grand|piano
attunement	consonance	great|organ
background	con|sordini	great|stave
ballad|horn	contrabass	Greek|modes
band|leader	cor|anglais	grind|organ
band|master	cornettist	ground|bass
band,waggon	Coryphaeus	harmonicon
barcarolle	cradlesong	harmonizer
basset|horn	dance|music	homophonic
basset|oboe	diminuendo	hornplayer
bassoonist	diminution	horse|opera
bell,ringer	disc|jockey	humoresque
Benedictus	dissonance	hurdy,gurdy
binary|form	doodlesack	incidental
bottom|note	dotted|note	instrument
brass|winds	double|bass	intermezzo
bridal|hymn	double|flat	intonation

jam session	musical ear	quick march
kettledrum	music lover	recitalist
leger lines	music maker	recitative
light music	musicology	recitativo
light opera	music paper	related key
long player	music stand	repertoire
lyre guitar	oboe d'amore	repetition
lyric drama	opera buffa	resolution
lyric tenor	opera score	responsory
mainstream	ophicleide	rhapsodist
major chord	orchestral	ritardando
major scale	organ point	ritornelle
major sixth	patter song	ritornello
major third	pedal board	round dance
major triad	pedal organ	sacred Nine
manuscript	pedal point	salicional
marimbaist	pentachord	saltarello
melody part	pentatonic	saxotromba
mezzo forte	percussion	scherzando
mezzo piano	perdendosi	scordatura
minor canon	phonograph	Scotch snap
minor chord	pianissimo	seguidilla
minor scale	pianoforte	semichorus
minor sixth	pianologue	semiquaver
minor third	piano score	set to music
minor triad	piano stool	shaped note
minstrelsy	piccoloist	sheet music
mixed times	plagal mode	short score
modal scale	Polyhymnia	silver disc
modern jazz	polyphonic	simple time
modulation	ponticello	sonata form
mouth music	pop concert	song leader
mouth organ	popular air	songstress
mouthpiece	portamento	songwriter
musical bow	prima donna	sound board
musical box	proportion	sousaphone

speaker|key	tweedledum	concertante
squeeze|box	twelve|note	concert|band
Stradivari	union|pipes	concert|hall
strathspey	variations	consecutive
street|band	vibraphone	contrapunto
stringendo	villanella	contredanse
submediant	vocal|music	counterbase
supertonic	vocal|score	damper|pedal
suspension	accelerando	decrescendo
swell|organ	accompanist	descant|viol
swell|pedal	Aeolian|harp	discography
symphonion	alla|tedesca	discotheque
symphonist	arrangement	divided|stop
syncopated	ballad|maker	dominant|key
syncopator	ballad|opera	Dorian|modes
tambourine	barrel|organ	dotted|minim
tarantella	bass|passage	double|chant
tetrachord	beat|a|tattoo	double|fugue
tin|whistle	beat|the|drum	double|sharp
tone|poetry	bell|ringing	double|touch
tonic|chord	blues|singer	dulcet|tones
tonic|major	broken|chord	ear|for|music
tonic|minor	calliophone	English|horn
tonic|sol,fa	campanology	equal|voices
transcribe	canned|music	eurhythmics
transition	capriccioso	extemporize
treble|clef	cat's|concert	faux|bourdon
treble|viol	chansonette	fiddlestick
tremolando	chanterelle	fife|and|drum
triple|time	choirmaster	figured|bass
trombonist	clarinetist	finger|board
troubadour	clarion|call	fipple|flute
tuning|fork	clavicymbal	first|fiddle
tuning|pipe	common|chord	first|violin
tuning|wire	compact|disc	French|pitch
tweedledee	composition	French|sixth

fundamental	opera|ballet	sacred|music
funeral|song	opera|bouffe	saxophonist
German|flute	orchestrate	scat|singing
German|sixth	orchestrion	Schottische
golden,toned	organophone	Scotch|catch
graphophone	organ|player	short|octave
great|octave	over|blowing	silver,toned
half|cadence	Pandean|pipe	singing|sand
harmonizing	partial|tone	small|octave
harpsichord	part|playing	solmization
hunting|horn	part|singing	soprano|clef
inscription	part|writing	sound|in|tune
in|the|groove	passacaglia	square|piano
keyed|guitar	passing|bell	Stabat|Mater
leading|note	passing|note	stopped|pipe
long|playing	percussives	street|organ
Lydian|mode	performance	street|piano
madrigalist	piano|player	string|music
major|second	piano,violin	string|plate
mandolinist	pitch|accent	subdominant
mellifluent	plagal|modes	sweet,voiced
mellifluous	player|piano	synchronism
mellisonant	polyphonism	syncopation
Minnesinger	popular|tune	temperament
minor|second	preparation	tempo|giusto
mixed|voices	prestissimo	ternary|form
morris|dance	progression	Terpsichore
musical|ficta	psalm|singer	time|pattern
musical|copy	quarter|note	Tin|Pan|Alley
musical|joke	quarter|rest	tonic|accent
musical|note	ragtime|band	torch|singer
music|lesson	rallentando	transposing
music,loving	relative|key	tunefulness
music|school	Requiem|mass	tuning|slide
nickelodeon	retardation	vicar|choral
normal|pitch	rock|and|roll	viola|d'amore

viol|da|gamba	concert|pitch	light|harmony
violin|pipe	Concertstuck	lyric|cantata
violoncello	conservatory	major|seventh
vivacissimo	contrapuntal	marching|song
voix|celeste	counterpoint	martial|music
wedding|song	counter|tenor	mean|semitone
willow|pipes	country|dance	medieval|mode
acciaccatura	cushion|dance	mellifluence
accompanyist	divertimento	melodic|minor
accordionist	dominant|note	mezzo,soprano
acoustic|bass	dotted|quaver	military|band
agogic|accent	drinking|song	minor|seventh
anticipation	extended|play	minstrel|song
appassionata	extravaganza	mixed|cadence
appoggiatura	false|cadence	monochordist
augmentation	fiddlesticks	musical|scale
balladmonger	fiddlestring	musical|score
ballad|singer	florid|phrase	musicianship
banjo|ukelele	funeral|march	musicologist
bass|baritone	glockenspiel	mutation|stop
bass|clarinet	gravicembalo	opening|notes
bass|trombone	harmonichord	opera|comique
beat|a|retreat	harmonic|tone	orchestra|pit
boogie|woogie	hidden|fifths	orchestrator
brass|section	hurdy|gurdist	organ|grinder
chamber|music	hymnographer	parlour|grand
chamber|organ	improvisator	passion|music
changing|note	instrumental	penny|whistle
chest|of|viols	introduction	perfect|fifth
chorus|singer	inverted|turn	perfect|pitch
clavicembalo	Italian|sixth	philharmonic
comedy|ballet	ivory|thumper	Phrygian|mode
compound|time	ivory|tickler	piobaireachd
concert|grand	jazz|musician	pipe|and|tabor
concertinist	key|signature	polytonality
concert|music	less|semitone	popular|music

reciting|note	choir|practice
record|player	choral|society
registration	choreographer
repercussion	concrete|music
rhythmic|mode	conductorship
sarrusophone	conservatoire
sesquialtera	contrabassoon
singl i n|chorus	contrafagotto
skiffle|group	contrapuntist
slow|movement	cornet|a|piston
speaking|stop	corps|de|ballet
steam|whistle	electric|organ
Stradivarius	Gregorian|mode
street|singer	harmonic|scale
stress|accent	kapellmeister
symphonic|ode	kettledrummer
tape|recorder	meistersinger
theatre|organ	melodiousness
thorough|bass	musicological
tintinnabula	orchestration
tone|measurer	piano|concerto
tone|painting	recorded|music
top|of the|pops	rhythm|section
tromba|marina	signature|tune
trumpet|major	singing|master
upper|partial	staff|notation
upright|piano	string|quartet
viola|da|gamba	string|quintet
vocalization	symphonic|poem
wedding|march	time|signature
wind|musician	transposition
Zigeunerlied	twelve|tone|row
accompaniment	violoncellist
American|organ	ballet|mistress
capellmeister	chromatic|scale
cello|concerto	

classical music	wind instrument
concerto grosso	Bachelor of Music
contrary motion	background music
demisemiquaver	Christy minstrel
double stopping	concert overture
electric guitar	concert platform
male voice choir	electronic music
musical prodigy	flutter tonguing
music publisher	incidental music
negro spiritual	instrumentalist
open air concert	instrumentation
piano accordion	Moog synthesiser
plantation song	perfect interval
reed instrument	string orchestra
smoking concert	symphony concert
violin concerto	

Mythology

Anu	Gog	nis	Sol	Adad	Ares
Ate	Hel	nix	Sri	Aeon	Argo
Aya	Hob	Nox	Tem	Afer	Askr
Bel	Ida	Nut	Tiu	Agni	Aten
Bor	imp	Nyx	Tiw	Ajax	Aton
Cos	Ino	obi	Tum	Alea	Auge
dea	Ira	Ops	Tyr	Amen	Baal
Dia	Leo	Ore	Ull	Amor	Bast
Dis	Ler	Oya	Vac	Amun	Bora
elf	Lok	Pan	Van	Anax	Bran
Eos	Lug	Ran	Zan	Anna	Bron
fay	Mab	Seb	Zio	Anta	Buto
god	Mot	Set	Ziu	Apis	Ceto

4/5 LETTERS

Ceyx	Hera	Ment	Tiki	Atlas	Dione
Civa	Hero	Mors	Troy	Atman	Diral
Clio	Hler	Muse	tyro	Baldr	Dirce
Cora	Hodr	Nabu	Ullr	Batea	Donar
deil	Hora	Naga	Upis	Belus	Dorus
deus	Hoth	Nana	Urth	Bhaga	Draco
Deva	huma	Nebo	Vach	bogey	dryad
Devi	icon	Neph	Vale	Bragi	Durga
Dewa	idol	Nike	Vali	Brute	dwarf
Dian	Idun	Nona	Vans	Cabal	Dyaus
Dido	Ilus	Norn	Vayu	Cacus	Dylan
Dike	Inar	Nott	Vili	Canis	Dymas
Echo	Iole	Odin	Wate	Capta	Egill
Edda	Iris	ogre	Yama	Caria	Ehlis
Eden	Isis	peor	yeti	Carpo	elves
Enyo	jinn	peri	Ymir	Ceres	Enlil
Erda	jinx	Ptah	Zemi	Cerus	Epona
Eric	joss	Puck	Zeus	Cetus	Erato
Eris	Jove	Rahu	Zion	Chaos	Erlik
Eros	juju	Rama	Aegir	charm	Etara
Erua	Juno	Rhea	aegis	Circe	Eurus
Fate	Kali	Rind	Aegle	Coeus	fable
Faun	Kama	Saga	Aeson	Comus	Fagus
Fons	kami	Sati	afrit	coven	fairy
Frey	Kapi	seer	Algol	Creon	Fauna
Fria	Leda	Seth	Ammon	Creus	Faust
Frig	Leto	Shri	angel	Crius	fetch
Fury	Loke	Siva	Arcas	Cupid	fiend
Gaea	Loki	Soma	Arges	Dagda	Flora
Gaia	Luna	Spes	Argos	Dagon	Freya
Gerd	Lyra	Styx	Argus	Damia	Frigg
Gere	magi	tabu	Ariel	Danae	Gauri
Goll	Maia	Tara	Aries	deify	genie
Hapi	mana	Tare	Arion	deity	ghost
Hebe	Mara	Thea	Artio	Devil	ghoul
hell	Math	Thor	Athor	Diana	giant

291

MYTHOLOGY

Gibil	Kotys	Notus	theos	Aglaia
gnome	Laius	nymph	Thoth	Alecto
Grace	lamia	obeah	Thrym	Alseid
Gyges	Lamos	Orcus	Thule	Amazon
Hadad	Lares	oread	Titan	Amen,Ra
Hades	larva	Orion	totem	Amenti
Harpy	Lepus	ouphe	Troad	Amores
Hatra	Lethe	Paean	troll	amulet
haunt	Liber	pagan	Tyche	Anubis
Helen	Libra	Pales	Uriel	Anytus
Helle	limbo	Parca	Vanir	Apollo
Herse	Lupus	Paris	Varah	Aquila
Hoder	Lycus	Pitys	Venus	Arthur
Holda	Lydia	pixie	Vesta	Asgard
Horae	Magog	Pluto	Vidar	Assama
Horus	magus	Poeas	Virgo	astral
houri	Marut	Priam	Vithi	Athena
Hyads	Mazda	Remus	Wabun	Athene
Hydra	Medea	Robur	weird	Atreus
Hylas	Metis	Satan	Wodan	Attica
Hymen	Midas	satyr	Woden	Auriga
Iasus	mimic	shade	Wotan	Aurora
ichor	Minos	Sheol	Yasna	Auster
Idmon	Moira	Shiva	zombi	Avalon
Iliad	Momos	Shree	Adonai	avatar
Indra	Momus	Sibyl	Adonis	Azrael
Irene	Morna	Sinon	Aeacus	Babbar
Irmin	Morta	siren	Aeetes	Balder
Istar	naiad	Siris	Aegeus	Baldur
Ister	Nanna	spell	Aegina	Baucis
Janus	Nerio	spook	Aeneas	Belial
Jason	Ninos	Surya	Aeneid	Beulah
jinni	Niobe	sylph	Aeolus	Bootes
Karna	nisse	taboo	Aethra	Boreas
kelpy	nixie	Terra	afreet	Brahma
Komos	Njord	Theia	Agenor	brewer

292

6 LETTERS

Buddha	Freyia	Isolde	Nereus	Saturn
Cabiri	Freyja	Ithunn	Nergal	Sciron
Cadmus	Frigga	jinnee	Nessus	Scylla
Cancer	Ganesa	jumart	Nestor	sealgod
Castor	Garuda	kelpie	Nimrod	Sekume
Chandi	Gawain	kobold	numina	Selene
Charis	Gemini	kraken	Oberon	Semele
Charon	genius	Kronos	obiman	seraph
cherub	Geryon	Laputa	occult	Simios
Chiron	goblin	Libera	Oeneus	Sinbad
Clotho	Gorgon	Lilith	ogress	Sirius
Corona	Graces	Locris	Oileus	skygod
Corvus	Graeae	Lucina	OldNed	Somnus
Crater	Haemon	Lugaid	Ondine	Sparta
Creusa	Hathor	maenad	oracle	Sphynx
Cronus	heaven	Mammon	Ormuzd	spirit
Crotus	Hebrus	manito	Osiris	sprite
Cybele	Hecate	Marduk	Ossian	Stator
Cygnus	Hector	Marmar	Pallas	Stheno
daemon	Hecuba	mascot	panisc	Strymo
Danaus	Hekate	Medusa	panisk	sungod
Daphne	Helios	Megara	Parcae	syrinx
Decuma	Hermes	Memnon	Peleus	Tammuz
dragon	Hobbit	Mentor	Pelias	Taurus
durgan	Hoenir	Merlin	Pelops	Tellus
Egeria	hoodoo	merman	Phocis	Tethys
Eirene	Hyades	Merope	Phoebe	Teucer
Epirus	Hyllus	Mithra	Pisces	Thalia
Erebus	Iasion	Moerae	Placia	Thallo
Erinys	Iasius	Moirai	Pollux	Thebus
Erotes	Icarus	Molech	Pontus	Themis
Etolia	Indara	Moloch	Pothos	Thetis
Europa	Iolcus	Myrrha	Psyche	thrall
Euryte	Iseult	nectar	Pythia	Thunor
Faunus	Ishtar	Neleus	Python	Titans
fetish	Ismene	Nereid	Rhodus	Tithon

Tityus	Ali Baba	Camelot	Eurytus
Tonans	Amphion	cantrip	Euterpe
Tophet	Antaeus	Capella	evil eye
Triton	Antenor	Cecrops	Evil one
Tydeus	Anteros	centaur	Faustus
Typhon	Antiope	Cepheus	firegod
undine	Aquilon	Cercyon	Fortuna
Urania	Arallis	charmer	Gabriel
Uranus	Arcadia	Chemosh	Galahad
Utopia	Argolis	chimera	Galatea
Varuna	Ariadne	Chloris	Gehenna
Vesper	Artemis	Cisseus	giantry
Victor	Astarte	Clymene	Glaucus
Vishnu	Athamas	Cocytus	Glitnir
vision	Atropos	Curetes	goatgod
voodoo	Avallon	cyclops	goddess
Vulcan	Avernus	Cynthia	godling
war god	Axierus	Cyzicus	gremlin
wizard	Azapane	Deasura	griffin
wraith	Bacchus	Deipyle	griffon
Wyvern	bad luck	Demeter	halfgod
Yahweh	bad peri	demigod	Hanuman
yelgods	banshee	dervish	Harpies
Zephyr	Bellona	dogstar	Helenus
Zethus	bewitch	Echidna	hellion
zombie	Bifrost	Electra	heroine
Abaddon	Boeotia	Eleusis	Hesione
Achalia	boggart	Elysian	Himeros
Achates	Bona Dea	Epigoni	Horatii
Acheron	Brontes	Erginus	Hygieia
Actaeon	brownie	Erinyes	Iacchus
Ahriman	bugaboo	erlking	Iapetus
Aladdin	bugbear	Eubulus	Icarius
Alcaeus	Cabeiri	Eunomia	Illyria
Alcmene	Calydon	Eupheme	incubus
Alcyone	Calypso	Euryale	inferno

294

Iuturna	OldNick	Savitri	Aidoneus
Jocasta	Olympus	Scorpio	ambrosia
Jupiter	Omphale	seamaid	Ameinias
Krishna	Orestes	Serapis	Anchises
Laertes	Orpheus	Serpens	Antigone
Lakshmi	Orthrus	serpent	Apollyon
Laocoon	Ouranos	Shaitan	Aquarius
Laodice	Pandion	Shamash	Arcturus
Laputan	Pandora	Sigmund	Argestes
Leander	Panthus	Silenus	Argonaut
limniad	Pegasus	sorcery	Arimaspi
Lorelei	Penates	spectre	Asmodeus
Lucifer	Perseus	sylphid	Asterope
Lynceus	Pervati	Taygete	Astraeus
Marsyas	Phaedra	Telamon	Astyanax
Megaera	phantom	Thaumus	Astyoche
Mercury	Philtre	thegods	Atalanta
mermaid	Phineus	Theseus	Atlantis
Michael	Phoebus	Titania	Baalpeor
Midgard	Phoenix	Tristan	bacchant
Miletus	Phorcys	Troilus	badfairy
Minerva	Phryxus	Ulysses	blackart
Mordred	Pleione	unicorn	Briareus
Mycenae	Pluvius	vampire	Cabeirus
Nariman	Procris	warlock	caduceus
Nemesis	Procyon	Wieland	Calliope
Nephele	Proteus	windgod	Callisto
Neptune	Pylades	Zadkiel	Capareus
Nerthus	Pyrrhus	Absyrtus	Castalia
Niflhel	raingod	Achelous	Cephalus
Nirvana	Raphael	Achernar	Cerberus
Nisroch	RigVeda	Achilles	Charites
nymphet	Romulus	Acrisius	cherubim
Oceanid	Sagitta	Adrastus	chimaera
Oceanus	Sammael	Aegyptus	Chrysaor
Oedipus	sandman	Aganippe	chthonic

Cimmerii	false|god	Marathon
Clymenus	Favonius	Marnaran
Cockayne	folklore	Melampus
colossus	Ganymede	Meleager
Corythus	giantess	Menelaus
Cretheus	Glasberg	Mephisto
Curiatii	good|luck	Merodach
Cyclopes	gramarye	Messenia
Cynosura	grimoire	Minotaur
Daedalus	Harmonia	morganes
Danaides	Harpinna	Morpheus
Dardanus	hell|fire	Myrtilus
Deiphyle	Hellotis	Nauplius
demiurge	Heracles	Nephthys
demonism	Hercules	Niflheim
Despoina	Hesperis	Odysseus
devaloka	Hiawatha	Oenomaus
devil|god	Himantes	Old|Harry
Diomedes	Horatius	Old|Horny
Dionysus	Hyperion	Olympian
Dioscuri	Iphicles	paganism
dream|god	Juventas	Pan|pipes
earth|god	Kalevala	Pantheon
El|Dorado	Lachesis	Paradise
elf|child	Laconica	Pasiphae
Epicaste	Lancelot	Penelope
Eridanus	Laomedon	Pentheus
Erinnyes	Laputian	Percival
Eriphyle	Leiriope	Pergamus
Erytheia	libation	Periboea
Eteocles	Lilliput	Persides
Eurayale	limoniad	PeterPan
Eurydice	Lycurgus	Phaethon
exorcise	Lyonesse	Philemon
exorcism	magician	Philotis
fabulous	Mahadeva	Pierides

Pittheus	zoolater	Cassandra
Pleiades	zoolatry	Centaurus
Podarces	Acarnania	Cephissus
Polyxena	Aegisthus	Charybdis
Portunus	Agamemnon	chthonian
Poseidon	Agapemone	Cimmerian
Quirinus	Aigialeus	Cleopatra
revenant	Aldebaran	cloudland
Sabazius	Alexander	Cockaigne
Sarpedon	Amphiarus	Concordia
Satanism	Andromeda	cupbearer
sea|nymph	Anticleia	Cupidines
Sharrapu	Aphrodite	Davy|Jones
Sisyphus	archangel	Deianeira
Sleipnir	archfiend	Delphinia
sorcerer	Argus|eyed	Delphinus
Steropes	Aristaeus	Dendrites
succubus	Asclepiad	Deucalion
talisman	Asclepios	devil|lore
Tantalus	Asclepius	diablerie
Tartarus	Ashtaroth	diabolism
Teraphim	Assaracus	Discordia
Thanatos	Astydamia	dreamland
the|Deuce	Atalantis	Electryon
the|Muses	Atargatis	enchanter
the|Seven	Atlantica	Eumenides
Thyestes	Attic|salt	Euphorbus
Tithonus	Autolycus	Excalibur
Tristram	Axiocersa	fairyfolk
Tristran	bacchante	fairyland
Valhalla	Beelzebub	fairy|ring
Valkyrie	bewitcher	Friar|Tuck
werefolk	Black|mass	Gilgamesh
werewolf	brimstone	golden|age
Ygdrasil	Britannia	golden|egg
Zephyrus	cacodemon	good|fairy

297

Great|Bear	Phantasus	Andromache
Guenevere	Philomelo	apotheosis
Guinevere	pied|piper	apparition
hamadryad	Polydorus	Arion's|lyre
Heimdallr	purgatory	Armageddon
Hippocoon	pyrolater	Axiocersus
Hippolyte	pyrolatry	bewitchery
Hobgoblin	Robin|Hood	black|magic
Holy|Grail	Ruritania	broomstick
Houyhnymn	Sangarius	Callirrhoe
Hyppolita	Sarasvati	Canis|major
Ilmarinen	Shangri,la	Cassiopeia
Immortals	sorceress	cast|a|spell
Jagannath	Sthenelus	changeling
Kumarpish	Strategis	Chrysippus
labyrinth	Teiresias	cloven|foot
Launcelot	Telegonus	Cockatrice
love|charm	the|Furies	Coriolanus
lucky|bean	Tisiphone	cornucopia
Lycomedes	totem|pole	Cretan|Bull
Lyonnesse	tree|nymph	Demogorgon
maelstrom	Trojan|War	demonology
magic|wand	Tyndareus	Electryone
magic|word	Ursa|major	Epimetheus
Marspiter	Ursa|minor	Erechtheus
Meilanion	Valkyries	Euphrosyne
Melpomene	Valkyriur	Euroclydon
Mnemosyne	winged|cap	Eurystheus
Myrmidons	wood|nymph	evil|genius
Narcissus	Yggdrasil	evil|spirit
occultism	Zernebock	fairy|queen
Palamedes	Zeus|Pater	Gargantuan
Palladium	Alexandros	ghost|dance
Pandareus	Amphiaraus	Greek|Fates
Parnassus	Amphitrite	hagiolatry
Parthenon	Amphitryon	Happy|Isles

heathen|god	Nebelkappe	sun|worship
heliolater	necromancy	Telemachus
heliolatry	Nemean|lion	the|Dickens
Hellespont	ocean|nymph	the|Tempter
Hephaestus	Oedipus|Rex	Thruthvang
Hesperides	old|soldier	Triangulum
Hippocrene	open|sesame	underworld
hippogriff	Orion's|belt	Vardhamana
hippogryph	Pantagruel	water|nymph
Hippolytus	Peripheles	water|witch
hippomanes	Persephone	white|magic
Hippomenes	Pheidippes	wishing|cap
Hitopadesa	Phlegethon	witchcraft
hocus|pocus	Phosphoros	Wonderland
Hyacinthus	phylactery	Yggdrasill
idolatrous	pipes|of|Pan	abracadabra
idolomancy	Polydectes	Aesculapius
invocation	Polydeuces	amphisbaena
ivory|tower	Polyhymnia	Aonian|fount
Juggernaut	Polymestor	Aonian|mount
Juno|Lucina	Polyneices	Aristomenes
King|Arthur	Polyphemus	bedevilment
leprechaun	Procrustes	Bellerophon
Little|Bear	Prometheus	Britomartis
Little|John	Proserpina	Brobdingnag
lucky|charm	rabbit|foot	Capricornus
lucky|piece	River|of|woe	charmed|life
magic|spell	round|table	demigoddess
Maid|Marion	salamander	demonolatry
Melicertes	Samothrace	enchantment
Memnonides	Santa|Claus	fetch|candle
Menestheus	Saturnalia	fire|worship
Midas|touch	Schamander	flower|nymph
minor|deity	sixth|sense	Gog|and|Magog
mumbo|jumbo	soothsayer	Golden|Bough
myrmidones	St|Nicholas	golden|goose

Gorgon's head	Prester John	Clytemnestra
Happy Valley	Rosicrucian	Doppelganger
Helen of Troy	Sagittarius	Dyanean rocks
hippocampus	Scamandrius	Erichthonius
Hypermestra	second sight	exsufflation
Juno Curitis	Shawandasee	Garden of Eden
Kabibonokka	spellbinder	golden apples
kingdom come	Stygian oath	golden fleece
Locrian Ajax	sylvan deity	Golden Legend
lotus eaters	Symplegades	heavenly host
lycanthrope	Terpsichore	Hesperethusa
magic carpet	the black art	hippocentaur
magic circle	three Graces	horn of plenty
meadow nymph	thunderbolt	household god
medicine man	Triptolemus	Hyperboreans
Megapenthes	Trojan horse	Isle of Apples
moon goddess	tutelary god	Juno Quiritis
Morган le Fay	ultima Thule	Kriss Kringle
mother earth	under a spell	Laestrygones
Mudjekeavis	ware animals	Lake Tritonis
necromancer	water spirit	Land of the Leal
Neoptolemus	water sprite	lap of the gods
nether world	wishing well	Lernean Hydra
Nymphagetes	witch doctor	little people
Orion's hound	wooden horse	Marathon bull
Orion's sword	Achilles heel	Mount Helicon
Pallantides	Aesop's fables	Mount Olympus
Pandemonium	Aladdin's lamp	ordeal by fire
Pandora's box	Amphion's lyre	Pallas Athene
pastoral god	Arcadian hind	Parthian shot
patron saint	Athena Pallas	Periclymenus
Persephassa	Augean stable	Promised Land
Philippides	avenging fury	Rhadamanthus
Philoctetes	Bower of Bliss	Serpentarius
poltergeist	Bull Poseidon	Stygian creek
Polymnestor	Chrysomallus	Stygian gloom

supernatural	metamorphosis
thaumaturgus	Phoebus|Apollo
Thesmophorus	apple|of|discord
vestal|virgin	Jupiter|Pluvius
Wandering|Jew	mythologically
Weird|Sisters	Never|Never|Land
Will|Scarlett	Walpurgis|Night
wishing|stone	Father|Christmas
witches|coven	Gotterdammerung
Augean|stables	Homeric|laughter
Elysian|fields	sword|of|Damocles

Occupations

AB	dux	bard	feed	peon	adult
BA	fan	beak	firm	poet	agent
CA	guy	bear	girl	pope	baker
DD	job	beau	Gman	sage	belle
GP	kid	boss	hack	salt	boots
MA	lad	bull	hand	seer	bosun
MC	man	chap	head	serf	boxer
MD	Mrs	char	hero	silk	buyer
MO	nun	chef	hobo	star	caddy
MP	pay	cook	host	task	cadet
Mr	rep	crew	lass	tyro	canon
PA	sir	cure	lead	wage	chief
PM	spy	dean	magi	ward	chips
BSc	tar	demy	maid	whip	chore
CID	vet	dick	miss	work	clerk
deb	aide	diva	monk	abbot	coach
doc	babe	doxy	page	actor	crier
don	baby	dyer	peer	adman	crone

301

OCCUPATIONS

crony	luter	sewer	bandit	codist
crook	madam	slave	banker	coheir
decoy	major	smith	barber	consul
demon	maker	sower	bargee	coolie
devil	Maori	staff	barker	cooper
diver	mason	tenor	barman	copier
donor	mayor	thief	batman	copper
doyen	medic	tiler	batter	costar
dummy	miner	tommy	beadle	coster
dutch	minor	trade	bearer	couper
elder	model	tramp	beater	cowboy
envoy	nanny	tuner	beggar	Creole
extra	navvy	tutor	beldam	critic
fakir	nurse	uhlan	Berber	curate
felon	odist	usher	bishop	cutler
fence	owner	valet	boffin	cutter
fifer	padre	vicar	bookie	damsel
friar	party	viner	bowman	dancer
Galen	pilot	wages	broker	deacon
garbo	pinup	wench	bugler	dealer
ghost	piper	witch	bursar	debtor
gipsy	posse	woman	busker	deputy
grass	prior	yokel	butler	divine
guard	proxy	youth	cabbie	docker
guest	pupil	abbess	caddie	doctor
guide	quack	admass	caller	double
hewer	quill	airlace	camper	dowser
issue	rabbi	airman	cantor	draper
judge	racer	albino	captor	drawer
juror	rider	alumna	career	driver
laird	rishi	archer	carter	drudge
limey	rival	artist	carver	duenna
local	rover	aupair	casual	editor
locum	saver	aurist	censor	ensign
loser	sawer	author	cleric	escort
lover	scout	backer	client	Eskimo

302

etcher	high‚up	mahout	oracle	rookie
expert	hippie	maiden	orator	runner
fabler	hosier	marine	ostler	sailor
factor	hunter	marker	outlaw	sapper
feeder	hussar	master	packer	sartor
fellow	hymner	matron	parson	savage
fitter	iceman	medico	pastor	savant
flunky	inmate	medium	patron	sawyer
flyman	intern	member	pedlar	scorer
forger	jailer	menial	penman	scouse
friend	jester	mentor	penpal	scribe
fuller	jet‚set	mercer	picket	seadog
gaffer	jobber	mikado	pieman	sealer
gagman	jockey	miller	pirate	seaman
ganger	joiner	minion	pitman	second
gaoler	jumper	mister	plater	seller
garcon	junior	moiler	player	senior
gaucho	junker	monger	Pommie	sentry
German	keener	moppet	porter	server
gigolo	keeper	mortal	potter	sexton
gillie	killer	mummer	prater	shadow
glazer	lackey	munshi	priest	sheila
glover	lancer	musico	punter	shower
golfer	lascar	mystic	purser	shrink
graver	lawyer	nannie	ragman	singer
grocer	leader	native	ranger	sister
grower	lector	Norman	rating	skater
gunman	legate	notary	reader	skivvy
gunner	lender	novice	reaper	skyman
hatter	lessee	nudist	rector	slater
hawker	Levite	nuncio	regius	slavey
healer	limner	oboist	rhymer	slayer
helper	living	odd‚job	rigger	sleuth
herald	lodger	office	ringer	smoker
hermit	lutist	oilman	rioter	sniper
het‚man	lyrist	optime	robber	soutar

OCCUPATIONS

souter	waiter	bandman	citizen
sowter	walkon	barmaid	cleaner
sparks	warden	baronet	climber
squire	warder	bassist	clippie
status	weaver	Bedouin	coalman
stoker	welder	beldame	cobbler
suitor	whaler	bellboy	cockney
sutler	winner	bellhop	colleen
tailor	wizard	bigname	collier
talent	worker	bigshot	colonel
tanner	wright	bitpart	commere
Tartar	writer	blender	company
taster	yeoman	boarder	compere
tatter	abetter	boatman	comrade
teller	abigail	bookman	convert
tenant	acolyte	bouncer	convict
Teuton	acrobat	breeder	copilot
tiller	actress	brigand	copyist
tinker	actuary	builder	copyman
tinner	admiral	burglar	coroner
toiler	adviser	bushman	corsair
trader	almoner	butcher	Cossack
truant	alumnus	buttons	counsel
turner	amateur	callboy	courier
tycoon	analyst	calling	cowherd
typist	apostle	cambist	cowpoke
tyrant	arbiter	captain	creator
umpire	artisan	captive	crofter
urchin	artiste	carrier	crooner
usurer	assayer	cashier	cropper
valuer	athlete	caulker	curator
vanman	attache	caveman	custode
vendor	auditor	cellist	cyclist
verger	aviator	chemist	danseur
victor	bailiff	chindit	daysman
Viking	ballboy	chorist	debater

denizen	gateman	lockman	patient
dentist	general	lookout	patroon
diviner	ghillie	lorimer	pearler
dominie	glazier	maestro	peasant
doorman	gleaner	magnate	pianist
dragoon	grownup	mailman	picador
drayman	gunmoll	manager	pierrot
dresser	gymnast	mariner	pilgrim
driller	handler	marshal	pioneer
drummer	hangman	masseur	planner
dustman	harpist	matador	planter
elogist	haulier	matelot	plumber
embassy	headboy	meatman	poacher
entrant	headman	midwife	poetess
equerry	heckler	milkman	pollman
escapee	heiress	mobsman	poloist
escaper	heroine	mobster	pontiff
esquire	hipster	modiste	poorman
farceur	histrio	monitor	popidol
farcist	hostess	moulder	popstar
farrier	hymnist	mourner	postboy
fiddler	imagist	mudlark	postman
fighter	invalid	navarch	prefect
fireman	Jacktar	newsboy	prelate
flagman	janitor	newsman	premier
flapper	jemedar	oarsman	presser
flesher	juggler	oculist	primate
florist	junkman	officer	printer
footboy	justice	oldsalt	privado
footman	knacker	omnibus	private
footpad	knitter	oratrix	proctor
foreman	knowhow	orderly	proofer
founder	learner	pageboy	prophet
frogman	lineman	painter	protege
furrier	linkboy	partner	provost
gambler	linkman	passman	prowler

305

OCCUPATIONS

puddler	sharper	trooper	banjoist
punster	shearer	trouper	bankrupt
pursuer	sheriff	tumbler	banksman
railman	shopman	turfman	bargeman
rancher	shopper	veteran	baritone
rat|race	showman	viceroy	beadsman
realtor	skinner	vintner	bedesman
redskin	skipper	visitor	bedmaker
referee	soldier	warrior	beginner
refugee	soloist	webster	benefice
regular	soprano	whipper	bigamist
remover	spartan	wiseman	blackleg
rentier	speaker	witness	blind|man
rescuer	spinner	wolf|cub	boardman
reserve	sponsor	woodman	Bohemian
retinue	spotter	woolman	bondsman
rich|man	stand|by	workman	boniface
routine	starlet	abductor	borrower
rustler	starman	adherent	botanist
saddler	starter	adjutant	bowmaker
sagaman	station	advocate	boxmaker
samurai	steward	aeronaut	boy|scout
sandman	stipend	alderman	brakeman
scalper	student	alienist	brunette
scenist	supremo	allopath	bummaree
scholar	surgeon	ambivert	business
scraper	swagman	anchoret	cabin|boy
sea|cook	tapster	armorist	call|girl
sea|king	teacher	armourer	caness
sea|lord	tipster	arranger	cardinal
sea|wolf	tourist	assassin	castaway
seminar	trainee	assessor	ceramist
senator	trainer	attacker	chairman
servant	trapper	attorney	chambers
service	trawler	axemaker	champion
settler	tripper	bagmaker	chandler

306

chaperon	dictator	filmstar	Hebraist
chaplain	diet|cook	finalist	helmsman
choirboy	diocesan	finisher	henchman
cicerone	diplomat	fishwife	herdsman
cicisbeo	director	flatfoot	hijacker
civilian	disciple	flautist	hired|gun
claimant	dogsbody	floorman	hired|man
clansman	domestic	forester	hireling
classman	dragoman	forgeman	home|help
clerkess	druggist	freshman	horseman
clothier	duettist	front|man	hotelier
co,author	educator	fugitive	houseboy
comedian	elegiast	fusilier	hula|girl
commando	embalmer	gangsman	huntsman
commoner	emeritus	gangster	identity
compiler	emigrant	gaolbird	idyllist
composer	emissary	gardener	importer
conjurer	employee	garroter	inceptor
convener	engineer	gendarme	informer
corporal	engraver	goatherd	initiate
coryphee	epic|poet	governor	inkmaker
cottager	essayist	gownsman	inventor
courtier	eulogist	graduate	investor
coxswain	examinee	guardian	islander
creditor	executor	guerilla	jailbird
croupier	explorer	gunmaker	jet|pilot
cupmaker	exponent	gunsmith	jeweller
cutpurse	fabulist	ham|actor	jongleur
dairyman	factotum	handmaid	juvenile
danseuse	falconer	handyman	knife,boy
dead,head	fanfaron	hatmaker	labourer
deck|hand	fanmaker	hawkshaw	landgirl
delegate	farm|hand	haymaker	landlady
deserter	ferryman	head|cook	landlord
designer	figurant	head|girl	landsman
detainee	film|idol	headship	lapidary

OCCUPATIONS

lawagent	modeller	perfumer	retainer
lawgiver	moralist	perjurer	reveller
lawmaker	motorist	picaroon	revenant
laywoman	muleteer	pilferer	reviewer
lecturer	muralist	pillager	rewriter
licensee	murderer	plagiary	rifleman
lifepeer	musician	poetling	rivetter
lifework	narrator	poisoner	roadgang
linesman	naturist	polisher	rotarian
linguist	neophyte	pontifex	rugmaker
listener	netmaker	position	saboteur
logician	newcomer	potmaker	salesman
loiterer	newshawk	practice	salvager
lookeron	nightman	preacher	satirist
lumberer	Norseman	pressman	sawbones
luminary	novelist	prioress	sawsmith
lyricist	objector	prisoner	sciolist
magician	observer	prizeman	scullion
mandarin	occupant	producer	sculptor
mapmaker	official	promoter	seafarer
marauder	onlooker	prompter	seedsman
marksman	opartist	psychist	selector
masseuse	operator	publican	sentinel
mechanic	opponent	pugilist	sergeant
mediator	optician	purveyor	servitor
melodist	oratress	quarrier	shepherd
mercator	ordinand	radarman	shipmate
merchant	organist	ragtrade	shopgirl
milkmaid	overlord	ragwoman	showgirl
millgirl	overseer	receiver	sidekick
millhand	pardoner	recorder	sidesman
milliner	parodist	reformer	silkgown
minister	partyman	reporter	sinecure
ministry	passerby	research	sketcher
minstrel	patentee	resident	skyscout
mistress	penmaker	retailer	smallfry

smuggler	torturer	alchemist
solitary	townsman	anatomist
songster	trainman	anchoress
sorcerer	trappist	anchorite
spaceman	tripeman	annotator
spearman	tunester	announcer
speed|cop	unionist	annuitant
sprinter	union|man	antiquary
stageman	vagabond	apologist
star|turn	valuator	applicant
stockman	vanguard	appraiser
storeman	virtuoso	arch|enemy
stowaway	vocalist	architect
stranger	vocation	archivist
stripper	waitress	art|critic
stroller	ward|maid	art|dealer
stunt|man	wardress	artificer
superior	watchman	assistant
superman	waterman	associate
supplier	wayfarer	astronaut
surveyor	wet|nurse	attendant
survivor	wheelman	authoress
swagsman	whiphand	authority
tallyman	whipjack	automaton
taxpayer	whittler	axlesmith
teddy|boy	wig|maker	balladist
teenager	woodsman	ballerina
thatcher	workfolk	bargainer
Thespian	workgirl	barrister
thurifer	workhand	barrow|boy
tin|miner	wrangler	beefeater
tinsmith	wrestler	bee|keeper
Tom|Thumb	yodeller	beermaker
tone|poet	aborigine	beggarman
top|brass	absconder	bellmaker
toreador	aerialist	biologist

309

bit|player	choralist	cupbearer
boatswain	chorus|boy	custodian
bodyguard	clergyman	cutthroat
bodymaker	clinician	cymbalist
boilerman	clogmaker	daily|help
boltsmith	coadjutor	day|labour
bookmaker	coal|miner	deaconess
bootblack	coenobite	dean|of|men
bootmaker	colleague	debutante
brass|hats	collector	decorator
brigadier	columnist	defendant
buccaneer	combatant	dependent
bunny|girl	commander	designate
bus|driver	commodore	desk|clerk
bush|pilot	companion	detective
byrewoman	concierge	dialogist
bystander	concubine	dietician
cab|driver	conductor	dispenser
cabin|crew	confessor	dog|walker
cafe|owner	confidant	dollmaker
cakemaker	conqueror	dramatist
cameraman	conscript	drum|major
candidate	constable	drysalter
canvasser	contender	ecologist
cardsharp	contralto	economist
caretaker	cornerboy	embezzler
carpenter	cosmonaut	emolument
casemaker	cost|clerk	enamelist
celebrity	costumier	enchanter
cellarman	court|fool	engrosser
centurion	couturier	entourage
chain|gang	covergirl	errand|boy
chartered	crackshot	espionage
charterer	cracksman	estimator
charwoman	crayonist	exchanger
chauffeur	cricketer	exchequer

exciseman	guest star	jitterbug
executive	guitarist	jobholder
eye doctor	gunrunner	key worker
fieldwork	hand sewer	kidnapper
figurante	harbinger	lacemaker
film actor	harbourer	lady's maid
financier	hard graft	lampmaker
film extra	harlequin	lampooner
film maker	harmonist	land agent
financier	harpooner	land force
fire guard	harvester	landowner
first mate	head clerk	landreeve
fisherman	herbalist	land shark
foreigner	hillbilly	larcenist
foundling	hired hand	launderer
free lance	hired help	laundress
freemason	historian	lawmonger
fruiterer	home maker	lay figure
furnisher	homeopath	lay reader
garreteer	Hottentot	lay sister
garrotter	house dick	legionary
gas fitter	housemaid	lensmaker
gazetteer	husbandry	librarian
gem cutter	hypnotist	lifeguard
geologist	immigrant	life's work
girl guide	increment	linotyper
gladiator	incumbent	liontamer
gluemaker	innkeeper	lip reader
go between	inscriber	liveryman
goldsmith	in service	loan agent
gondolier	inside man	lockmaker
governess	inspector	locksmith
grapevine	interview	log roller
grenadier	ironminer	lord mayor
guarantor	ironsmith	lowlander
guardsman	jay walker	lumberman
guerrilla		

311

machinist	outfitter	postulant
majordomo	panellist	postwoman
majorpoet	pantomime	poulterer
make,up,man	paparazzo	precentor
malemodel	part,owner	precursor
malenurse	passenger	prelector
man,at,arms	patrolman	presbyter
manFriday	patroness	president
medallist	paymaster	priestess
mendicant	paysagist	principal
mercenary	pedagogue	privateer
mesmerist	penfriend	professor
messenger	penpusher	profiteer
middleman	pensioner	prud'homme
minorpoet	performer	publicist
modelgirl	personage	publisher
monitress	personnel	puppeteer
moonraker	phonegirl	raconteur
mortician	physician	rainmaker
muscleman	physicist	ransacker
musketeer	picksmith	ranzelman
mythmaker	Pierrette	ratefixer
navigator	pistoleer	ratepayer
neighbour	pitwright	recordist
newsagent	plaintiff	reference
newshound	plasterer	registrar
nursemaid	ploughboy	residency
occultist	ploughman	rhymester
oddjobman	plunderer	ringsider
officeboy	poetaster	roadmaker
oldmaster	policeman	rocketeer
oldstager	popartist	rocketman
ombudsman	popsinger	ropemaker
operative	portrayer	roundsman
osteopath	portreeve	rumrunner
otologist	possessor	ruraldean

sackmaker	spiderman	volunteer
sacristan	spokesman	wassailer
safemaker	sportsman	waxworker
sailmaker	stagehand	weekender
salesgirl	stageidol	wheelsman
salesteam	stargazer	winemaker
sassenach	statesman	woodreeve
scarecrow	stationer	workwoman
scavenger	steersman	yachtsman
scenarist	stevedore	youngster
scientist	strikepay	zitherist
scrapegut	subaltern	zoologist
scribbler	subeditor	ableseaman
scrivener	suffragan	accomplice
sealawyer	swineherd	accountant
secretary	tablemaid	advertiser
seneschal	tailoress	aeronomist
sentryman	tapdancer	agrologist
seraskier	taxevader	agronomist
serenader	tentmaker	aidedecamp
sermonist	testpilot	airhostess
servitude	therapist	airsteward
shoemaker	timberman	amanuensis
signaller	toolsmith	ambassador
signalman	townclerk	AngloSaxon
situation	towncrier	anvilsmith
skindiver	tradesman	apothecary
solicitor	traveller	apprentice
songsmith	tribesman	arbitrator
sonneteer	troubador	archbishop
sophister	trumpeter	archdeacon
sophomore	tympanist	archpriest
sorceress	undergrad	aristocrat
soubrette	usherette	astrologer
spacecrew	vigilante	astronomer
speedster	violinist	auctioneer

313

audit|clerk	bootlegger	clocksmith
au|pair|girl	brain|drain	clog|dancer
babe|in|arms	brakemaker	cloisterer
baby|sitter	brass|smith	cloistress
ballet|girl	breadmaker	clothmaker
ballplayer	bricklayer	clubmaster
bandmaster	brickmaker	coachmaker
bank|robber	broom|maker	coastguard
baseballer	brushmaker	co|director
bassoonist	bulb|grower	collar|work
bear|leader	bumbailiff	coloratura
beautician	bureaucrat	colporteur
bellringer	burlesquer	comedienne
benefactor	camera|team	commandant
billbroker	campaigner	commission
billposter	cartoonist	competitor
biochemist	cat|breeder	compositor
biographer	cat|burglar	concertist
blacksmith	catechumen	consultant
bladesmith	cavalryman	contestant
blockmaker	ceramicist	contractor
bludgeoner	chainmaker	controller
bluebottle	chairmaker	copyreader
bluejacket	chancellor	copywriter
boatwright	changeling	corn|doctor
bogtrotter	chargehand	cornettist
bombardier	charity|boy	coryphaeus
bonesetter	chauffeuse	councillor
bonus|clerk	chorus|girl	counsellor
bookbinder	chronicler	country|boy
book|dealer	cider|maker	countryman
bookfolder	cigar|maker	couturiere
bookholder	claim|agent	cover|agent
bookkeeper	clapper|boy	crackbrain
bookseller	cloakmaker	cultivator
bookwright	clockmaker	customs|man

cytologist	flag bearer	hatchet man
day tripper	flight crew	headhunter
demoiselle	flower girl	headmaster
dilettante	folk singer	head porter
dirty nurse	footballer	head waiter
disc jockey	foot doctor	hedgesmith
discounter	forecaster	henchwoman
discoverer	forerunner	highjacker
dishwasher	forty niner	highlander
dispatcher	frame maker	high priest
dog breeder	freebooter	highwayman
donkey work	fund raiser	hitchhiker
doorkeeper	gamekeeper	holy orders
dramatizer	game warden	honorarium
dramaturge	garage hand	horn player
dressmaker	gatekeeper	horologist
drug pusher	gatewright	house agent
drummer boy	geisha girl	husbandman
dry cleaner	geneticist	impresario
duty roster	geochemist	incendiary
early riser	geographer	incumbency
empiricist	glassmaker	inhabitant
employment	glossarist	inquisitor
equestrian	goalkeeper	instructor
evangelist	gold beater	ironmaster
experience	gold digger	ironmonger
eye witness	goldworker	ironworker
fabricator	grammarian	jewel thief
faith curer	grand prior	job hunting
farmer's boy	grindstone	job printer
fellmonger	groceryman	journalist
fictionist	gubernator	junk dealer
film editor	gunslinger	kennelmaid
firemaster	hall porter	kitchenboy
fire raiser	handmaiden	kitchenman
fishmonger	handshaker	knifesmith

land|holder	millwright	peacemaker
land|jobber	mind,curist	pearl|diver
landlubber	mind|healer	pearly|king
land|pirate	mindreader	pedestrian
land|waiter	ministress	pediatrist
lapidarist	missionary	pedicurist
laundryman	model|maker	penologist
law|officer	monopolist	perruquier
lay|brother	moonshiner	petitioner
leading|man	motley|fool	pharmacist
legislator	mouthpiece	piano|tuner
liberty|man	naturalist	piccoloist
librettist	nautch|girl	pickpocket
licentiate	naval|cadet	piermaster
lieutenant	negotiator	plagiarist
lighterman	neutralist	platelayer
lime|burner	newscaster	playbroker
linotypist	news|editor	playwright
livelihood	newsvendor	playwriter
lobsterman	newswriter	poet|artist
lock|keeper	night|float	poet,farmer
loggerhead	night|nurse	poet,priest
loomworker	notability	politician
lumber|jack	nurseryman	postmaster
machineman	obituarist	prebendary
magistrate	occupation	priesthood
mail|robber	oil|painter	prima|donna
management	pallbearer	private|eye
manageress	pantomimic	procurator
manicurist	pantry|maid	profession
manservant	papermaker	programmer
medical|man	park|keeper	prolocutor
medicaster	park|ranger	proprietor
message|boy	pastrycook	prospector
midshipman	pathfinder	proveditor
militiaman	pawnbroker	questioner

316

quizmaster	songstress	timekeeper
railwayman	soundmixer	trafficker
rawrecruit	spacewoman	translator
recitalist	specialist	tripehound
researcher	speculator	tripewoman
retirement	spycatcher	trombonist
revenueman	staffnurse	tweedledee
revivalist	starmonger	tweedledum
rhapsodist	steelmaker	typesetter
ringmaster	stepdancer	typingpool
roadmender	stewardess	underagent
ropedancer	stickupman	understudy
ropewalker	stockrider	undertaker
safeblower	stocktaker	vegetarian
salesclerk	stonemason	versemaker
salesforce	storesmith	versesmith
saleswoman	strategist	veterinary
saltworker	submariner	viceconsul
sanddancer	subscriber	vicemaster
schoolmaam	substitute	victualler
scrutineer	supercargo	vinegrower
sculptress	supervisor	wageearner
seacaptain	supplicant	wageworker
seamstress	swordsmith	wainwright
secondmate	symphonist	watchmaker
seminarian	syncopator	waterguard
sempstress	tallyclerk	wharfinger
serologist	tallywoman	wholesaler
serviceman	taskmaster	winebibber
sessionman	taxidriver	winewaiter
shanghaier	technician	wireworker
shipwright	technocrat	woodcarver
shopfitter	televiewer	woodcutter
shopkeeper	tenderfoot	woodworker
signwriter	thirdparty	woolcarder
sinologist	tilewright	woolcomber

wool|sorter	bridgemaker	delivery|man
wool|winder	broadcaster	demographer
workfellow	bronzesmith	distributor
working|man	bullfighter	double|agent
workmaster	bushfighter	draughtsman
workpeople	businessman	drill|master
worshipper	candlemaker	drug|peddler
abecedarian	car|salesman	duty|officer
academician	chamberlain	electrician
accompanist	chambermaid	embroiderer
actor's|agent	charcoalist	enlisted|man
antiquarian	cheerleader	entertainer
appointment	cheesemaker	estate|agent
army|officer	chiropodist	etymologist
astrologist	choirmaster	executioner
astronomist	clairvoyant	extortioner
audio|typist	clergywoman	factory|hand
backroom|boy	coachwright	faith|healer
bag|snatcher	co|authoress	field|worker
bank|cashier	coffinmaker	fifth|column
bank|manager	cognoscenti	fighting|man
bargemaster	commentator	filing|clerk
basketmaker	congressman	fingersmith
beauty|queen	conspirator	fire|brigade
bell|founder	contributor	fire|watcher
beneficiary	conveyancer	flag|captain
billsticker	co|ordinator	flag|officer
bingo|caller	coppersmith	flat|dweller
bird|fancier	court|jester	flying|squad
bird|watcher	crane|driver	foot|soldier
board|member	crimewriter	fruit|picker
body|builder	crown|lawyer	funambulist
body|servant	cub|reporter	functionary
boilermaker	cypher|clerk	galley|slave
boilersmith	day|labourer	games|master
breadwinner	dean|of|women	gentlewoman

ghostwriter	laundrymaid	night|sister
ginger|group	leading|lady	night|worker
glass|blower	leaseholder	novelettist
glass|cutter	ledger|clerk	numismatist
grave|digger	lifeboatman	office|party
greengrocer	locum|tenens	onion|Johnny
gunman's|moll	lollipop|man	optometrist
haberdasher	Lord|Provost	ornamentist
hairdresser	lorry|driver	orthopedist
hair|stylist	madrigalist	palaestrian
hammersmith	maidservant	pamphleteer
handservant	mandolinist	panelbeater
hardwareman	manipulator	panel|doctor
head|teacher	masquerader	papal|nuncio
hedgepriest	master|baker	paperhanger
high|sheriff	matinee|idol	paragrapher
high|society	mechanician	parish|clerk
home|crofter	medicine|man	parlourmaid
horse|doctor	memorialist	pathologist
horse|trader	merchantman	pearlfisher
housekeeper	metalworker	pearly|queen
housemaster	methodactor	penny|a|liner
housemother	military|man	petrologist
housewright	millionaire	philatelist
ice|cream|man	mimographer	philologist
illuminator	miniaturist	philosopher
illusionist	money|lender	phonologist
illustrator	moonlighter	piece|worker
infantryman	mother's|help	police|cadet
interpreter	mountaineer	policewoman
interviewer	music|critic	portraitist
iron|founder	naval|rating	predecessor
kitchenmaid	needlewoman	prizewinner
lamplighter	neurologist	probationer
landscapist	night|hunter	protagonist
land|steward	night|porter	proof|reader

purseholder	ship's writer	testimonial
questionist	shop steward	ticket agent
quill driver	silversmith	toastmaster
radiologist	sister tutor	tobacconist
rag merchant	slaughterer	Tommy Atkins
rank and file	slave labour	tooth doctor
rear admiral	slave trader	tooth drawer
relic monger	smallholder	town planner
research man	sociologist	toxophilite
resignation	space doctor	train bearer
rhetorician	spacewriter	train robber
river keeper	speechmaker	transcriber
roadsweeper	stage player	travel agent
rocket pilot	stagewright	tree surgeon
rugby player	stallholder	truck farmer
safebreaker	steeplejack	typographer
safecracker	stenotypist	upholsterer
sandwich man	stereotyper	van salesman
saxophonist	stipendiary	versemonger
school nurse	stockbroker	vice admiral
scorekeeper	stockfarmer	vine dresser
scoutmaster	stock jobber	viola player
scrap dealer	stonecutter	war reporter
scythesmith	storekeeper	washerwoman
search party	storyteller	water doctor
secret agent	straight man	water finder
semanticist	stripteaser	welfare work
semaphorist	subordinate	whalefisher
semi skilled	surrebutter	wheelwright
senior clerk	swordmaster	white collar
sharebroker	talent scout	white hunter
sheep farmer	taxidermist	witch doctor
shepherdess	telegrapher	woodchopper
shipbuilder	telepathist	wool stapler
ship's cooper	telephonist	working girl
ship's tailor	terpsichore	workmanlike

xylophonist	cerographist	escapologist
youth|leader	check|weigher	exhibitioner
actor|manager	chicken|thief	experimenter
advance|party	chief|cashier	ex|service|man
air|commodore	chief|justice	exterminator
aircraftsman	chief|mourner	family|doctor
air|sea|rescue	chief|of|staff	father|figure
ambulance|man	chimney|sweep	field|marshal
anaesthetist	chirographer	field|officer
armour|bearer	chiropractor	figure|dancer
artilleryman	churchwarden	filibusterer
balladmonger	circuit|rider	film|director
ballad|singer	civil|servant	film|producer
ballet|dancer	civil|service	first|officer
bibliologist	clarinettist	first|reserve
bibliopegist	clerk|of|works	flying|column
board|meeting	coachbuilder	flying|doctor
body|snatcher	collaborator	footplateman
booking|clerk	commissioner	garret|master
bookstitcher	confectioner	general|agent
border|sentry	conquistador	geriatrician
bottle|washer	contemporary	globetrotter
boulevardier	corn|chandler	grandstander
bridgemaster	costermonger	group|captain
brigade|major	customs|clerk	guest|speaker
brinkmanship	deep|sea|diver	gynecologist
cabinet|maker	demonstrator	headmistress
calligrapher	desk|sergeant	headshrinker
camp|follower	doctor's|round	heir|apparent
candlewright	dramaturgist	high|official
caricaturist	ecclesiastic	hockey|player
carpet|bagger	electrotyper	holidaymaker
carpet|fetter	elocutionist	hotel|manager
cartographer	entomologist	housebreaker
casual|labour	entrepreneur	housepainter
cattle|lifter	equestrienne	hydropathist

immunologist	manual|worker	prison|warder
impersonator	manufacturer	prison|worker
improvisator	mass|producer	quarrymaster
in|conference	master|at|arms	racing|driver
inseparables	mastersinger	radiodontist
instructress	metallurgist	radiographer
intermediary	metropolitan	receptionist
jazz|musician	mezzo|soprano	remuneration
junior|rating	mineralogist	restaurateur
juvenile|lead	money|changer	retaining|fee
king's|counsel	monographist	sales|manager
kitchen|staff	motorcyclist	scene|painter
knifegrinder	musicologist	scene|shifter
knifethrower	naval|officer	schoolmaster
lady|superior	newspaperman	screenwriter
landed|gentry	notary|public	scriptwriter
land|surveyor	nutritionist	scullery|maid
law|stationer	obstetrician	sister|german
lay|out|artist	office|bearer	site|engineer
leader|writer	office|junior	snake|charmer
leathernecks	pastoral|poet	social|worker
legal|adviser	patent|office	soil|mechanic
letter|writer	pediatrician	sole|occupant
lexicologist	penitentiary	special|agent
line|sergeant	petty|officer	speechwriter
literary|hack	photographer	spiritualist
literary|lion	physiologist	sports|master
lithographer	plant|manager	sportscaster
longshoreman	ploughwright	sports|writer
loss|adjuster	plumber's|mate	staff|officer
maid|of|honour	poet|laureate	stage|manager
maitre|d'hotel	post|graduate	statistician
major|general	postmistress	steel|erector
make|up|artist	practitioner	stenographer
man|of|letters	press|officer	stereotypist
man|of|science	principal|boy	stonedresser

stormtrooper	church officer
street trader	civil engineer
tax collector	coastguardman
technologist	common law wife
telegraph boy	contortionist
telephone man	contrabandist
tennis player	cook housemaid
test engineer	cotton spinner
theatre nurse	counter jumper
ticket holder	craftsmanship
ticket writer	cryptographer
top executive	dancing master
trained nurse	dental surgeon
trichologist	district nurse
trick cyclist	feature editor
trout breeder	fellow servant
undermanager	fencing master
vaudevillist	fortune teller
vice director	guardian angel
vice governor	gynaecologist
warehouseman	harbour master
water diviner	health visitor
wind musician	industrialist
wine merchant	lady in waiting
wood engraver	lift attendant
worker priest	lighthouseman
working party	livery servant
workmistress	livery servant
works manager	lollipop woman
alongshoreman	maid of all work
antique dealer	master builder
archaeologist	master mariner
articled clerk	night watchman
audio engineer	office manager
barber surgeon	old clothes man
campanologist	poultry farmer

OCCUPATIONS

printer's devil	house detective
prison visitor	king's messenger
process server	labour exchange
rag and bone man	maintenance man
rent collector	market gardener
scrap merchant	marriage broker
ship's chandler	matron of honour
shop assistant	mining engineer
shop detective	munition worker
skeleton staff	naval architect
skilled worker	nursing officer
still room maid	opposite number
street sweeper	prison governor
toastmistress	research worker
traffic warden	Reverend Mother
universal aunt	ship's carpenter
window cleaner	sports reporter
window dresser	stage carpenter
accomplishment	stamp collector
apprenticeship	standard bearer
audiometrician	station manager
black marketeer	store detective
bus conductress	street musician
busman's holiday	superintendent
casual labourer	tobacco planter
charcoal burner	troubleshooter
chimney sweeper	turf accountant
clerical worker	valet de chambre
coastguardsman	blast furnaceman
commissionaire	Bow street runner
common informer	colliery manager
dramatic critic	commission agent
elder statesman	crossing sweeper
gentleman usher	customs official
hotel detective	district visitor
house decorator	Father Christmas

15 LETTERS

funeral director
gentleman farmer
gossip columnist
Jack of all trades
old age pensioner
one parent family
ophthalmologist
planning officer
police constable
police inspector
programme seller
Queen's messenger
research chemist

shorthand typist
shorthand writer
slave trafficker
stamp collection
stretcher bearer
surrogate father
surrogate mother
surrogate parent
ticket collector
tightrope walker
undercover agent
youth club leader

Oceans and Seas

Aegean
Arctic
Baltic
Red Sea
Aral Sea
Dead Sea
Java Sea
Kara Sea
Oresund
Ross Sea
Sulu Sea
Wash, The
Adriatic
Atlantic
Black Sea
Bosporus

Coral Sea
Kattegat
Korea Bay
Minch, The
North Sea
Spithead
Timor Sea
Azov, Sea of
Bantry Bay
Foxe Basin
Hudson Bay
Ionian Sea
Scapa Flow
Skagerrak
Solent, The
Yellow Sea

Zuider Zee
Aden, Gulf of
Andaman Sea
Arabian Sea
Bass Strait
Caspian Sea
Celebes Sea
Cook Strait
Delagoa Bay
Fundy, Bay of
Oman, Gulf of
Palk Strait
Riga, Gulf of
Siam, Gulf of
Aqaba, Gulf of
Beaufort Sea

325

OCEANS AND SEAS

Bengal, Bay of	Panama, Gulf of
Bismarck Sea	Tonkin, Gulf of
Cabot Strait	Torres Strait
Dardanelles	Bothnia, Gulf of
Indian Ocean	Corinth, Gulf of
Korea Strait	Finland, Gulf of
Lions, Gulf of	Fonseca, Gulf of
Menai Strait	Mediterranean
Persian Gulf	Pentland Firth
Plenty, Bay of	South China Sea
Saronic Gulf	Taranto, Gulf of
Solway Firth	Tyrrhenian Sea
Benin, Bight of	Van Diemen Gulf
Darien, Gulf of	Albemarle Sound
East China Sea	Bristol Channel
Greenland Sea	English Channel
Guinea, Gulf of	Macassar Strait
Mannar, Gulf of	Magellan Strait
Marmora, Sea of	Malacca, Strait of
Mexico, Gulf of	Messina, Strait of

Physical Sciences

AU	coil	lens	unit	cycle	light
amp	core	mass	volt	field	meson
erg	echo	phon	wane	flame	optic
lab	flex	pile	watt	focus	orbit
ray	flux	pion	wave	force	phase
wow	foam	pole	X,ray	gauss	polar
atom	foci	rays	anion	henry	power
beam	fuse	rule	anode	hertz	quark
cell	heat	tone	curie	laser	radar

relay	siphon	density	science
solve	solder	diagram	Sputnik
sound	stress	Doppler	tensile
spark	syphon	dry|cell	tension
steam	theory	elastic	torsion
A|blast	thrust	entropy	vernier
aerial	torque	EURATOM	voltage
albedo	vacuum	fall|out	aerology
ampere	vortex	fatigue	aerostat
atomic	weight	fissile	alpha|ray
baffle	actinon	fission	angstrom
boffin	adaptor	gilbert	anode|ray
bolide	aerator	gimbals	antinode
cation	airlock	gravity	armature
charge	air|pump	heating	atmology
degree	ammeter	impulse	atomizer
dipole	aneroid	inertia	Avogadro
dynamo	angular	isotone	beta|rays
energy	antenna	isotope	betatron
Geiger	aphotic	kiloton	bevatron
H|blast	atomics	megaton	cassette
ignite	atomism	missile	constant
isobar	aureole	monitor	delta|ray
kation	azimuth	neutron	detector
magnet	battery	nuclear	deuteron
megohm	beta|ray	nucleon	dew|point
metric	binocle	nucleus	electron
micron	bipolar	off|peak	enthalpy
mirror	capsule	ohmeter	equation
nuclei	cathode	physics	eutectic
opaque	chamber	positon	excitant
optics	circuit	project	fast|pile
proton	control	quantum	filament
quasar	crystal	radical	formulae
radome	current	reactor	freezing
sensor	decibel	rontgen	friction

327

fuel|cell	pressure	apparatus
gamma|ray	radiator	atom|blast
gas|laser	reaction	atomicity
half₁life	reactive	atomology
harmonic	receiver	barograph
heat|sink	recorder	barometer
hologram	red|shift	baroscope
ignition	research	binocular
impeller	resistor	blast|wave
inductor	rheostat	bolometer
infra₁red	roentgen	Boyle's|law
injector	scanning	canal|rays
ion|drive	scissile	capacitor
ionizing	sine|wave	capillary
iriscope	slow|pile	cold|short
klystron	Space|age	condenser
laser|gun	spectrum	conductor
magic|eye	sub₁atoms	converter
mesotron	thruster	cosmic|ray
molecule	unit|cell	cosmogony
momentum	velocity	cosmology
negative	watt₁hour	cosmotron
negatron	wave|form	countdown
neutrino	X₁ray|tube	cryoscope
nucleate	zoetrope	ctyogenic
ohmmeter	zoom|lens	cyclotron
overload	acoustics	dead|point
paradigm	activated	deflector
particle	activator	deionizer
peak|load	adiabatic	detonator
physical	advection	dineutron
pinacoid	air|pocket	discharge
polarity	altimeter	elastance
positive	amplitude	electrode
positron	annealing	equipoise
power|cut	aperiodic	explosion

field|coil	megascope	stability
flotation	mesic|atom	stop|clock
flow|meter	mesotrons	subatomic
focimeter	microfilm	telephony
frequency	microtron	telescope
galvanize	microwave	threshold
gamma|rays	moderator	time|clock
gyroscope	molecular	tolerance
heat|index	monatomic	triatomic
heliostat	multipole	video|tape
holograph	Newtonian	voltmeter
hydration	phonemics	wattmeter
hydrostat	photocell	wave|guide
hygrostat	physicist	wire|gauge
indicator	pitot|tube	wire|photo
induction	plumb|line	air|cooling
inelastic	pneumatic	amphoteric
inventory	polar|axis	antiproton
isosteric	potential	atmosphere
kilohertz	power|pack	atomic|mass
laser|beam	proton|gun	atomic|pile
Leyden|jar	radiation	atomic|unit
libration	radiology	atom|rocket
light|wave	radio|rays	battery|jar
light|year	recording	biophysics
long|waves	reflector	bleep|bleep
lubricant	reservoir	Bohr|theory
Mach|front	resonance	calorifier
macrodome	scientist	carbonated
magnetism	scintilla	carbon|atom
magnetron	short|wave	catenation
magnifier	side|chain	cathode|ray
manometer	sound|wave	Centigrade
mechanics	spaceship	centrifuge
megacurie	spacesuit	cine|camera
megacycle	spacewalk	cobalt|bomb

collimator	laboratory	resistance
combustion	latent|heat	resolution
compressor	light|valve	rutherford
controller	Mach|number	scientific
convection	macroprism	short|waves
corrugated	magnet|pole	space|craft
cryogenics	mass|defect	spallation
curiescopy	mass|energy	stabilizer
deep|freeze	mass|number	step|rocket
degaussing	megaparsec	supersonic
desiccator	megascopic	synchroton
Dewar|flask	metacentre	tagged|atom
distortion	microcurie	technology
elasticity	micrograph	telegraphy
electronic	microphone	television
elongation	microscope	tetratomic
energetics	millicurie	thermistor
epithermal	multicurie	thermopile
estimation	nanosecond	thermostat
evaporator	nucleonics	three|phase
excitation	pentatomic	time|switch
experiment	polycyclic	transistor
Fahrenheit	power|plant	transition
filter|pump	projectile	triniscope
filter|tube	pronucleus	trochotron
geophysics	propellant	voltameter
gravimeter	propulsion	volt|ampere
heat|shield	radiogenic	water|gauge
horse|power	radiometer	water|level
hydraulics	radiometry	wave|length
hypothesis	radioscope	white|light
hypsometer	radioscopy	wind|tunnel
inductance	radio|sonde	xerography
ionosphere	reactivity	X|radiation
isonuclear	reluctance	zwitterion
isothermal	resilience	accelerator

accumulator	free|radical	supercooled
achromatism	gravitation	technocracy
actinic|rays	gravity|cell	temperature
actinometer	ground|state	thermionics
anticathode	heat|barrier	thermoduric
antineutron	high|voltage	thermograph
atom|counter	iridescence	thermometer
atomic|clock	irradiation	transformer
atomologist	isochronism	transmitter
atom|smasher	kinetic|body	tripod|stand
Auger|effect	landing|beam	troposphere
baffle|plate	light|shield	ultrasonics
barycentric	lyophilizer	vacuum|flask
bifocal|lens	macroscopic	acceleration
capillarity	manipulator	acceptor|atom
carnot|cycle	opeidoscope	actinic|glass
cathode|rays	open|circuit	aerodynamics
coefficient	photography	afterburning
conductance	photosphere	Angstrom|unit
crystalline	polarimeter	antineutrino
cytophysics	polarimetry	antiparticle
diffraction	polarograph	astronautics
dynamometer	positive|ray	astrophysics
echo|sounder	primary|cell	atomic|energy
Einsteinium	quantum|jump	atomic|number
electricity	radiant|heat	atomic|theory
electrolyte	radioactive	atomic|weight
electronics	radio|beacon	atom|smashing
engineering	radiologist	boiling|point
epidiascope	reactor|pile	burning|glass
fast|breeder	regenerator	burning|point
fibre|optics	retro|rocket	carat|balance
fissionable	Rontgen|rays	central|force
fluorescent	rule|of|thumb	chain|reactor
fluoroscope	space|rocket	cloud|chamber
fluoroscopy	stroboscope	condensation

critical|mass
crystallites
deceleration
deflagration
displacement
electric|cell
electric|lamp
electron|pair
electronvolt
electroscope
experimental
extranuclear
fluorescence
galvanometer
geomagnetism
high|fidelity
hyperphysics
iatrophysics
infra,red|lamp
interference
law|of|gravity
luminescence
macrophysics
microammeter
microphysics
millerontgen
mirror|nuclei
nuclear|force
nuclear|power
optical|laser
oscilloscope
photofission
photoneutron
polarization
positive|rays
power|reactor

power|station
quantization
radio|compass
reactivation
refrigerator
Roentgen|rays
scintillator
selenium|cell
short|circuit
smash|the|atom
solar|battery
solar|physics
space|station
specific|heat
split|the|atom
stereophonic
stereopticon
stratosphere
thermoscopic
transmission
unified|field
Van|Allen|belt
vaporization
wave|function
X,ray|spectrum
amplification
Appleton|layer
astrophysical
Auger|electron
camera|obscura
chain|reaction
compressed|air
critical|angle
decompression
demonstration
direct|current

discharge|tube	cathode,ray|tube
Doppler|effect	circuit|breaker
electric|field	counter,current
electric|light	disintegration
electric|meter	eigen|frequency
electromagnet	electronically
electrostatic	heavier|than|air
ferromagnetic	Heaviside|layer
freezing,point	magnetic|needle
Geiger|counter	microcomponent
graticulation	nuclear|fission
heat,resistant	nuclear|physics
high|frequency	nuclear|powered
hydroelectric	nuclear|reactor
kinetic|energy	phantom|circuit
magnetic|field	printed|circuit
magnetic|north	radio|telescope
magnetic|poles	surface|tension
magnetisation	thermodynamics
non,conducting	torsion|balance
photo,electric	transverse|wave
quantum|theory	trickle|charger
radioactivity	tuner|amplifier
radiolocation	centre|of|gravity
semiconductor	crystallography
spring|balance	electrification
telephoto|lens	electroanalysis
thermonuclear	electrodynamics
tracer|element	electrokinetics
under|pressure	electromagnetic
anacoustic|zone	horseshoe|magnet
applied|science	magneto,electric
astrophysicist	microtechnology
audio,frequency	nuclear|reaction
bioelectricity	optical|illusion
breeder|reactor	Planck's|constant

potential|energy   specific|gravity
specific|gravity   ultra,violet|rays

Plants

bur	ling	blade	panic	borage
fog	lint	bract	plant	bryony
hay	mint	camas	radix	burnet
ivy	moly	canna	ramie	cacoon
mow	moss	caper	rubia	cactus
poa	otto	clary	scrub	camass
rue	peat	clove	sedge	catnip
sod	rape	couch	senna	caulis
tea	reed	cumin	sisal	clover
balm	rhea	cycad	sprig	cockle
bent	rush	dagga	starr	coffee
bixa	rust	dulse	stoma	corkir
burr	sage	erica	sward	cotton
cane	soma	fitch	tansy	crotal
culm	star	frond	thyme	croton
dill	tare	fucus	umbel	cummin
dock	taro	fungi	vetch	darnel
fern	tuft	gemma	wrack	eringo
flax	turf	gloom	yeast	fescue
gale	weed	grass	yucca	fucoid
gall	woad	halfa	acacia	fungus
hemp	abaca	heath	agaric	hedera
herb	abrus	lemna	albino	hyssop
jute	algae	liana	arabis	indigo
kelp	anise	musci	aralia	jungle
lawn	aspic	orpin	balsam	kissme
leaf	basil	osier	bamboo	knawel

lalang	twitch	dogbane	seaweed
lichen	acerose	esparto	seedbox
madder	alecost	foxtail	sorghum
mallee	alfalfa	frogbit	spignel
manioc	alkanet	genista	spurrey
maquis	allheal	ginseng	statice
marram	amanita	guarana	stipule
marrum	aniseed	guayule	tanghin
medick	armilla	hawkbit	tarweed
myrica	auricle	hayseed	tendril
nettle	benthos	heather	thistle
nostoc	bistort	hemlock	timothy
origan	bogbean	henbane	tobacco
orpine	bogmoss	herbage	trefoil
oxalis	bracken	hogweed	truffle
pampas	bugloss	honesty	tussock
pappus	bulrush	labiate	vanilla
phylum	burdock	linseed	verdant
raffia	calamus	lucerne	verdure
ramson	caltrop	lycopod	vervain
redtop	cambium	mayweed	zedoary
sapium	caraway	melilot	zizania
seamat	carline	milfoil	abutilon
sesame	cassava	mudwort	acanthus
simple	catmint	mustard	angelica
sobole	cat's-ear	opuntia	asphodel
sorrel	clivers	osmunda	bedstraw
spurge	clotbur	papyrus	bignonia
spurry	cowbane	pinguin	bindweed
squill	cowweed	redroot	blueweed
stolon	creeper	rhizome	boggrass
storax	crinoid	rootage	buckbean
sundew	crottle	saguaro	canaigre
tangle	curcuma	sampire	cardamom
teasel	deutzia	seareed	cat'sfoot
thrift	dittany	seatang	cat'stail

335

caulicle	knapweed	samphire
centaury	knapwood	sargasso
charlock	knotweed	seaberry
cleavers	lady|fern	sea|blite
clubmoss	licorice	seagrape
clubrush	mandrake	sea|holly
cocculus	marjoram	sea|wrack
conferva	medicago	seedcase
costmary	meristem	seed|leaf
cow|grass	milkweed	shamrock
cow|plant	milkwort	soapwort
cow|wheat	moonwort	spergula
cut|grass	mushroom	spigelia
death|cap	offshoot	spikelet
death|cup	origanum	starwort
dicentra	peat|moss	take|root
dock|leaf	phyllome	tamarisk
dog|grass	pillwort	tarragon
dog|wheat	pinkroot	toad|flax
dropwort	plantage	tree|fern
duckweed	plantain	tree|lily
eel|grass	plant|pot	tree|moss
egg|plant	plantule	tremella
fernshaw	plumbago	tuberose
fireweed	pokeweed	turmeric
flaxseed	pondweed	valerian
gas|plant	puffball	vasculum
glory|pea	purslane	waybread
goatweed	ratsbane	xanthium
greenery	red|algae	acrospire
gulfweed	reed|mace	arrowhead
hedgerow	ribgrass	arrowroot
hepatica	rockweed	arrowroot
hibiscus	root|knot	artemisia
honeydew	ryegrass	astrofell
ice|plant	saltwort	baldmoney

336

bearberry	flagellum	mesophyte
beech|fern	fly|agaric	milk|vetch
bent|grass	galingale	mistletoe
bird's|foot	gama|grass	monk's|hood
bird's|nest	gemmation	musk|plant
birthwort	germander	navelwort
bloodroot	glasswort	overgrown
bluegrass	goosefoot	pellitory
bog|myrtle	gramineae	pennywort
bog|orchid	green,weed	plant|life
bracteole	ground|ivy	poison|ivy
broomrape	groundsel	polygonum
cane|sugar	hair|grass	portulaca
carrageen	halophyte	quillwort
catchweed	herbarium	reed|grass
centaurea	holly|fern	rocambole
chain|fern	holy|grass	rock|brake
chickweed	horehound	rockcress
China|root	hornwrack	rock|plant
cockscomb	horsetail	royal|fern
coral|root	house|leek	sand|grain
coriander	idioblast	sand|grass
crab|grass	involucre	scale|moss
crazyweed	Irish|moss	screw|pine
crosswort	knotgrass	seabottle
cryptogam	laserwort	seagirdle
cup|lichen	leaf|mould	sea,tangle
desert|pea	lemon,weed	silk|grass
dittander	liquorice	sisal|hemp
dock|cress	liverwort	smartweed
duck's|meat	luxuriant	snakeroot
dyer's|weed	lyme|grass	snowplant
earth|star	mare's|tail	spearmint
euphorbia	marijuana	spikenard
fairy|ring	marsh|fern	star|grass
fenugreek	marshwort	stinkweed

PLANTS

stonecrop	goat's beard	sea lettuce
stonewort	golden seal	sea whistle
sugar cane	goosegrass	second crop
sun spurge	grama grass	seed vessel
sweet flag	grasswrack	semination
sweetgale	green algae	shield fern
teargrass	greenhouse	sisal grass
toadstool	greensward	slime mould
toothwort	hemp nettle	spear grass
vernation	herb garden	spiderwort
water fern	Indian hemp	springwort
water leaf	indigenous	stitchwort
water vine	Jimson weed	strike root
waterweed	lemon grass	sword grass
wire grass	lycopodium	thale cress
wormgrass	maidenhair	transplant
aftergrass	maidenweed	tree mallow
arrow grass	malaguetta	tumbleweed
aspidistra	mandragora	vegetation
beard grass	Manila hemp	wall pepper
bitterroot	manna grass	waterbloom
brown algae	motherwort	wilderness
bunch grass	musk mallow	wild indigo
butterwort	new mown hay	willow weed
Canada rice	nipplewort	Adam's needle
China grass	orangeroot	alpine plant
couch grass	penny cress	bell heather
cow chervil	pennyroyal	blue thistle
cow parsley	peppermint	bur marigold
cow parsnip	pepperwort	canary grass
dead nettle	photometry	chanterelle
dog parsley	planthouse	chive garlic
dog's fennel	plume grass	cotton grass
dyer's broom	restharrow	cotton plant
elecampane	sand binder	cruciferous
glasshouse	sea burdock	cypress knee

338

dame's|violet	sea|milkwort
dog's|mercury	sea|purslane
dyer's|rocket	sesame|grass
false|acacia	Spanish|moss
finger|grass	swallow|wort
French|berry	switch|grass
fuller's|herb	thistle|down
garden|stuff	tree|creeper
germination	viper's|grass
giant|cactus	water|meadow
graft|hybrid	water|pepper
green|dragon	water|violet
guinea|grass	wintergreen
hart's|tongue	witches|meat
horseradish	bladderwrack
Iceland|moss	buffalo|grass
kidney|vetch	climbing|fern
lady's|finger	conservatory
leopardbane	esparto|grass
luxuriation	feathergrass
manna|lichen	fool's|parsley
marram|grass	forcing|house
myrtle|grass	green|fingers
oyster|plant	hassock|grass
pampas|grass	hound's|tongue
pepper|grass	Jacob's|ladder
potting|shed	lady's|fingers
pullulation	lady's|thistle
ribbon|grass	orchard|grass
Roman|nettle	sheep's|fescue
root|climber	skunk|cabbage
rubber|plant	snuffbox|bean
salad|burnet	Spanish|cress
scurvy|grass	Spanish|grass
sea|furbelow	staghorn|moss
sea|lavender	Timothy|grass

PLANTS

tobacco|plant	Scotch|thistle
umbelliferae	water|crowfoot
Venus|fly|trap	chincherinchee
waterhemlock	circumnutation
watermilfoil	classification
white|heather	evergreen|plant
zantedeschia	flowering|plant
elephant|grass	mountain|sorrel
golden|thistle	Shepherd's|purse
horse|mushroom	wood|nightshade
lady's|bedstraw	Virginia|creeper
meadow|saffron	virgin|territory
noli|me|tangere	woody|nightshade

Political Leaders

Fox	Bevan	Caesar	Allende
Blum	Bevin	Carson	Ataturk
Eden	Botha	Castro	Baldwin
Grey	Derby	Cripps	Balfour
Hess	Heath	Curzon	Bolivar
Marx	Laval	Dulles	Canning
Meir	Lenin	Franco	Goering
More	Nehru	Gandhi	Hampden
Nagy	North	Hitler	Hertzog
Peel	Obote	Kaunda	Himmler
Pitt	Peron	Mobutu	Kosygin
Tito	Smuts	Nasser	Luthuli
Tojo	Spaak	Pelham	Mandela
Banda	Attlee	Stalin	Masaryk
Benes	Brandt	Wilson	Menzies
Beria	Bright	Wolsey	Molotov

Nkrumah	Verwoerd
Nyerere	BenGurion
Parnell	Bonaparte
Reynaud	ChouenLai
Russell	Churchill
Salazar	Gaitskell
Trotsky	Garibaldi
Trudeau	Gladstone
Walpole	Gorbachev
Aberdeen	HoChiMinh
Adenauer	Kissinger
Andropov	Lafayette
Augustus	Liverpool
Bismarck	Macdonald
BonarLaw	Macmillan
Brezhnev	Melbourne
Bulganin	Mussolini
Burghley	Richelieu
Caligula	Salisbury
Cosgrave	Shelburne
Cromwell	Stevenson
Crossman	Vishinsky
deGaulle	Alcibiades
deValera	CheGuevara
Disraeli	Clemenceau
Goebbels	MaoTsetung
Kenyatta	Metternich
Kruschev	Palmerston
Malenkov	Ribbentrop
McCarthy	Stresemann
Napoleon	Talleyrand
Perceval	Castlereagh
Pericles	Chamberlain
Poincaré	Demosthenes
Rosebery	DouglasHome
Thatcher	Machiavelli

POLITICAL LEADERS

Robespierre Bandaranaike Mendes France
Shaftesbury Julius Caesar Themistocles

Presidents of the USA

Ford	Pierce	Coolidge
Polk	Reagan	Fillmore
Taft	Taylor	Garfield
Adams	Truman	Harrison
Grant	Wilson	McKinley
Hayes	Harding	Van Buren
Nixon	Jackson	Cleveland
Tyler	Johnson	Jefferson
Arthur	Kennedy	Roosevelt
Carter	Lincoln	Eisenhower
Hoover	Madison	Washington
Monroe	Buchanan	

Relations

<table>
<tr><td>ma</td><td>mother</td><td>divorcee</td></tr>
<tr><td>pa</td><td>nephew</td><td>grandson</td></tr>
<tr><td>dad</td><td>nuncle</td><td>helpmeet</td></tr>
<tr><td>kin</td><td>orphan</td><td>relation</td></tr>
<tr><td>mum</td><td>parent</td><td>relative</td></tr>
<tr><td>son</td><td>senior</td><td>son‚in‚law</td></tr>
<tr><td>aunt</td><td>sister</td><td>spinster</td></tr>
<tr><td>heir</td><td>spouse</td><td>triplets</td></tr>
<tr><td>kith</td><td>suitor</td><td>boy|friend</td></tr>
<tr><td>sire</td><td>best‖man</td><td>firstborn</td></tr>
<tr><td>twin</td><td>brother</td><td>forebears</td></tr>
<tr><td>mater</td><td>cognate</td><td>godfather</td></tr>
<tr><td>mummy</td><td>consort</td><td>godmother</td></tr>
<tr><td>niece</td><td>dowager</td><td>grand‚aunt</td></tr>
<tr><td>pater</td><td>fiancée</td><td>great‚aunt</td></tr>
<tr><td>scion</td><td>heiress</td><td>kid|sister</td></tr>
<tr><td>sonny</td><td>husband</td><td>kinswoman</td></tr>
<tr><td>twins</td><td>kindred</td><td>next|of|kin</td></tr>
<tr><td>uncle</td><td>kinsman</td><td>offspring</td></tr>
<tr><td>widow</td><td>mankind</td><td>patriarch</td></tr>
<tr><td>agnate</td><td>partner</td><td>antecedent</td></tr>
<tr><td>auntie</td><td>progeny</td><td>babe|in|arms</td></tr>
<tr><td>cousin</td><td>sibling</td><td>bridegroom</td></tr>
<tr><td>father</td><td>stepson</td><td>bridesmaid</td></tr>
<tr><td>fiancé</td><td>widower</td><td>forefather</td></tr>
<tr><td>frater</td><td>ancestor</td><td>grandchild</td></tr>
<tr><td>godson</td><td>bachelor</td><td>grand‚niece</td></tr>
<tr><td>infant</td><td>children</td><td>grand‚uncle</td></tr>
<tr><td>junior</td><td>daughter</td><td>grass|widow</td></tr>
</table>

great|uncle	blood|relation
half|sister	Bob's|your|uncle
kid|brother	brotherliness
kith|and|kin	close|relative
maiden|aunt	consanguinity
seventh|son	daughter|in|law
son|and|heir	direct|descent
stepfather	distant|cousin
stepmother	family|reunion
stepsister	first|begotten
sweetheart	flesh|and|blood
blood|sister	foster|brother
father|in|law	granddaughter
first|cousin	great|grandson
foster|child	identical|twin
grandfather	intermarriage
grandmother	marriage|lines
grandnephew	materfamilias
grandparent	progenitorial
half|brother	fairy|godmother
mother|in|law	foster|daughter
sister|in|law	husband|and|wife
step|brother	identical|twins
blood|brother	in|loco|parentis
brother|in|law	mother|and|child
cousin|german	mother's|darling
Darby|and|Joan	distant|relative
foster|father	every|mother's|son
foster|mother	great|grandchild
foster|parent	honeymoon|couple
foster|sister	mother|and|father
heir|apparent	rude|forefathers
natural|child	surrogate|father
near|relation	surrogate|mother
second|cousin	surrogate|parent
stepdaughter	wife|and|children
blood|brothers	

Religions

alb	halo	tomb	chela	Hades
ark	harp	tope	choir	Islam
goy	Hell	veil	cotta	Jewry
pew	holy	vows	credo	judge
pie	hymn	wake	creed	knell
pye	icon	zeal	cross	Koran
pyx	idol	abbey	crypt	lauds
RIP	joss	abbot	curse	laver
see	keen	agape	demon	leper
sin	kirk	aisle	Devil	Logos
vow	lama	Allah	dogma	magus
alms	mass	almug	druid	Maker
ambo	monk	Alpha	dulia	manna
amen	naos	altar	elder	manse
apse	nave	ambry	ephod	Mazda
bell	oath	amice	exile	Mecca
bema	pall	angel	extol	Medes
bier	Pope	apron	faith	Media
bull	pray	apsis	fanon	mitre
cant	pyre	banns	feral	motet
cell	raga	beads	Flood	mound
cope	rite	Bible	friar	myrrh
cowl	robe	bigot	frock	Negeb
cure	rood	bless	glebe	nones
dean	sect	cairn	glory	Omega
dome	seer	canon	goyim	padre
fast	sext	carol	grace	paean
font	soul	cella	grail	pagan
guru	text	chant	grave	paten

345

RELIGIONS

piety	cantor	Israel	papacy
pious	casket	Jesuit	parish
prior	censer	Jewish	parson
psalm	chapel	Jordan	pastor
rabbi	cherub	Josiah	plague
relic	chimer	josser	postil
saint	chrism	jubbah	prayer
Satan	church	keener	preach
scarf	clergy	latria	priest
Solon	cleric	lector	primus
spire	coffin	lemuel	priory
staff	corban	litany	pulpit
stall	curacy	litany	Quaker
stole	curate	magian	rector
stoup	deacon	manger	ritual
stupa	Deluge	mantle	rochet
Sumer	devout	mantra	rosary
synod	diadem	manual	rubric
taber	divine	martyr	sacred
tiara	dolmen	matins	satrap
Torah	Easter	maundy	schism
tract	embalm	missal	Scribe
tunic	eunuch	Mormon	sedile
vault	famine	Moslem	Semite
vicar	fannel	mosque	sermon
abbess	Father	mullah	sexton
amulet	flamen	mystic	shaman
anoint	gospel	nimbus	shrine
anthem	hallow	nipter	shroud
armlet	hearse	novena	sinner
barrow	Heaven	novice	sister
beadle	Hebrew	office	stalls
bishop	heresy	ordain	Sunday
Brahma	hermit	orison	suttee
Buddha	homage	pagoda	tablet
burial	homily	palace	talent

346

Talmud	chaplet	godhead	mourner
temple	chapman	goodman	muezzin
tierce	chapter	gradino	mummify
tippet	charity	heathen	narthex
unholy	charnel	Hebrews	nunnery
vakass	chimere	heretic	obelisk
verger	chorale	holyday	oratory
vestry	collect	holysee	ossuary
vigils	complin	holywar	pallium
vision	convent	Hosanna	papyrus
zealot	convert	hymnary	parable
acolyte	cortege	Ichabod	periapt
Alcoran	Creator	impiety	pietism
almoner	crosier	impious	pilgrim
angelic	crozier	incense	piscina
angelus	crusade	infidel	pontiff
apostle	daysman	introit	prayers
ascents	DeadSea	Jehovah	prebend
atheist	deanery	jubilee	prelate
Babylon	deodate	Judaism	primate
baptism	devotee	keening	profane
Baptist	diocese	Lambeth	prophet
biretta	diptych	Lebanon	psalter
blessed	diviner	lectern	Puritan
bondage	doubter	lection	pyramid
bondman	DryMass	liturgy	pyxveil
brother	Eleazar	LowMass	rabboni
burying	epitaph	maniple	raiment
buskins	Essenes	mastaba	Ramadan
cabbala	fanatic	memoria	Rameses
calotte	fasting	Messiah	rectory
Cantuar	frontal	Messias	religio
capuche	funeral	minaret	requiem
cassock	gaiters	minster	reredos
chancel	gentile	miracle	retable
chantry	glorify	mission	Sabbath

sanctum	beadsman	delubrum	hymn|book
sandals	bedesman	disciple	idolater
Saviour	believer	divinity	idolatry
sceptic	blessing	doctrine	Immanuel
scourge	bless|you	doxology	inner|man
secular	bondmaid	druidess	Jonathan
sedilia	brethren	embolism	lamasery
Semitic	breviary	Emmanuel	lay|vicar
serpent	Buddhist	Epiphany	lich|gate
service	canonics	Epistles	Lord's|day
session	canonize	evensong	Lutheran
Shammah	canticle	exegesis	marabout
sistrum	capuchin	exequial	Mass|book
soutane	cardinal	exequies	mediator
steeple	catholic	exorcism	megalith
stipend	cemetery	faithful	memorial
tonsure	cenotaph	funerary	menology
Trinity	ceremony	funereal	minister
tumulus	chaplain	Gentiles	ministry
tunicle	chasuble	God's|acre	monachal
unction	cherubim	Good|Book	monastic
Vatican	choirboy	governor	monolith
vespers	chrismal	Hail|Mary	monument
Vulgate	cincture	hallowed	mourning
worship	cloister	hecatomb	mozzetta
atheist	compline	here|lies	neophyte
agnostic	conclave	hic|jacet	Noah's|Ark
Akeldama	corporal	High|Mass	obituary
Almighty	covenant	holiness	oblation
anathema	Creation	holy|city	offering
Anglican	credence	holy|coat	orthodox
antipope	credenda	Holy|Land	Paradise
Apostles	cromlech	holyrood	Parousia
Ave|Maria	crucifix	Holy|Week	Passover
basilica	Crusader	Holy|Writ	penitent
beadroll	dalmatic	Huguenot	Pharisee

pontifex	altardesk	confessor
praisebe	altarrail	converted
preacher	Apocrypha	cremation
predella	archangel	cupbearer
priedieu	archdruid	deaconess
province	archenemy	decalogue
psaltery	archfiend	deigratia
publican	Ascension	desecrate
pyxcloth	atonement	devotions
religion	baldachin	dignitary
Romanism	barbarian	dogcollar
roodloft	Beatitude	dogmatics
sacellum	Beelzebub	Dominican
sacristy	blackmass	embalming
sanctity	blasphemy	episcopal
scapular	Calvinist	episcopus
seraphic	canonical	Eucharist
seraphim	cantharus	exchanger
Shepherd	canticles	familypew
skullcap	Carmelite	firmament
SonofMan	carpenter	firstborn
surplice	cartulary	firstling
tenebrae	catacombs	fisherman
theology	catechism	footstone
thurible	cathedral	godfather
thurifer	celebrant	godliness
transept	cerecloth	godmother
versicle	cerements	godparent
vestment	Christian	goodworks
viaticum	churchman	gospeller
vicarage	claustral	graveside
Wesleyan	clergyman	graveyard
ziggurat	cloisters	hagiarchy
Aaron'srod	coadjutor	hagiology
adoration	Communion	headstone
Allelujah	concubine	Hereafter

heterodox	mummy|case	sacrarium
Hexateuch	Mussulman	sacrifice
hierarchy	mysticism	sacrilege
hierology	obsequial	sacristan
high|altar	obsequies	sainthood
holocaust	offertory	saintship
holy|cross	officiant	salvation
Holy|Ghost	orthodoxy	Samaritan
Holy|Grail	ossuarium	sanctuary
holy|table	Palestine	scapegoat
holy|water	papal|bull	scapulary
incumbent	Paraclete	schoolman
interment	parchment	Scripture
Israelite	parsonage	sepulchre
Jerusalem	patriarch	sepulture
joss\,house	payhomage	shewbread
joss\,stick	Pentecost	Shintoist
Judas|kiss	prayer|mat	shovel|hat
Lamb|of|God	prayer|rug	spiritual
land|of|Nod	precentor	suffragan
last|rites	presbyter	synagogue
laudation	priestess	Synoptics
lay|reader	prime|song	testament
lay|sister	profanity	tombstone
loincloth	proselyte	triforium
Lost|Sheep	proseuche	undersong
mactation	prothesis	unfrocked
Magdalene	psalmbook	Unitarian
martyrdom	reliquary	unworldly
mausoleum	reverence	venerable
mercy|seat	righteous	Zoroaster
Methodist	rood|stair	zucchetta
monastery	rood|tower	zucchetto
Monsignor	rural|dean	absolution
mortcloth	sackcloth	allocution
Mosaic|law	sacrament	allotheist

almsgiving	clerestory	high|places
altar|cloth	cloistered	high|priest
altar|front	collection	Holy|Family
altar|mound	Colossians	Holy|Father
altarpiece	confession	Holy|Orders
amen|corner	consecrate	Holy|Spirit
Anabaptist	conversion	Holy|Willie
antichrist	dedication	House|of|God
Apocalypse	diaconicon	hyperdulia
archbishop	divination	iconoclast
archdeacon	doctrinism	idolatrous
arch|flamen	Douay|Bible	immolation
arch|priest	encyclical	incumbency
Armaggedon	entombment	inhumation
Band|of|Hope	episcopacy	in|memoriam
baptistery	episcopant	irreligion
bar|mitzvah	Evangelist	Jacob's|Well
battle|hymn	Evil|Spirit	Lady|chapel
Beatitudes	exaltation	Last|Supper
benedicite	false|piety	lay|brother
benefactor	fellowship	lectionary
Bible|class	Franciscan	lie|in|state
birthright	funeral|ode	lip|service
blind|faith	funeral|urn	Lord's|house
canonicals	godfearing	Lord's|table
Carthusian	golden|calf	magnificat
catafalque	goody|goody	mantel|lone
catechumen	gravestone	Mark|of|Cain
chartulary	hagiolatry	missionary
choirstall	hagioscope	Mohammedan
Church|Army	Hallelujah	Mount|Sinai
church|bell	Heptateuch	Mount|Tabor
churchgoer	hierolatry	necropolis
churchyard	hieromancy	Needle's|eye
Cistercian	hierophant	pallbearer
clearstory	high|church	papal|brief

Papal Court	soothsayer	Christendom
paraphrase	superaltar	christening
Pentateuch	synthronus	church court
Pharisaism	tabernacle	church mouse
Philistine	tartuffery	City of David
phylactery	temperance	commandment
pilgrimage	temptation	communicant
pontifical	theologian	conventicle
poor sinner	theologist	Convocation
praetorium	unbeliever	crematorium
prayer bead	undertaker	crucifixion
prayer book	veneration	Curia Romana
prebendary	watch night	decanal side
Presbytery	widow's mite	Divine right
priesthood	wilderness	Epistle side
procurator	worshipper	eschatology
prophetess	Wycliffite	family bible
Protestant	agnosticism	first fruits
Providence	altar carpet	funeral pile
regenerate	altar facing	funeral pyre
Revelation	apologetics	Geneva bands
Roman Curia	arch heretic	Geneva cloak
rood screen	arch prelate	good tidings
Sabbath day	aspergillum	graven image
sacerdotal	Augustinium	Greek Church
sacredness	Benedictine	hagiographa
sacrosanct	benediction	hagiologist
sanctimony	bishop's ring	hierography
Scepticism	bitter herbs	incarnation
Schismatic	blasphemous	irreligious
scholastic	body and soul	Kingdom Come
Scriptures	Book of Book	kirk session
secularism	burning bush	last offices
Septuagint	Catholicism	lawn sleeves
sepulchral	chapel royal	Lord of Hosts
shibboleth	choir stalls	Lord's prayer

352

Lord's|supper	burial|ground
missal|stand	canonization
monasterial	cardinal's|hat
Nicene|Creed	chancel|table
nullifidian	chapel|of|ease
original|sin	chapter|house
parish|clerk	charnel|house
paternoster	Charterhouse
patron|saint	Chosen|People
pillar|saint	Christianity
pontificals	church|living
pontificate	churchmaster
prayer|wheel	church|nation
Prodigal|Son	church|parade
protomartyr	churchwarden
pure|in|heart	City|of|Refuge
reading|desk	collectarium
Reformation	Commandments
religiosity	Common|Prayer
remembrance	confessional
requiem|mass	confirmation
rest|in|peace	congregation
river|Jordan	consecration
Sacred|Heart	Coptic|church
saintliness	Damascus|road
Sanctus|bell	Day|of|the|Lord
sarcophagus	denomination
soteriology	ecclesiastic
take|the|veil	enshrinement
theological	fiery|serpent
triple|crown	frankincense
Vatican|City	Garden|of|Eden
vine|of|Sodom	Good|Shepherd
Virgin's|Well	hagiographer
Wise|Virgins	herald|angels
Annunciation	Holy|Alliance

Holy|of|Holies	Apostles|creed
Holy|Thursday	archbishopric
hot|gospeller	archidiaconal
Jacob's|ladder	beatification
jot|and|tittle	bidding|prayer
Judgment|Hall	bottomless|pit
Judgment|Seat	church|officer
Last|Judgment	church|service
major|prophet	communion|card
marriage|vows	co,religionist
minor|prophet	day|of|judgment
money|changer	divine|justice
New|Testament	divine|service
Old|Testament	ecumenicalism
prayer|carpet	eschatologist
Promised|Land	excommunicate
resting|place	high|churchman
Resurrection	holy|innocents
Rose|of|Sharon	household|gods
sacred|ground	household|gods
sacrilegious	incense|burner
Sea|of|Galilee	infant|baptism
Second|Coming	Lambeth|degree
Sunday|school	light|of|nature
thanksgiving	moral|theology
theologician	morning|prayer
Three|Wise|Men	nonconformist
Tower|of|Babel	nonconformity
ultramontane	pantheistical
wear|the|cloth	pantheologist
winding|sheet	pectoral|cross
Abraham's|bosom	prayer|meeting
aggiornamento	reincarnation
Ancient|of|days	Salvation|Army
Anglo|Catholic	Zarathustrism
anthroposophy	Anglican|church

apostolic|vicar
archiepiscopal
beatific|vision
cardinal|virtue
church|militant
communion|bread
communion|table
Dean|and|chapter
denominational
devil's|advocate
ecclesiastical
eschatological
evangelicalism
extreme|unction
fisherman's|ring
forbidden|fruit
high|priesthood
intercommunion
Latter|day|saint
mark|of|the|Beast
morning|service
mother|superior
Orthodox|Church
pastoral|letter
recording|angel
reformed|church
Revised|Version
sabbatarianism
sabbath|breaker
sign|of|the|cross
Society|of|Jesus

Tridentine|Mass
Zoroastrianism
anthropomorphic
anticlericalism
archiepiscopacy
archiepiscopate
articles|of|faith
chapter|and|verse
Christadelphian
Church|of|England
confessionalist
devil|worshipper
divine|messenger
episcopalianism
excommunication
General|Assembly
harvest|festival
Holy|Roman|Empire
Jehovah's|witness
laying|on|of|hands
Moral|Rearmament
new|English|Bible
odour|of|sanctity
Plymouth|brother
Presbyterianism
religious|belief
seven|deadly|sins
synoptic|gospels
ten|commandments
transfiguration

Rivers

Ob	Lena	Congo	Rhone	Ganges
Po	Maas	Douro	Saône	Hudson
Si	Main	Drava	Seine	Humber
Bug	Milk	Dvina	Siang	Iguaçú
Dee	Nile	Forth	Snake	Ijssel
Don	Oder	Foyle	Snowy	Irtysh
Ems	Ohio	Green	Somme	Japura
Esk	Oise	Havel	Spree	Jhelum
Exe	Ouse	Indus	Swale	Jordan
Han	Oxus	Ishim	Tagus	Kolyma
Lys	Para	James	Tiber	Leitha
Oka	Prut	Jumna	Torne	Liffey
Red	Saar	Jurua	Trent	Medway
Tay	Spey	Kasai	Tweed	Mekong
Usk	Suir	Lagan	Vitim	Mersey
Wye	Swan	Liard	Volga	Moldau
Aire	Taff	Loire	Volta	Murray
Arno	Tana	Marne	Weser	Neckar
Avon	Tees	Meuse	Xingú	Neisse
Ebro	Tyne	Negro	Yukon	Orange
Eden	Ural	Niger	Abdiel	Ottawa
Elan	Vaal	Osage	Amazon	Parana
Elbe	Wear	Peace	Angara	Ribble
Gila	Yalu	Pearl	Atbara	Sabine
Göta	Adige	Pecos	Chenab	Salado
Juba	Aisne	Piave	Danube	Sambre
Kama	Argun	Plate	Donets	Severn
Kura	Boyne	Purus	Fraser	StlJohn
Lech	Clyde	Rhine	Gambia	Struma

Sutlej	Waitaki
Thames	Yangtze
Tigris	Yenisei
Vilyui	Zambezi
Wabash	AmuDarya
Wharfe	Arkansas
Alabama	Cheyenne
Berbice	Chindwin
Bighorn	Colorado
Darling	Columbia
Derwent	Delaware
Dnieper	Dniester
Dubawnt	Dordogne
Garonne	Eastmain
Helmand	Flinders
Hooghly	Godavari
HwangHo	Hamilton
Krishna	Illinois
Lachlan	Missouri
Limpopo	Paraguay
Madeira	Parnaiba
Maritsa	Putumayo
Moselle	Savannah
Orinoco	Suwannee
Pechora	Wanganui
Potomac	Athabaska
Roanoke	Churchill
Salween	Euphrates
Scheldt	Irrawaddy
Senegal	Mackenzie
Shannon	Macquarie
SiKiang	Magdalena
Tsangpo	Murchison
Uruguay	Porcupine
Vistula	RioGrande
Waikato	Tennessee

RIVERS

Wisconsin	Brahmaputra	Murrumbidgee
Republican	Mississippi	Saskatchewan
Sacramento	Yellowstone	
St Lawrence	Guadalquivir	

Shakespearean Characters

Ely	Jamy	Bigot	Feste	Philo
Nym	John	Blunt	Flute	Pinch
Say	Juno	Boult	Froth	Poins
Adam	Kent	Boyet	Ghost	Priam
Ajax	Lear	Bushy	Goffe	Regan
Anne	Luce	Butts	Gower	Robin
Bawd	Lucy	Caius	Green	Romeo
Bona	Moth	Casca	Helen	Rugby
Cade	Page	Celia	Henry	Sands
Cato	Peto	Ceres	Hymen	Snare
Davy	Puck	Cinna	Julia	Snout
Dick	Ross	Cleon	Lafeu	Speed
Dion	Snug	Corin	Lewis	Timon
Dull	Vaux	Court	Lovel	Titus
Eros	Wart	Cupid	Lucio	Tubal
Fang	York	Curan	March	Varro
Fool	Aaron	Curio	Maria	Viola
Ford	Alice	Denny	Melun	Adrian
Grey	Angus	Derby	Menas	Aegeon
Hero	Anjou	Diana	Mopsa	Aeneas
Hume	Ariel	Edgar	Osric	Albany
Iago	Bagot	Egeus	Paris	Alonso
Iden	Bates	Elbow	Percy	Amiens
Iras	Belch	Essex	Peter	Angelo
Iris	Bevis	Evans	Phebe	Antony

Armado	Gremio	Quince	Bedford
Arthur	Grumio	Rivers	Berowne
Audrey	Gurney	Rumour	Bertram
Banquo	Hamlet	Scales	Bourbon
Basset	Hecate	Scarus	Brandon
Bianca	Hector	Scroop	Calchas
Blanch	Helena	Seyton	Caliban
Blount	Hermia	Shadow	Camillo
Boleyn	Horner	Silius	Capulet
Bottom	Imogen	Silvia	Cassius
Brutus	Isabel	Simple	Catesby
Bullen	Jaques	Siward	Cerimon
Cadwal	Juliet	Strato	Charles
Caesar	Launce	Surrey	Chatham
Caphis	LeBeau	Talbot	Claudio
Cassio	Lennox	Tamora	Conrade
Chiron	Lovell	Taurus	Costard
Cicero	Lucius	Thaisa	Cranmer
Cimber	Marina	Thomas	deBurgh
Clitus	Morgan	Thurio	Dionyza
Cloten	Morton	Tranio	Douglas
Cobweb	Mouldy	Tybalt	Dumaine
Curtis	Mutius	Ursula	Eleanor
Dennis	Nestor	Verges	Escalus
Dorcas	Oberon	Vernon	Escanes
Dorset	Oliver	Wolsey	Flavius
Dromio	Olivia	Abraham	Fleance
Duncan	Orsino	Aemilia	Francis
Edmund	Oswald	Afriana	Gallius
Edward	Oxford	Agrippa	Goneril
Elinor	Pandar	Alarbus	Gonzalo
Emilia	Pedant	Alencon	Gregory
Exeter	Philip	Antenor	Helenus
Fabian	Pistol	Antonio	Herbert
Feeble	Pompey	Arragon	Holland
Fenton	Portia	Aumerle	Horatio

SHAKESPEAREAN CHARACTERS

Hotspur	Orleans	William	Eglamour
Iachimo	Othello	Abhorson	Falstaff
Jessica	Paulina	Achilles	Florence
Laertes	Perdita	Aemilius	Florizel
Lavache	Phrynia	Aufidius	Fluellen
Lavinia	Pisanio	Auvergne	Gadshill
Leonato	Proteus	Baptista	Gargrave
Leonine	Provost	Bardolph	Gertrude
Leontes	Publius	Bassanio	Grandpre
Lepidus	Quintus	Beatrice	Gratiano
Lorenzo	Richard	Beaufort	Griffith
Lucetta	Rutland	Belarius	Harcourt
Luciana	Salanio	Benedick	Hastings
Lymoges	Sampson	Benvolio	Hermione
Macbeth	Shallow	Berkeley	Isabella
Macduff	Shylock	Bernardo	JackCade
Malcolm	Silence	Borachio	Jourdain
Marcade	Silvius	Bullcalf	Laurence
Marcius	Simpcox	Burgundy	Leonardo
Mardian	Slender	Campeius	Leonatus
Mariana	Solinus	Canidius	Ligarius
Martext	Stanley	Capucius	Lodovico
Martius	Suffolk	Carlisle	Lucentio
Messala	Theseus	Charmian	Lucilius
Michael	Thyreus	Clarence	Lucullus
Miranda	Titania	Claudius	Lysander
Montano	Travers	Clifford	Maecenas
Montjoy	Tressel	Cominius	Malvolio
Morocco	Troilus	Cordelia	Margaret
Mowbray	Tyrrell	Cornwall	Marullus
Nerissa	Ulysses	Cressida	Menelaus
Nicanor	Urswick	Cromwell	Menteith
Norfolk	Valeria	Dercetas	Mercutio
Octavia	Varrius	Diomedes	Montague
Ophelia	Vaughan	Dogberry	Mortimer
Orlando	Warwick	DonPedro	Overdone

Pandarus	Woodvile	Erpingham
Pandulph	Agamemnon	Ferdinand
Panthino	Aguecheek	Fitzwater
Parolles	Alexander	Flaminius
Patience	Antigonus	Francisca
Pembroke	Antiochus	Francisco
Pericles	Apemantus	Frederick
Philario	Archibald	Glansdale
Philemon	Arvigarus	Glendower
Philotus	Autolycus	Guiderius
Pindarus	Balthasar	Guildford
Polonius	Balthazar	Helicanus
Polydore	Bassianus	Hippolyta
Prospero	Biondello	Hortensio
Rambures	Boatswain	Katharina
Ratcliff	Bourchier	Katharine
Reignier	Brabantio	Lancaster
Reynaldo	Caithness	Lychorida
Richmond	Calpurnia	Macmorris
Roderigo	Cambridge	Mamillius
Rosalind	Cassandra	Marcellus
Rosaline	Chatillon	Nathaniel
Salarino	Cleomenes	Patroclus
Seleucus	Cleopatra	Petruchio
Somerset	Coleville	Polixenes
Stafford	Constance	Posthumus
Stephano	Cornelius	Rotherham
Thaliard	Cymbeline	Rousillon
Timandra	Dardanius	Salisbury
Titinius	Deiphobus	Sebastian
Trinculo	Demetrius	Servilius
Violenta	Desdemona	Simonides
Virgilia	Dolabella	Southwell
Volumnia	Donalbain	Thersites
Whitmore	Elizabeth	Trebonius
Williams	Enobarbus	Valentine

Ventidius	Abergavenny
Vincentio	Artemidorus
Voltimand	Bolingbroke
Volumnius	Brackenbury
Worcester	Caius Lucius
Young Cato	John of Gaunt
Alcibiades	Lady Capulet
Andromache	Mayor of York
Andronicus	Mustardseed
Anne Boleyn	Philostrate
Antipholus	Plantagenet
Apothecary	Rosencrantz
Barnardine	Young Siward
Brakenbury	Decius Brutus
Buckingham	Guildenstern
Coriolanus	Julius Caesar
Duke of York	Junius Brutus
Euphronius	Marcus Brutus
Fortinbras	Peaseblossom
Gloucester	Popilius Lena
Holofernes	Sir Toby Belch
Hortensius	Titus Lartius
Jaquenetta	Westmoreland
Longaville	Doll Tearsheet
Lysimachus	Faulconbridge
Margarelon	Joan la Pucelle
Mark Antony	Young Clifford
Menecrates	Christopher Sly
Montgomery	Launcelot Gobbo
Proculeius	Metellus Cimber
Saturninus	Northumberland
Sempronius	Octavius Caesar
Somerville	Sextus Pompeius
Starveling	Tullus Aufidius
Touchstone	Menenius Agrippa
Willoughby	Mistress Quickly

Robin|Goodfellow   Titus|Andronicus
Sicinius|Velutus

Sports, Games and Pastimes

KO	jig	away	deck	hand	lido
PT	kit	bail	dice	hank	lift
TT	lap	bait	dive	heat	lock
ace	lbw	ball	doll	hike	loom
aim	leg	bank	drag	hold	loop
bat	let	base	draw	hole	love
bet	lie	beat	duck	home	ludo
bid	lob	bend	duel	hook	luge
bow	loo	bias	epee	hoop	lure
box	net	bike	fall	hunt	mall
bye	par	bind	fare	hype	meet
cap	peg	blow	file	iron	meld
cat	pin	blue	fish	I|spy	mile
cox	Pit	bout	fist	jack	nock
cue	pot	bowl	foil	jape	Oaks
cup	run	brag	fore	jest	oars
dan	set	buck	form	jive	odds
die	shy	calx	foul	joke	Oval
DIY	ski	card	gaff	judo	over
fan	tag	chip	gala	jump	pace
fun	tie	chop	game	kail	pack
gin	ton	club	gate	kill	pass
gym	top	coup	gear	king	pawn
hit	toy	crew	goal	kite	play
hop	try	dart	golf	lane	polo
jab	win	dash	grid	lark	pool
jeu	ante	deal	grip	leap	port

puck	trot	catch	fives	notch
putt	turf	chase	fling	ombre
quiz	walk	check	frame	ouija
race	whip	chess	going	pairs
raft	wide	chips	grass	parry
reel	wing	chute	green	pilot
reel	wire	climb	guard	pique
ring	wood	clubs	guide	pitch
rink	yoyo	coach	gully	piton
rook	alley	conge	halma	pivot
ruck	angle	count	heave	point
ruff	arena	coupe	hobby	poker
rule	arrow	court	inner	polka
sail	baffy	craps	jetty	pools
seat	bathe	crawl	joker	prank
seed	baths	cycle	joust	proam
shot	baton	dance	kails	punto
side	bingo	darts	kayak	quart
skat	blade	debut	kendo	queen
skid	blind	decoy	kitty	racer
skip	bluff	Derby	knave	rally
skis	board	deuce	links	range
slam	bogey	diver	lists	relay
slip	bound	divot	loose	rouge
snap	bower	dormy	loser	rough
solo	bowls	drive	lotto	round
spin	boxer	dummy	lunge	rover
spot	break	eagle	mambo	rugby
suit	bully	evens	march	rules
sumo	caber	event	match	rumba
swim	caddy	eyass	medal	rummy
tack	cadge	fault	midon	sabre
team	canoe	feint	miler	samba
tice	caper	field	monte	scent
toss	cards	fight	morra	score
trap	carom	final	nobid	screw

scrum	whist	castle	glider	marina
scull	abseil	centre	gobang	mascot
serve	akimbo	cestus	gobble	mashie
shaft	anchor	cha,cha	go,kart	maxixe
shoot	angler	chasse	golfer	merils
sight	anorak	cherry	googly	mid,off
skier	archer	chukka	ground	minuet
skiff	ascent	circus	gutter	misere
slide	at|ease	conker	hammer	morris
slips	attack	corner	hand,in	mud|pie
smash	bailer	course	hazard	murder
spear	banker	cradle	header	nelson
spoon	bidder	crambo	hearts	no|ball
sport	birdie	crease	helmet	opener
stake	bishop	crosse	hiking	paddle
stalk	bisque	cruise	hockey	pelota
steer	blocks	cup|tie	honour	period
strip	bookie	curler	hooker	piquet
sweep	borrow	dealer	hookey	player
swing	boston	dedans	hoop,la	plunge
sword	bowled	diving	hurdle	pocket
tally	bowler	dog|leg	hurley	pommel
tango	bowman	dormie	ice|axe	popgun
tarot	boxing	driver	jesses	puppet
title	bracer	dry|f|ly	jigsaw	putter
ton,up	bricks	eleven	jockey	puzzle
touch	bridge	equipe	jostle	quarry
track	bulger	euchre	jumper	quarte
trick	bumper	fencer	karate	quinze
trump	bunker	fisher	knight	quoits
twist	caddie	flight	lariat	rabbit
valse	can,can	flying	leader	racing
venue	cannon	gallop	leg,bye	racket
wager	canter	gambit	mallet	raffle
waltz	car|run	gaming	manege	ramble
wedge	casino	glider	marble	rapids

rapier	squash	yoicks	bubbles
rave up	stakes	yorker	camp bed
record	stance	ace high	camping
remise	sticks	acrobat	captain
replay	stilts	address	capture
result	strike	also ran	carioca
rhumba	stroke	amateur	cassino
riddle	stroll	angling	catcher
riding	stumps	archery	century
roll in	stymie	arm hold	charade
roquet	sweeps	arm lock	charter
rowing	swivel	assault	Chicago
rubber	tackle	athlete	chicane
rugger	target	back row	chimney
runner	tarots	bad calx	chipper
safari	tennis	balance	chukker
savate	threes	ballast	circuit
scorer	thrust	balloon	classic
sculls	thwart	bar bell	compass
seance	tickle	bathing	couloir
second	tipcat	batsman	counter
seesaw	tiptoe	beguine	crampon
shimmy	tivoli	bezique	creases
shinny	torero	bicycle	cricket
shinty	touche	bidding	croquet
shorts	toygun	big game	cue ball
skater	trophy	bivouac	curb bit
skiing	truant	bladder	curling
slalom	TTrace	blaster	cushion
sledge	umpire	boating	cutlass
soccer	versus	bonfire	cycling
spades	volley	bowling	cyclist
spikes	wicket	box kite	dancing
spiral	willow	bracing	day trip
sports	winger	bran tub	decider
sprint	winner	brassie	declare

defence	goggles	leg|hold	pinball
descent	golf,bag	leg|side	pinfall
diabolo	golfing	let|ball	pin,high
diamond	golf|tie	line|out	pinocle
dicebox	good|fun	longbow	pitcher
discard	grounds	long,hop	pit|stop
doubles	guy|rope	long,leg	play,off
drawing	gymnast	lottery	poloist
dribble	hacking	marbles	pontoon
driving	hairpin	matador	potshot
end|game	hand,off	maypole	press|up
end|play	harpoon	mazurka	prowess
en|prise	harrier	meccano	pyramid
entrant	hawking	melding	quarter
fairway	holster	midiron	rackets
fan|club	honours	netball	rag|doll
fencing	hunting	net|cord	rebound
fielder	hurdler	niblick	referee
fifteen	hurling	ninepin	regatta
fine|leg	ice|pick	no|trump	reserve
finesse	ice|rink	oarsman	ripcord
fishing	ikebana	offside	riposte
fixture	infield	old|maid	rockers
fly|half	innings	one,step	rosette
foot|bow	jackpot	on|guard	rowlock
formula	j,adoube	overarm	rubicon
forward	javelin	over|par	running
fox|hunt	jogging	paddock	sailing
foxtrot	joy|ride	pallone	sand|pie
freehit	ju,jitsu	partner	sand|pit
Frisbee	keep|fit	passade	scooter
frogman	kick,off	passado	scratch
funfair	knock,up	pastime	service
gallery	lancers	penalty	seven|up
gavotte	landing	picador	shot|put
gliding	last|lap	picquet	shuffle

shuttle	Torpids	body|blow	cross,bat
singles	tourney	bonspiel	cruising
singlet	trainer	boundary	cup|final
skating	tumbler	brackets	dark|blue
skid,lid	twosome	bullring	dead|ball
snaffle	two,step	bull's|eye	dead|heat
snooker	vantage	bully|off	deadlock
snorkel	vaulter	cakewalk	dead|shot
society	walking	campfire	delivery
soft|toy	war|club	camp|site	diamonds
sparrer	war|game	canoeing	dominoes
squails	workout	card|game	doubling
stadium	wrestle	carnival	dragster
stamina	ziganka	carousel	draughts
starter	aerobics	car|rally	draw|lots
stirrup	all,fours	castling	dressage
St|Leger	approach	catapult	drop|goal
striker	apres,ski	cat|stick	drop|kick
stumped	aqualung	champion	drop|shot
sub,aqua	aquatics	charades	dumb|bell
sun|bath	armguard	checkers	even|keel
tacking	away|game	chequers	even|odds
tactics	baccarat	chessman	exercise
take,off	backhand	chess|set	face|card
tally|ho	backheel	chin|hold	fair|play
tangram	backspin	chip|shot	falconer
tantivy	bail|ball	climbing	falconry
tenpins	balk|line	coasting	fandango
tent|peg	ball|game	contract	fast|ball
The|Oaks	baseball	cottabus	field|day
The|Oval	baseline	counters	finalist
throw,in	beagling	coursing	firework
tie|game	biathlon	coxswain	fistiana
tilting	biathlon	crap|game	fivepins
toe|hold	blocking	cribbage	flapping
tombola	boat|race	crossbar	flat|race

flippers	half|ball	left|wing	pall|mall
floating	half|blue	leg|break	pass|line
foilsman	half|mile	leg|guard	pass|roll
foothold	half|shot	lifeline	patience
foot|race	half|time	linesman	pike|dive
footwork	handball	long|game	ping|pong
forehand	handicap	long|jump	pinochle
forfeits	hat|trick	long|odds	pin|table
foul|goal	haymaker	long|rush	playmate
foul|line	headlock	long|shot	playroom
foul|play	helmsman	long|stop	plunging
foursome	high|dive	lost|ball	polo|ball
foxhound	high|jump	love|game	polo|pony
free|kick	holed|out	lucky|bag	pony|trek
fretwork	hole|high	lucky|dip	pool|room
front|row	home|game	mah|jongg	port|tack
full|back	hornpipe	marathon	pugilism
full|draw	horseman	marksman	pugilist
full|toss	how's|that	marriage	pushball
gambling	hula|hoop	monopoly	pyramids
gamester	hula|hula	motorist	quintain
gauntlet	huntsman	multi|gym	quiz|game
gin|rummy	hurdling	napoleon	racegoer
goal|kick	ice|yacht	natation	radio|ham
goalpost	Irish|jig	ninepins	rambling
golfball	iron|shot	nose|dive	reaching
golf|club	jiu|jitsu	no|trumps	recovery
golliwog	joystick	off|break	red|cloak
good|calx	knock|out	off|drive	redouble
good|shot	korfball	Olympiad	ricochet
gridiron	lacrosse	open|file	rink|polo
guarding	lawn|game	opponent	rope|ring
gymkhana	leapfrog	outfield	roulette
gym|shoes	left|back	outsider	rounders
habanera	left|half	oval|ball	rucksack
halfback	left|hook	paddling	runner|up

Ruy|Lopez	stations	all,comers
sack|race	stoccado	all|square
sand|iron	stock|car	anchor|man
sand|trap	stop|shot	arabesque
saraband	straddle	arrow|shot
sardines	straight	astrodome
Scrabble	tap|dance	athletics
scramble	team|game	Aunt|Sally
scrum|cap	tent|pole	back|court
sculling	The|Ashes	back|edges
selector	the|field	back|swing
set|point	third|man	badminton
shell|out	thole|pin	bagatelle
shooting	tie|break	bandalore
short|leg	toreador	bandy|ball
side,blow	Totopoly	barn|dance
side|line	tracking	baulk|line
ski|ngame	trailing	beach|ball
ski|slope	training	best|bower
ski|stick	train|set	biathlete
skittles	tug,of|war	big|dipper
sledging	underarm	billiards
slow|ball	undercut	black|belt
snapshot	under|par	blackjack
snowball	upper|cut	black|pawn
snow|line	vaulting	bladework
softball	venation	boarhound
southpaw	walkover	boar|spear
sparring	wall|game	bobsleigh
speedway	wing|area	body|check
spoon|oar	wood|club	body|punch
sporting	wood|shot	bossa|nova
sprinter	wrestler	bowstring
stalking	yachting	brown|belt
stand|off	acey|deucy	caddie|car
stand|pat	advantage	camel|spin

370

card|trick	equalizer	grand|prix
cartwheel	exercises	grand|slam
cavalcade	extra|time	gum|shield
cha|cha|cha	face|guard	gymnasium
chair|lift	favourite	handstand
challenge	field|game	hard|court
checkmate	fieldsman	high|jinks
chess|game	first|half	hill|climb
clock|golf	first|seed	hitch|hike
clog|dance	first|slip	hit|wicket
closing|in	fisherman	hopscotch
club|house	fisticuff	horseback
collector	five|a|side	horseplay
combatant	fletching	horse|race
conjuring	flight|bow	ice|hockey
contender	flyweight	ice|skates
cotillion	foot|fault	infielder
court|card	fore|royal	jackknife
crackshot	forty|love	judo|throw
cricketer	free|reach	kennelman
cross|jack	freestyle	king's|rook
crossword	freewheel	lawn|bowls
cycle|race	full|house	left|bower
cycle|tour	galleries	left|inner
dance|step	game|point	leg|before
dartboard	gardening	leg|spread
decathlon	gladiator	light|blue
decoy|duck	goalposts	long|loser
disengage	go|karting	long|tacks
dog|racing	gold|medal	loose|ball
doll's|pram	golf|links	loose|maul
drawn|game	golf|range	loose|rein
dribbling	golf|shoes	love|forty
enclosure	golf|widow	love|match
en|passant	good|loser	low|volley
en|tout|cas	good|sport	match|play

medallist	quadrille	silver|cup
medal|play	quickstep	singleton
mid|mashie	race|track	skin|diver
motocross	racing|car	sky|diving
music|hall	relay|race	small|bore
Newmarket	relay|team	snow|climb
Nuts|in|May	right|back	solitaire
orienteer	right|half	solo|whist
pacemaker	right|hook	spectator
palaestra	right|wing	speedboat
panel|game	ringsider	spin|parry
pantomime	rock|climb	split|shot
paper|doll	roundelay	spoon|bait
parachute	round|game	sports|day
party|game	round|trip	sportsman
paso|doble	rover|hoop	spot|dance
passepied	safety|net	square|leg
Paul|Jones	sand|yacht	stable|boy
pelmanism	sauna|bath	stalemate
pen|friend	schnorkel	starboard
penthouse	score|card	steersman
philately	scrapbook	step|dance
pickaback	screw|dive	stopwatch
pilot|ball	scrimmage	stud|poker
pinch|draw	scrum|half	surfboard
pirouette	scrummage	sweatband
pitch|camp	second|row	swordplay
plaything	semi|final	swordsman
pogo|stick	shaftment	teddy|bear
poker|dice	shamateur	tennis|net
pole|vault	shinguard	terracing
polonaise	short|game	test|match
potholing	short|odds	the|sticks
puissance	shortstop	three|jump
punchball	shrimping	threesome
push|parry	signal|gun	three|turn

tight|rein	blood|sport	drop|cannon
tip,and,run	booby|prize	drop|volley
torch|race	boxing|ring	equitation
touch|down	catch|a|crab	Eskimo|roll
touch|goal	cat's|cradle	fairground
touch|line	centre|half	fantoccini
track|suit	challenger	fast|bowler
trump|card	changeover	feathering
trump|suit	charleston	fianchetto
turnstile	checkpoint	field|event
twenty,one	chessboard	field|sport
twist|dive	Chinese|box	first|blood
vingt,et,un	christiana	fishing|net
water|polo	clay|pigeon	fishing|rod
whirligig	coconut|shy	flat|racing
white|pawn	competitor	fly|fishing
wrist|lock	contestant	flying|mare
yacht|club	contractor	flying|shot
yacht|race	counted|out	footballer
yachtsman	cover|point	forced|move
youth|club	cricket|bat	foundation
acrobatics	cricket|net	fox|hunting
aerobatics	crown|green	free,for,all
agility|mat	cyclo|cross	full|nelson
agonistics	daily|dozen	gambit|pawn
backgammon	decathlete	ghost|train
back|marker	deck|quoits	goal|circle
back|stroke	deck|tennis	goal|crease
balneation	discobolus	goalkeeper
banderilla	diving|bell	goal|tender
basketball	doll's|house	golf|course
battledore	dolly|catch	grandstand
bee|keeping	double|axle	gymnastics
betting|man	double|game	half|bisque
binoculars	double|peel	half|nelson
blind|poker	draw|stumps	half|volley

373

halieutics	kewpie|doll	playground
halved|hole	kite|flying	point|of|a|im
handspring	kriegspiel	poker|chips
hard|tackle	lansquenet	polo|ground
Harrow|game	lawn|tennis	potato|race
hazard|side	league|game	prize|fight
headhunter	little|slam	prize|money
health|club	loaded|dice	punch|drunk
health|farm	loose|scrum	push|stroke
heel|and|toe	love|thirty	queen's|pawn
high|diving	maiden|over	queen's|rook
hitch|hiker	marionette	racecourse
hobbyhorse	marker|buoy	racing|cars
hockey|team	mashie|iron	ratcatcher
hog|hunting	match|point	real|tennis
horseshoes	middle|spot	recreation
horsewoman	minor|piece	relaxation
hunting|bow	non|starter	relegation
ice|dancing	object|ball	rifle|range
ice|skating	off|the|hook	right|bower
Indian|club	opening|bat	right|inner
Indian|file	open|season	right|swing
indoor|golf	open|target	ring|o|roses
injury|time	Ouija|board	rod|and|reel
inside|home	outfielder	roundabout
inside|lane	pancration	round|dance
inside|left	pancratium	rowing|boat
inside|lock	paper|chase	royal|flush
in|the|rough	par|contest	rubber|ball
in|training	pari|mutuel	rubber|duck
isometrics	passed|pawn	rugby|union
jackstones	penalty|try	rumpus|room
jackstraws	pentathlon	run|through
Jockey|Club	philatelic	rush|stroke
jump|the|gun	pigeon|loft	sand|castle
karate|chop	planchette	scoreboard

second|half	suspension	willow|wand
second|slip	sweepstake	win|by|a|head
seconds|out	switchback	winning|gun
second|wind	sword|dance	Yarborough
seven|a|side	take|a|trick	young|entry
short|tacks	tarantella	accumulator
show|jumper	team|spirit	baseball|bat
sidesaddle	tennis|ball	bearbaiting
side|stroke	tennis|shoe	bellringing
silly|mid|on	thirty|love	Bengal|spear
silly|point	thrown|goal	betting|ring
single|file	tiger|badge	biased|bowls
single|game	timekeeper	big|game|hunt
skateboard	time|thrust	boating|pond
ski|jumping	tin|soldier	Bombay|spear
skin|diving	title|fight	bow|and|arrow
ski|running	toe|scratch	boxing|match
sky|jumping	tournament	bronze|medal
slow|bowler	tour|skiing	bull|baiting
somersault	toy|soldier	canoe|slalom
speed|trial	track|event	casual|water
spike|shoes	trampoline	Channel|swim
spin|bowler	trial|match	chariot|race
sportswear	triple|jump	cheer|leader
spot|stroke	triple|peel	cinder|track
square|ring	true|to|form	class|racing
stamp|album	tumble|turn	close|season
stock|cards	turkey|trot	compact|disc
stop|thrust	twelfth|man	country|walk
strathspey	vantage|set	county|match
strike|camp	Vardon|grip	coup|de|grace
stroke|play	volleyball	court|tennis
submission	water|wings	crash|helmet
substitute	whippers|in	crawl|stroke
sun|bathing	whist|drive	cricket|ball
surf|riding	wilful|foul	cricket|pads

croquet|arch	fox|and|geese	modern|waltz
croquet|ball	free|skating	morris|dance
croquet|hoop	fun|and|games	motor|racing
croquet|lawn	gambit|piece	mountaineer
cross|swords	gambling|man	mystery|tour
curling|pond	gaming|house	nailed|boots
curling|rink	gaming|table	neck|and|neck
cycle|racing	garden|party	offside|rule
daisy|cutter	glove|puppet	Olympic|team
deck|of|cards	gone|fishing	out|of|bounds
deep|fine|leg	good|innings	outside|home
direct|party	grand|salute	outside|left
diving|board	groundsheet	pack|of|cards
diving|dress	hairpin|bend	pair|skating
double|check	half|passage	palaestrian
double|fault	halfway|line	pancake|race
downhill|run	heavyweight	pancratiast
driving|iron	hide\,and\,seek	parlour|game
egg|and|spoon	hitch\,hiking	pawn|and|move
envelopment	hockey|match	penalty|area
eurhythmics	hockey|stick	penalty|goal
false|attack	home|and|away	penalty|kick
fencing|mask	horse|racing	penalty|line
Ferris|wheel	horse|riding	photo|finish
field|events	ice|yachting	picture|card
fifteen|love	inside|right	pigeon|flier
figure|eight	jumping|bean	pigeon|house
first|attack	king's|bishop	pigeon|timer
first|eleven	king's|knight	pig|sticking
fishing|line	lap|of|honour	pillow|fight
flick|stroke	league|table	piscatology
flying|start	lightweight	pitch|and|run
football|fan	lock|forward	playing|card
forced|error	loop|the|loop	playing|line
forward|line	love\,fifteen	play|the|game
forward|pass	malibu|board	pole|vaulter

prizewinner	snow|glasses	training|run
prop|forward	snowshoeing	transfer|fee
public|games	soft|landing	triple|crown
pyramid|spot	spade|mashie	Turkish|bath
quarterback	speculation	waiting|game
rabbit|punch	spinning|top	walking|race
race|meeting	sportswoman	water|hazard
racing|craft	spreadeagle	water|skiing
racing|shell	springboard	water|sports
racket|court	square|dance	Western|roll
record|break	square|tango	wine|tasting
riddle|me|ree	squash|court	wing|forward
Roman|candle	staghunting	winning|post
rouge|et|noir	starting|gun	winning|time
round|of|golf	straight|bat	win|on|points
royal|tennis	striker|ball	wooden|horse
rugby|league	sudden|death	world|record
Schottische	swallow|dive	youth|hostel
seam|bowling	sweep|rowing	anchor|cannon
self|defence	table|tennis	approach|shot
service|grip	target|arrow	back|straight
service|hold	tennis|court	bantamweight
service|line	tennis|match	batting|order
service|side	tent|pegging	beachcombing
shinty|stick	Terpsichore	Becher's|brook
shovelboard	theatregoer	billiard|ball
show|jumping	the|Olympics	billiard|hall
shuttlecock	third|player	billiard|room
sightseeing	three|legged	billiard|spot
silver|medal	tiddlywinks	bingo|session
simple|parry	time|sharing	bird|watching
singing|game	tobogganing	body|building
skating|rink	totalisator	bowling|alley
skiing|field	touring|club	bowling|green
sleeping|bag	toxophilite	boxing|gloves
slow|foxtrot	track|record	break|dancing

break|the|bank fast|and|loose long|distance
breast|stroke field|glasses loose|forward
bull|fighting figure|skater losing|hazard
butterfly|net first|defence maiden|stakes
callisthenic first|innings marathon|race
century|break first|reserve medicine|ball
championship first|service melding|score
change|bowler flying|tackle merry|go|round
change|of|ends foursome|reel mincing|steps
changing|room free|wheeling mixed|doubles
checkerboard French|boxing National|Hunt
classic|races fruit|machine nature|ramble
climbing|rope game|of|chance noble|science
cockfighting game|of|points nursery|slope
consequences gamesmanship obstacle|race
country|dance gone|to|ground old|time|dance
cradle|cannon ground|stroke Olympic|games
crapshooting guessing|game Olympic|title
cricket|boots handicap|race Olympic|torch
cricket|pitch head|scissors opposing|side
croquet|court hill|climbing ordinary|foul
cross|country home|straight orienteering
curling|stone homing|pigeon orienteering
cut|and|thrust horsemanship outside|right
dead|ball|line housey|housey paddling|pool
deep|sea|diver hundred|yards parallel|bars
direct|cannon hunting|groom penalty|bully
directors|box in|the|running penalty|throw
disqualified investigator physical|jerk
do|it|yourself jack|in|the|box pigeon|flying
double|sculls kaleidoscope ping|pong|ball
doubles|match knucklebones pitch|and|putt
double|threes lampada|dromy pitch|and|toss
dressing|room landing|stage playing|cards
earth|stopper level|pegging playing|field
Eton|wall|game London|Bridge pleasure|trip

378

point to point	simple attack
pole position	single combat
pony trekking	single sculls
prize fighter	singles match
professional	skating boots
Punch and Judy	skipping rope
punto reverso	slice service
putting green	slippery pole
quarter final	soapbox derby
queen's bishop	speed skating
queen's knight	sporting life
raffle ticket	sport of kings
receiving end	stabbing blow
record holder	stand off half
redoublement	starting grid
referee's hold	starting post
return crease	steeplechase
ride to hounds	sticky wicket
riding school	stilt walking
rock climbing	straddle jump
rocking horse	stranglehold
roller skates	strong finish
running strip	Sunday driver
sandy achting	sweep oarsman
sandy achting	swimming gala
scissors jump	swimming pool
second attack	sword fencing
second eleven	table turning
second player	tennis player
shadow boxing	tennis racket
sharpshooter	tennis stroke
short pinocle	three quarter
shove ha'penny	tiddley winks
shrimping net	toss the caber
shuffleboard	train spotter
side chancery	trapshooting

treasure|hunt
treble|chance
trick|cyclist
trigger|happy
tunnel|of|love
umpire's|chair
vantage|point
Virginia|reel
weight|lifter
welter|weight
wicket|keeper
winter|sports
all|in|wrestler
auction|bridge
beauty|contest
big|game|hunter
billiard|table
blanket|finish
blind|man's|buff
bowling|crease
callisthenics
centre|forward
change|ringing
chequered|flag
climbing|frame
coarse|fishing
county|cricket
cribbage|board
cruiser|weight
double|or|quits
equestrianism
feather|weight
figure|of|eight
figure|skating
finishing|post
fishing|tackle

follow|through
football|match
football|pools
funny|peculiar
ghetto|blaster
Grand|National
half|time|score
hare|and|hounds
helter|skelter
hide|and|go|seek
Highland|fling
Highland|games
hunting|ground
international
mashie|niblick
mixed|foursome
nightwatchman
nursery|slopes
peace|offering
physical|jerks
popping|crease
prisoner's|base
prize|fighting
return|service
roller|skating
rough|shooting
rugby|football
Russian|ballet
second|innings
shooting|range
shooting|stick
sitting|target
skateboarding
sleight|of|hand
Space|Invaders
sportsmanlike

sportsmanship	greyhound Derby
sports stadium	grouse shooting
square dancing	halloween party
squash rackets	high cockalorum
stalking horse	hop, skip and jump
starting price	hunt the slipper
starting stall	marathon runner
steeplechaser	master of hounds
straight flush	mountaineering
surface worker	nine men's morris
table skittles	nineteenth hole
tenpin bowling	opening batsman
three day event	pig in the middle
train spotting	prima ballerina
ventriloquism	putting the shot
ventriloquist	ride a cock horse
vulnerability	shove halfpenny
weight lifting	sit on the splice
aerobic dancing	smoking concert
approach stroke	solitaire board
bathing costume	spectator sport
bathing machine	speedway racing
billiard marker	squash racquets
catherine wheel	starting blocks
champion jockey	starting stalls
channel swimmer	steeplechasing
cock a doodle doo	stock car racing
conjuring trick	supporters club
contract bridge	three card trick
country dancing	winter Olympics
crown and anchor	wrestling match
fancy dress ball	amusement arcade
follow my leader	appearance money
football ground	Australian rules
football league	bodyline bowling
golf tournament	catch as catch can

cross,country,run
crossword,puzzle
duplicate,bridge
egg,and,spoon,race
fancy,dress,dance
firework,display
game,,set,and,match
glorious,Twelfth
hit,below,the,belt
Indian,rope,trick
king,of,the,castle
leg,before,wicket
nursery,handicap
odds,on,favourite
pipped,at,the,post
puss,in,the,corner

rain,stopped,play
Roger,de,Coverley
Royal,and,Ancient
Russian,roulette
shooting,gallery
sparring,partner
sports,equipment
stable,companion
stamp,collecting
stamp,collection
swimming,costume
three,day,eventer
three,legged,race
three,ring,circus
throw,in,the,towel
women's,institute

Theatre

act	foil	solo	enact	stagy
bit	fool	spot	extra	stall
bow	gods	star	farce	stand
box	grid	tail	flies	still
cue	hall	text	floor	stunt
fan	hero	turn	focus	usher
gag	idol	tutu	foots	wings
ham	joke	unit	foyer	absurd
hit	lead	wing	front	acting
mug	line	zany	heavy	action
pit	loft	actor	house	act|out
rag	loge	ad|lib	lines	appear
rep	mask	agent	mimer	backer
run	mime	angel	mimic	ballet
set	mute	arena	odeum	barker
tab	part	aside	on|cue	Big|Top
bill	play	barre	opera	boards
bowl	plot	break	piece	border
busk	prop	buffo	props	buskin
cast	rant	cloth	Punch	chaser
clap	rave	clown	put|on	chorus
dais	ring	comic	queue	circle
diva	role	corps	revue	circus
dock	rush	debut	rodeo	claque
dots	shot	decor	scena	comedy
drop	show	drama	scene	critic
epic	side	drill	score	dancer
flat	skit	dry|up	spout	depict
flop	sock	eclat	stage	direct

383

effect	review	callboy	manager
encore	ring|up	casting	marquee
Equity	satire	cat|call	matinee
exodus	scenic	cat|walk	mimicry
farcer	script	charade	miracle
feeder	season	chorine	mummery
filler	singer	circuit	musical
finale	sketch	clapper	mystery
floats	speech	close|up	New|Wave
flyman	stager	comedia	No|drama
gagman	stalls	commere	on|stage
guiser	stanza	company	overact
jester	stooge	compere	pageant
Kabuki	talent	costume	perform
lights	teaser	cothurn	Pierrot
limber	Thalia	coxcomb	play|act
lyceum	ticket	curtain	playing
make|up	tights	dancing	playlet
masque	timing	danseur	pop|idol
method	tragic	deadpan	pop|star
motley	troupe	dress|up	portray
mummer	up|left	drive|in	present
number	walk|on	fan|club	preview
one|act	warm|up	farceur	produce
on|tour	writer	farcist	proverb
patron	acrobat	gallery	re|enact
patter	act|drop	gate|man	rep|show
person	actress	grimace	Roscius
pit|man	all|star	ham|it|up	rostrum
player	artiste	heroine	scenery
podium	balcony	histrio	scenist
prompt	benefit	ingenue	showman
puppet	bit|part	last|act	show|off
relief	booking	leg|show	soapbox
repeat	buffoon	leotard	spieler
re|take	cabaret	long|run	stadium

stagery	coulisse	off|stage
staging	danseuse	operatic
stand|by	dialogue	operetta
stand|in	Dionysus	overture
stardom	director	paradise
starlet	disguise	parterre
support	down|left	pastoral
tableau	dramatic	peep|show
theatre	dumb|show	pit|stall
the|gods	duologue	platform
Thespis	entr'acte	playbook
tragedy	entrance	playgoer
trouper	epilogue	playland
tumbler	epitasis	playwork
up|right	exit|line	practice
upstage	farceuse	premiere
vehicle	farcical	producer
antimask	fauteuil	prologue
applause	festival	prompter
audience	figurant	property
audition	filmgoer	protasis
backdrop	film|unit	rehearse
balletic	first|act	ring|down
big|scene	front|row	scenario
Broadway	funny|man	sceneman
burletta	gridiron	set|piece
business	grimacer	showboat
carnival	ham|actor	side|show
clapping	headline	smash|hit
claqueur	interval	stagedom
clowning	juvenile	stageman
coliseum	libretto	stage|set
comedian	live|show	star|turn
conjuror	location	stasimon
coryphee	magician	straight
costumer	morality	stroller

subtitle	cothurnus	Melpomene
take|a|bow	criticism	menagerie
the|dance	cyclorama	minor|role
Thespian	dead|stage	monodrama
the|stage	direction	monologue
third|act	discovery	music|hall
tragical	down|right	night|club
travesty	downstage	old|stager
typecast	dramatics	orchestra
usheress	dramatist	panel|game
wardrobe	dramatize	pantaloon
wigmaker	drop|scene	pantomime
wireless	entertain	parabasis
absurdist	entrechat	pas|de|deux
animation	epirrhema	patronage
announcer	featuring	patroness
arabesque	figurante	performer
astrodome	floor|show	personage
backcloth	greenroom	Pierrette
backstage	guest|star	pirouette
ballerina	ham|acting	play|actor
bandstand	harlequin	playhouse
barnstorm	headliner	portrayal
bit|player	heavy|lead	programme
box|office	hoardings	prompt|box
breakaway	horseshoe	publicity
burlesque	incognito	punch|line
carpenter	interlude	raw|comedy
character	left|stage	rehearsal
chorus|boy	limelight	repertory
chorus|man	live|stage	represent
cinematic	love|scene	scenarist
clip|joint	low|comedy	scene|plot
Colosseum	major|role	second|act
Columbine	make|up|man	side|scene
costumier	melodrama	slapstick

soliloquy	comedienne	milk|a|scene
soubrette	comic|opera	mimologist
spectacle	continuity	motley|fool
spectator	coryphaeus	mountebank
spotlight	costumiere	music|drama
stage|door	crowd|scene	on|the|stage
stagehand	denouement	opera|buffa
stageland	disc|jockey	opera|house
stage|name	drama|group	pantomimic
stage|play	dramalogue	pass|holder
staginess	dramatizer	performing
superstar	dramaturge	play|acting
take|a|part	dramaturgy	playbroker
tap|dancer	engagement	playreader
theatrics	exhibition	playwright
the|big|top	expository	playwriter
the|boards	fantoccini	presenting
title|role	first|name	prima|donna
tragedian	first|night	production
triologue	footlights	promptbook
usherette	get|the|bird	properties
wisecrack	high|comedy	proscenium
act|curtain	hippodrome	Pulcinella
act|the|goat	histrionic	puppet|show
act|the|part	impresario	put|on|a|show
afterpiece	impression	rave|notice
appearance	intermezzo	repertoire
apron|stage	in|the|round	right|stage
arena|stage	in|the|wings	Scaramouch
auditorium	leading|man	shadow|show
bandwaggon	legitimate	soci·o|drama
buffoonery	librettist	stage|boxes
chorus|girl	management	stagecraft
chorus|show	marionette	stage|fever
clog|dancer	masquerade	step|dancer
clown|white	microphone	strip|tease

substitute	dramaticism	play|the|fool
tap|dancing	dramaturgic	play|the|part
tear|jerker	dress|circle	practicable
theatre|box	drop|curtain	protagonist
theatreman	electrician	psychodrama
theatrical	entertainer	Punchinello
the|critics	exeunt|omnes	scene|change
the|unities	fire|curtain	scenewright
tragicomic	galantly|show	set|designer
trial|scene	grease|paint	set|the|scene
understudy	Greek|chorus	set|the|stage
utility|man	histrionics	showmanship
variety|act	histrionism	show|stopper
vaudeville	illusionist	Simon|Legree
walk|on|part	impersonate	skirt|dancer
actor's|agent	jack|pudding	sound|effect
actor's|lines	kitchen|sink	spectacular
all|star|bill	leading|lady	stage|design
all|star|cast	light|comedy	stage|effect
a|star|is|born	low|comedian	stage|fright
bag|of|tricks	make|believe	stage|player
balletomane	matinee|idol	stage|school
barnstormer	merry|andrew	stagestruck
black|comedy	method|actor	stageworthy
broad|comedy	mimographer	stagewright
cap|and|bells	miracle|play	star|billing
catastrophe	mise|en|scene	star|quality
charity|show	off|Broadway	star|studded
cliff|hanger	on|the|boards	star|vehicle
comedy|drama	pantomimist	straight|man
comic|relief	pas|de|quatre	strip|teaser
commentator	Passion|play	talent|scout
concert|hall	performance	terpsichore
curtain|call	personality	theatregoer
drama|school	personation	theatreland
dramatic|art	play|actress	theatricals

theatrician	introduction
Thespian|art	juvenile|lead
tragedienne	make,up|artist
tragic|drama	masked|comedy
tragicomedy	melodramatic
upper|circle	method|acting
ventriloquy	minstrel|show
waiting|line	modern|ballet
walking|part	morality|play
walk,through	old|stage|hand
word|perfect	opera|glasses
academy|award	orchestra|pit
acting|device	Pepper's|ghost
actor|manager	presentation
advance|agent	principal|boy
amphitheatre	publicity|man
ballet|dancer	Punch|and|Judy
balletomania	scene|painter
booking|agent	scene|shifter
borderlights	scene|stealer
characterize	scenic|effect
character|man	screenwriter
choreography	season|ticket
comedy|ballet	show|business
concert|party	show|must|go|on
dramatic|play	song|and|dance
dramaturgist	sound|effects
dressing|room	stage|manager
entrepreneur	stage|setting
extravaganza	stage|whisper
first,nighter	standing|room
Grand|Guignol	starring|role
Greek|theatre	steal|the|show
harlequinade	stock|company
hold|the|stage	stole|the|show
impersonator	straight|part

take|the|floor
theatrecraft
theatromania
top|of|the|bill
vaudevillian
vaudevillist
curtain|raiser
curtain|speech
dramatic|irony
dramatisation
emergency|exit
entertainment
impersonation
melodramatist
musical|comedy
one|night|stand
pantomime|dame
safety|curtain
theatre|school
theatricalism
walking|on|part
world|premiere
character|actor
dramatic|critic
dress|rehearsal
open|air|theatre

orchestra|stall
pantomime|horse
prima|ballerina
property|master
proscenium|arch
smoking|concert
speech|training
stage|carpenter
stage|direction
supporting|cast
supporting|part
supporting|role
touring|company
variety|theatre
behind|the|scenes
dramatic|society
gala|performance
legitimate|drama
National|Theatre
orchestra|stalls
raise|the|curtain
shadow|pantomime
situation|comedy
slapstick|comedy
strolling|player
tightrope|walker

Time

AD	mo	ago	due	eld	ere
am	pm	aye	e'en	Eos	eve
BC	age	day	e'er	era	May

oft	soon	never	Aurora
old	span	night	autumn
sec	term	nonce	Bairam
ult	then	often	brumal
yet	tick	passe	coeval
aeon	tide	pause	coming
ages	till	point	crisis
anon	time	prime	curfew
ante	unto	prior	decade
date	week	Purim	dotage
dawn	when	ready	during
dial	Xmas	shake	Easter
dusk	year	sharp	elapse
even	yore	short	ere|now
ever	Yule	since	extant
fall	again	so|far	ferial
fast	annum	space	Friday
fore	April	spell	future
Ides	as|yet	still	gnomon
inst	brief	style	heyday
jiff	clock	sunup	hiemal
July	cycle	tempo	hourly
June	daily	today	Ice|age
late	dekad	trice	in|time
Lent	delay	until	jet|age
moon	diary	watch	Julian
morn	early	while	Lammas
next	epact	years	lapsed
Noel	epoch	young	lately
noon	fasti	youth	latest
once	flash	actual	latish
over	jiffy	advent	lustre
past	later	always	manana
post	March	annual	May|day
prox	matin	at|once	midday
slow	month	August	minute

TIME

modern	yearly	expired	onetime
moment	yester	extinct	overdue
Monday	abiding	fastday	pending
morrow	ackemma	flagday	pipemma
newday	ageless	forever	postwar
o'clock	agesago	forgood	present
offday	allover	forlife	proximo
oflate	almanac	harvest	quarter
oldage	already	highday	quondam
oneday	ancient	history	Ramadan
ontime	anytime	holiday	ripeage
period	archaic	holyday	Sabbath
presto	atnight	infancy	secular
prewar	bedtime	instant	shortly
prompt	belated	interim	sinedie
pronto	betimes	IronAge	someday
protem	boyhood	January	stretch
rarely	byandby	journal	Sukkoth
recent	calends	jubilee	sundial
season	century	justnow	sundown
second	chiliad	kalends	sunrise
seldom	current	Ladyday	teenage
sooner	dawning	longago	tertian
spring	daylong	longrun	thisday
sudden	daypeep	lustrum	timelag
summer	daytime	manhood	timewas
Sunday	diurnal	manhour	tonight
sunset	dogdays	matinal	toolate
timely	earlier	midweek	toosoon
todate	elapsed	monthly	Tuesday
update	endless	morning	twinkle
vernal	epochal	newborn	twotwo's
vesper	equinox	NewYear	unready
weekly	estival	nightly	uptonow
whilst	evening	noonday	usually
winter	exactly	October	weekday

weekend	February	lifelong
whereon	fleeting	life,span
whitsun	foredawn	lifetime
abruptly	forenoon	livelong
allong|day	formerly	long|time
antedate	frequent	Lord's|day
as|soon|as	gain|time	lose|time
biannual	gloaming	lunation
biennial	half|hour	make|time
birthday	half|past	mark|time
biweekly	Hanukkah	meantime
blue|moon	hereunto	mean|time
Brumaire	hibernal	medieval
calendar	high|time	menology
darkling	hitherto	meridian
date|line	Hogmanay	meteoric
daybreak	holy|days	midnight
daylight	Holy|week	momently
deadline	horology	natal|day
December	ill,timed	New|Style
Derby|day	in|a|flash	next|week
directly	in|a|trice	noontide
dogwatch	infinity	noontime
doomsday	in|future	not|often
duration	in|no|time	November
egg,timer	in|season	nowadays
enduring	interval	obsolete
entr'acte	juncture	occasion
Epiphany	keep|time	oft|times
eternity	kill|time	old|times
eventide	lang|syne	on|the|dot
evermore	last|time	our|times
every|day	last|week	Passover
evil|hour	lateness	pass|time
fast|time	latterly	postdate
feast|day	leap|year	postpone

393

previous	yoretime	epochally
promptly	Yuletide	erstwhile
punctual	adulthood	ever|since
recently	afternoon	every|hour
right|now	after|that	far|future
ringtime	after|time	first|time
Saturday	all|at|once	foregoing
seasonal	antiquity	forthwith
seedtime	Atomic|Age	fortnight
semester	at|present	from|now|on
solar|day	bimonthly	gnomonics
solstice	Boxing|Day	Golden|Age
some|time	Bronze|Age	great|year
Space|Age	Candlemas	Gregorian
sporadic	canicular	Hallowe'en
Steel|Age	centenary	Hallowmas
Stone|Age	childhood	happy|days
suddenly	Christmas	hereafter
take|time	chronicle	honeymoon
temporal	civil|time	hourglass
this|week	civil|year	immediacy
Thursday	clepsydra	immediate
timeless	continual	in|a|second
time|worn	crepuscle	in|due|time
tomorrow	days|of|old	instanter
too|early	dayspring	instantly
twilight	decennary	interlude
ultimate	decennial	in|the|past
until|now	decennium	Julian|day
untimely	due|season	Lammas|day
up|to|date	earliness	later|date
weeklong	early|bird	latter|day
whenever	ember|days	light|year
year|book	Empire|Day	local|time
yearlong	ephemeral	longevity
years|ago	ephemeris	long|lived

long|since	preceding	timepiece
long|spell	precisely	times|past
long|while	premature	timetable
lunar|year	presently	to|this|day
many|a|time	quarterly	transient
many|times	quarter|to	triennial
Mardi|Gras	quotidian	twinkling
Martinmas	recurrent	two|shakes
mature|age	regularly	upon|which
matutinal	remote|age	vicennial
meanwhile	right|time	waste|time
mediaeval	Saint's|day	Wednesday
menstrual	salad|days	well|timed
metronome	sandglass	wherefore
midday|sun	semestral	whereunto
middle|age	September	whereupon
midsummer	short|term	wrong|time
midwinter	short|time	yesterday
mistiming	solar|time	afterwards
momentary	solar|year	after|which
monthlong	sometimes	alarm|clock
nevermore	space|time	Allhallows
nightfall	spare|time	all|the|time
nightlong	spend|time	anno|Domini
nighttide	stopwatch	at|all|times
night|time	Swiss|plan	at|that|time
nocturnal	temporary	at|this|time
octennial	temporize	beforehand
oftentime	therewith	before|long
opportune	till|death	beforetime
out|of|date	time|being	behindhand
overnight	time|check	behind|time
Pentecost	time|clock	better|days
perennial	time|flies	break|of|day
permanent	time|limit	bygone|days
postcenal	time|of|day	by|the|clock

centennial	incidental	ripe|old|age
childermas	in|good|time	Sabbath|day
chronogram	invariably	seasonable
chronology	isochronon	semiweekly
close|of|day	Julian|year	septennial
common|time	just|in|time	sextennial
consequent	Lammastide	short|spell
constantly	last|chance	small|hours
continuous	last|minute	soon|enough
cosmic|time	Lententide	springtide
crepuscule	lunar|month	springtime
days|gone|by	Methuselah	subsequent
days|of|yore	Michaelmas	summertide
Eastertide	middle|aged	summertime
Easter|time	Middle|Ages	thereafter
evanescent	midmorning	this|minute
eventually	millennium	time|keeper
Father's|day	moratorium	timeliness
Father|Time	Mother's|day	time|signal
fiscal|year	near|future	time|to|come
fleetingly	nick|of|time	time|to|kill
frequently	now|or|never	transitory
futuristic	occasional	tricennial
generation	of|the|clock	triple|time
Good|Friday	olden|times	ultimately
half|a|jiffy	one|fine|day	very|seldom
half|an|hour	on|occasion	vespertime
half|a|shake	on|the|eve|of	water|clock
hardly|ever	Palm|Sunday	wedding|day
hebdomadal	posthumous	whensoever
Hebrew|year	prehistory	Whitmonday
henceforth	present|day	Whitsunday
here|and|now	previously	wintertide
heretofore	proper|time	wintertime
historical	repeatedly	with|the|sun
immemorial	retrospect	wristwatch

years|on|end	former|times	on|the|morrow
yesteryear	fortnightly	opportunely
adjournment	Gay|Nineties	opportunity
adolescence	golden|hours	out|of|season
after|dinner	good|old|days	Passion|week
against|time	halcyon|days	penultimate
ahead|of|time	half|a|second	perennially
All|Fools|day	hebdomadary	perfect|year
All|Souls|day	hereinafter	perpetually
anachronism	ides|of|March	play|for|time
anniversary	immediately	point|of|time
at|intervals	in|an|instant	present|time
bicentenary	incessantly	prime|of|life
bygone|times	in|due|course	promptitude
ceaselessly	interregnum	punctuality
chronograph	Judgment|day	quadrennial
chronometer	lapse|of|time	quarter|past
chronoscope	leisure|time	sands|of|time
coincidence	little|while	semi|monthly
concurrence	livelong|day	shining|hour
continually	long,lasting	short|notice
crack|of|dawn	long|overdue	some|time|ago
crepuscular	march|of|time	split|second
cuckoo|clock	microsecond	straightway
day|after|day	middle|years	synchronism
day|and|night	millisecond	synchronize
day|in|day|out	modern|times	tempus|fugit
dead|of|night	momentarily	thenceforth
endless|time	morningtide	the|other|day
ever|and|a|day	morning|time	this|morning
ever|and|anon	never,ending	this|very|day
everlasting	New|Year's|day	time|and|tide
every|moment	New|Year's|eve	time|drags|by
fin|de|siècle	night|and|day	time|machine
flower|of|age	once|or|twice	time|to|spare
for|evermore		turret|clock

twelvemonth	Indian summer
ultramodern	Innocents' day
waiting time	in olden times
Whitsuntide	intermission
with the lark	late in the day
Year of Grace	long standing
all of a sudden	many a long day
All Saints' day	metachronism
a long time ago	nychthemeron
ancient times	occasionally
Annunciation	old-fashioned
antediluvian	once in a while
antemeridian	on the instant
ante meridiem	parachronism
Armistice day	periodically
Ascension day	postdiluvian
Ash Wednesday	postmeridian
auld lang syne	post meridiem
bide one's time	postponement
calendar year	postprandial
Christmas day	Quadragesima
Christmas eve	quinquennial
consequently	quinquennium
contemporary	rare occasion
course of time	red letter day
decisive hour	sempiternity
decline of day	sidereal time
donkey's years	sidereal year
eleventh hour	simultaneous
Feast of Weeks	stall for time
following day	standard time
fourth of July	still of night
from that time	stitch in time
Greek calends	tercentenary
Holy Thursday	the dawn of day
in days of yore	then and there

398

the|year|round
time|and|again
time|honoured
timelessness
time|will|tell
turning|point
Twelfth|night
twelve|o'clock
unseasonable
witching|hour
without|delay
again|and|again
All|Hallow's|eve
April|fool's|day
Ascensiontide
at|short|notice
broad|daylight
calendar|month
Christmas|tide
Christmas|time
chronographer
chronological
days|of|the|week
every|few|hours
every|few|years
every|other|day
financial|year
for|the|present
from|the|outset
from|the|word|go
generation|gap
getting|on|a|bit
golden|jubilee
golden|wedding
Greenwich|time
Michaelmas|day

old|as|the|hills
once|upon|a|time
Passion|Sunday
quincentenary
Quinquagesima
retrospective
right|up|to|date
round|the|clock
Shrove|Tuesday
silver|jubilee
silver|wedding
some|of|the|time
some|other|time
sooner|or|later
speaking|clock
St|Crispin's|day
St|Luke's|summer
St|Swithin's|day
summer|holiday
synchronology
the|time|is|ripe
time|after|time
time|marches|on
time|of|arrival
time|out|of|mind
tomorrow|night
Trinity|Sunday
tropical|month
turn|of|the|year
up|to|the|minute
up|with|the|lark
vernal|equinox
week|in,|week|out
year|in,|year|out
advancing|years
before|and|after

399

behind|schedule
breathing|space
chronometrical
day|in|and|day|out
daylight|saving
declining|years
diamond|jubilee
diamond|wedding
during|the|night
Easter|holidays
for|ever|and|a|day
for|ever|and|ever
for|the|duration
from|time|to|time
fullness|of|time
geological|time
in|ancient|times
in|course|of|time
interval|of|time
in|the|afternoon
in|the|beginning
in|the|meanwhile
Julian|calendar
keep|early|hours
Maundy|Thursday
midsummer|night
month|of|Sundays
Pancake|Tuesday
past|and|present
Remembrance|Day
Rogation|Sunday
sabbatical|year
septuagenarian
Walpurgis|night

witches|Sabbath
against|the|clock
ahead|of|schedule
chronologically
contemporaneity
contemporaneous
continental|time
continuation|day
dominical|letter
equinoctial|year
every|now|and|then
for|a|year|and|a|day
fourth|dimension
how|goes|the|enemy
in|the|nick|of|time
month|after|month
months|and|months
months|of|the|year
Mothering|Sunday
night|after|night
once|in|a|blue|moon
once|in|a|lifetime
put|back|the|clock
put|the|clock|back
quatercentenary
retrospectively
spur|of|the|moment
St|Valentine's|day
Thanksgiving|day
the|morning|after
this|year|of|grace
tomorrow|evening
tomorrow|morning
world|without|end

Tools

awl	lever	roller	pincers
axe	mower	scythe	riffler
bit	plane	shaver	rotator
cow	punch	shears	scalpel
die	scoop	shovel	scraper
dig	spade	sickle	shuttle
hod	tongs	spigot	spanner
hoe	wedge	stylus	spatula
jig	bob|saw	tedder	sprayer
saw	bodkin	trowel	stapler
adze	chaser	wrench	toolbox
file	chisel	bandsaw	woodsaw
fork	dibble	bradawl	air|drill
hose	digger	buzz|saw	billhook
jack	eolith	cadrans	calipers
mole	gadget	chopper	cant|hook
pick	gimlet	cleaver	chainsaw
pump	grater	cold|saw	clippers
rake	hammer	crowbar	cross|bit
tool	harrow	forceps	dividers
auger	jigsaw	fretsaw	Dutch|hoe
brace	mallet	gripper	edge|tool
burin	muller	hacksaw	flash|gun
delve	oil|gun	handsaw	flat|iron
drill	pliers	hatchet	handtool
gouge	plough	hayfork	penknife
jemmy	ramrod	hayrake	polisher
jimmy	riddle	mattock	power|saw
knife	rip|saw	pickaxe	saw|knife

401

TOOLS

scissors	cold chisel
spray gun	compass saw
tommy bar	cultivator
tweezers	drop hammer
air hammer	edging tool
arc welder	garden fork
belt punch	garden hose
blow torch	goat sallow
can opener	hole cutter
cement gun	keyhole saw
corkscrew	pantograph
die sinker	paper knife
drop drill	peen hammer
eidograph	pipe wrench
excavator	powder mill
fly cutter	twist drill
grease gun	whirl drill
hair drier	brace and bit
hand drill	butcher's saw
handspike	circular saw
implement	dovetail saw
jack knife	drilling rig
lawn mower	electric saw
pitchfork	electron gun
plumb line	garden spade
road drill	glass cutter
rock drill	machine tool
secateurs	pillar drill
steam iron	ploughshare
telescope	pocket knife
tin opener	power shovel
tyre lever	pruning bill
bowie knife	pruning hook
box spanner	ring spanner
claw hammer	rotary drill
coal shovel	safety razor

sanding disc	hydraulic ram
screwdriver	marlinespike
steam hammer	masonry drill
steam shovel	palette knife
surgeon's saw	pruning knife
tamping iron	ratchet drill
watering can	sledgehammer
wheelbarrow	soldering gun
battering ram	two-handed saw
carving knife	pick and shovel
electric iron	precision tool
garden roller	hammer and tongs
garden shears	pneumatic drill
garden trowel	hammer and sickle
hedge trimmer	

Trade

CA	due	pro	bank	chip	dues
co	dun	put	bear	coin	dump
HP	EEC	rig	body	co-op	dust
rd	fee	sag	bond	corn	duty
bag	IOU	SET	boom	cost	earn
bar	job	sum	buck	crop	EFTA
bid	lot	tag	bulk	curb	fair
bob	Ltd	tax	bull	deal	fees
BOT	net	tin	bury	dear	file
buy	oof	tip	call	debt	fine
cap	owe	VAT	cant	desk	fire
COD	par	wad	cash	dibs	firm
con	pay	agio	cess	dole	fisc
dot	pit	back	char	drug	free

fund	pawn	ware	chips	miser
gain	PAYE	work	chore	money
game	peag	agent	clear	ochre
gift	perk	amass	clerk	offer
gild	pool	angel	costs	order
gilt	post	assay	craft	owing
giro	rags	asset	crash	panic
glut	raid	at|par	cycle	paper
gold	rate	audit	debit	piece
good	reap	baron	depot	pitch
haul	rent	batch	Dives	plant
hawk	risk	beans	dough	pound
heap	roll	bears	dowry	price
hire	roup	bid|up	draft	prize
hive	ruin	block	entry	purse
hold	sack	blunt	Ernie	queer
hype	safe	board	exact	quota
idle	sale	bogus	files	quote
IOUs	salt	bones	float	rails
item	save	bonus	forge	rally
lend	scab	boost	funds	rebuy
levy	sell	booth	gilts	remit
line	shop	brand	gnome	repay
list	sink	brass	goods	rhino
loan	slug	broke	gross	rocks
long	sold	bucks	guild	salve
loss	stag	bulls	hoard	scalp
make	swap	bunce	house	scoop
mart	tare	buyer	index	score
meed	task	buy|up	ingot	scrip
milk	tick	by|bid	issue	setup
mill	till	cadge	lease	share
mint	tout	cargo	lucre	shark
nail	vend	cheap	maker	shift
note	visa	check	means	short
paid	wage	chink	Midas	skill

5/6 LETTERS

slash	accept	change	garage	nugget
slump	accrue	charge	gazump	octroi
smash	admass	cheque	godown	odd|job
smith	afford	client	go|slow	odd|lot
snide	agency	coffer	gratis	office
spend	agenda	consol	grease	on|call
spiel	amount	copper	growth	oncost
spots	appeal	corner	guinea	on|tick
stake	arrear	costly	haggle	option
stall	assets	coupon	hammer	outbid
stand	at|cost	cowrie	hard|up	outcry
stint	avails	credit	hawker	outlay
stock	backer	crisis	import	outlet
store	banker	custom	impose	output
strop	barker	dealer	impost	packet
tally	barter	deal|in	in|bulk	parity
taxes	bazaar	debtee	in|cash	patron
terms	bearer	debtor	income	pauper
tithe	boodle	defray	in|debt	pay|day
token	borrow	demand	in|tray	pay|for
trade	bought	dicker	jobber	paying
treat	bounce	drawer	job|lot	pay|off
trend	bounty	dunner	labour	payola
truck	bourse	emptio	leader	pay|out
trust	branch	enrich	ledger	peddle
usury	broker	equity	lender	pedlar
utter	budget	errand	liable	picket
value	bureau	estate	living	pirate
venal	bursar	excise	luxury	pledge
wages	button	expend	mammon	plunge
wares	buying	export	merger	Plutus
welsh	buy|out	figure	minute	pocket
works	cambio	fiscal	moneys	policy
worth	career	fold|up	monger	profit
yield	cartel	freeze	monies	public
abacus	cash|in	future	notice	purvey

racket	spread	arrears	concern
raffle	stable	article	consols
rating	staker	atelier	contact
ration	stocks	auction	convert
realty	strike	auditor	coppers
rebate	sundry	automat	corn|pit
recoup	supply	average	cottons
redeem	surtax	backing	counter
refund	swings	bad|debt	Croesus
reject	tariff	balance	cumshaw
remedy	taxman	ballast	Customs
render	teller	banking	customs
rental	tender	bargain	cut,rate
resale	tenths	berries	damages
resell	ticker	bidding	daybook
resign	ticket	bonanza	dealing
retail	towage	bondage	declare
retire	trader	boycott	default
return	treaty	bullets	deficit
reward	tycoon	bullion	deflate
rialto	unload	bursary	deposit
riches	unpaid	buy|back	deviser
ruined	usurer	cabbage	dockage
salary	valuta	calling	draw|out
save|up	vendor	cambist	due|bill
saving	vendue	capital	dumping
sell|up	wallet	cash|box	economy
settle	wampum	cashier	effects
shares	wealth	ceiling	embargo
shorts	worker	chapman	emption
silver	wright	charity	endorse
simony	abscond	chinker	engross
smithy	account	clinker	entrust
specie	actuary	coinage	expense
spiral	allonge	coining	exploit
sponge	annuity	company	exports

factory	jobless	payroll	rollers
failure	journal	payslip	room|man
fall|due	killing	peddlar	rouleau
finance	land|tax	pending	royalty
flutter	leading	pension	sacking
foot|lot	lending	pet|bank	salable
foreman	lettuce	plunger	salt|tax
forgery	limited	poll|tax	salvage
for|sale	lockout	poor|man	savings
fortune	Lombard	portage	seconds
foundry	long|run	pre|empt	selling
freebie	lottery	premium	sell|out
freight	lump|sum	prepaid	service
full|lot	manager	pricing	shekels
futures	man|made	produce	shopman
gabelle	mintage	profits	shopper
gift|box	mission	promote	skilled
go|broke	moneyed	pro|rata	smelter
good|buy	nest|egg	prosper	solvent
good|sum	net|gain	provide	sponger
go|under	notions	pursuit	squeeze
guerdon	nummary	pyramid	stipend
half|day	oddment	realize	storage
harvest	on|offer	realtor	striker
haulage	on|terms	receipt	subsidy
head|tax	on|trust	refusal	surplus
holding	opening	regrate	swindle
imports	opulent	reissue	takings
inflate	out|tray	release	taxable
in|funds	package	requite	tax|free
intrust	parlour	reserve	terrier
invoice	parvenu	retiral	the|city
iron|men	payable	returns	tidy|sum
jingler	pay|cash	revenue	trade|in
jobbers	payment	rich|man	trading
jobbing	pay|rise	rigging	traffic

407

tranche	basic|pay	credit|to	gazumper
trustee	bear|pool	currency	gift|shop
utility	bear|raid	customer	gilt|edge
vacancy	beat|down	cut|price	giveaway
vending	below|par	day|shift	gold|mine
venture	blackleg	dealings	gold|rush
voucher	blue|chip	defrayal	good|will
walkout	board|lot	director	gratuity
war|bond	boardman	disburse	grow|rich
warrant	bondager	discount	hallmark
wealthy	boom|town	disposal	hard|cash
welfare	borrower	dividend	hard|sell
well|off	boutique	dry|goods	hardware
welsher	breakage	earnings	hoarding
wildcat	brochure	embezzle	homework
workday	bull|pool	employee	hot|money
above|par	bull|raid	employer	huckster
accredit	business	emporium	importer
affluent	buying|in	entrepot	in|arrear
after|tax	campaign	estimate	increase
agiotage	carriage	evaluate	indebted
agronomy	cashbook	exchange	industry
amortize	cash|down	expended	in|pocket
appraise	cash|sale	expenses	interest
at|a|price	circular	exporter	in|the|red
auditing	clientry	face|ruin	investor
automate	close|out	finances	issuance
badly|off	cold|cash	fire|sale	issue|par
bad|money	commands	flat|rate	jeweller
ballyhoo	commerce	floorman	junkshop
bankbook	consumer	for|a|song	keep|shop
bank|loan	contango	free|gift	kitemark
bank|note	contract	free|port	knitwork
bank|roll	converts	function	labourer
bankrupt	counting	gasworks	lame|duck
base|coin	creditor	gazetted	largesse

8 LETTERS

large|sum	overhaul	rent|roll
legation	overhead	requital
levanter	overseer	reserves
lifework	overtime	retailer
live|high	par|value	retainer
live|well	passbook	richesse
long|side	pawn|shop	richling
low|price	pay|talks	round|lot
low|water	pin|money	round|sum
make|a|bid	pipeline	rush|hour
make|good	pittance	salaried
manifest	position	saleroom
man|power	post|paid	salesman
mark|down	poundage	salt|down
material	practice	sanction
maturity	premises	scalping
merchant	price|cut	scarcity
mint|drop	price|war	schedule
monetary	proceeds	security
money|bag	producer	self|made
money|box	property	shipment
monopoly	prospect	shipyard
mortgage	purchase	shopping
net|price	put|price	short|run
net|worth	quit|rent	showcase
no|charge	rack|rent	showroom
notation	rag|trade	sideline
note|case	rainy|day	sinecure
oddments	receipts	small|sum
off|price	reckoner	soft|cell
on|credit	recorder	solatium
on|demand	recovery	solidity
on|strike	refinery	solvency
operator	register	spending
opulence	regrater	spot|cash
ordinary	rent|free	spot|sale

square up	workshop	cable code
sterling	write off	cable rate
sundries	absconder	call price
supertax	ad valorem	cash grain
supplies	affiliate	catalogue
swapping	affluence	cellarage
takeover	aggregate	cheapjack
tallyman	allowance	check rate
taxation	amount due	clearance
tax dodge	appraisal	clientage
taxpayer	arbitrage	clientele
time bill	arrearage	coemption
tolbooth	avocation	coin money
tool shop	back shift	commodity
toolwork	bad cheque	costerman
top price	bank clerk	cost price
trade gap	bank stock	craftsman
trade off	barrow boy	death duty
treasure	bartering	debenture
Treasury	bear panic	deduction
turnover	blind pool	defaulter
underbid	board room	deflation
undercut	bond issue	depositor
usufruct	bon marché	dime store
valorize	bonus bond	directors
valuable	borrowing	direct tax
venality	box office	dirt cheap
vendible	brand name	discharge
vocation	breadline	dishonour
wash sale	brokerage	dismissal
watchdog	bucketing	dollar gap
well to do	bull panic	draw wages
wharfage	buy in bulk	drug store
workaday	by auction	easy money
work late	by bidding	easy terms
workroom	by product	economics

410

economies	hard goods	make a sale
economise	hard money	market day
emolument	head buyer	marketing
establish	heavy cost	means test
exchequer	high price	middleman
exciseman	high value	money bags
excise tax	holy stone	money belt
executive	hot market	mortgagee
expansion	hush money	mortgager
expensive	import tax	neat price
exploiter	in arrears	negotiate
export tax	incentive	net income
extortion	income tax	night safe
face value	in deficit	officiate
fair price	indemnity	off market
fair trade	inflation	on account
fat profit	insolvent	on the nail
fiat money	insurance	operative
financial	in the city	order book
financier	invention	outgoings
firm offer	inventory	out of debt
firm price	job of work	out of work
flash note	joint bank	outworker
flat broke	keep books	overdraft
flotation	knock down	overdrawn
free trade	late shift	overheads
full purse	legal bond	overspend
gilt edged	liability	patronage
going rate	life's work	patronize
gold piece	liquidate	pay dearly
good price	list price	pay in kind
greenback	long purse	paymaster
guarantee	loss maker	pecuniary
guarantor	low priced	pecunious
half price	luxury tax	penniless
handiwork	mail order	penny wise

411

petty|cash	sacrifice	take|stock
piecework	sale|block	tax|return
piggy|bank	salesgirl	technical
plutocrat	sales|talk	the|actual
poorly|off	secretary	the|market
portfolio	sell|short	the|street
pound|note	shift|work	tie,i|n|sale
pourboire	shop|floor	timocracy
practical	short|sale	tollbooth
priceless	short|side	trade|fair
price|list	sight|bill	trademark
price|ring	single|tax	trade|name
price|rise	situation	trade|sale
prime|cost	soft|goods	tradesman
principal	sole|agent	traffic|in
profiteer	soundness	treadmill
promotion	speculate	treasurer
purchaser	spendings	undersell
qualified	spot|grain	union|card
quittance	spot|price	unit|trust
quotation	stability	unsalable
ratepayer	stamp|duty	unskilled
ready|cash	statement	up|for|sale
real|wages	stock|list	utilities
recession	stockpile	utterance
reckoning	stock|rate	valuation
reduction	strike|pay	vendition
redundant	strongbox	wage|claim
reference	subsidize	wage|scale
refinance	substance	warehouse
reflation	sumptuary	wash|sales
registrar	surcharge	wealth|tax
reimburse	sweatshop	well,lined
repayment	sweet|shop	whitewash
resources	syndicate	wholesale
restraint	synthetic	work|force

workhouse	capitalism	department
work|study	capitalist	depository
World|Bank	capitalize	depreciate
acceptance	chain|banks	depression
accountant	chain|store	direct|cost
accounting	chancellor	dirty|money
accumulate	chargeable	dividend|on
adjustment	chargehand	dollar|bill
advertiser	cheapening	dummy|share
appreciate	cheap|skate	Dutch|treat
apprentice	cheque|book	easy|market
assessment	chrematist	economizer
assignment	chrysology	efficiency
at|a|bargain	closed|shop	employment
at|a|premium	closing|bid	encumbered
at|the|spear	collateral	end|product
auctioneer	colporteur	enterprise
auction|off	commercial	estate|duty
automation	commission	Eurodollar
average|out	compensate	evaluation
bank|credit	conference	ex|dividend
bankruptcy	consortium	exorbitant
bearer|bond	contraband	exposition
bear|market	cost|centre	false|money
best|seller	coupon|bond	fancy|goods
bill|broker	credit|card	fancy|price
bill|of|sale	credit|slip	fancy|stock
blood|money	curb|broker	filthy|rich
bondholder	curb|market	first|offer
bonus|stock	daily|bread	fiscal|year
bookkeeper	dead|market	fixed|price
bucket|shop	deep|in|debt	fixed|trust
bulk|buying	defalcator	flat|market
buy|and|sell	defrayment	floor|price
buy|futures	del|credere	forced|sale
calculator	demand|bill	free|gratis

free market	joint stock	numismatic
free sample	jumble sale	obligation
free trader	laboratory	occupation
freightage	lighterage	off licence
full stocks	liquidator	oil of palms
funded debt	livelihood	on the block
give credit	living wage	on the cheap
gold nugget	loan market	on the rocks
go on strike	long market	on the shelf
go shopping	long seller	opening bid
government	loss leader	open market
green pound	management	out of funds
grindstone	man of means	overcharge
half stocks	marked down	paper money
handicraft	marketable	pawnbroker
hand market	market hall	peppercorn
have in hand	mass market	percentage
head office	meal ticket	picket duty
heavy purse	member bank	pig in a poke
high priced	mercantile	pilot plant
hold office	merchantry	plutocracy
honorarium	Midas touch	pocketbook
import duty	monetarism	power plant
imposition	monetarist	pre emption
in business	moneyed man	preference
income bond	money order	prepayment
incumbered	monopolist	price index
incur a debt	monopolise	price level
industrial	moratorium	printworks
insolvency	negotiable	Prix unique
instalment	never never	production
in the black	nightshift	profession
in the money	nominal fee	profitable
investment	nominal par	prospector
job hunting	nonpayment	prospectus
joint bonds	note of hand	prosperity

414

provide|for	short|bonds	trade|price
purchasing	sick|market	trade|route
pure|profit	skilled|man	trade|union
put|and|call	slave|trade	treaty|port
ration|book	slow|market	typewriter
ready|money	smart|money	typing|pool
real|estate	soft|market	underwrite
recompense	sole|agency	unemployed
recoupment	speciality	upset|price
redeemable	speculator	wad|of|notes
redundancy	split|shift	wage|freeze
remittance	spondulies	wage|policy
remunerate	statistics	walk|of|life
repair|shop	steelworks	Wall|Street
reparation	steep|price	waterworks
repository	stock|issue	wealthy|man
repurchase	stockpiles	well|afford
retail|shop	stony|broke	well|heeled
retirement	straitened	wholesaler
rock|bottom	stronghold	window|shop
round|trade	strongroom	working|day
run|up|a|bill	sum|of|money	work|to|rule
salability	swap|horses	written|off
sales|force	take|a|flier	accountancy
saving|bank	taskmaster	account|book
saving|game	tax|evation	acquittance
scrip|issue	technician	advertising
second|hand	technocrat	agriculture
securities	the|needful	antique|shop
serial|bond	thin|margin	appointment
settlement	Third|World	asking|price
settle|with	ticker|tape	association
share|index	tour|of|duty	at|face|value
shoestring	trade|board	auction|ring
shopkeeper	trade|cycle	bank|account
shop|window	trade|guild	bank|balance

bank|holiday	common|stock	endorsement
bank|manager	company|rule	established
bank|of|issue	competition	estate|agent
Barclaycard	competitive	expenditure
bargain|sale	comptometer	fabrication
bear|account	consumption	fetch|a|price
bear|the|cost	cool|million	filthy|lucre
betting|shop	co,operative	fixed|assets
big|business	co,operative	fixed|income
billionaire	copperworks	floor|broker
bill|of|costs	corporation	floor|trader
black|market	cost,benefit	fluctuation
blank|cheque	counterfeit	foot|the|bill
bonus|scheme	cover|charge	foreclosure
book|keeping	cum|dividend	free|harbour
bottom|price	custom|house	future|grain
bread|winner	customs|duty	future|price
brisk|market	danger|money	gingerbread
budget|price	defence|bond	gross|income
bull|account	delinquence	hard|bargain
businessman	demand|curve	high|finance
capital|gain	demarcation	horse|market
carbon|paper	deposit|slip	hypermarket
cash|account	devaluation	impecunious
catallactic	display|case	indirect|tax
caught|short	distributor	industrials
central|bank	dividend|off	inexpensive
certificate	double|entry	institution
chamberlain	down|payment	intercourse
chancellery	drive|a|trade	ironmongery
chemist|shop	earn|a|living	joint|return
chrysocracy	economic|law	key|industry
circulation	economic|man	king's|ransom
closing|down	economy|size	lap|of|luxury
come|to|terms	embarrassed	legal|tender
commodities		liberty|bond

life savings	out of pocket	restriction
line of goods	outstanding	retiring age
liquidation	overpayment	risk capital
local branch	package deal	rummage sale
local office	paper credit	run into debt
long account	partnership	sales ledger
long service	pay cash down	sales person
loose change	pay on demand	savings bank
machine made	pay spot cash	self service
machine shop	pay the piper	sell at a loss
made of money	piece of work	sell forward
manufactory	pilot scheme	sell futures
manufacture	place of work	share broker
market place	pocket money	shareholder
market price	polytechnic	share ledger
mass produce	possessions	shopping bag
merchandise	postal order	short change
millionaire	pots of money	short seller
minimum wage	poverty line	single entry
mint of money	poverty trap	sinking fund
money broker	premium bond	slot machine
money dealer	pretty penny	small change
money lender	price fixing	small trader
money's worth	price freeze	sole emption
money to burn	price spiral	speculation
negotiation	price ticket	sponsorship
nest factory	property tax	stagflation
net interest	proposition	stockbroker
net receipts	provided for	stock dealer
nuisance tax	purchase tax	stockholder
numismatics	put up market	stock jobber
on easy terms	Queer Street	stock ledger
on good terms	quoted price	stock market
on the market	raw material	stockpiling
open account	reserve bank	stocktaking
open end bond	resignation	

storekeeper	auction|stand	costermonger
subsistence	balance|sheet	cost|of|living
supermarket	bank|examiner	counting|room
take|home|pay	bargain|offer	credit|rating
take|over|bid	bargain|price	critical|path
Tattersall's	barter|system	currency|note
tax|assessor	be|in|business	current|price
tax|gatherer	bill|of|lading	customs|union
technocracy	board|meeting	depreciation
the|have|nots	Board|of|Trade	direct|labour
tight|budget	bond|to|bearer	disbursement
tight|market	bottom|dollar	discount|rate
time|bargain	bottomry|bond	distribution
tired|market	branch|office	dollar|crisis
to|the|tune|of	broker's|agent	durable|goods
trade|school	brokers|board	Dutch|auction
trading|post	business|deal	early|closing
transaction	business|life	earned|income
travel|agent	businesslike	econometrics
truck|system	buyer's|market	economy|drive
undercharge	buying|public	entrepreneur
underwriter	callable|bond	exchange|rate
vendibility	capital|gains	exhaust|price
wherewithal	capital|goods	extend|credit
working|life	capital|stock	extravagance
workmanlike	cash|and|carry	fair|exchange
workmanship	cash|register	fill|an|office
works|outing	casual|labour	first|refusal
world|market	catallactics	fiscal|policy
active|market	circular|note	fixed|capital
ad|valorem|tax	clearing|bank	floating|debt
amalgamation	closing|price	folding|money
amortization	common|market	foreign|trade
amortizement	compensation	gate|receipts
arithmometer	consumer|good	general|store
assembly|line	cook|the|books	

get|rich|quick money|matters redeployment
going|concern mortgage|bond regional|bank
gold|standard national|bank remuneration
goods|for|sale nearest|offer remunerative
great|expense nine|till|five reserve|price
haberdashery nominal|price retaining|fee
hard|currency nominal|value retrenchment
high|pressure nouveau|riche rigged|market
hire|purchase odd|lot|dealer rig|the|market
hungry|market offered|price rising|prices
impulse|buyer offer|for|sale rolling|stock
in|conference office|junior rubber|cheque
indebtedness open|end|trust sale|by|outcry
interest|rate opening|price sale|or|return
internal|bond organization sales|gimmick
in|the|gazette packing|house sales|manager
joint|account pay|as|you|earn salesmanship
keep|accounts pay|in|advance satisfaction
labour|of|love pegged|market sell|on|credit
laissez|faire peg|the|market severance|pay
leather|goods ply|one's|trade share|company
line|of|credit porte|monnaie shareholding
live|in|clover pressure|belt short|account
lively|market price|ceiling show|business
long|interest price|control slender|means
make|a|bargain price|current sliding|scale
make|a|fortune price|of|money state|lottery
make|delivery price|rigging steady|market
make|one's|pile productivity sterling|area
manipulation professional stock|company
manufacturer profiteering stock|dealing
marginal|cost profit|margin stockholding
mass|produced profit|in|trade stock|in|trade
mercantilism purse|strings stock|jobbery
monetization rags|to|riches street|market
money|changer rate|of|growth strike|action

strike|it|rich	cash|in|advance
strong|market	cash|on|the|nail
superannuate	clearance|sale
sustain|a|loss	clearing|house
tax|collector	commercialism
tax|exemption	commercialist
ten|cent|store	company|report
the|long|green	concessionary
ticker|market	confetti|money
trade|balance	confidence|man
trade|mission	consumer|goods
trading|stamp	copartnership
travel|agency	cost|effective
treasury|bill	counting|house
treasury|note	credit|account
trial|balance	credit|balance
trustee|stock	credit|company
unemployment	credit|squeeze
variety|store	crossed|cheque
watered|stock	current|assets
Welfare|State	depressed|area
without|a|bean	discount|house
working|class	discount|store
working|order	excess|profits
advertisement	eye|to|business
asset|stripper	falling|prices
bank|messenger	filing|cabinet
Bank|of|England	financial|year
bank|overdraft	fire|insurance
bank|statement	free|trade|area
budget|account	fringe|benefit
budget|surplus	going|for|a|song
bulls|and|bears	impulse|buying
burial|society	incorporation
business|hours	industrialism
cash|dispenser	in|Queer|Street

life|assurance	tax|deductible
life|insurance	trade|discount
Lombard|Street	trade|unionism
man|of|business	trade|unionist
millionairess	trading|estate
modernisation	value|added|tax
money|no|object	white|elephant
multinational	wild|cat|strike
multiple|store	accident|policy
Parkinson's|Law	asset|stripping
payment|in|kind	balance|of|trade
payment|in|lieu	bargain|counter
penalty|clause	bill|discounter
petticoat|lane	capitalisation
price|increase	cash|on|delivery
private|income	certain|annuity
private|sector	clearance|house
profitability	company|meeting
profit|and|loss	concessionaire
profit|sharing	consumer|demand
protectionism	corporation|tax
protectionist	cost|accountant
public|company	cost|accounting
purchase|price	cost|efficiency
raise|the|money	current|account
rate|for|the|job	deposit|account
rates|and|taxes	direct|debiting
regular|income	discount|broker
sellers|market	distressed|area
service|charge	expense|account
small|business	eye|for|business
small|investor	family|business
spending|spree	finance|company
stock|exchange	free|enterprise
strike|breaker	free|of|interest
subcontractor	full|employment

gnomes|of|Zurich
holding|company
imprest|account
inertia|selling
letter|of|credit
lighting|up|time
limited|company
Lloyd's|register
market|research
mass|production
merchant|banker
monthly|payment
national|income
national|wealth
ordinary|shares
over|production
over|the|counter
penny|in|the|slot
peppercorn|rent
Peter|principle
private|company
production|line
pyramid|selling
quality|control
rate|of|exchange
rate|of|interest
second|hand|shop
shopping|centre
simple|interest
superannuation
surrender|value
tariff|reformer
three|mile|limit
under|the|hammer
unearned|income
vending|machine

vested|interest
visible|exports
window|shopping
working|capital
American|Express
bargain|basement
building|society
business|as|usual
business|circles
business|contact
business|manager
business|studies
business|venture
capital|gains|tax
carriage|forward
cash|transaction
closing|down|sale
commission|agent
company|director
company|promoter
complete|annuity
cottage|industry
deferred|annuity
deferred|payment
department|store
development|area
distress|warrant
dividend|warrant
do|a|roaring|trade
electricity|bill
endowment|policy
entrepreneurial
exchange|control
family|allowance
floating|capital
foreign|exchange

422

franking machine	non profit making
friendly society	preference stock
golden handshake	public ownership
income tax demand	purchasing power
income tax rebate	registration fee
income tax relief	regular customer
income tax return	reserve currency
insurance broker	rock bottom price
insurance policy	service industry
investment trust	settle an account
invisible import	sleeping partner
labour intensive	supply and demand
lightning strike	suspense account
marine insurance	under the counter
money for old rope	unemployment pay
national savings	world of commerce
no claim discount	

Transport and Communications

A1	cab	guy	leg	rut	UFO
AA	cam	HMS	log	sea	van
go	car	hop	map	ski	via
GT	cat	hoy	MOT	SOS	way
M1	cog	hub	mph	STD	yaw
ABC	cox	jet	oar	sub	ahoy
ace	fan	jib	oil	tar	A one
aft	fin	jog	ply	ton	auto
air	fly	key	ram	top	axle
ark	gad	lag	rev	tow	back
bay	gas	lap	rig	tub	bail
bus	gig	lee	run	tug	bank

bark	flow	luff	sail	warp	cleat
beak	ford	Mach	salt	wash	climb
beam	fore	mail	scow	wire	coach
bend	fork	mast	ship	yard	coast
biga	gaff	mini	sink	yawl	coble
bike	gait	moke	skid	zoom	coupe
bitt	gear	mole	skip	abaft	craft
blip	gyro	moor	skis	afoot	crank
boat	hack	navy	sled	afoul	crash
boom	haul	nose	span	alley	crate
boot	head	oars	spar	aloft	cycle
brig	heel	pace	spin	amble	dandy
bunk	helm	park	stay	araba	davit
buoy	hike	pass	stem	avion	ditch
buss	hold	path	step	awash	dodge
cart	hood	pier	tack	balsa	dolly
case	horn	poop	tail	barge	drift
code	hove	port	tank	beach	drive
cork	hulk	post	taxi	below	drome
crew	hull	pram	tide	berth	E-boat
curb	idle	prop	toll	bilge	embus
dash	jack	prow	tour	blimp	facia
deck	jeep	pull	tram	board	fanal
dhow	junk	punt	trap	bosun	ferry
dial	keel	push	trek	brail	flare
dive	kerb	quay	trim	brake	fleet
dock	kite	raft	trip	buggy	flier
dory	knot	rail	trot	byway	float
drag	land	reef	tube	cabby	flota
draw	lane	ride	tyre	cabin	fluke
dray	lift	ring	vang	cable	foist
duck	line	road	veer	canal	forth
fare	list	roam	vent	canoe	glide
fast	lock	roll	wain	cargo	going
flee	loop	rove	wake	choke	guard
flit	lost	saic	walk	chute	guide

haste	pylon	stage	adrift	bumper
hatch	Q|boat	stall	afloat	busman
hawse	racer	stamp	airbus	by|lane
hiker	radar	start	airing	by|pass
hobby	radio	steam	air|log	bypath
hoist	rally	stern	airman	byroad
horse	range	stray	air|ram	caique
hurry	reach	strip	airway	calash
jaunt	relay	strut	alight	call|up
jetty	rev|up	stunt	anchor	camber
jolly	rider	sweep	argosy	canard
jumbo	ropes	Telex	armada	canter
kayak	rotor	thole	arrive	careen
kedge	route	ton|up	artery	career
ketch	royal	track	ascent	carfax
lay|by	sally	trail	astern	carina
leech	screw	train	avenue	chaise
lie|to	sedan	tramp	aweigh	clutch
light	shaft	tread	back|up	coaler
liner	sheer	trike	banger	cobble
loran	sheet	truck	bargee	cockle
lorry	shell	trunk	barque	conner
march	shift	U|boat	barrow	con|rod
morse	shunt	umiak	basket	convoy
motor	sidle	U|turn	bateau	copter
mount	skiff	valve	beacon	course
naval	skirt	visit	berlin	cruise
nomad	skull	way|in	big|end	cut|out
on|tow	slips	wharf	bireme	cutter
orbit	sloop	wheel	boatel	decked
pedal	smack	xebec	bomber	de|icer
pilot	smash	yacht	bonnet	depart
pitch	spars	Z|bend	bowser	detour
plane	speed	aboard	braces	dinghy
praam	spill	abroad	bridge	divert
prang	sprit	access	bucket	

425

diving	hurtle	nip|off	saloon
dogger	hustle	nose|up	sampan
driver	idling	octane	sculls
dry|run	impact	on|deck	seaman
dugout	intake	one|way	seaway
earing	in|trim	on|foot	sender
egress	island	onward	set|out
elevon	jalopy	outing	sheets
embark	jet|lag	outset	shoran
engine	jetsam	oxcart	shroud
escape	jet|set	packet	siding
exodus	jib|guy	paddle	signal
fender	jigger	petrol	skates
fiacre	jostle	pharos	skyway
flight	junket	pickup	sledge
flying	kit|bag	pile|up	sleigh
fo'c'sle	klaxon	piston	smoker
funnel	landau	porter	sortie
galiot	lascar	propel	sparks
galley	lateen	pursue	spiral
gallop	launch	radial	splice
garage	leeway	ramble	spring
gas|jet	letter	ram|jet	stocks
gasket	litter	randem	stoker
glider	lock|up	rating	strake
gocart	lorcha	ratlin	street
gunnel	lugger	reefer	stride
hangar	mahout	return	stroll
hansom	marina	rigged	subway
haul|to	marker	rigger	surrey
hawser	mayday	ring|up	swerve
hearse	mirror	rocket	tackle
hooker	mizzen	rudder	tandem
hot|rod	mobile	runner	tanker
hove|to	module	runway	tannoy
hubcap	motion	sailor	tartan

426

6/7 LETTERS

tender	airfoil	bollard	chopper
ticker	air|jump	bomb|bay	chutist
ticket	air|lane	booking	circuit
tiller	air|legs	booster	clipper
timber	airlift	bow|fast	coaster
tin|can	airline	bowline	cockpit
toddle	air|miss	boxhaul	collide
toggle	airpark	box|kite	collier
torque	airport	boxseat	commute
totter	airship	britzka	compass
towbar	airsick	bulwark	contact
travel	air|taxi	busline	co|pilot
troika	ambages	bus|stop	coracle
trudge	arrival	buzzing	courier
tunnel	autobus	buzz|off	crack|up
turret	autocar	caboose	crewman
unmoor	autovac	call|box	crock|up
valise	aviator	capsize	cruiser
vessel	aviette	capstan	cyclist
volant	baby|jib	capsule	day|trip
voyage	baggage	captain	descent
waggon	bail|out	caravan	detrain
wander	ballast	caravel	dodgems
way|out	balloon	cariole	dogcart
whaler	banking	carpark	draught
wherry	barge|in	carport	drayman
whisky	battery	carrack	dredger
address	bay|line	carrier	drifter
aerobus	beeline	catboat	drive|in
aground	bicycle	cat|head	droshky
aileron	biplane	cat's|eye	dry|dock
air|base	birdman	catwalk	dry|land
airboat	blister	channel	ejector
air|crew	boating	chariot	emplane
airdrop	boatman	charter	engaged
air|flow	bobstay	chassis	en|route

TRANSPORT AND COMMUNICATIONS

entrain	gunboat	killick	monitor
exhaust	gun|deck	killock	mooring
explore	guy,rope	landing	mud|hook
express	gyro,car	lanyard	nacelle
fairing	hackney	L,driver	no|entry
fairway	halyard	learner	oarsman
felucca	hammock	lee|helm	odyssey
fetch|up	handbag	lee|tack	offside
flattop	harbour	leeward	old|salt
flivver	hardtop	leewide	omnibus
flyboat	harness	lift,off	on|board
flyover	haywain	lighter	ongoing
fly|past	head|for	logbook	on|the|go
foretop	head|off	L,plates	opening
formula	headset	luggage	orbital
founder	headway	lugsail	outride
four,oar	heave|to	lymphad	painter
freeway	helibus	Mae|West	parking
frigate	helipad	magneto	parting
frogman	highway	mail|van	passage
futtock	holdall	maintop	pathway
galleon	hot|line	make|for	payload
galleys	hurry|up	make|off	phaeton
gangway	iceboat	man,o,war	pig|boat
gearbox	impetus	mariner	pillion
getaway	impulse	marline	pinnace
get|lost	ingress	Martian	piragua
gliding	Jack|Tar	matelot	pirogue
go|ahead	jaw|rope	meander	polacca
go|below	jet|pipe	migrant	polacre
go|by|air	jib|boom	milk|run	pontoon
go,devil	jibstay	minibus	postage
gondola	journey	minicab	postman
grapnel	joy|ride	minicar	precede
growler	keelson	minisub	proceed
guichet	keep|off	mission	Pullman

pull|out	set|sail	tonneau	volante
push|car	shallop	top|deck	voyager
railway	shipway	topmast	wanigan
ratline	shuttle	topsail	warship
rebound	side|car	topside	waybill
reentry	skid|pan	torsion	wayfare
retrace	skipper	tourist	wayworn
retreat	skysail	towards	welcome
reverse	sleeper	towboat	winging
ride|out	slipway	towpath	wingtip
rigging	smash|up	towrope	wrecker
ring|off	spanker	tractor	yardarm
ripcord	sputnik	traffic	zooming
road|hog	starter	trailer	aerodyne
road|map	start|up	traipse	aerofoil
road|tax	station	tramcar	aerogram
rolling	steamer	tramway	aeronaut
rope|tow	steward	transit	aerostat
ropeway	stopway	travels	airborne
rowboat	surface	trawler	air|brake
rowlock	sweeper	tripper	air|coach
run|away	swifter	trireme	aircraft
run|into	tackler	trolley	airfield
runners	tail|end	trundle	airframe
sailing	tail|fin	trysail	airliner
satchel	take|off	tugboat	air|route
saunter	tartane	tumbrel	air|scout
scamper	taxicab	tumbril	airscrew
scooter	taxiing	turning	airspace
scupper	taxiway	twin|jet	air|speed
scuttle	telpher	vagrant	airstrip
sea|lane	Telstar	vehicle	airwoman
sea|legs	termini	viaduct	all|at|sea
seasick	test|hop	vis|a|vis	alleyway
seaward	tilbury	visitor	altitude
send|off	to|horse	voiture	approach

area|code	caracole	drag|wire	fore|jack
arterial	carriage	driftway	fore|lift
at|anchor	cast|away	drive|off	foremast
autobahn	catapult	driveway	foresail
autogyro	cat's|eyes	dust|cart	foreship
aviation	causeway	eight|oar	forestay
aviatrix	clarence	elevator	foretack
backfire	clearway	emigrant	foreyard
back|seat	coachbox	emigrate	forkroad
backstay	coachman	entrance	fuel|ship
backwash	coachway	envelope	full|load
bargeman	coasting	equipage	fuselage
barnacle	cockboat	Europort	gad|about
barouche	commuter	evacuate	galleass
beam|ends	Concorde	even|keel	garboard
bearings	converge	exchange	gasoline
becalmed	corridor	excursus	get|ahead
bilander	corvette	fall|back	go|aboard
binnacle	coxswain	farewell	go|ashore
black|box	crabbing	fast|line	go|astray
boat|deck	crescent	ferryman	go|before
boat|hook	crossing	fireboat	go|by|rail
boat|line	crossply	flagging	Godspeed
bodywork	cruising	flagship	gradient
bolt|rope	culde|sac	flatboat	grounded
bowsprit	curricle	flat|spin	half|deck
Bradshaw	cylinder	flat|tyre	handcart
brancard	dahabeah	floating	hang|back
broach|to	deck|hand	flotilla	hatchway
brougham	derelict	flywheel	hawse|bag
bulkhead	dipstick	fogbound	head|fast
bulwarks	dismount	footfall	head|into
cabin|boy	ditty|bag	footpath	heel|over
cable|car	downhaul	footslog	heliport
cableway	dragoman	footstep	helmsman
camshaft	dragster	forefoot	highroad

430

8 LETTERS

high|seas	level|off	motorist	porthole
homeward	life|belt	motorway	portside
horse|box	lifeboat	muleteer	port|tack
horseman	life|buoy	multi|jet	post|boat
icebound	life|line	navarchy	postcard
ice|yacht	life|raft	nearside	postcode
ignition	lift|wire	nose|cone	progress
in|flight	log|canoe	nosedive	pulse|jet
in|motion	longbeat	nose|down	puncture
inner|jib	longeron	nose|into	pushcart
intercom	long|haul	oil|gauge	put|to|sea
ironclad	loose|box	old|crock	quadriga
jackstay	mail|boat	oleo|gear	radiator
jerrican	main|deck	oncoming	railroad
jet|pilot	main|lift	one|horse	receiver
jet|plane	mainline	on|the|run	red|light
jet|power	mainmast	open|road	reef|band
jettison	main|road	operator	reef|knot
journeys	mainstay	ordinary	rickshaw
joy|rider	main|yard	outboard	ring|road
joystick	manifold	outer|jib	road|sign
jumbo|jet	man|of|war	overhaul	roadster
junction	maritime	overland	rockaway
jurymast	masthead	overpass	roof|rack
jury|sail	mine|ship	overseas	ropeband
kamikaze	momentum	overtake	ropework
keel|over	monorail	overturn	rucksack
kickback	moon|base	passer|by	runabout
knapsack	moonsail	passover	run|ahead
land|ahoy	moon|ship	passport	rush|hour
landfall	moonshot	pavement	sailboat
larboard	moonwalk	periplus	sail|free
lateener	moorings	pilotage	sail|loft
launcher	motorbus	platform	schedule
leeboard	motorcar	Plimsoll	schooner
lee|sheet	motoring	poop|deck	scout|car

seafarer	staysai̇l	under|way
seagoing	steerage	unicycle
seaplane	steering	velocity
sea|route	sternway	victoria
set|forth	stock|car	volatile
shanghai	stopover	volplane
sheer|leg	stowaway	wagon|lit
sheer|off	straggle	wardroom
ship|ahoy	straying	warplane
shipmate	stunt|man	water|bus
ship|oars	suitcase	waterway
shipping	tackling	wayfarer
short|hop	tag|along	way|train
shoulder	tail|boom	wear|ship
show|a|leg	tailpipe	wheelies
showboat	tail|skid	wind|cone
side|road	tail|spin	wind|drag
sideslip	taxi|rank	wind|sock
side|step	telegram	windward
sidewalk	teletype	wing|over
silencer	terminal	wireless
skidding	terminus	withdraw
skid|mark	thole|pin	yachting
slip|road	throttle	Zeppelin
slow|down	toboggan	zero|hour
slow|lane	tollgate	about|ship
snap|roll	tramline	addressee
sociable	traverse	aerodrome
spaceman	tricycle	aeromotor
spar|deck	trimaran	aeroplane
speeding	trim|sail	after|deck
squad|car	trim|ship	air|bridge
staff|car	turbojet	air|pocket
stanhope	turn|away	air|sleeve
start|off	turn|over	airworthy
start|out	turnpike	all|aboard

altimeter	cablegram	deceleron
ambulance	cabriolet	departure
amidships	canalboat	depot|ship
amphibian	cargo|boat	destroyer
anchorage	carpet|bag	diesel|oil
applecart	cartwheel	diligence
astrodome	catamaran	dining|car
astronaut	charabanc	dip|switch
atom|liner	chauffeur	direction
autopilot	chief|mate	dirigible
autopista	clearance	dirt|track
backropes	clew|lines	disembark
backwater	coach|road	diversion
bandwagon	coachwork	dodgem|car
bargepole	collision	drag|force
basic|load	combat|car	drift|wire
Bath|chair	concourse	drive|away
below|deck	conductor	drop|a|line
bilge|keel	cosmonaut	duffel|bag
bilge|pump	couchette	Early|Bird
black|gang	countdown	earphones
blockship	crankcase	empennage
blue|peter	crash|boat	escalator
boathouse	crash|land	esplanade
boatswain	crocodile	estate|car
boat|train	crossjack	excursion
bobsleigh	cross|road	extension
bon|voyage	crosstree	false|keel
boulevard	crowd|sail	family|car
bowl|along	crow's|nest	fare|stage
box|waggon	curbstone	ferryboat
broadside	cut|and|run	first|mate
bubble|car	dashboard	first|rate
bulldozer	Davy|Jones	flying|jib
bus|driver	day|letter	footropes
cab|driver	day|return	forebrace

foreroyal	headphone	lower|boom
foresheet	helidrome	lower|deck
freeboard	hit|and|run	lunar|base
free|wheel	hitch|hike	Mach|meter
freighter	hoist|sail	mail|coach
French|lug	hook|a|ride	mainbrace
front|seat	horseback	mainroyal
fuel|gauge	houseboat	mainsheet
funicular	hump|speed	major|road
gain|speed	hydrofoil	make|haste
gallivant	ice|skates	manoeuvre
gangplank	immigrant	mass|media
gather|way	immigrate	milestone
gear|lever	inch|along	milkfloat
ghost|ship	indicator	milometer
give|a|ring	itinerant	mine|layer
globe|trot	itinerary	miss|stays
go|aground	jaunty|car	mizzentop
gondolier	jaywalker	monoplane
goose|step	jet|bomber	moonraker
grand|tour	jollyboat	morse|code
grapevine	kerb|drill	motorbike
gross|lift	kerbstone	motorboat
groundhog	kick|start	motorcade
guard|ship	lag|behind	mule|train
guard|s|van	landaulet	multi|prop
guess|warp	landplane	navigable
guest|rope	land|rover	navigator
gyropilot	launching	newsflash
gyroplane	launch|pad	nosewheel
handbrake	leave|home	ocean|lane
hansom|cab	letter|box	ocean|trip
hatchback	leviathan	on|the|move
haversack	lightship	on|the|wing
hawse|hook	limousine	orientate
hawsepipe	lose|speed	orlop|deck

434

outrigger	river|boat	sidetrack
overboard	road|block	sight|land
overdrive	road|sense	sightseer
overshoot	roadstead	signal|box
packhorse	road|works	signalman
palanquin	rocket|car	single|jet
pancaking	rocket|man	skyriding
parachute	rotor|ship	slowcoach
party|line	round|trip	slow|train
passenger	royal|mast	small|boat
patrol|car	royal|road	snowshoes
periscope	royal|sail	sonic|boom
phone|book	rudder|bar	sonic|wall
phone|call	saddlebag	space|crew
pillar|box	sailplane	spacedock
pilot|boat	sally|port	spaceport
point|duty	saloon|car	spaceship
police|car	sandyacht	space|suit
police|van	satellite	spacewalk
portfolio	saucerman	spare|part
post,haste	sea|anchor	speedboat
postilion	seafaring	speedster
powerboat	sea|gasket	spinnaker
power|dive	seaworthy	sports|car
pressgang	semaphore	spritsail
privateer	set|on|foot	stage|boat
prize,crew	sharp|bend	stanchion
promenade	sheer,hulk	starboard
propeller	shipboard	stateroom
racing|car	ship|of|war	steal|away
radar|nose	ship|plane	steamboat
radio|beam	ship|route	steam|line
radiogram	ship's|crew	steamship
ram|rocket	shipshape	steersman
reach|land	shipwreck	step|aside
reef|point	sidelight	stern|fast

sternpost	tramlines	air|control
stevedore	transport	air|cruiser
stokehold	traveller	air|hostess
storeship	triptyque	air|service
storm|boat	troopship	air|steward
stratojet	trunk|call	air|support
streetcar	trunk|line	A|at|Lloyd's
stretcher	trunk|road	amber|light
strike|out	turboprop	ambulation
stringers	turbopump	ambulatory
sub|chaser	turn|aside	anchor|deck
submarine	turn|round	antifreeze
surfacing	turret|top	automobile
surfboard	twin|screw	ballooning
switch|off	two|seater	balloonist
tailboard	ufologist	ball|turret
tail|light	underpass	barkentine
tailplane	under|sail	barrel|roll
tail|rotor	upper|deck	batten|down
tail|shaft	vehicular	battleship
take|leave	war|galley	bear|down|on
taximeter	water|line	Bermuda|rig
taxiplane	whaleback	Black|Maria
tea|waggon	whaleboat	blind|alley
telegraph	wheel|base	boneshaker
telemotor	wheel|spin	branch|line
telepathy	white|line	breakwater
telephone	wirephoto	bridge|deck
telephony	yachtsman	bridle|path
telephoto	able|seaman	brigantine
test|pilot	aboard|ship	bubble|hood
third|mate	access|road	bucket|seat
timenoguy	adventurer	bus|service
timetable	aerobatics	bus|station
touch|down	aeronautic	cabin|plane
traipsing	a|head|start	camouflage

cantilever	drift along	ground loop
cargo plane	drift angle	hackney cab
cast anchor	drop anchor	hawsepiece
catch a crab	dusk rocket	headlights
catch a ride	emigration	heatshield
chapel cart	evacuation	heave round
clear house	expedition	heave short
clew garnet	expressway	helicopter
coach horse	fall behind	High street
cockleboat	feed system	hitch hiker
column gear	fire engine	hit the deck
command car	first class	home and dry
congestion	flight deck	homecoming
connection	flight path	hovercraft
contraflow	flight plan	hydroplane
control rod	flight time	icebreaker
conveyance	floatplane	inflatable
cosmodrome	fly by night	inter urban
country bus	flying boat	invalid car
covered way	flying wing	jaywalking
cow catcher	footbridge	jet fatigue
crankshaft	fore and aft	jet fighter
crossroads	forecastle	jiggermast
dandy horse	forerunner	Jolly Roger
dawn rocket	foresheets	Joyce stick
day tripper	forge ahead	juggernaut
decampment	four in hand	jury rigged
delta wings	four master	jury rudder
dickey seat	gain ground	knockabout
disemplane	gather head	landing run
dive bomber	gear change	landlubber
diving bell	glass coach	lateen sail
double bend	go in the van	lead the way
double prop	goods train	lettergram
double reef	green light	lie athwart
downstream	ground crew	life jacket

lighthouse	patrol|boat	round|house
locomotion	pedestrian	roustabout
luggage|van	Penny|Black	rowing|boat
main|artery	petrol|pump	safety|belt
make|tracks	petrol|tank	safety|wire
manipulate	picket|boat	sail|teaser
manoeuvres	pilgrimage	sally|forth
marker|buoy	pilot|house	seamanship
martingale	pilot|plane	second|mate
middle|deck	pipe|aboard	sedan|chair
midshipman	port|anchor	sens|unique
mizzenmast	port|of|call	servo|pilot
mizzen|sail	post|chaise	set|the|pace
mizzen|stay	Post|Office	sheepshank
monkey|deck	propellant	shipmaster
monkey|rail	propulsion	sidesaddle
motorcoach	public|walk	side|street
motorcycle	quadrireme	single|prop
motor|truck	quadruplex	skyscraper
naval|cadet	radial|tyre	sky|writing
navigation	rear|mirror	slipstream
nose|turret	reduce|sail	sloop|of|war
ocean|going	rendezvous	smoking|car
ocean|liner	repair|ship	solo|flight
on|a|bowline	rescue|boat	spacecraft
on|the|march	rev|counter	spare|wheel
on|the|rocks	ride|and|tie	speed|limit
open|waggon	ride|a|storm	square|away
outer|space	right|of|way	square|sail
overbridge	road|safety	stagecoach
packet|boat	roadworthy	stand|first
packet|line	robot|plane	state|barge
packet|ship	rocket|boat	static|tube
paddle|boat	rocket|ship	step|rocket
parcel|post	rope|bridge	stewardess
pathfinder	roundabout	streamline

submariner	two|wheeler	assault|boat
sun|compass	undershoot	attack|plane
supercargo	under|steam	balloon|sail
supersonic	useful|lift	battleplane
supply|ship	vanity|case	beaten|track
suspension	velocipede	belaying|pin
switchback	veteran|car	bid|farewell
tachometer	V|formation	blind|corner
tanker|ship	vintage|car	blind|flying
target|boat	volitation	break|ground
tea|clipper	volplaning	built|up|area
telegraphy	wanderings	bullock|cart
telepathic	wanderlust	carburetter
television	watercraft	card|compass
telewriter	water|plane	carriageway
telpherage	watertight	carrick|bend
test|flight	way|station	catch|a|train
test|rocket	way|traffic	caterpillar
thumb|a|lift	wheelchair	cat's|whisker
ticker|tape	wheelhouse	centreboard
tip|up|lorry	whirlybird	close|hauled
toll|bridge	windjammer	club|topsail
topgallant	windscreen	coach|driver
touring|car	wing|mirror	cockleshell
tracklayer	abandon|ship	combat|plane
traffic|jam	accelerator	come|forward
train|ferry	aeronautics	compartment
trajectory	afterburner	contraprops
travelling	after|shroud	convertible
travel|sick	air|controls	country|road
travel|worn	airsickness	cover|ground
triaconter	air|terminal	crash|helmet
triphibian	air|umbrella	crash|waggon
trolley|bus	anchor|fluke	crowd|of|sail
true|course	armoured|car	delivery|van
turret|ship	articulated	destination

distributor	hit|the|trail	minesweeper
double|march	horse|litter	mizzen|royal
dreadnought	hug|the|shore	montgolfier
driving|test	ignition|key	moon|landing
ejector|seat	immigration	moon|station
engaged|line	interceptor	mooring|buoy
engine|gauge	in|the|saddle	mooring|mast
entrainment	in|the|wake|of	morse|signal
escape|hatch	jaunting|car	Moses|basket
escape|route	journeyings	motor|launch
exhaust|pipe	journey's|end	motor|vessel
fares|please	kedge|anchor	mystery|tour
find|one's|way	keep|station	naval|rating
fishing|boat	kite|balloon	naval|vessel
fishing|dory	laminar|flow	near|the|wind
fishtailing	landing|deck	night|letter
fleet|of|foot	landing|skis	orientation
flight|strip	lazy|painter	ornithopter
flying|kites	leading|edge	out|of|the|way
flying|speed	leave|taking	outside|loop
flying|visit	limber|board	package|tour
forced|march	line|engaged	paddle|wheel
fore|topsail	loop|the|loop	parachutist
forward|deck	lorry|driver	paratrooper
galley|slave	lose|one's|way	penteconter
gather|speed	luggage|rack	peregrinate
get|under|way	lunar|module	peripatetic
go|alongside	magic|carpet	petrol|gauge
goods|waggon	main|skysail	phone|number
go|overboard	main|topsail	pick|up|speed
GranTurismo	make|headway	pillion|seat
ground|speed	make|sea|room	pony|and|trap
gyrocompass	make|strides	portmanteau
hawse|timber	man|from|Mars	private|line
head|for|home	merchantman	push|bicycle
highway|code	mess|steward	put|into|port

quarter deck	sightseeing	telpher line
quarter jack	sinking ship	testing area
quinquereme	skysail mast	three in hand
racing shell	sleeping bag	three master
radio beacon	sleeping car	ticking over
radio mirror	soft landing	torpedo boat
request stop	solar rocket	trafficator
rescue plane	space centre	transmitter
reservation	space flight	transporter
retroaction	space island	travel agent
retro rocket	space patrol	true heading
reverse turn	space rocket	trysail gaff
road haulage	space travel	tube station
road licence	spanker boom	under canvas
road traffic	spanker gaff	underground
rocket motor	speedometer	vapour trail
rocket plane	stagger wire	waggon train
rocket power	standing lug	waggon wheel
rotor blades	steal a march	waiting room
running knot	steam engine	walking tour
sailing boat	steam launch	weather deck
sailing ship	step rockets	weather side
scuttle butt	stern anchor	weigh anchor
search plane	stern sheets	wheel barrow
seasickness	straphanger	wing loading
second class	string a long	wrong number
self starter	stunt flying	aircraftsman
send packing	submersible	airfreighter
set in motion	subsonic jet	air sea rescue
Shanks's mare	switchboard	all systems go
Shanks's pony	synchromesh	approach road
sheet anchor	tailless jet	arrester hook
shelter deck	take the lead	arterial road
ship the oars	tandem plane	autorotation
shroud lines	telecontrol	baby carriage
shuttle trip	teleprinter	Bailey bridge

```
beaching|gear entrance|lock landing|strip
beacon|lights escape|rocket launching|pad
bearing|plate fighter|pilot level|landing
belly|landing fishing|fleet light|cruiser
between|decks fishing|smack long|distance
blind|landing flight|tester longshoreman
cabin|cruiser flying|circus lost|and|found
cable|railway flying|saucer luggage|label
caulking|iron flying|tanker luggage|train
centre|anchor forestaysail maiden|flight
change|course forward|march maiden|voyage
channel|patch free|wheeling main|staysail
chart|a|course freight|train make|good|time
citizen's|band fuel|injector make|progress
clear|the|land Gladstone|bag manned|rocket
coach|and|four glide|landing man|overboard
coach|and|pair globetrotter merchant|ship
coachbuilder go|by|the|board monkey|rigged
companionway ground|tester motor|scooter
conning|tower hackney|coach night|fighter
control|stick happy|landing off|like|a|shot
control|tower harbour|light overnight|bag
counter|march heavy|cruiser pantechnicon
crash|barrier hedgehopping parking|light
crash|landing hospital|ship parking|meter
cylinder|head inclinometer parking|orbit
desobligeant in|the|train|of passing|place
dialling|code inverted|spin perambulator
dialling|tone Jacob's|ladder petty|officer
dispatch|boat jet|propelled pilot|balloon
double|decker king's|highway plain|sailing
draught|horse landing|craft platform|deck
dual|controls landing|field pleasure|boat
East|Indiaman landing|light pleasure|trip
ejection|seat landing|speed Plimsoll|line
end|of|the|line landing|stage Plimsoll|mark
```

postage|stamp	space|station
pressure|suit	spanker|sheet
puddle|jumper	sparking|plug
pursuit|plane	speed|of|sound
quarter|light	square|rigged
radar|scanner	square|rigger
radar|station	stall|landing
radio|compass	steer|clear|of
radio|monitor	steering|gear
radio|station	stream|anchor
raise|the|dead	streamlining
return|ticket	Sunday|driver
ride|at|anchor	sunshine|roof
ride|bareback	survival|suit
road|junction	take|bearings
rocket|assist	take|off|strip
rocket|engine	tally|ho|coach
rocket|glider	tearing|hurry
roller|skates	tender|rocket
rolling|stock	the|bitter|end
rolling|stone	thoroughfare
rough|passage	three|wheeler
running|board	through|train
running|light	ticket|office
sailing|barge	touch|the|wind
sailing|canoe	tourist|class
sailing|yacht	traffic|light
season|ticket	train|service
shape|a|course	transmission
shipping|line	travel|agency
shoot|ballast	trolley|track
single|decker	tubeless|tyre
slacken|speed	upset|the|boat
sonic|barrier	utility|plane
sound|barrier	VIP|transport
space|capsule	walk|the|plank

Wandering Jew	jet propulsion
weatherboard	landing ground
weather sheet	left hand drive
windward side	level crossing
aerial railway	number engaged
armoured train	paddle steamer
begging letter	panda crossing
Belisha beacon	penny farthing
booking office	peregrination
breakdown gang	peripatetical
bridge of sighs	petrol station
bush telegraph	pontoon bridge
carriage drive	postal address
Channel tunnel	postal service
coach building	poste restante
command module	power steering
communication	press campaign
conducted tour	press cuttings
conductor rail	pressure cabin
container port	printing press
container ship	promenade deck
corridor train	public address
distant signal	public highway
driving lesson	Queen's highway
driving mirror	radiotelegram
driving school	railway engine
electric train	railway system
excess luggage	railway tunnel
express letter	restaurant car
flying machine	return journey
foot passenger	road transport
forced landing	roller coaster
globe trotting	roll on roll off
ground control	rule of the road
homeward bound	sailing orders
horse and buggy	scenic railway

shock|absorber	first|class|post
shooting|brake	flight|recorder
space|platform	floating|bridge
speed|merchant	full|steam|ahead
station|master	inland|waterway
steering|wheel	luggage|carrier
stepping|stone	no|thoroughfare
strato,cruiser	observation|car
telegraph|pole	package|holiday
telegraph|wire	passenger|train
telephone|book	personal|column
telephone|call	person|to|person
telephone|line	platform|ticket
through|ticket	quarantine|flag
traffic|island	radio|telegraph
traffic|lights	radio|telephone
transportable	rear,view|mirror
transport|cafe	registered|mail
transport|ship	registered|post
transshipping	reversing|light
trunk|dialling	road|traffic|act
turning|circle	running|repairs
turn|the|corner	service|station
unadopted|road	shuttle|service
undercarriage	space|traveller
zebra|crossing	steering|column
automatic|pilot	telegraph|cable
breakdown|truck	telephone|kiosk
catenary|system	telephotograph
coaling|station	three,point|turn
deadman's|handle	three,speed|gear
diesel,electric	through|traffic
disembarkation	traction|engine
excursion|train	traffic|manager
filling|station	traffic|signals
first|class|mail	transportation

trustee|account
wild|goose|chase
carriage|and|pair
double|white|line
dual|carriageway
excursion|ticket
express|delivery
Grand|Union|canal
hackney|carriage
invalid|carriage
marshalling|yard
message|received
motorway|madness
mountain|railway
moving|staircase
pelican|crossing
picture|postcard
pleasure|steamer
point|of|no|return

prairie|schooner
press|conference
public|transport
radiotelegraphy
railway|carriage
railway|crossing
refreshment|room
road|fund|licence
second|class|mail
second|class|post
special|delivery
stamping|machine
telephone|number
temperance|hotel
ticket|collector
ticket|inspector
vertical|take|off
victualling|ship
windscreen|wiper

Trees

ash	sal	coca	sorb	alder	briar
bay	sap	coco	teak	algum	brier
ben	yew	cone	tree	almug	broom
box	akee	cork	twig	arbor	brush
elm	bark	dhak	upas	aspen	cacao
fig	bass	dita	whin	balsa	carob
fir	bast	ilex	wood	beech	cedar
gum	bole	palm	abele	birch	copse
log	bosk	pine	abies	bough	cubeb
oak	bush	root	acorn	brake	ebony

elder	banyan	sallow	foliage
frith	baobab	sapota	foliose
furze	bog,oak	sappan	genipap
glade	bo,tree	souari	gum|tree
gorse	bransh	spruce	hickory
grove	carapa	sumach	holm,oak
hedge	cassia	sylvan	hop|tree
henna	catkin	timber	juniper
holly	caudex	walnut	leafage
hurst	cornel	wattle	leaflet
jarul	daphne	willow	lentisk
kokra	deodar	ailanto	logwood
kokum	forest	ambatch	madrona
larch	gingko	arbutus	margosa
lilac	jarool	babussu	oakling
maple	jarrah	bebeeru	palmyra
myrrh	jujube	blue,gum	pinetum
palay	jungle	boscage	platane
pipal	kalmia	boxwood	pollard
plane	kittul	bullace	pruning
ramus	laurel	cajuput	rampick
roble	lignum	catalpa	rampike
roots	linden	chamise	red|pine
rowan	loquat	chamiso	redwood
sapan	manuka	conifer	sapling
shrub	myrtle	coppice	sapwood
sumac	papaya	coquito	sequoia
thorn	pinery	cork,oak	service
tilia	platan	cow,tree	spinney
trunk	poplar	cypress	sundari
zamia	privet	dagwood	syringa
abroma	prunus	dogwood	taproot
aca jou	queach	duramen	tea|tree
antiar	rattan	durmast	thicket
arbute	red,bud	fig|leaf	wax|tree
arolla	red|fir	fir|cone	wych,elm

447

TREES

Yule|log	kingwood	tamarind
ailantus	laburnum	viburnum
alburnum	lavender	witch|elm
allspice	magnolia	woodland
arboreal	mahogany	wood|pulp
ash|plant	mangrove	adansonia
barberry	manna|ash	albespyne
basswood	mesquite	algarroba
beam|tree	milk|tree	aloes|wood
beefwood	milkwood	alpine|fir
caatinga	oleander	andromeda
calamite	palmetto	arboretum
carnauba	palm|tree	balsam|fir
chestnut	pear|tree	balsa|wood
cinchona	piassava	brier|bush
cinnamon	pinaster	brushwood
clearing	pine|cone	buckthorn
coco|tree	pine|tree	bully|tree
coco|wood	quandong	bussu|palm
cork|tree	rain|tree	butternut
date|palm	rambutan	casuarina
date|tree	red|cedar	chaparral
deadwood	red|maple	chincapin
dendroid	rosemary	cocoa|wood
forestry	rosewood	crowberry
Greek|fir	royal|oak	deciduous
guaiacum	sago|palm	dwarf|tree
hardwood	sapindus	evergreen
hawthorn	shadbush	forsythia
hemp|palm	sloetree	grape|tree
hemp|tree	softwood	greenwood
holly|oak	sweet|bay	ground|ash
hornbeam	sweetsop	heartwood
iron|bark	sycamine	hydrangea
ironwood	sycamore	in|blossom
jack|tree	tamarack	ivory|palm

448

ivory|tree	whitebeam	orange|wood
Judas|tree	widow|wail	palm|branch
lancewood	wych|hazel	paper|birch
lilac|tree	almond|tree	pine|needle
maple|leaf	annual|ring	plantation
outer|bark	blackbully	prickly|ash
paulownia	blackthorn	quercitron
peach|palm	bladder|nut	raffia|palm
petty|whin	bottle|tree	rain|forest
pitch|pine	brazilwood	red|sanders
plane|tree	bullet|tree	rose|laurel
poison|oak	butter|tree	sandalwood
pyracanth	button|bush	silver|bell
quebracho	buttonwood	silver|tree
rose|apple	calamander	spring|wood
rowan|tree	chinquapin	sugar|maple
royal|palm	coniferous	tallow|tree
sagebrush	coral|berry	tree|of|life
sapodilla	cowrie|pine	tree|tomato
sassafras	crown|graft	turpentine
satinwood	dead|finish	underbrush
Scotch|elm	dendrology	white|cedar
Scotch|fir	Diana's|tree	white|thorn
Scots|pine	Douglas|fir	witch|hazel
shade|tree	dragon|tree	yellow|wood
shrubbery	Durmast|oak	African|teak
silver|fir	eucalyptus	amboyna|wood
sloethorn	fiddlewood	American|elm
snowberry	goat's|thorn	burning|bush
soapberry	greasewood	cabbage|palm
star|anise	greenheart	cabbage|tree
stone|pine	hackmatack	cajuput|tree
thorn|tree	laurustine	camel's|thorn
tulip|tree	manna|larch	coconut|palm
underwood	nothofagus	copper|beech
wax|myrtle	olive|grove	cotoneaster

honey|locust
hound's|berry
Japan|laurel
juniper|tree
laurustinus
lignum|vitae
mammoth|tree
mountain|ash
olive|branch
palm|cabbage
poison|sumac
prickly|pear
purpleheart
pussy|willow
shittah|tree
silver|birch
slippery|elm
spindle|tree
sweet|willow
undergrowth
varnish|tree
white|poplar
wintersweet
xanthoxylum
balsam|of|Peru
balsam|of|Tolu
bougainvilia
calabash|tree
Canada|balsam
checkerberry
chestnut|tree
Christ's|thorn
cucumber|tree
decorticated
dragon's|blood
frankincense

massaranduba
monkey|puzzle
Norway|spruce
Philadelphus
piassava|palm
plantain|tree
poison|laurel
quaking|aspen
ramification
rhododendron
sea|buckthorn
snowdrop|tree
Spanish|broom
spurge|laurel
tree|of|heaven
umbrella|tree
virgin|forest
wellingtonia
afforestation
almond|blossom
amygdalaceous
arboriculture
bird's|eye|maple
Christmas|tree
cranberry|tree
deforestation
dendrological
horse|chestnut
savanna|forest
weeping|willow
arboricultural
cedar|of|Lebanon
flowering|shrub
Lombardy|poplar
maidenhair|tree
mistletoe|bough

15 LETTERS

arboriculturist Spanish|chestnut
Dutch|elm|disease tree|of|knowledge

Vegetables

cos	cress	murphy	pumpkin
pea	cubeb	pea|pod	salsify
pod	kraut	pepper	seakale
rue	onion	potato	seed|pod
sot	patch	radish	shallot
bean	pease	runner	skirret
beet	roots	savory	soybean
cole	salad	sprout	spinach
dill	savoy	tomato	sprouts
herb	swede	turnip	succory
kale	thyme	bay|leaf	weed|out
leek	tuber	blewits	beetroot
mace	borage	cabbage	borecole
mint	carrot	caraway	brassica
okra	celery	cardoon	broccoli
peas	chilli	chervil	camomile
root	cow|pea	chicory	capsicum
sage	endive	collard	celeriac
sium	fennel	gherkin	chick|pea
slaw	floret	haricot	coleslaw
spud	garden	lettuce	cole|wort
basil	garlic	olitory	crucifer
caper	ginger	oregano	cucumber
chard	greens	parsley	dill|seed
chive	growth	parsnip	egg|apple
cibol	legume	potherb	egg|fruit
clove	marrow	produce	egg|plant

451

VEGETABLES

escarole	love apple
greenery	navy beans
green pea	new potato
kohlrabi	pinto bean
Lima bean	red pepper
mad apple	snap beans
main crop	soya beans
marjoram	sugar beet
peasecod	sword bean
plantain	tree onion
potherbs	vegetable
root crop	alexanders
rosemary	broad beans
rutabaga	butter bean
scallion	coffee bean
soy beans	cos lettuce
split pea	cotton tree
tuberose	cotton wood
turmeric	cruciferae
zucchini	French bean
artichoke	garden peas
asparagus	green beans
aubergine	jardiniere
beet sugar	kidney bean
carob bean	potato peel
chick peas	red cabbage
cold frame	runner bean
cole garth	salad plant
colocynth	sauerkraut
coriander	Scotch kale
crucifera	sea cabbage
dried peas	string bean
garden pea	vanilla pod
green bean	water cress
green peas	Welsh onion
Lima beans	wolf's peach

452

butter|beans   lamb's|lettuce
cauliflower   mangel|wurzel
celery|stick   market|garden
French|beans   marrowfat|pea
green|pepper   marrow|squash
horseradish   Spanish|onion
runner|beans   spring|greens
scarlet|bean   St|John's|bread
sea|colewort   water|parsnip
spring|onion   kitchen|garden
string|beans   mangold|wurzel
sweet|potato   root|vegetable
winter|cress   cabbage|lettuce
asparagus|tip   green|vegetable
cabbage|patch   Brussels|sprouts
chilli|pepper   globe|artichokes
corn|on|the|cob vegetable|garden
Covent|Garden   vegetable|marrow
haricot|beans

Virtues

hope   charity   fortitude
love   justice   temperance
faith   prudence

Visual Arts

ART	glue	batik	model	study
cut	head	block	motif	style
dye	kiln	brush	mould	throw
gum	lake	burin	mural	tinct
hue	lens	cameo	op|art	tinge
lac	limn	carve	paint	trace
oil	line	chalk	photo	turps
pen	mark	chase	piece	virtu
pot	mask	china	pin|up	wheel
sit	nude	craft	plate	artist
urn	oils	crock	point	azo|dye
arty	oven	curio	prime	bedaub
boss	pose	delft	print	bisque
bust	roll	drawn	prism	bite|in
calk	seal	dryer	pupil	blazon
cast	shot	easel	rough	blow|up
clay	show	fired	scape	bronze
copy	snap	frame	scene	calque
daub	soup	genre	sculp	camera
dope	tile	glass	shade	canvas
draw	tint	glaze	shape	carved
etch	tone	gloss	slide	carver
film	tool	glyph	smear	chased
fire	turn	grave	Spode	chaser
flat	turn	hatch	spool	chisel
flux	vase	image	stain	chroma
form	view	inlay	stamp	colour
gild	wash	Japan	still	crayon
gilt	work	lines	stone	crible

cubism	pastel	coating	off¡tone
cubist	pencil	collage	outline
dauber	plaque	colours	painter
déjà¡vu	pop¡art	copyist	palette
depict	poster	Dadaism	pattern
design	potter	dash¡off	picture
doodle	primer	develop	pigment
drawer	relief	diorama	plaster
dyeing	rococo	draught	portray
eat¡out	school	drawing	pottery
effigy	screen	ebauche	preview
enamel	sculpt	ecorche	primary
engild	shadow	enchase	profile
etcher	sketch	engrave	realism
figure	statue	enlarge	relievo
filter	studio	etching	scenist
firing	symbol	faience	scratch
fresco	talent	fast¡dye	shading
glazed	tripod	Fauvism	shutter
graven	viewer	furnace	spatula
graver	acid¡dye	gallery	stencil
incise	acushla	gilding	stipple
limner	aniline	glyphic	tableau
madder	art¡deco	glyptic	tachism
magilp	art¡form	gouache	tempera
mallet	art¡work	graphic	tessera
marble	atelier	graving	the¡arts
master	baroque	gravure	thinner
medium	biscuit	high¡art	tinting
megilp	camaieu	imagism	tintype
mobile	cartoon	incised	tooling
mock¡up	carving	lacquer	touch¡up
mosaic	ceramic	linocut	tracery
museum	chasing	montage	tracing
opaque	classic	moulded	varnish
parget	close¡by	moulder	woodcut

abstract	eclectic	majolica
acid|kiln	eggshell	mandorla
aesthete	emblazon	modelled
airscape	emulsion	modeller
anaglyph	enchased	monument
aquatint	engraved	movement
art|autre	engraver	negative
art|class	enlarger	original
artcraft	exposure	paint|box
artefact	exterior	paintbox
artifact	fair|copy	painting
artiness	figurine	panorama
artistic	fine|arts	pargeter
artistry	fire|clay	pastiche
art|paper	fixative	pastille
autotype	freehand	pastoral
autotypy	frescoes	photomap
Barbizon	fretwork	picturer
basic|dye	futurism	plein|air
burinist	glyptics	portrait
calotype	graffiti	positive
ceramics	graffito	potsherd
charcoal	graphics	printing
chromism	Greek|urn	repousse
ciselure	grouping	sculptor
clayware	half|tint	seapiece
colorama	half|tone	seascape
creation	hatching	sketcher
curlicue	in|relief	skiagram
dark|room	inscribe	skyscape
demitint	intaglio	slapdash
depicter	interior	snapshot
designer	intimism	spectrum
dry|paint	lapidary	staining
dry|plate	likeness	statuary
dyestuff	limekiln	stop|bath

symbolic	cityscape	lithotint
tachisme	clean|line	lithotype
tapestry	cloisonné	low|relief
tessella	collodion	manual|art
the|brush	collotype	medallion
tinction	colorific	mezzotint
tincture	colourful	microcopy
turn|a|pot	colouring	microfilm
vignette	colourist	miniature
virtuoso	crayonist	modelling
zoom|lens	cyanotype	modern|art
aesthetic	cyclorama	modernism
anastasis	decorator	objet|d|art
anastatic	delftware	off|colour
aquarelle	designing	oil|paints
art|critic	developer	old|master
art|lesson	distemper	oleograph
art|minded	enameller	paintress
art|school	encaustic	paper|clip
bas|relief	enchasing	pargeting
beaux|arts	engraving	parge|work
blackware	ferrotype	pasticcio
blueprint	flash|bulb	pen|and|ink
box|camera	flash|tube	photocopy
bric|a|brac	glassware	photogram
brick|kiln	goldsmith	photostat
brushwork	Gothicism	pictorial
cameo|ware	grisaille	porcelain
cameraman	grotesque	portrayal
cartridge	headpiece	portrayer
cerograph	heliotype	prefigure
champleve	heliotypy	prismatic
china|clay	inscriber	projector
chinaware	kalamkari	reflector
chiseller	landscape	represent
chromatic	lay|figure	rice|paper

rotograph	xylograph	crosshatch
rough|copy	zinc|plate	crouch|ware
scrimshaw	acid|colour	Crown|Derby
sculpture	aesthetics	dead,colour
secondary	anaglyphic	decoration
sgraffito	aniline|dye	delineator
sketching	art|gallery	draughting
sketch|pad	art|nouveau	drawing|pin
skiagraph	arty,crafty	emblazonry
statuette	automatism	embossment
still,life	avant|garde	enamel|kiln
stippling	background	enamelling
stoneware	beaten|work	enamellist
symbolism	Berlin|ware	enamelware
symbology	bibliofilm	exhibition
tablature	block|print	figuration
tailpiece	cameo|glass	figurehead
talbotype	caricature	flashlight
technique	carmagnole	foreground
telephoto	cartoonist	full|colour
tenebrist	cement|kiln	functional
throw|a|pot	ceramicist	futuristic
townscape	cerography	glazed|ware
treatment	china|stone	grand|stone
triquetra	chiselling	graphic|art
undercoat	chromatics	Grecian|urn
vitascope	chromatism	half|relief
vorticism	chromogram	handicraft
wax|f igure	chromotype	heliograph
whiteware	cinecamera	high|colour
whitewash	classicism	high|relief
wirephoto	cloudscape	illuminate
wood|block	coloration	illustrate
woodcraft	colour|film	impression
woodprint	colourless	jasper|ware
work|of|art	comic|strip	kinetic|art

lightmeter	proportion	zincograph
linography	pure|colour	zylography
linseed|oil	queen'sware	abstract|art
lithograph	Raphaelite	abstraction
luminarist	repoussage	achromatism
lustreware	rich|colour	alto,relievo
masterwork	riverscape	anaglyptics
metalcraft	Rockingham	brush|stroke
micrograph	scenograph	cavo,relievo
microprint	sculptress	ceramic|ware
monochrome	sculptural	cerographer
monumental	sculptured	ceroplastic
mordant|dye	sculpturer	charcoalist
natural|dye	Sèvres|ware	chef|d|oeuvre
naturalism	shadowgram	chiaroscuro
neoclassic	show|of|work	Chinese|clay
oil|colours	silhouette	cloisonnage
oil|painter	sketchbook	coat|of|paint
ornamental	sling|paint	colorimeter
paintbrush	statuesque	colouration
pastellist	steel|plate	colour|blind
pedal|wheel	stereotype	colour|cycle
photoflash	stonecraft	colour|gamut
photoflood	stovehouse	colour|print
photogenic	surrealism	composition
photograph	surrealist	connoisseur
photometer	terra|cotta	copperplate
photomural	tessallate	delineation
photoprint	turpentine	dichromatic
phylactery	view|finder	discoloured
picaresque	warm|colour	draughtsman
pigmentary	water|glass	earthenware
plasticine	waterscape	eclecticism
polychrome	wax|etching	electrotype
port,crayon	wax|process	engravement
power|wheel	wood|carver	enlargement

459

etching|ball	pointillism	candid|camera
flash|camera	pointillist	caricaturist
French|chalk	portraiture	cave|painting
gild|the|lily	potter's|clay	ceramography
glass|blower	press|camera	ceroplastics
glyphograph	primitivism	chaleography
graphic|arts	proportions	chiaro,oscuro
heliochrome	psychedelic	Chinese|paper
ichnography	range|finder	chromaticity
illuminator	romanticism	colour|circle
illustrator	rotogravure	colour|filter
in|low|relief	rough|sketch	cottage|china
insculpture	Satsuma|ware	design|centre
landscapist	scenewright	drawing|board
life|drawing	scenography	drawing|paper
Limoges|ware	sculpturing	Dresden|china
linographer	shadowgraph	Elgin|marbles
lithography	silversmith	etching|point
living|image	snap|shooter	fashion|plate
local|colour	snapshotter	genre|painter
madder|bloom	solid|colour	glyphography
masterpiece	still|camera	heliogravure
Meissen|ware	tile|painter	hollow|relief
miniaturist	tissue|paper	illumination
museum|piece	water|colour	illustration
object|of|art	wood|carving	in|high|relief
objet|trouvé	xylographer	kaleidoscope
oil|painting	zincography	lantern|slide
ornamentist	aestheticism	lignographer
papier|mâché	architecture	line|engraver
perspective	artist's|model	lithographer
photography	artist's|proof	lithographic
photorelief	basso,relievo	lithogravure
picturesque	brass,rubbing	magic|lantern
pinacotheca	bright|colour	metallograph
plein,air ist	camera|lucida	mezzo,relievo

old|Worcester	wall|painting
opaque|colour	water|colours
paint|the|lily	wax|engraving
palette|knife	wax|modelling
panchromatic	Wedgwood|ware
photoengrave	well|composed
photoetching	white|pottery
photographer	zincographer
photographic	action|painter
photogravure	art|exhibition
photomontage	black|and|white
picture|frame	calligraphist
pointelliste	cross|hatching
pointillisme	daguerreotype
portrait|bust	expressionism
poster|colour	expressionist
potter's|earth	Flemish|school
potter's|wheel	glass|printing
reflex|camera	impressionism
reproduction	impressionist
riot|of|colour	pre|Raphaelite
rough|draught	primary|colour
rough|outline	willow|pattern
scene|painter	action|painting
sculptograph	art|for|art's|sake
self|portrait	foreshortening
shadow|figure	pavement|artist
sneak|preview	picture|gallery
spectrograph	vanishing|point
stained|glass	abstract|painter
stereo|camera	charcoal|drawing
street|artist	draughtsmanship
technicolour	picture|restorer
time|exposure	portrait|gallery
tracing|paper	portrait|painter
tripod|camera	

Warfare

AB	van	dart	impi	rout	arrow
GI	vet	D-day	jack	rush	at bay
GI	war	dike	jamb	shot	at war
MP	ally	dirk	jeep	slug	baton
RA	ammo	dove	Jock	spit	beset
RE	Ares	duck	keep	spur	blade
RN	arms	duel	kill	stab	blank
arm	army	dump	kris	stab	blast
axe	A-war	duty	levy	tank	blitz
bow	AWOL	epee	load	tuck	Boche
cap	ball	exon	lock	unit	bolas
cut	band	feud	mail	WAAF	brave
dud	barb	file	Mars	WACS	broch
foe	bard	fire	mere	wage	Buffs
gat	bill	fish	mine	wall	burst
gun	bird	flak	MIRV	ward	cadre
Hun	bola	foil	moat	WAVE	chute
NCO	bolt	fort	mole	wing	clash
POW	bomb	fray	navy	WRNS	corps
RAF	bone	guns	Odin	yomp	cover
ram	bout	hate	peel	zone	ditch
rat	Bren	hawk	peon	Zulu	draft
rod	butt	helm	pike	A-gun	drive
row	camp	hero	post	A-bomb	enemy
sap	club	hilt	rack	aegis	feint
spy	cock	hold	rank	arena	fence
sub	coif	host	rath	armed	field
TNT	Colt	H-war	riot	armet	fight
Tyr	cosh	ICBM	rock	array	flail

flank	rebel	tommy	battle	enlist
fleet	recce	tommy	beaver	ensign
foray	redan	train	bellum	escarp
fosse	repel	troop	biggun	escort
front	rifle	truce	billet	Exocet
fusee	rowel	U,boat	bomber	fewter
fusil	sally	uhlan	breech	flight
grape	salvo	visor	bugler	foeman
guard	scarp	WAACS	bullet	forage
harry	scene	WAAFS	bunker	forces
H,bomb	scout	waddy	camail	gabion
H,hour	sepoy	Woden	cannon	galoot
jerid	serve	wound	casque	glacis
Jerry	shaft	WRACS	castle	glaive
jihad	shako	Wrens	casual	gorget
jingo	shell	abatis	charge	greave
knife	shoot	ack,ack	cohort	gunner
kukri	siege	action	column	gun,shy
lager	skean	air,arm	combat	Gurkha
lance	sling	air,gun	convoy	gusset
leave	snake	alpeen	cordon	hagbut
Luger	sowar	Amazon	corium	hammer
melee	spahi	ambush	creese	hanger
mound	spear	animus	cudgel	hanjar
onset	spike	Anzacs	cuisse	harass
orgue	spray	archer	curfew	heaume
parry	spurs	Archie	curtal	helmet
pavis	squad	argosy	dagger	hot,war
plate	staff	armada	defeat	hussar
poilu	steel	armour	defend	impact
posse	stick	askari	detail	impale
power	stone	assail	donjon	in,arms
Provo	storm	attack	dry,run	inroad
rally	sword	barbel	duello	jereed
range	targe	barrel	dugout	jingal
ranks	tasse	batman	dumdum	laager

labrys	rapier	tom,tom	bayonet
lancer	rappel	trench	bazooka
legion	ray|gun	troops	beat|off
lorica	razzia	tulwar	Bellona
mailed	rebuff	turret	big|guns
maquis	reduit	vallum	big|shot
marine	report	valour	blowgun
Mauser	revolt	Vandal	Boer|War
merlon	rioter	victor	bombard
minnie	rocket	volley	bombing
morion	rookie	war|cry	booster
mortar	salade	war|dog	bravado
musket	sallet	war|god	Bren|gun
muster	salute	weapon	bricole
muzzle	sangar	womera	brigade
oilcan	sapper	yeoman	buckler
outfit	sconce	Zouave	bulldog
panzer	scutum	abattis	bulwark
parade	sentry	advance	caisson
parole	set|gun	air|raid	caitiff
patrol	shield	amnesty	calibre
pavise	slogan	archery	caliver
pellet	sniper	armoury	caltrop
pepper	sortie	arsenal	cap,a,pie
petard	sparth	assault	carbine
picket	spying	assegai	carcass
pierce	strafe	atom|gun	carrier
pistol	strike	atom|war	cashier
pogrom	swivel	baldric	cavalry
pompom	talion	barrack	chamade
powder	target	barrage	chamber
pow,pow	tenail	barrier	charger
quiver	thrust	bar|shot	chicken
rafale	to|arms	basinet	citadel
Rajput	tocsin	bastion	cold|war
ramrod	Toledo	battery	command

464

company	gas|bomb	javelin	petrary
conchie	gas|mask	jollies	phalanx
conquer	germ|war	jump|jet	pikeman
cordite	gisarme	knifing	pillbox
corslet	go|to|war	kremlin	platoon
cossack	grapnel	lambast	poleaxe
coupure	grenade	lamboys	poniard
courage	gunboat	longbow	private
courser	gundeck	Long|Tom	quarrel
crusade	gunfire	lookout	rampage
cudgels	gunlock	lunette	rampart
cuirass	gunnage	lyddite	ravelin
curtain	gunnery	machete	recruit
curtana	gunning	make|war	red|army
cutlass	gun|park	maniple	redcoat
dastard	gunplay	mantlet	redoubt
defence	gun|port	marines	regular
disband	gunroom	martial	repulse
distaff	gunshot	matross	retreat
dragoon	hackbut	megaton	riposte
draught	halberd	militia	Sabaoth
dry|fire	handjar	missile	sabaton
dudgeon	harness	mission	salient
dueller	hatchet	morrion	samurai
dungeon	hauberk	neutral	sandbag
echelon	heroism	offence	Seabees
enomoty	Hessian	on|guard	section
fall|out	heyduck	open|war	self|bow
fend|off	hold|off	outpost	service
fighter	holster	outwork	shoot|at
firearm	holy|war	paladin	shooter
fortify	hostage	panoply	shotgun
fortlet	invader	parados	soldier
foxhole	jackman	parapet	Spartan
gallant	jambeau	patriot	sparthe
gallery	jankers	pedrero	spinner

465

sten|gun	aceldama	bomb|site	drumhead
supremo	activate	brattice	duellist
tactics	air|force	brickbat	dynamite
teargas	air|rifle	broadaxe	embattle
tenable	air,to,air	Browning	enfilade
testudo	all,clear	buckshot	enlistee
theatre	alliance	buttress	entrench
the|fray	ammo|dump	buzzbomb	envelope
torpedo	anabasis	campaign	errantry
traitor	anti|mine	cannonry	escalade
trigger	arbalest	casemate	exercise
trooper	armament	catapult	falchion
tumbril	armature	cavalier	falconet
uniform	armoured	chaffron	fasthold
veteran	arms|race	chamfron	fastness
victory	arquebus	champion	fencible
wage|war	art|of|war	chasseur	field|gun
war|club	atom|bomb	chivalry	fighting
ward|off	attacker	civil|war	file|fire
war|drum	aventail	claymore	fireball
warfare	ballista	cold|feet	fire|bomb
war|game	banderol	commando	firelock
warhead	barbette	conflict	fire|upon
warlike	barbican	corselet	flotilla
warlord	barracks	crossbow	fortress
warpath	bartisan	cry|havoc	fugleman
warring	baselard	culverin	furlough
warrior	battalia	cylinder	fusilier
warship	battling	defender	gambeson
war|song	bear|arms	demilune	garrison
weapons	besieger	deserter	gauntlet
wind|gun	betrayer	destrier	Great|War
woomera	blockade	division	guerilla
wounded	blowpipe	doughboy	gunflint
yatagan	bludgeon	drum|call	gunmetal
yomping	bomb|rack	drumfire	gunpoint

gunsmith	marksman	reveille
gunstick	martello	revolver
gunstock	massacre	ricochet
hang|fire	Maxim|gun	rifleman
heavy|gun	melinite	risalder
hedgehog	militant	runagate
herisson	military	safehold
hill|fort	mobilize	scabbard
hireling	muniment	scimitar
hornwork	munition	sentinel
howitzer	mushroom	shrapnel
infantry	musketry	side|arms
informer	nerve|gas	siege|cap
invading	open|fire	skean|dhu
invasion	ordnance	skirmish
invasive	orillion	soldiery
ironclad	outguard	solleret
janizary	overkill	space|gun
jazerant	pacifist	spadroon
jingoism	palisade	spearman
jump|area	palstaff	spontoon
kill|adar	palstave	squadron
knuckles	partisan	stabbing
lancegay	password	stalwart
land|army	pauldron	Star|Wars
land|mine	petronel	stave|off
langrage	pikehead	stiletto
last|post	poltroon	stockade
launcher	puncheon	strafing
Leon|mine	quisling	strategy
Lewis|gun	quo|vadis	struggle
loophole	recreant	surprise
magazine	regiment	surround
mailclad	renegade	take|arms
man|of|war	repulsor	tenaille
mantelet	reserves	the|front

the|sword	army|corps	brown|bill
time|bomb	army|issue	camouflet
tomahawk	army|lists	cannonade
Tommy|gun	arrowhead	cannoneer
total|war	artillery	caparison
transfix	assailant	carronade
trenches	atomic|gun	carry|arms
turnback	atomic|war	cartouche
turncoat	attacking	cartridge
turntail	attrition	casemated
up|in|arms	automatic	castellan
uprising	auto|rifle	cease|fire
vambrace	backplate	chain|mail
vamplate	ballistic	chain|shot
vanguard	banderole	challenge
vanquish	bandolier	chamfrain
vendetta	bastinado	chassepot
war|cloud	battalion	cold|steel
warcraft	battleaxe	combatant
war|dance	battlecry	combative
warfarer	beachhead	conquerer
war|horse	beefeater	conscript
war|hound	beleaguer	crackshot
war|paint	bellicism	cross|fire
war|whoop	bellicose	defensive
Waterloo	Big|Bertha	derringer
wayfarer	blackjack	desert|rat
weaponry	bloodshed	deterrent
world|war	bomb|happy	detonator
yeomanry	bombs|away	discharge
zero|hour	bombshell	doodlebug
accoutred	bombsight	double|sap
aggressor	booby|trap	drop|a|bomb
air|to|ship	boomerang	earthwork
ambuscade	broadside	embattled
arch|enemy	Brown|Bess	encompass

enemy camp	heavy fire	munitions
enemy fire	heroic act	musketeer
escopette	Home Guard	musketoon
espionage	hostility	needle gun
explosive	hydrobomb	nose guard
face guard	incursion	nosepiece
fence wall	incursive	offensive
field army	in defence	onslaught
fieldwork	ironbound	open order
fire a shot	irregular	operation
firepower	irruption	other side
fireworks	janissary	overthrow
first line	jesserant	panoplied
flintlock	katabasis	parachute
flying sap	keep guard	peel house
fortalice	keep vigil	peel tower
fortified	lance jack	pikestaff
fourth arm	langridge	prick spur
free lance	last ditch	projector
front line	legionary	protector
fulgurite	levy war on	pugnacity
fusillade	lie in wait	pyroxylin
gas attack	lionheart	ram rocket
gelignite	logistics	rearguard
gladiator	long range	rebel call
grapeshot	Luftwaffe	rebellion
grenadier	make war on	rerebrace
guardsman	man at arms	ressaldar
guerrilla	manoeuvre	rifle ball
gun battle	march past	rocket gun
guncotton	matchlock	rocket man
gunpowder	mercenary	roundhead
gun turret	militancy	round shot
habergeon	minefield	rowel spur
harquebus	minuteman	Royal Navy
headpiece	monomachy	sally port

469

saltpetre	task|force	armed|truce
sea|battle	tit|for|tat	armigerous
seat|of|war	torpedoed	armipotent
sentry|box	torpedoer	arm's|length
shellfire	trainband	atomic|bomb
signalman	trench|gun	atomic|pile
single|sap	troopship	atom|rocket
ski|troops	truncheon	ballistics
skyrocket	under|arms	barbed|wire
sky|troops	under|fire	battle|flag
slaughter	vigilante	battle|hymn
slingshot	volunteer	battle|line
slung|shot	warmonger	battlement
small|arms	War|Office	battleship
small|bore	war|rocket	blitzkrieg
small|shot	watchword	blockhouse
smoke|bomb	white|flag	bold|stroke
soldierly	woomerang	bombardier
soldier|on	zumbooruk	bowie|knife
sonic|mine	activation	box|barrage
son|of|a|gun	active|army	breastwork
spearhead	active|duty	bridgehead
spring|gun	active|list	brigandine
stand|fire	adventurer	broadsword
stink|bomb	aerial|bomb	bugle|corps
strategic	aerial|mine	call|to|arms
subaltern	aggression	camel|corps
submarine	aggressive	camouflage
super|bomb	Air|Command	campaigner
surprisal	air|service	cannon|ball
surrender	ambushment	cannon|shot
swivel|gun	ammunition	cantonment
sword|play	antagonism	carabineer
take|sides	Armageddon	carry|on|war
tank|corps	armed|force	cavalryman
target|day	armed|guard	coastguard

470

coat of mail	ground zero	operations
combat area	halberdier	other ranks
combat team	heavy armed	over the top
commandant	impalement	oyster mine
contingent	incendiary	paratroops
cross staff	investment	percussion
cuirassier	jingoistic	petrol bomb
declare war	knighthood	picket duty
defendable	knobkerrie	point blank
defensible	kriegspiel	portcullis
demobilize	lambrequin	private war
detachment	lay siege to	projectile
direct fire	Life Guards	raking fire
dragonnade	light armed	rally round
dragoonade	line of fire	raw recruit
drawbridge	loaded cane	Resistance
drummer boy	long knives	revolution
embankment	lookout man	rifle range
encampment	machine gun	rocket bomb
engarrison	martiality	rocket fire
eprouvette	militarism	rules of war
escalation	militarize	run through
expedition	militiaman	second line
faint heart	missile man	sentry duty
fieldpiece	mob tactics	serviceman
field train	mount guard	shellshock
fiery cross	mural crown	shillelagh
fire trench	musket shot	short range
firing area	mustard gas	siegecraft
flying bomb	napalm bomb	siege train
flying tank	no man's land	six shooter
Foot Guards	nuclear war	slit trench
foot rifles	obsidional	smallsword
Gatling gun	occupation	smooth bore
ground fire	old soldier	spill blood
ground mine	on the march	stand guard

state|of|war	bersaglieri	fire|tactics
strategist	besiegement	firing|party
stronghold	blockbuster	firing|squad
submarine	bloody|shirt	firing|table
sure|as|a|gun	blunderbuss	first|strike
sword|fight	bombardment	fission|bomb
swordstick	bomber|pilot	flare|rocket
sworn|enemy	bomb|release	flying|corps
take|to|arms	bow|and|arrow	footed|arrow
tenderfoot	breastplate	footslogger
ten|pounder	British|Army	foot|soldier
test|rocket	British|Navy	forced|march
touch|paper	buck|private	force|of|arms
trajectile	bulletproof	friend|or|foe
trajectory	buoyant|mine	full|harness
under|siege	bushwhacker	full|of|fight
vanquisher	cameraderie	gang|warfare
volunteers	castellated	generalship
war|goddess	castle|guard	germ|warfare
Winchester	caterpillar	giant|powder
air|to|ground	change|sides	ground|to|air
anti|missile	combat|train	guerrillero
anti|tank|gun	contentious	guncarriage
area|bombing	countermine	hair|trigger
armed|combat	crack|troops	hand|grenade
armed|forces	declaration	heavy|armour
armoured|car	demi|bastion	heavy|bomber
auxiliaries	depth|charge	high|dudgeon
barnstormer	dive|bombing	hill|station
battle|array	emplacement	Horse|Guards
battledress	enemy|action	horse|pistol
battlefield	engine|of|war	hostilities
battle|order	enlisted|man	infantryman
battle|plane	envelopment	Irish|Guards
battle|royal	fighting|man	iron|rations
beach|master	fire|a|volley	land|warfare

light|bomber	safe,conduct	up|and|at|them
lionhearted	safety|catch	warlikeness
Lochaber|axe	Scots|Guards	war|of|nerves
loggerheads	service|call	warriorlike
look|daggers	ship|to|shore	war|to|end|war
magazine|gun	shock|troops	water|cannon
Maginot|line	shooting|war	wooden|horse
Marine|Corps	shoot|to|kill	wooden|walls
might|of|arms	shuttle|raid	acoustic|mine
military|man	Signal|Corps	anti|aircraft
mine|thrower	smell|powder	appeal|to|arms
moral|defeat	smoke|rocket	armour|plated
mountain|gun	smoke|screen	army|reserves
naval|bomber	sneak|attack	artilleryman
naval|forces	soldatesque	atomic|cannon
nitre|powder	soldierlike	awkward|squad
nitrocotton	soldiership	banzai|charge
nuclear|bomb	spent|bullet	battering|ram
open|warfare	stand|at|ease	battleground
pattern|bomb	stand|of|arms	beat|a|retreat
peace|treaty	step|rockets	belligerence
picket|guard	storm|troops	breakthrough
plate|armour	stray|bullet	breechloader
platoon|fire	subdivision	buccaneering
postern|gate	Swiss|Guards	bushfighting
powder|grain	sword|in|hand	cannon|fodder
Provisional	take|by|storm	cannon's|mouth
put|to|flight	thin|red|line	civil|defence
rallying|cry	Tommy|Atkins	council|of|war
rank|and|file	torpedo|boat	counter|march
rebel|action	trench|knife	court|martial
reconnoitre	trigger|talk	cut|and,thrust
recruitment	true|colours	daggers|drawn
regular|army	trusty|sword	deadly|weapon
retro,rocket	under|attack	demi,culverin
rolling|fire	Underground	dumdum|bullet

Dutch|courage	Medical|Corps
electron|bomb	medium|bomber
encirclement	military|zone
engines|of|war	mine|detector
entrenchment	mobilization
escaramouche	moral|courage
false|colours	moral|support
field|of|blood	moral|victory
flame,thrower	muzzle,loader
floating|mine	naval|militia
flying|column	naval|reserve
forward|march	naval|warfare
fowling|piece	on|the|warpath
gladiatorial	Parthian|shot
go|over|the|top	Pearl|Harbour
grand|tactics	picked|troops
ground|forces	pioneer|corps
guerrilla|war	plunging|fire
guided|weapon	powder|charge
heavy|dragoon	pyrotechnics
home|reserves	quarterstaff
homing|rocket	reactivation
horse|and|foot	religious|war
horse|marines	rifled|cannon
hydrogen|bomb	rifle|grenade
lady|from|hell	rocket|attack
launching|pad	second|strike
leathernecks	sharpshooter
Light|Brigade	shock|tactics
light|dragoon	shoulder|a|gun
line|of|action	shoulder|arms
line|of|battle	siege|warfare
machicolated	signal|rocket
magnetic|mine	single|combat
march|against	standing|army
marching|song	stormtrooper

474

stouthearted	cheval de frise
sudden attack	Churchill tank
supply troops	cobelligerent
sword bayonet	combat fatigue
tactical unit	comrade in arms
take the field	counter attack
theatre of war	desert warfare
tooth and nail	disengagement
trench mortar	dispatch rider
trigger happy	drill sergeant
under the flag	evasive action
vertical fire	Exocet missile
virus warfare	field hospital
warmongering	field of battle
white feather	fighter patrol
who goes there	first world war
yellow streak	Flammenwerfer
active service	flying colours
Andrew Ferrara	flying officer
armaments race	force de frappe
armed conflict	foreign legion
arms and the man	fortification
army exercises	generalissimo
articles of war	guard of honour
assault course	guided missile
baptism of fire	gunnery school
battle cruiser	high explosive
battle honours	lance corporal
battle scarred	light infantry
bayonet charge	line of defence
beleaguerment	listening post
bomber command	machine gunner
breechloading	Messerschmitt
British Legion	Military Cross
cartridge belt	Military Medal
cavalry charge	mine detection

mini,submarine
muzzle|loading
non,resistance
nuclear|weapon
order|of|battle
order|of|the|day
passage|of|arms
Peninsular|War
pitched|battle
prisoner|of|war
put|to|the|sword
quarter|gunner
quartermaster
reinforcement
royal|air|force
running|battle
sabre,rattling
scorched|earth
senior|service
sergeant|major
Siegfried|line
staff,sergeant
striking|force
sublieutenant
submachine|gun
trench|warfare
two,edged|sword
unarmed|combat
Victoria|Cross
war|department
war|to|the|death
wing|commander
yeoman|service
action|stations
airborne|forces
airborne|troops

aircraftswoman
Air|Vice|Marshal
ammunition|dump
army|cadet|force
army|manoeuvres
barrage|balloon
battle|stations
blank|cartridge
blockade|runner
captain|general
cavalry|officer
chevaux|de|frise
cloak|and,dagger
coastal|battery
coastal|command
colonel,in,chief
colour|sergeant
comrades|in|arms
conquering|hero
demobilisation
field|ambulance
field|artillery
fifth|columnist
fighter|command
fight|to|a|finish
flag,lieutenant
freedom|fighter
guerrilla|chief
guerrilla|force
heavy|artillery
horse|artillery
incendiary|bomb
liaison|officer
light|artillery
marching|orders
militarisation

military police
military tattoo
muzzle velocity
non operational
nuclear warfare
nuclear warhead
operations room
orderly officer
ordinary seaman
pincer movement
powder magazine
Pyrrhic victory
reconnaissance
regimental band
Royal Artillery
Royal Engineers
Royal Fusiliers
Royal Tank Corps
squadron leader
street fighting
supreme command
unknown soldier
unknown warrior
urban guerrilla
warrant officer
Wars of the Roses
winter quarters
adjutant general
air chief marshal
aircraft carrier
Anderson shelter
armed to the teeth
armoured cruiser

Brigade of Guards
chemical warfare
displaced person
first lieutenant
gentleman at arms
Grenadier Guards
light machinegun
military mission
military service
Molotov cocktail
Morrison shelter
Mulberry harbour
national defence
national service
naval engagement
naval operations
non commissioned
observation post
officer of the day
on active service
orderly corporal
orderly sergeant
parachute troops
rearguard action
recruiting drive
regimental march
second in command
spoils of victory
sword and buckler
telescopic sight
territorial army
up guards and at em

Weight

lb	long|ton
oz	quintal
cwt	scruple
ton	tonneau
dram	assay|ton
gram	decagram
kilo	decigram
mass	gram|atom
carat	gross|ton
gerah	kilogram
grain	short|ton
libra	centigram
livre	hectogram
minim	metric|ton
pound	milligram
scale	myriagram
stone	ounce|troy
tonne	troy|ounce
uncia	carat|grain
denier	troy|weight
dirhem	avoirdupois
drachm	centigramme
gramme	gram|molecule
net|ton	hundredweight
shekel	imperial|weight

Wonders of the World

Colossus,|The	Hanging|Gardens
Pyramids,|The	Tomb|of|Mausolus
Pharos|Lighthouse	Statue|of|Zeus,|The
Temple|of|Diana	

478

Works of Literature and Music

Job	Lolita	Giselle	Carnival
Kim	Martha	Ivanhoe	Catriona
She	Mignon	Lord|Jim	Cenci,|The
Aida	Nuages	Lycidas	Coppelia
Emma	Oberon	Macbeth	Cranford
Lulu	Otello	Manfred	Endymion
Maud	Rienzi	Marmion	Everyman
Brand	Rob|Roy	Ma|Vlast	Falstaff
Comus	Rokeby	Mazeppa	Gloriana
Faust	Salome	Messiah	Hay|Fever
Fetes	Semele	Nabucco	Hiawatha
Kipps	Sylvia	Othello	Hudibras
La|Mer	Trilby	Rebecca	Hyperion
Manon	Utopia	Ring,|The	Idiot,|The
Medea	Walden	Shirley	Idomeneo
Norma	Adonais	Sirenes	Iliad,|The
Scoop	Aladdin	Ulysses	In|the|Wet
Tosca	Amadeus	Volpone	Iolanthe
Alcina	Babbitt	Werther	Jane|Eyre
Amelia	Beowulf	Wozzeck	King|Lear
Becket	Camilla	Adam|Bede	La|Boheme
Ben|Hur	Candida	Adam|Zero	L'Allegro
Carmen	Candide	Alcestis	Lavengro
En|Saga	Don|Juan	Anabasis	Les|Noces
Ghosts	Dracula	Antigone	Lucky|Jim
Hassan	Electra	Arabella	Moby|Dick
Helena	Erewhon	Bells,|The	Parsifal
Iberia	Euphues	Born|Free	Patience
Jenufa	Fidelio	Carnaval	Peer|Gynt

WORKS OF LITERATURE AND MUSIC

Pericles	Lohengrin	InMemoriam
Rasselas	MeinKampf	Intermezzo
SeaDrift	MenatArms	IPagliacci
SwanLake	Mikado,The	JamaicaInn
TomJones	NoHighway	JohnGilpin
Turandot	OnLiberty	Kenilworth
Villette	Papillons	Kingdom,The
Waves,The	Prince,The	LaGioconda
Aeneid,The	Pygmalion	LaTraviata
Agamemnon	Rigoletto	LesTroyens
BeauGeste	Rivals,The	LornaDoone
BillyBudd	Ruddigore	Lysistrata
BriggFair	SaintJoan	MyFairLady
Capriccio	Siegfried	MySon,MySon
Cavalcade	TomSawyer	NelsonMass
Checkmate	Venusberg	Odyssey,The
Choephori	ViceVersa	OedipusRex
Coningsby	Warden,The	OnlyWay,The
CoxandBox	AllforLove	OntheBeach
Critic,The	AnimalFarm	OurVillage
Cymbeline	Appalachia	Pantagruel
DandyDick	BleakHouse	Persuasion
DonCarlos	Borough,The	Petroushka
DrZhivago	CanneryRow	Planets,The
Dubliners	Casabianca	Prelude,The
EastLynne	Cinderella	PrinceIgor
Egoist,The	Citadel,The	Relapse,The
Eumenides	Coriolanus	RuralRides
Euryanthe	DasKapital	Seagull,The
HardTimes	DieWalkure	Seasons,The
Hobbit,The	DonQuixote	Semiramide
I,Claudius	Dunciad,The	Tannhauser
IPuritani	Dynasts,The	Tempest,The
Kidnapped	HowardsEnd	TonoBungay
KublaKhan	IlSeraglio	Trojans,The
LesBiches	Inferno,The	UncleRemus

Uncle Vanya	Love for Love	Alchemist, The
Vanity Fair	Luisa Miller	Anna Karenina
Vile Bodies	Mary Poppins	Antiquary, The
War Requiem	Middlemarch	Apple Cart, The
Water Music	Minute Waltz	Archduke Trio
Westward Ho!	Mrs Dalloway	Areopagitica
American, The	Mr Standfast	Ash Wednesday
Apostles, The	Newcomes, The	Barnaby Rudge
As You Like It	Now We Are Six	Blithe Spirit
Big Sleep, The	Noye's Fludde	Brighton Rock
Black Beauty	Ode to Autumn	Buddenbrooks
Blue Bird, The	Oliver Twist	Caretaker, The
Boule de Suif	Peter Grimes	Charley's Aunt
Cakes and Ale	Peter Simple	Childe Harold
Creation, The	Pippa Passes	Cosi fan Tutte
Cruel Sea, The	Princess Ida	Danse Macabre
Doll's House, A	Princess, The	Decameron, The
Don Giovanni	Puss in Boots	Dogs of War, The
Don Pasquale	Redgauntlet	Dombey and Son
Firebird, The	Rosmersholm	Epithalamion
Georgics, The	Salut d'Amour	Eugene Onegin
Greenmantle	Sea Symphony	Excursion, The
Harp Quartet	Silas Marner	Four Quartets
Hedda Gabler	Sorcerer, The	Frankenstein
High Windows	South Riding	Golden Ass, The
HMS Pinafore	Stalky and Co	Grand Duke, The
Hymn of Jesus	Stenka Razin	Guy Mannering
I Like it Here	Tale of a Tub, A	Handley Cross
Il Penseroso	Talisman, The	Julius Caesar
Il Trovatore	Tam o'Shanter	Karelia Suite
Jack and Jill	Trial by Jury	Khovanshchina
Journey's End	What Katy Did	Kinderscenen
Judith Paris	Wild Duck, The	Kreisleriana
Little Eyolf	William Tell	La Sonnambula
Little Women	Women in Love	Le Pere Goriot
Loved One, The	Wrong Box, The	Les Huguenots

WORKS OF LITERATURE AND MUSIC

Les Sylphides
Linz Symphony
Little Dorrit
Locksley Hall
Lost Chord, The
Madame Bovary
Major Barbara
Manon Lescaut
Moll Flanders
Moonstone, The
Old Mortality
Owen Wingrave
Paradise Lost
Piers Plowman
Porgy and Bess
Precious Bane
Private Lives
Prothalamion
Rheingold, Das
Rip Van Winkle
Rogue Herries
Romany Rye, The
Sardanapalus
Spring Sonata
Trout Quintet
Twelfth Night
Valkyries, The
Whisky Galore
Albert Herring
Almayer's Folly
Andrea Chenier
Angel Pavement
Arms and the Man
Art of Fugue, The
Bab Ballads, The
Black Arrow, The

Black Mischief
Blue Danube, The
Boris Godounov
Brave New World
Cancer Ward, The
Carmina Burana
Chanson de Nuit
Clock Symphony
Crown Imperial
Death in Venice
Der Freischutz
Dido and Aeneas
Doctor Faustus
Doctor Zhivago
Fame is the Spur
Finnegans Wake
Ghost Train, The
Gondoliers, The
Harold in Italy
Hatter's Castle
Jungle Book, The
Just So Stories
La Cenerentola
L'Elisir d'Amore
Mabinogion, The
Magic Flute, The
Magistrate, The
Mansfield Park
Metamorphosen
Nutcracker, The
Odessa File, The
Orb and Sceptre
Path to Rome, The
Peg Woffington
Private Angelo
Religio Medici

Schindler's Ark	Four Just Men, The
Sketches by Boz	Gay Lord Quex, The
Songs of Travel	Golden Bough, The
Sons and Lovers	Goodbye Mr Chips
Stamboul Train	Great Gatsby, The
Tarka the Otter	Handful of Dust, A
Timon of Athens	Horse's Mouth, The
Under Milk Wood	Jude the Obscure
Utopia Limited	Kreutzer Sonata
Virginians, The	Le Morte d'Arthur
White Devil, The	London Symphony
Winnie the Pooh	Loom of Youth, The
Winslow Boy, The	Lord of the Flies
Zuleika Dobson	Lord of the Rings
Ambassadors, The	Lost Horizon, The
Andrea del Sarto	Lyrical Ballads
Battle Symphony	Madam Butterfly
Bees Wedding, The	Man and Superman
Book of Snobs, The	Masterman Ready
Brief Encounter	National Velvet
Chanson de Matin	Nightmare Abbey
Choral Symphony	Nine Tailors, The
Cider with Rosie	Of Human Bondage
Claudius the God	Our Man in Havana
Coral Island, The	Pickwick Papers
Country Wife, The	Plain Dealer, The
Crotchet Castle	Prague Symphony
Darkness at Noon	Quentin Durward
Decline and Fall	Rhapsody in Blue
Deep Blue Sea, The	Rights of Man, The
Die Zauberflote	Robinson Crusoe
Ein Heldenleben	Roderick Random
Emperor Quartet	Romeo and Juliet
Entertainer, The	Separate Tables
Eroica Symphony	Shropshire Lad, A
Forsyte Saga, The	Siegfried Idyll

Sinister Street	From the New World
Sins of my Old Age	Golden Legend, The
Slavonic Dances	Gone with the Wind
Spring Symphony	Goodbye to Berlin
Stones of Venice	Gotterdammerung
Time Machine, The	Haffner Symphony
Town Like Alice, A	Hansel and Gretel
Tragic Symphony	Heartbreak House
Treasure Island	Huckleberry Finn
Tristram Shandy	Iceman Cometh, The
Uncle Tom's Cabin	Invisible Man, The
Venus and Adonis	Italian Symphony
Vicar of Bray, The	Jupiter Symphony
Voices of Spring	Le Nozze di Figaro
Water Babies, The	Letters of Junius
Widowers Houses	Life for the Tsar, A
Winter's Tale, The	Look Back in Anger
Woodlanders, The	Moonlight Sonata
African Queen, The	Northanger Abbey
Allan Quatermain	Old Wives Tale, The
Ariadne auf Naxos	Our Mutual Friend
Bartholomew Fair	Passage to India, A
Beggar's Opera, The	Pearl Fishers, The
Child of our Time, A	Peregrine Pickle
Christmas Carol, A	Peter and the Wolf
Clarissa Harlowe	Puck of Pook's Hill
Dangerous Corner	Put out More Flags
Daphnis and Chloe	Raindrop Prelude
Divine Comedy, The	Rite of Spring, The
Emperor Concerto	Rupert of Hentzau
Emperor Waltz, The	Samson Agonistes
Essays of Elia, The	Samson and Dalila
Faerie Queene, The	Scholar Gipsy, The
Fanny by Gaslight	Serenade to Music
Farewell to Arms, A	Simon Boccanegra
Frenchman's Creek	Soldier's Tale, The

Tanglewood|Tales Waldstein|Sonata
Three|Men|in|a|Boat Weir|of|Hermiston
Titus|Andronicus Woman|in|White,|The
To|the|Lighthouse Yarrow|Revisited
Waiting|for|Godot You|Never|Can|Tell

Writers

Fry	Hume	West	Freud	Moore
Hay	Hunt	Wren	Gogol	Noyes
Kyd	Kant	Zola	Gorki	Orczy
Lee	Knox	Aesop	Grimm	Ouida
Poe	Lamb	Auden	Hardy	Paine
Amis	Lang	Bacon	Heine	Pater
Baum	Lear	Bates	Henry	Pepys
Bell	Livy	Behan	Henty	Plato
Bolt	Loos	Blake	Homer	Pliny
Buck	Lyly	Burke	Ibsen	Pound
Cary	Mann	Burns	Innes	Reade
Dane	Marx	Byron	James	Rilke
Dell	Mill	Camus	Jeans	Scott
Elia	More	Capek	Jones	Shute
Eyre	Muir	Clare	Joyce	Smart
Ford	Nash	Dante	Kafka	Smith
Gide	Ovid	Defoe	Keats	Spark
Glyn	Owen	Donne	Lewis	Stein
Gray	Pope	Doyle	Locke	Stern
Hall	Saki	Dumas	Lodge	Stowe
Home	Sand	Eliot	Lorca	Swift
Hood	Shaw	Ellis	Lucan	Synge
Hope	Snow	Evans	Mason	Tasso
Hugo	Webb	Frayn	Milne	Twain

WRITERS

Verne	Cooper	Mailer	Anouilh
Waugh	Coward	Malory	Aquinas
Wells	Crabbe	Miller	Beckett
Wilde	Cronin	Milton	Bennett
Woolf	Daudet	Morgan	Blunden
Yeats	Davies	Morris	Boswell
Young	Dekker	Musset	Bridges
Zweig	Dryden	Newman	Campion
Anstey	Empson	O'Neill	Carlyle
Archer	Evelyn	Orwell	Carroll
Arnold	Farnol	Parker	Chaucer
Asimov	France	Pascal	Chekhov
Austen	Frazer	Pindar	Cobbett
Bailey	Gibbon	Pinero	Cocteau
Balzac	Goethe	Pinter	Colette
Barham	Gordon	Proust	Collins
Barrie	Graham	Racine	Corelli
Belloc	Graves	Ruskin	Dickens
Benson	Greene	Sappho	Dodgson
Binyon	Hawkes	Sartre	Douglas
Borrow	Hemans	Sayers	Drayton
Brecht	Henley	Seneca	Dunsany
Bridie	Hesiod	Sidney	Durrell
Bronte	Hobbes	Squire	Emerson
Brooke	Holmes	Steele	Erasmus
Browne	Holtby	Sterne	Flecker
Bryant	Horace	Tagore	Forster
Buchan	Howard	Thomas	Gallico
Bunyan	Hughes	Villon	Gaskell
Burney	Huxley	Virgil	Gilbert
Butler	Jerome	Waller	Golding
Caesar	Jonson	Walton	Haggard
Chekov	Landor	Wesker	Harnett
Cicero	Larkin	Wilcox	Hartley
Clough	London	Wilson	Hazlitt
Conrad	Lytton	Addison	Herbert

Herrick	Spencer	Koestler
Hopkins	Spender	Lawrence
Housman	Spenser	Lovelace
Ionesco	Spinoza	Macaulay
Johnson	Surtees	MacNeice
Juvenal	Tacitus	Mallarme
Kipling	Terence	Melville
Leacock	Thomson	Meredith
Lehmann	Thoreau	Merriman
Lessing	Thurber	Mirabeau
Malraux	Tolkien	Mortimer
Marlowe	Tolstoy	Petrarch
Marryat	Ustinov	Plutarch
Martial	Wallace	Rabelais
Marvell	Walpole	Rattigan
Maugham	Webster	Rossetti
Mauriac	Whitman	Rousseau
Maurois	Andersen	Schiller
Merimee	Apuleius	Sheridan
Moliere	Beaumont	Sinclair
Murdoch	Beerbohm	Smollett
Nabokov	Berkeley	Stendhal
Newbolt	Betjeman	Stoppard
Nichols	Browning	Strachey
Osborne	Campbell	Suckling
Patmore	Catullus	Tennyson
Peacock	Christie	Thompson
Pushkin	Congreve	Tibullus
Rimbaud	DayLewis	Trollope
Russell	DelaMare	Turgenev
Saroyan	Disraeli	Vanburgh
Sassoon	Faulkner	Verlaine
Shelley	Fielding	Voltaire
Simenon	Fletcher	Whittier
Sitwell	Forester	Xenephon
Southey	Kingsley	Aeschylus

WRITERS

Aristotle	Wycherley
Blackmore	Ayckbourne
Boccaccio	Ballantyne
Cervantes	Baudelaire
Churchill	Chatterton
Coleridge	Chesterton
Corneille	ConanDoyle
DelaRoche	Drinkwater
DeQuincey	Fitzgerald
Descartes	Galsworthy
DuMaurier	LaFontaine
Euripides	Longfellow
Goldsmith	Maupassant
Hemingway	Pirandello
Herodotus	Propertius
Isherwood	Quintilian
Linklater	Richardson
Lucretius	Strindberg
Mackenzie	Thucydides
Masefield	Wordsworth
Middleton	Dostoievsky
Mitchison	Maeterlinck
Montaigne	OmarKhayyam
Nietzsche	Shakespeare
Pasternak	Yevtushenko
Priestley	Aristophanes
Sophocles	Beaumarchais
Steinbeck	Macchiavelli
Stevenson	QuillerCouch
Suetonius	RiderHaggard
Swinburne	Solzhenitsin
Thackeray	Wittgenstein
Trevelyan	SackvilleWest
Wodehouse	MarcusAurelius

Signs of the Zodiac

Leo	Cancer	Scorpio
Aries	Gemini	Aquarius
Libra	Pisces	Capricorn
Virgo	Taurus	Sagittarius

NOTES

NOTES

NOTES

NOTES

NOTES

NOTES

NOTES

INDEX

LITERATURE
Drugs: MEDICINE

Ecclesiastical: RELIGIONS
Employment: TRADE
Engineering:
    MACHINERY or
    PHYSICAL SCIENCES
Entertainment: CINEMA
    or THEATRE
Examinations:
    EDUCATION

Fabrics: CLOTHES
Fashion: CLOTHES
Festivals: RELIGIONS
Figures of Speech:
    LITERATURE
Finance: MONEY or
    TRADE
Flags: HERALDRY
Footwear: CLOTHES

Games: SPORTS
Geology: GEOGRAPHY
Geometry:
    MATHEMATICS
Grammar: LITERATURE

Headgear: CLOTHES
Herbs: VEGETABLES

History: LITERATURE
Hobbies: PASTIMES
Hospitals: MEDICINE

Illnesses: MEDICINE
Instruments: MUSIC

Journalism:
    LITERATURE

Kitchen: HOUSEHOLD
    ITEMS

Land Formations:
    GEOGRAPHY
Language: LITERATURE
Legal Terms: LAW

Maps: GEOGRAPHY
Market Terms: TRADE
Metals: MINERALS
Monuments:
    ARCHITECTURE
Motoring: TRANSPORT

Nautical: MARINE or
    TRANSPORT
Numbers:
    MATHEMATICS

Operas: WORKS OF
    MUSIC

COLLINS GEM

BABIES' names

a z

?

a mine of information

COLLINS GEM

BEER

a mine of information

COLLINS GEM

BIRDS

a mine of information

COLLINS GE

CALORI Counter

a mine of information

COLLINS GEM

FACT FILE

?

a mine of information

COLLINS GEM

FENG SHUI

a mine of information

COLLINS GEM

FLAGS

a mine of information

COLLINS GE

Healthy **EATING**

a mine of information

COLLINS GEM

QUOTATIONS

"

"

a mine of information

COLLINS GEM

SAS Self-Defence

a mine of information

COLLINS GEM

SAS Survival Guide

a mine of information

COLLINS GE

SEASHOR

a mine of information

COLLINS GEM

TREES

a mine of information

COLLINS GEM

Understanding **DREAMS**

a mine of information

COLLINS GEM

WILD flowers

a mine of information

COLLINS GE

WINE Dictionary

a mine of information